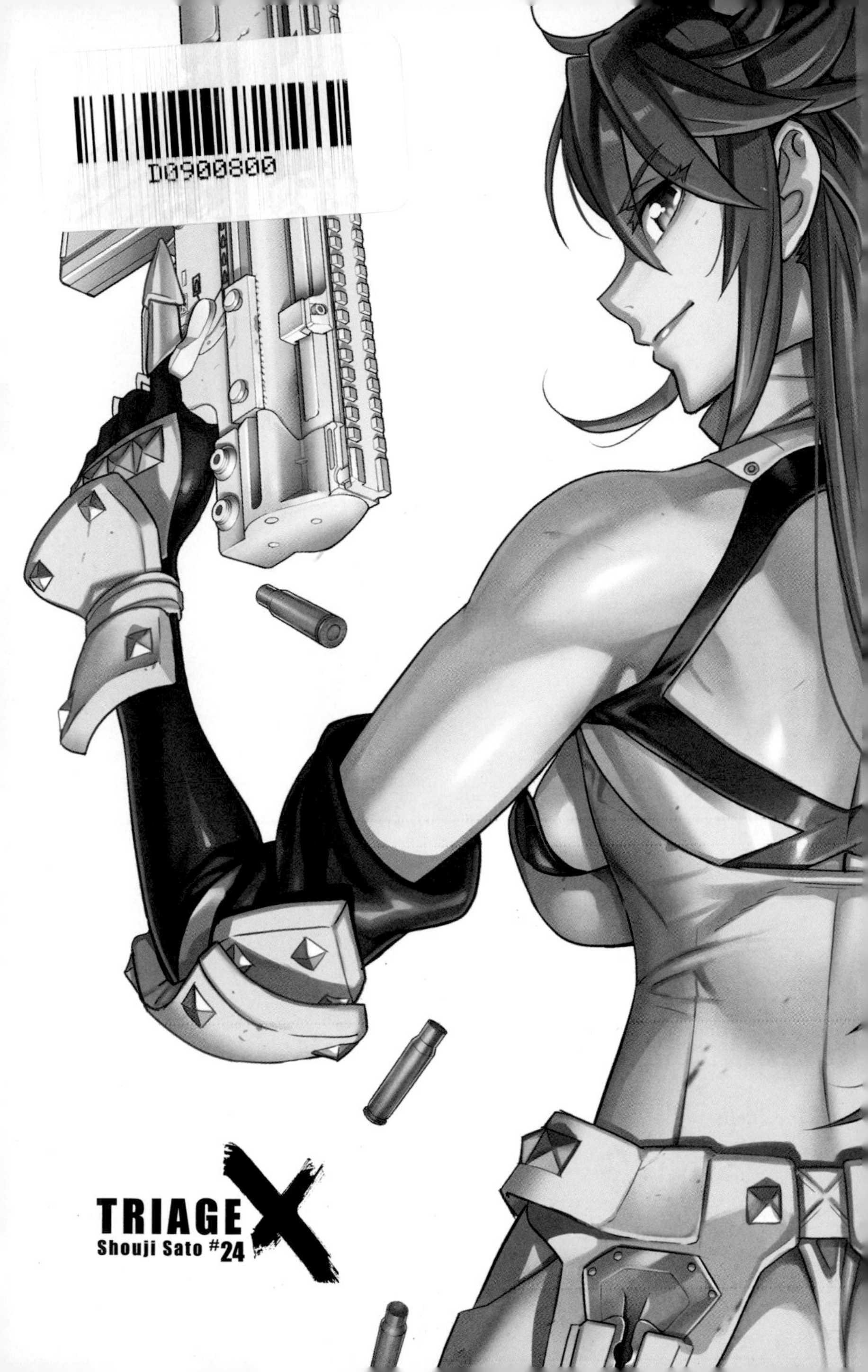
TRIAGE X
Shouji Sato #24

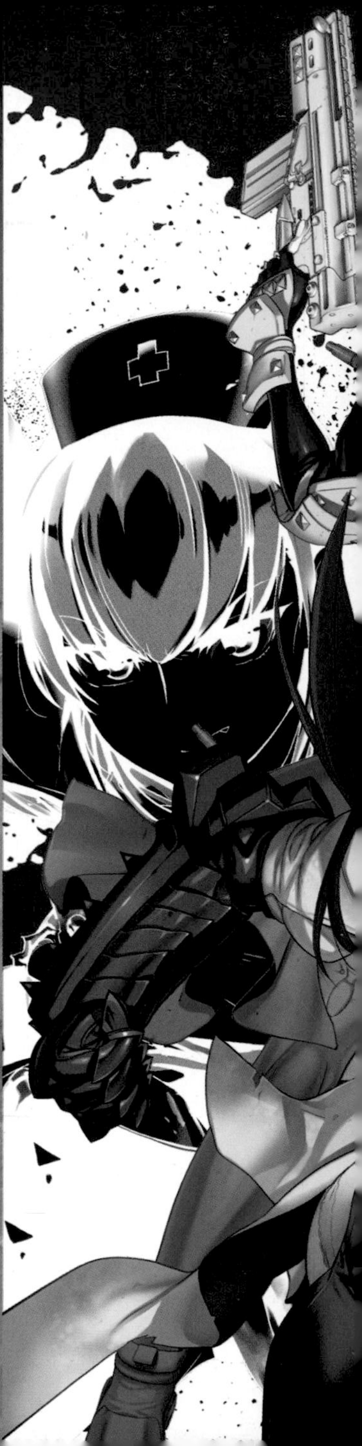

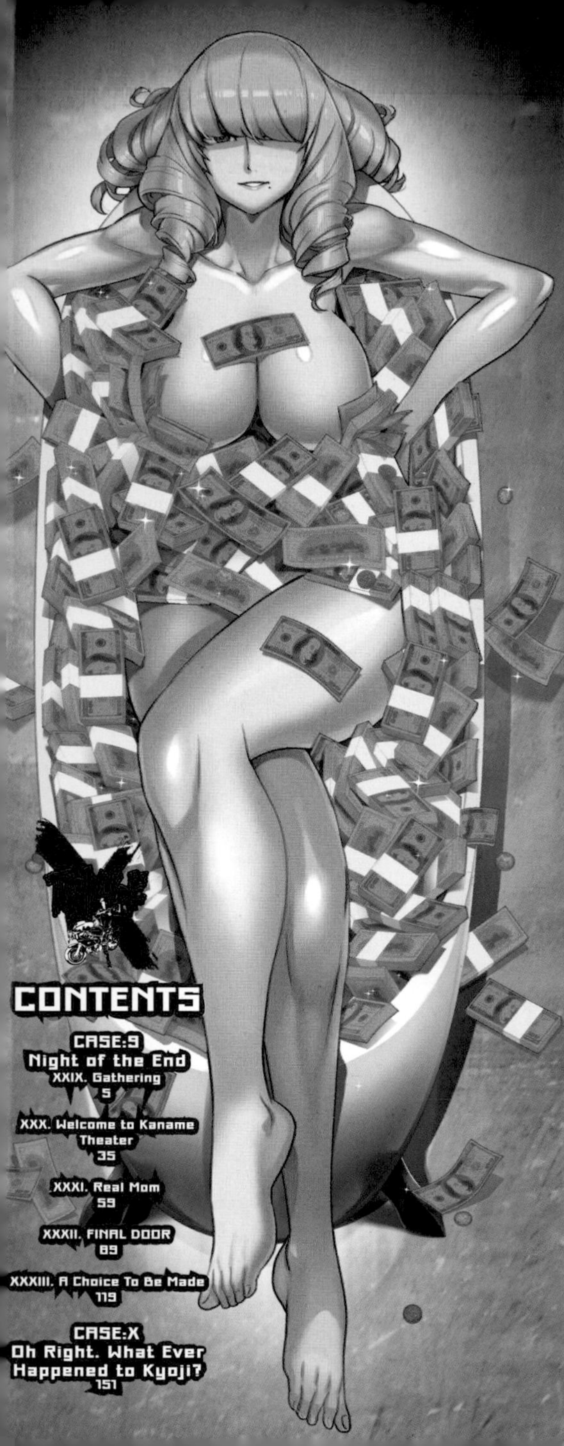

CONTENTS

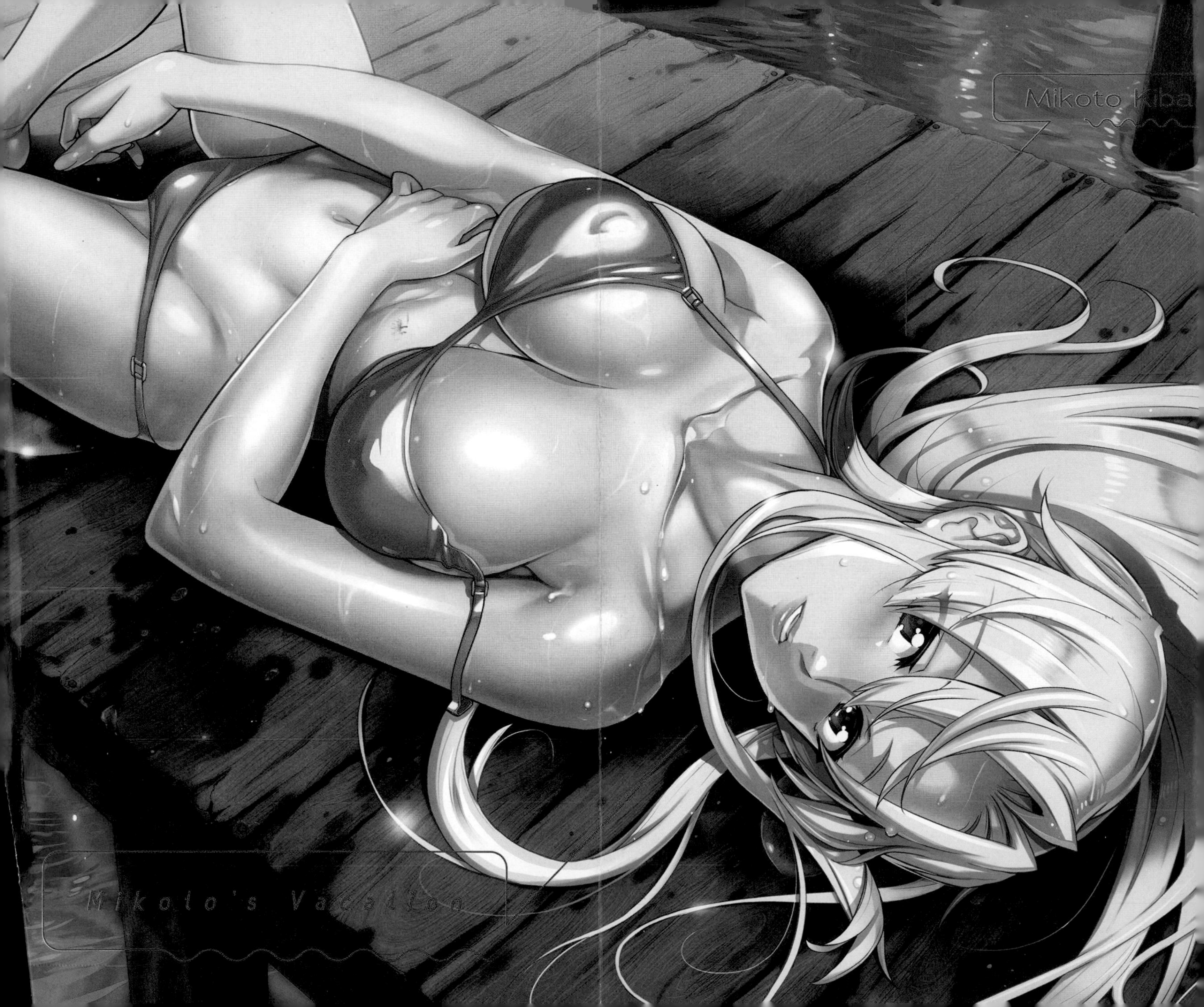
Mikoto Kiba
Mikoto's Vacation

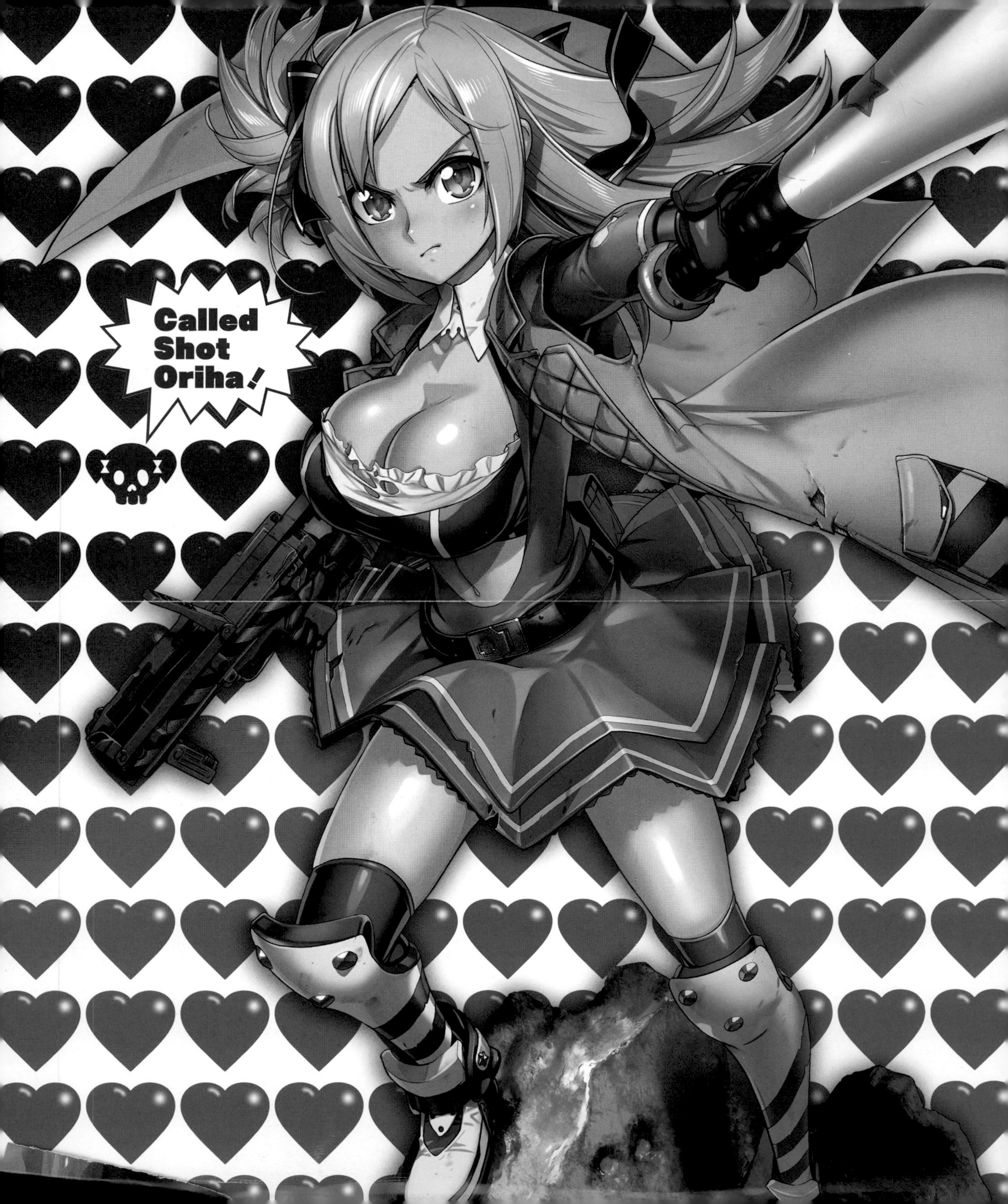
Called Shot Oriha!

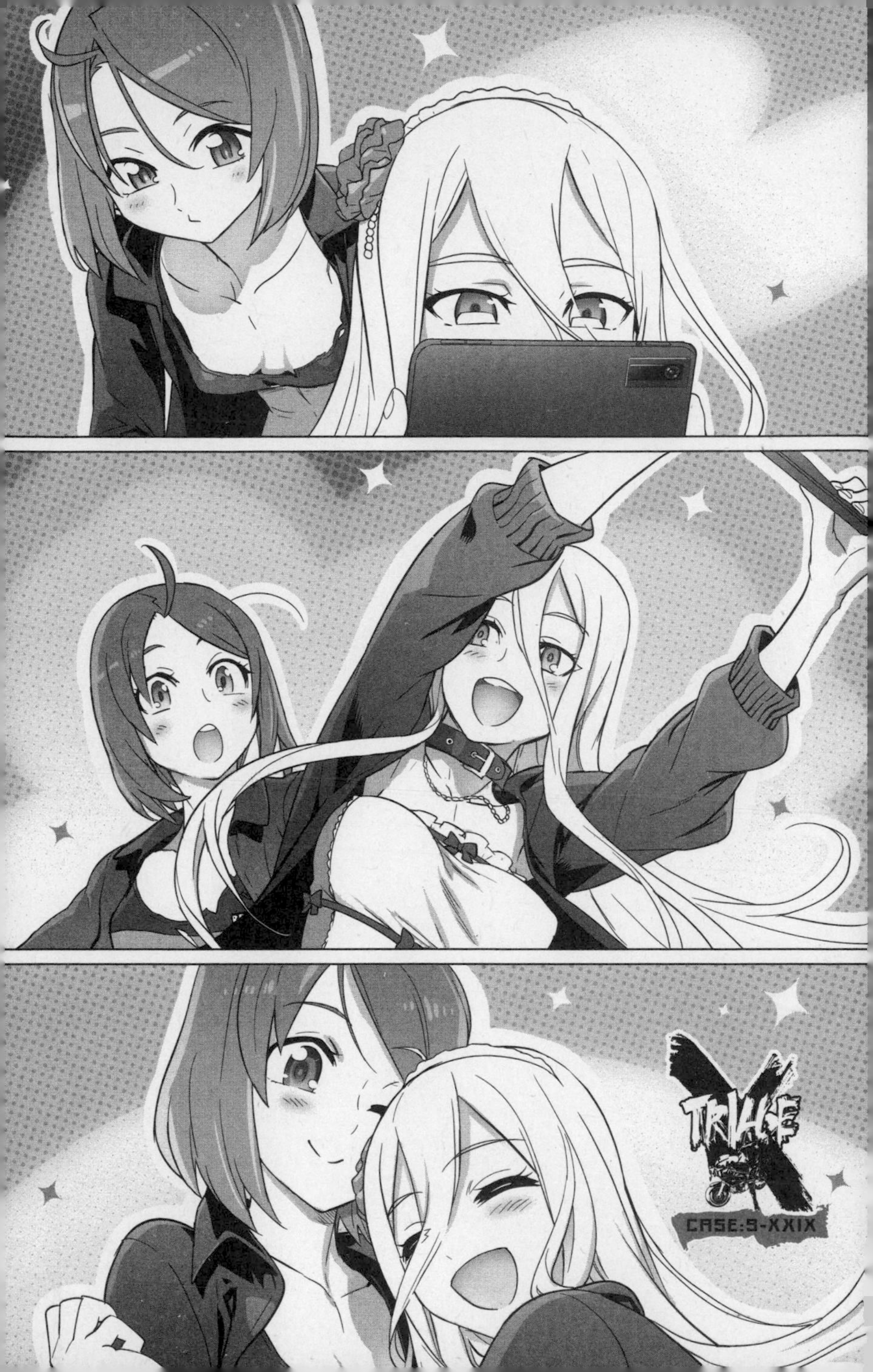
TRIAGE X
CASE:5-XXIX

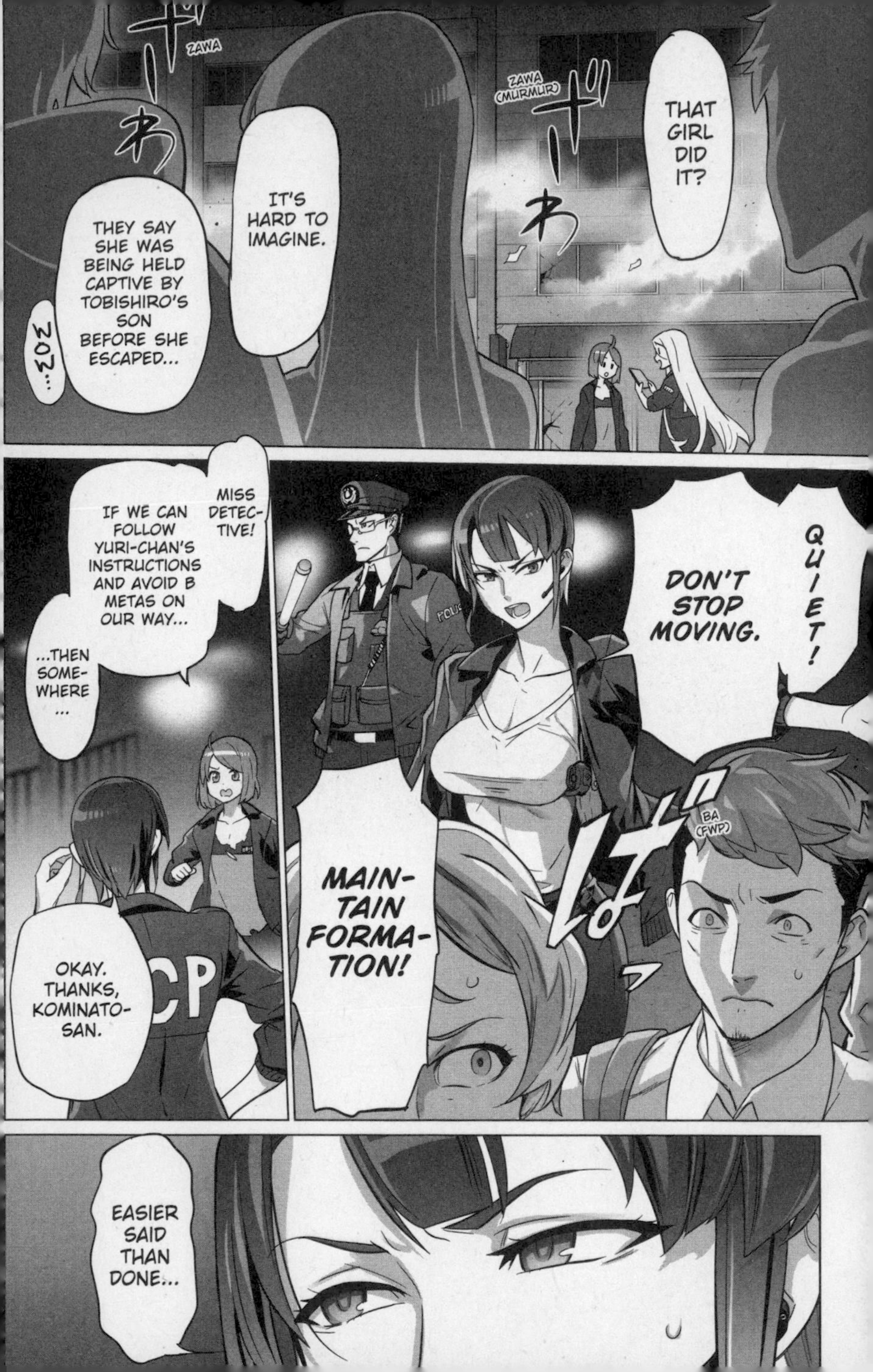
THAT GIRL DID IT?
ZAWA (MURMUR)
IT'S HARD TO IMAGINE.
ZAWA
THEY SAY SHE WAS BEING HELD CAPTIVE BY TOBISHIRO'S SON BEFORE SHE ESCAPED...
WOW...
QUIET!
DON'T STOP MOVING.
BA (FWP)
MAIN-TAIN FORMA-TION!
MISS DETEC-TIVE!
IF WE CAN FOLLOW YURI-CHAN'S INSTRUCTIONS AND AVOID B METAS ON OUR WAY...
...THEN SOME-WHERE ...
OKAY. THANKS, KOMINATO-SAN.
EASIER SAID THAN DONE...

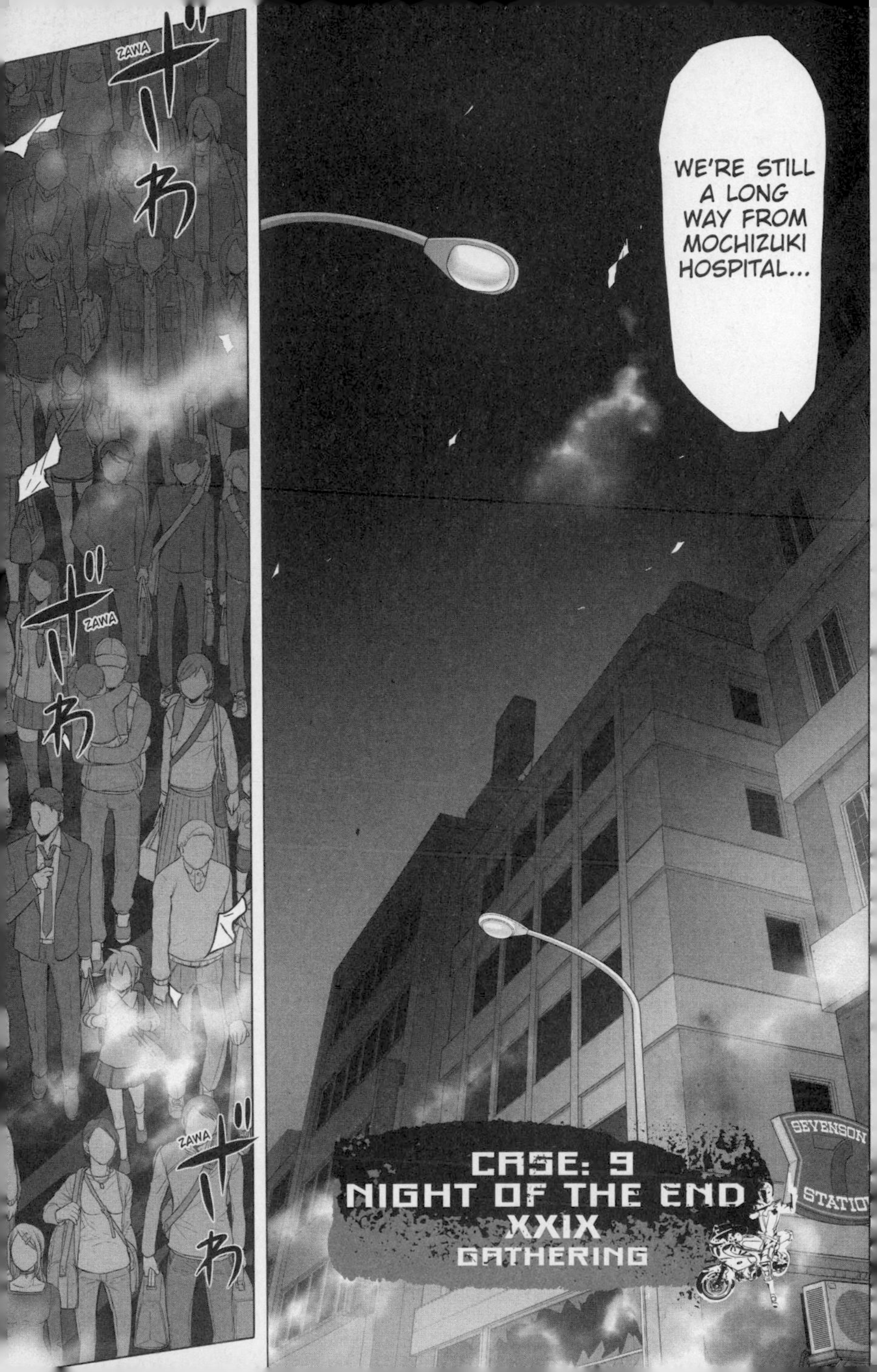
WE'RE STILL A LONG WAY FROM MOCHIZUKI HOSPITAL...
SEVENSON
CASE: 9
NIGHT OF THE END
XXIX
GATHERING
ZAWA
ザわ
ZAWA
ザわ
ZAWA
ザわ

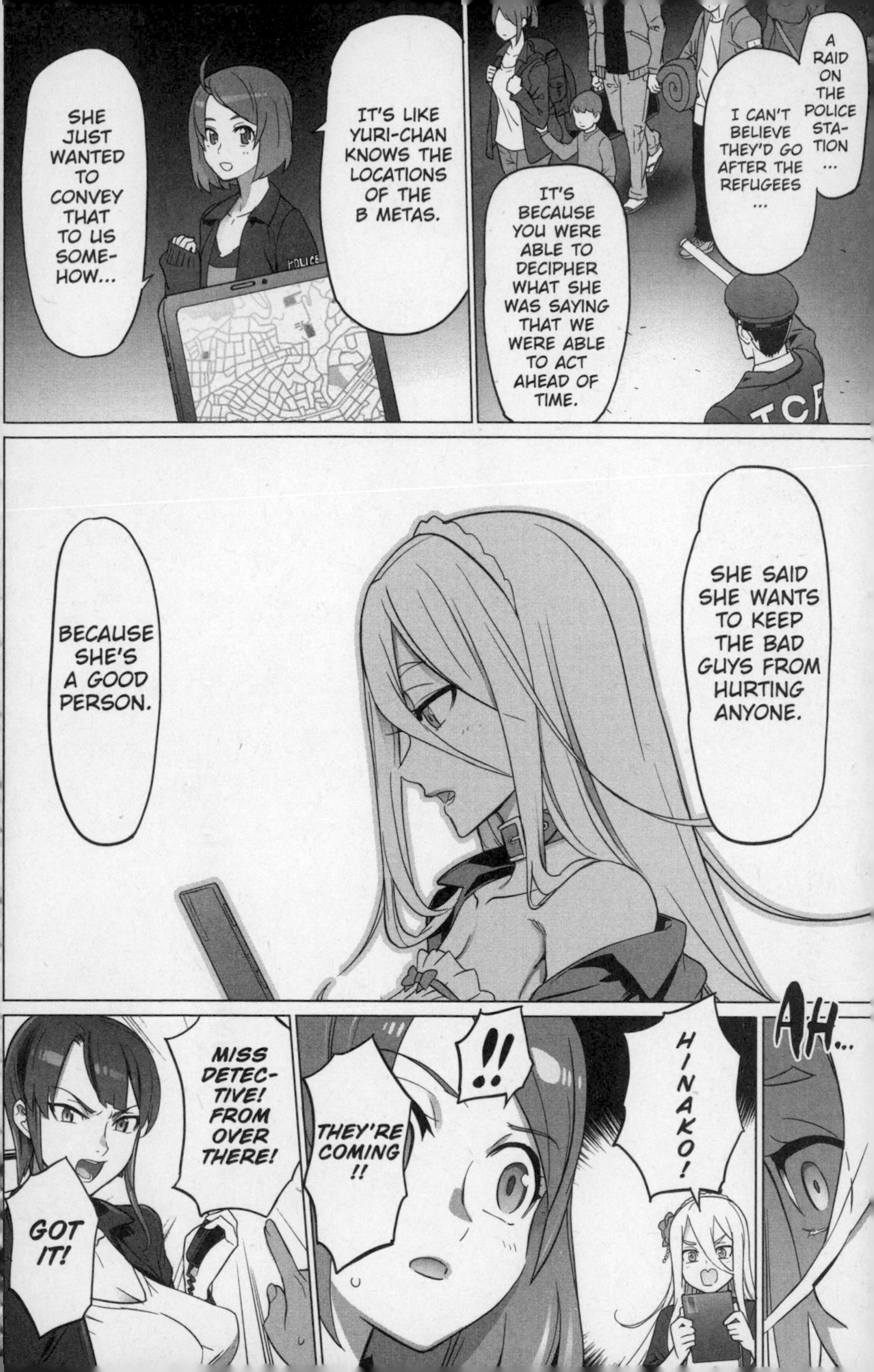

A RAID ON THE POLICE STATION...
I CAN'T BELIEVE THEY'D GO AFTER THE REFUGEES...
IT'S BECAUSE YOU WERE ABLE TO DECIPHER WHAT SHE WAS SAYING THAT WE WERE ABLE TO ACT AHEAD OF TIME.
TCP
IT'S LIKE YURI-CHAN KNOWS THE LOCATIONS OF THE B METAS.
POLICE
SHE JUST WANTED TO CONVEY THAT TO US SOMEHOW...
SHE SAID SHE WANTS TO KEEP THE BAD GUYS FROM HURTING ANYONE.
BECAUSE SHE'S A GOOD PERSON.
AH...
HINAKO!
!!
THEY'RE COMING!!
MISS DETECTIVE! FROM OVER THERE!
GOT IT!

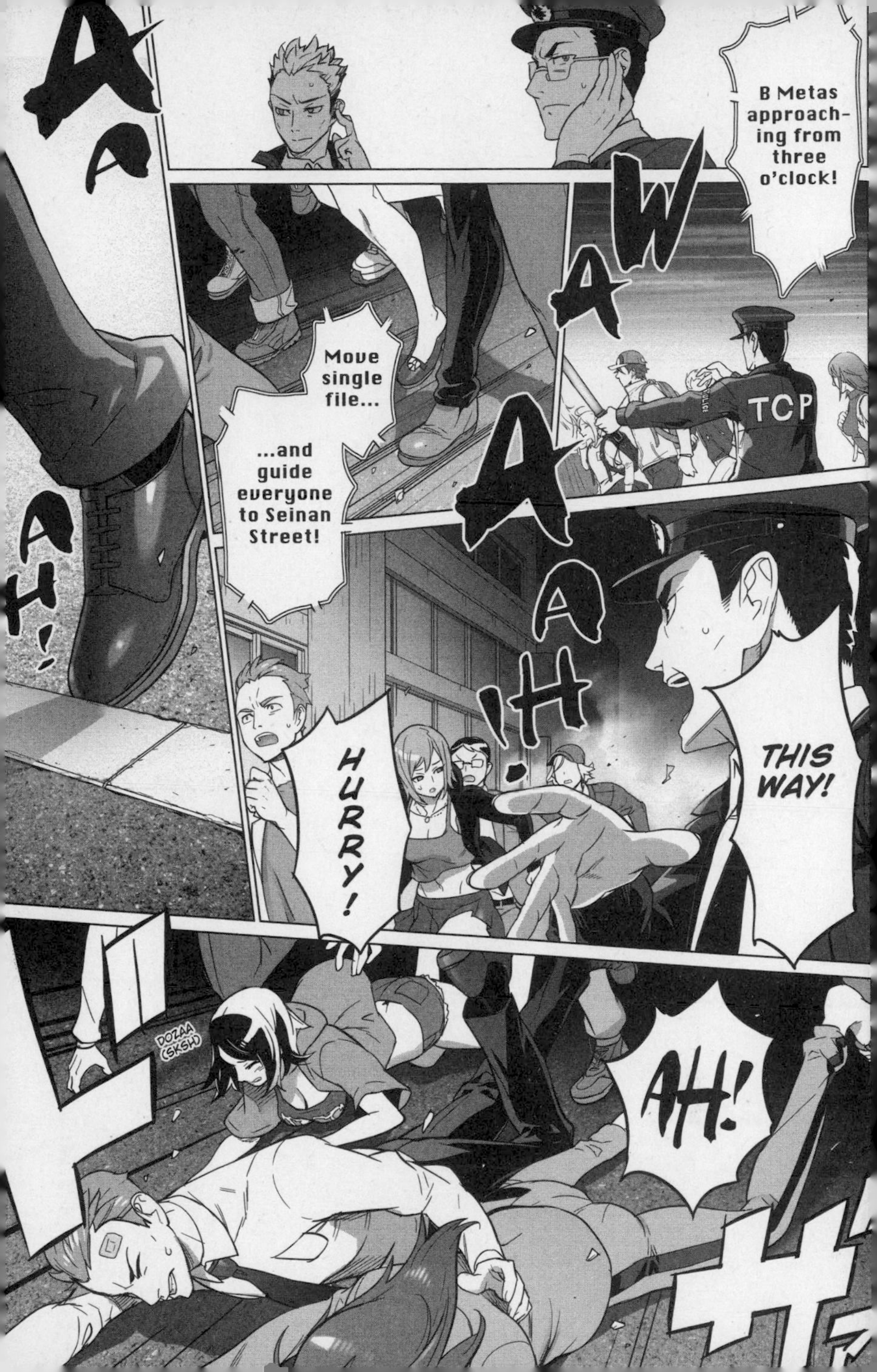
B Metas approaching from three o'clock!
Move single file...
...and guide everyone to Seinan Street!
TCP
AAAH!
THIS WAY!
HURRY!
AH!
DOZAA (SKSH)

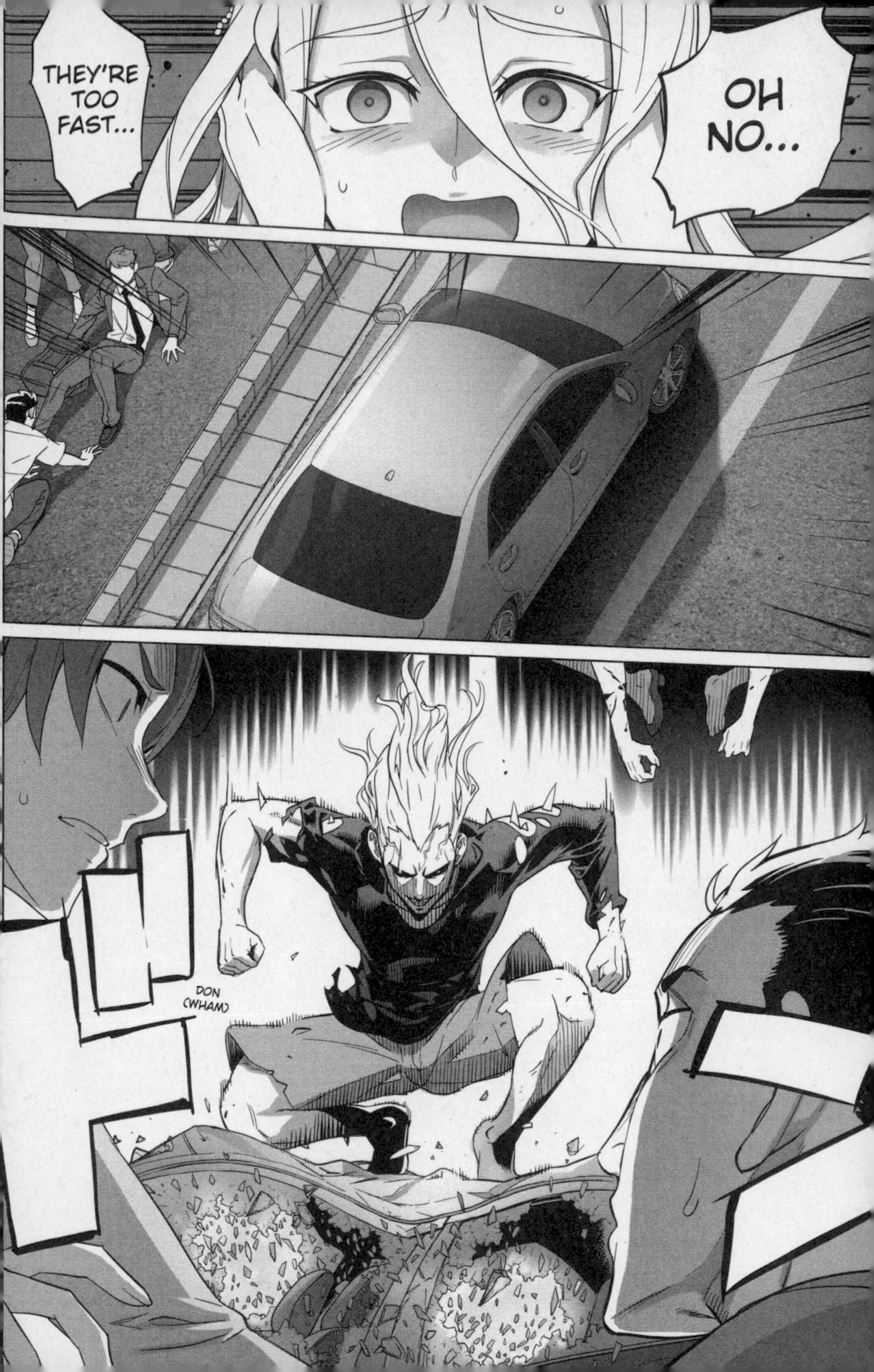
OH NO...
THEY'RE TOO FAST...
DON (WHAM)

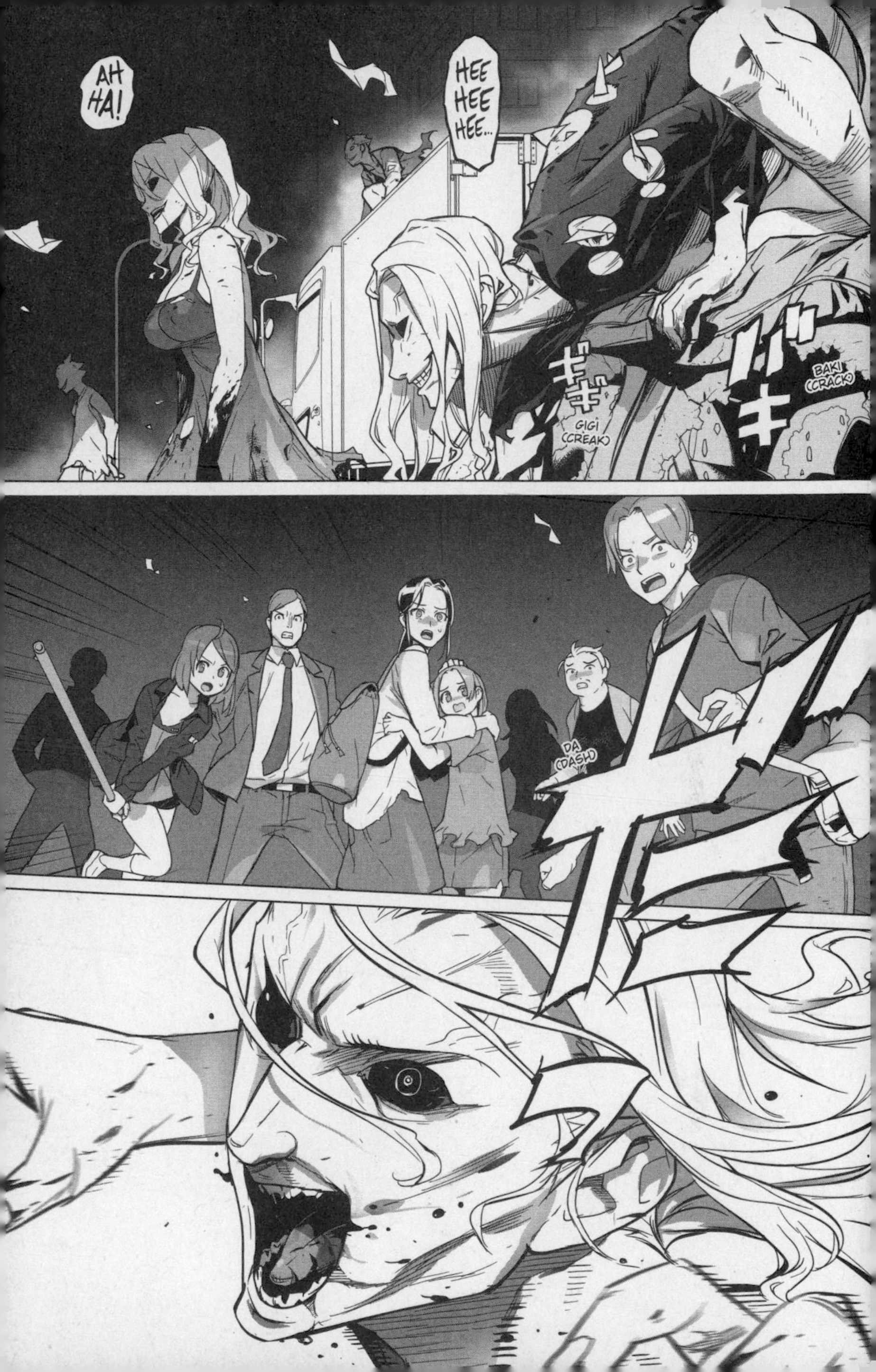
HEE HEE HEE...
AH HA!
BAKI (CRACK)
GIGI (CREAK)
DA (DASH)

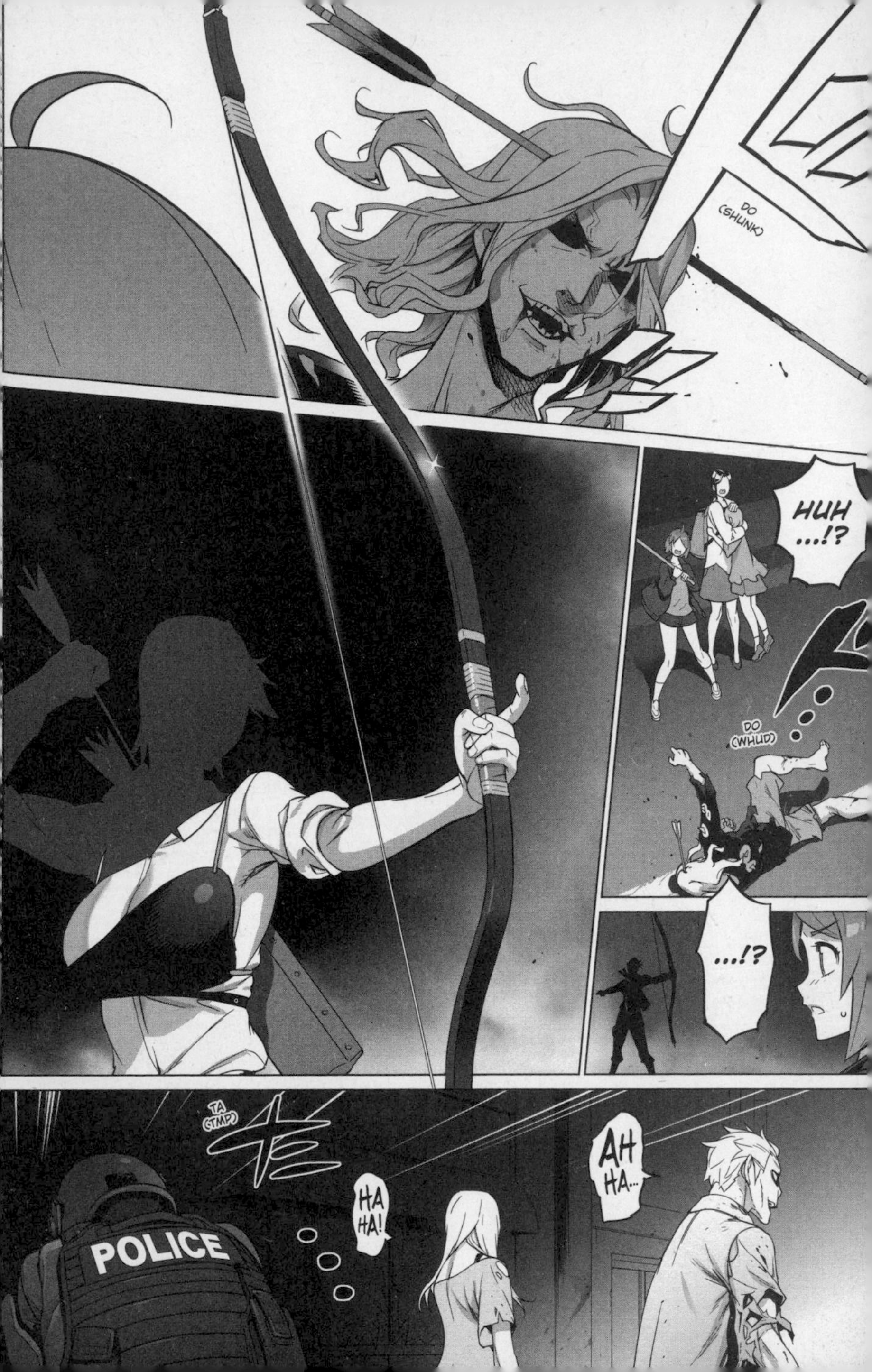
DO (SHUNK)
HUH ...!?
DO (WHUD)
...!?
AH HA...
HA HA!
TA (TMP)
POLICE

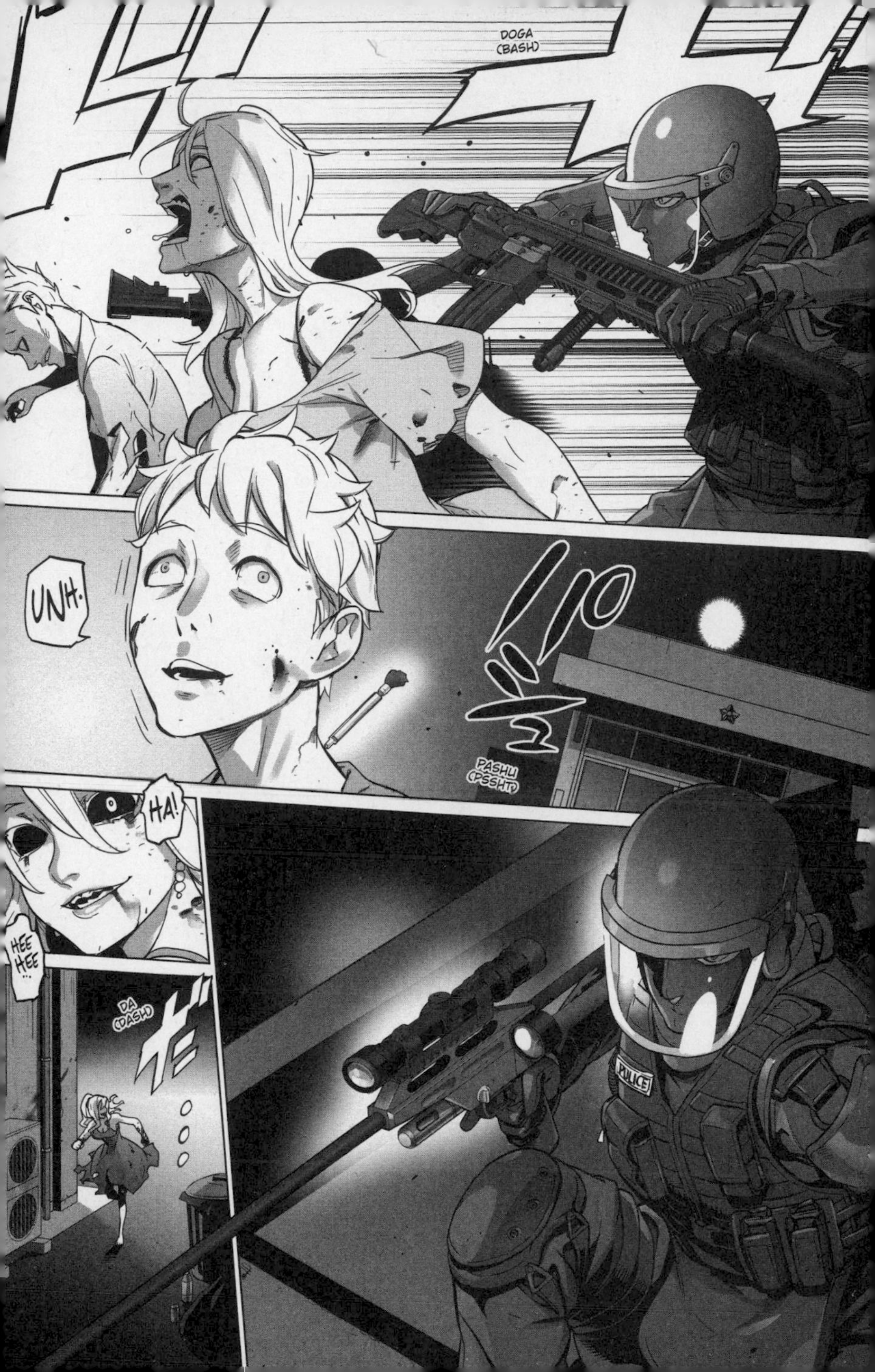
DOGA (BASH)
UNH.
PASHU (PSSHT)
HA!
HEE HEE ...
DA (DASH)

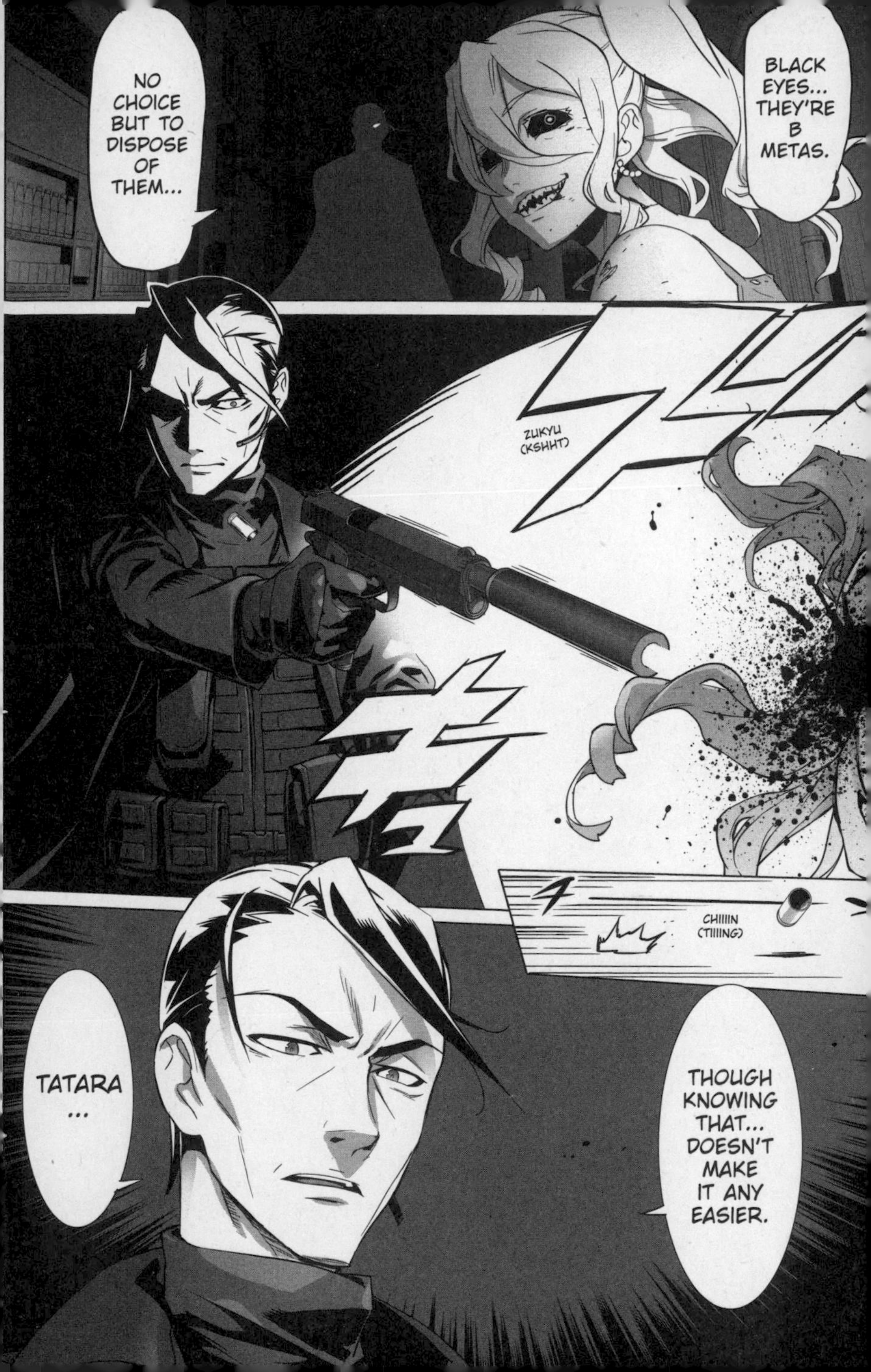
BLACK EYES... THEY'RE B METAS.
NO CHOICE BUT TO DISPOSE OF THEM...
ZUKYU (KSHHT)
CHIIIIN (TIIIING)
THOUGH KNOWING THAT... DOESN'T MAKE IT ANY EASIER.
TATARA ...

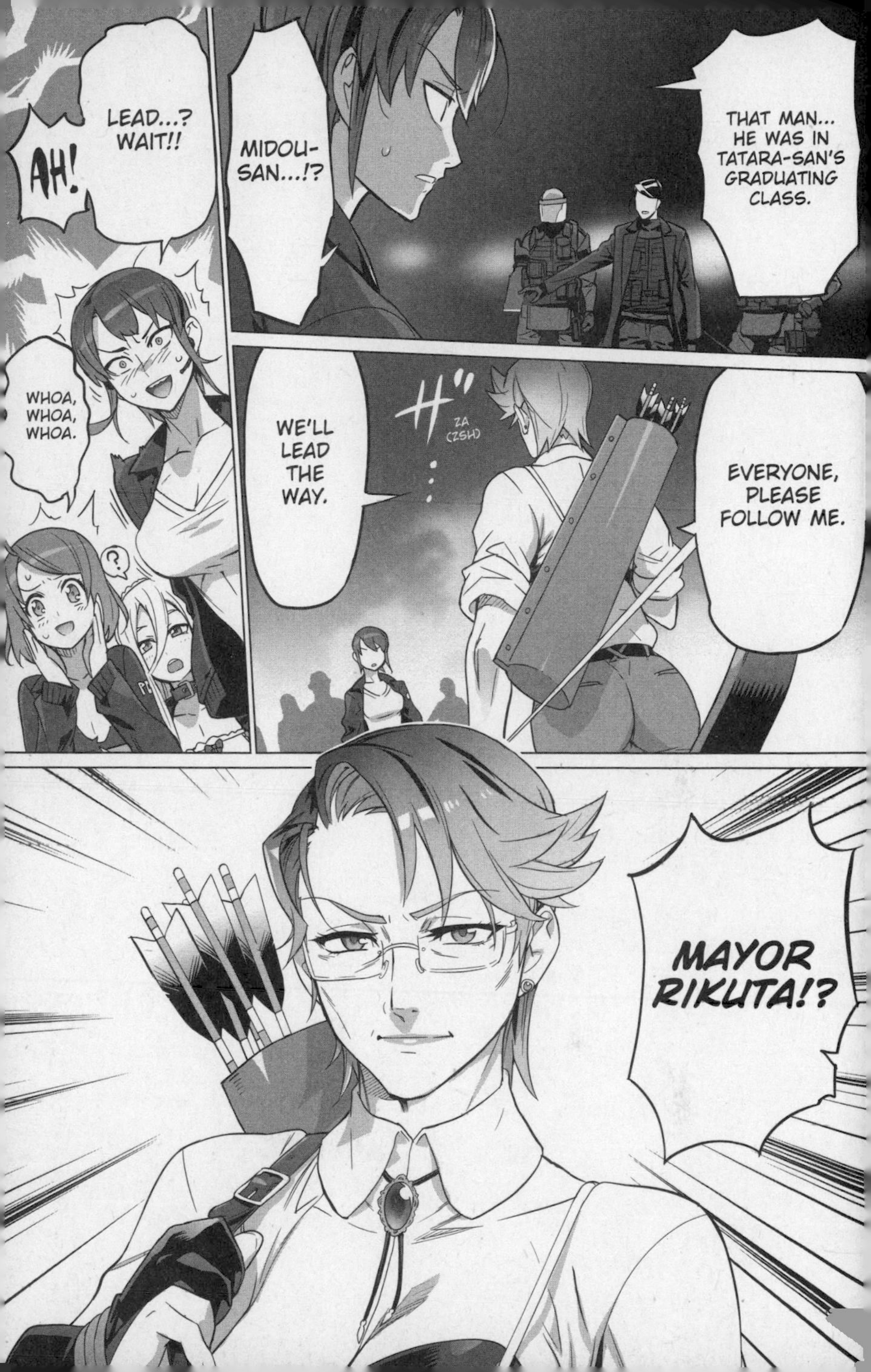
THAT MAN... HE WAS IN TATARA-SAN'S GRADUATING CLASS.
MIDOU-SAN...!?
EVERYONE, PLEASE FOLLOW ME.
ZA (ZSH)
WE'LL LEAD THE WAY.
LEAD...? WAIT!!
AH!
WHOA, WHOA, WHOA.
MAYOR RIKUTA!?

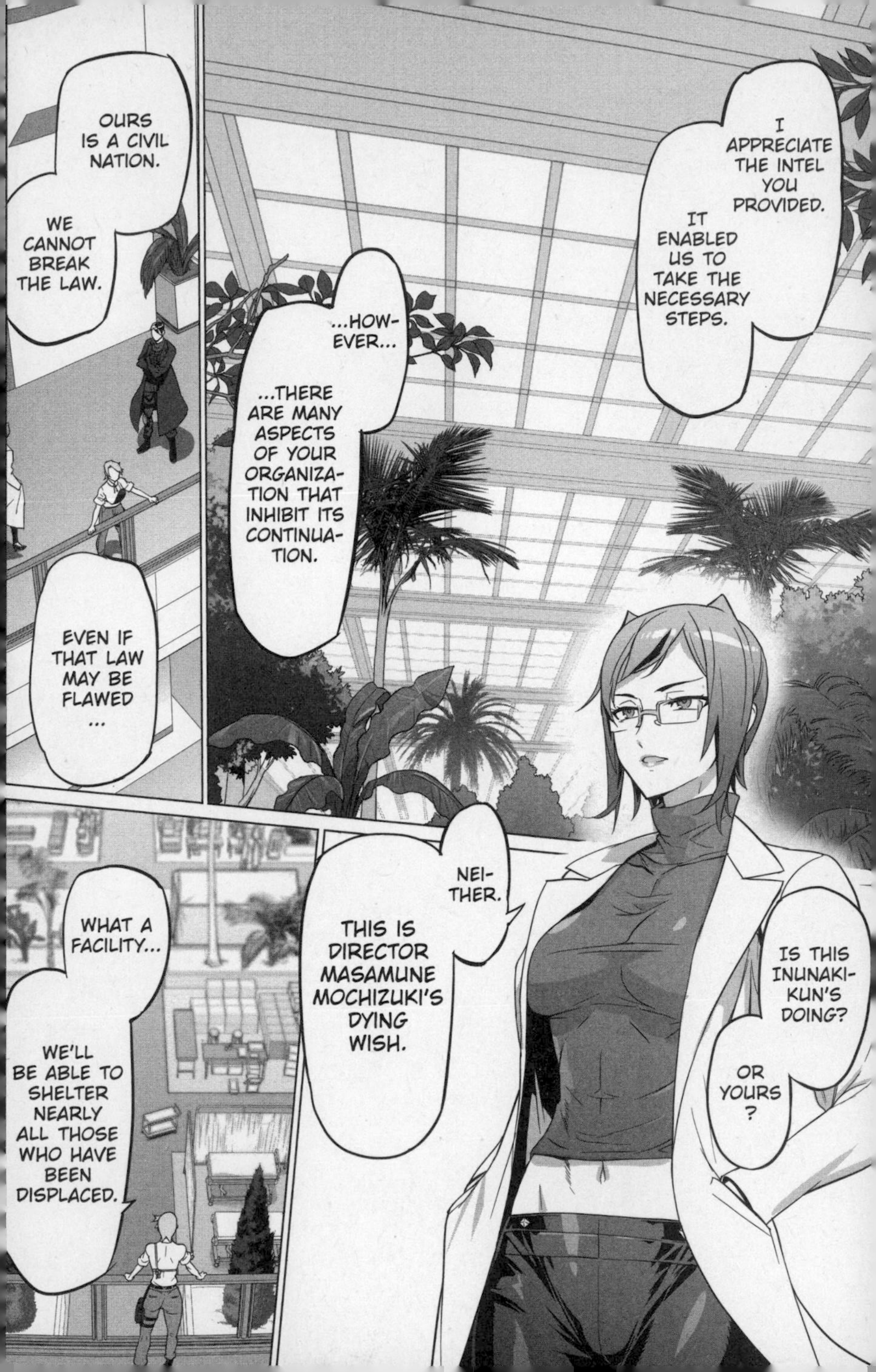
I APPRECIATE THE INTEL YOU PROVIDED.
IT ENABLED US TO TAKE THE NECESSARY STEPS.
...HOWEVER...
...THERE ARE MANY ASPECTS OF YOUR ORGANIZATION THAT INHIBIT ITS CONTINUATION.
OURS IS A CIVIL NATION.
WE CANNOT BREAK THE LAW.
EVEN IF THAT LAW MAY BE FLAWED...
IS THIS INUNAKI-KUN'S DOING?
OR YOURS?
NEITHER.
THIS IS DIRECTOR MASAMUNE MOCHIZUKI'S DYING WISH.
WHAT A FACILITY...
WE'LL BE ABLE TO SHELTER NEARLY ALL THOSE WHO HAVE BEEN DISPLACED.

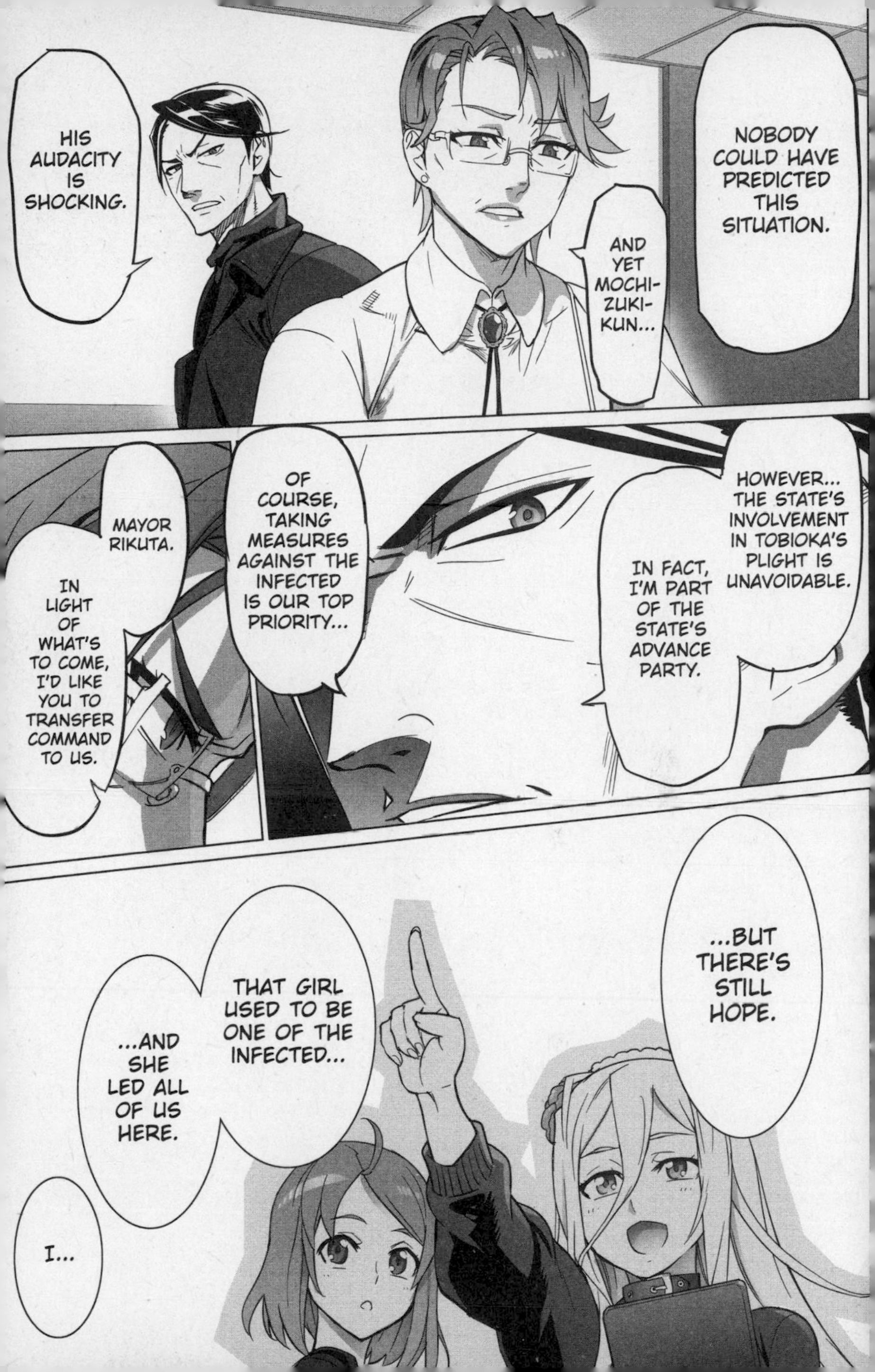
NOBODY COULD HAVE PREDICTED THIS SITUATION.
AND YET MOCHI-ZUKI-KUN...
HIS AUDACITY IS SHOCKING.
HOWEVER... THE STATE'S INVOLVEMENT IN TOBIOKA'S PLIGHT IS UNAVOIDABLE.
IN FACT, I'M PART OF THE STATE'S ADVANCE PARTY.
OF COURSE, TAKING MEASURES AGAINST THE INFECTED IS OUR TOP PRIORITY...
MAYOR RIKUTA.
IN LIGHT OF WHAT'S TO COME, I'D LIKE YOU TO TRANSFER COMMAND TO US.
...BUT THERE'S STILL HOPE.
THAT GIRL USED TO BE ONE OF THE INFECTED...
...AND SHE LED ALL OF US HERE.
I...

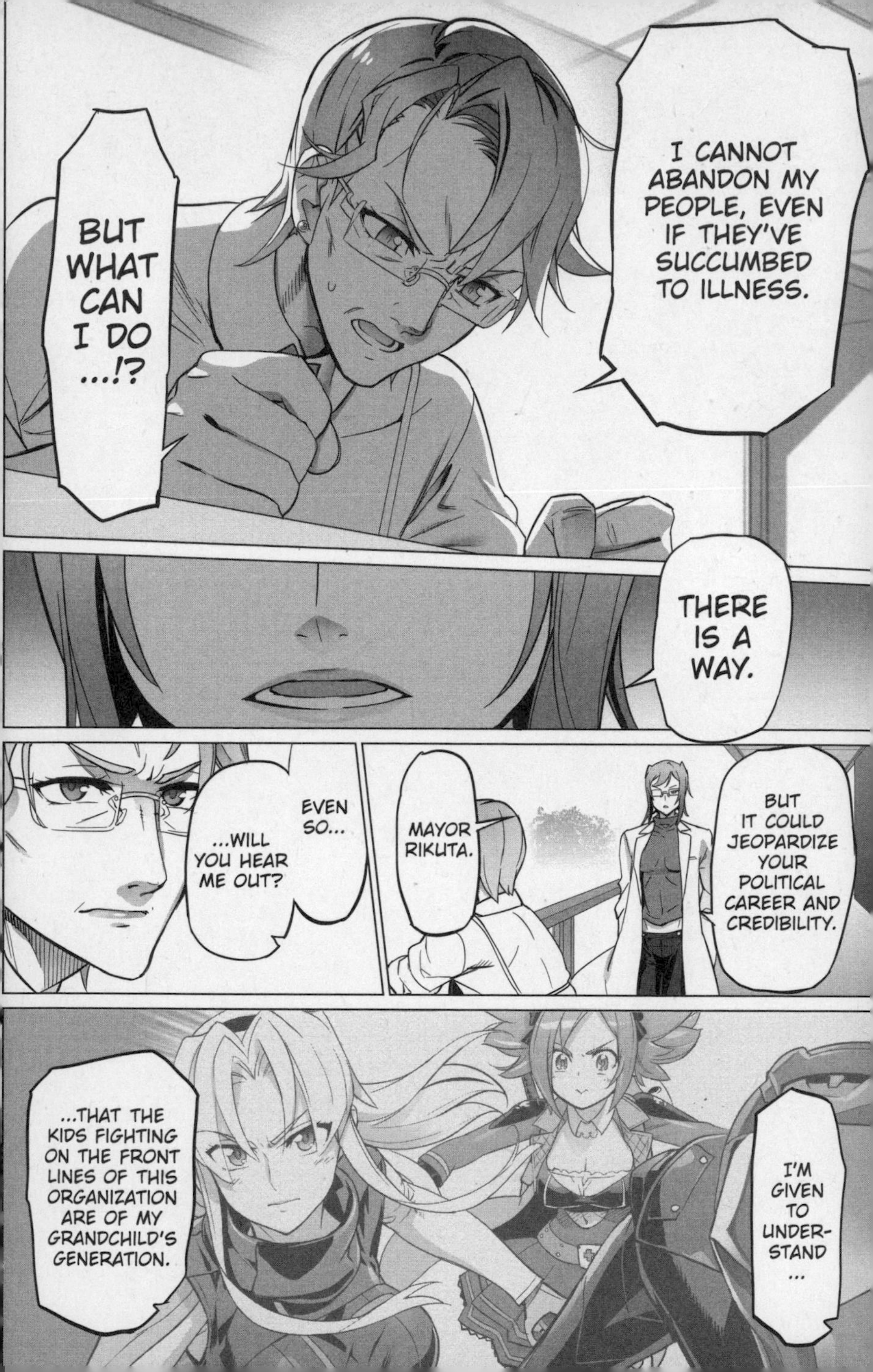
I CANNOT ABANDON MY PEOPLE, EVEN IF THEY'VE SUCCUMBED TO ILLNESS.
BUT WHAT CAN I DO ...!?
THERE IS A WAY.
BUT IT COULD JEOPARDIZE YOUR POLITICAL CAREER AND CREDIBILITY.
MAYOR RIKUTA.
EVEN SO...
...WILL YOU HEAR ME OUT?
I'M GIVEN TO UNDER-STAND ...
...THAT THE KIDS FIGHTING ON THE FRONT LINES OF THIS ORGANIZATION ARE OF MY GRANDCHILD'S GENERATION.

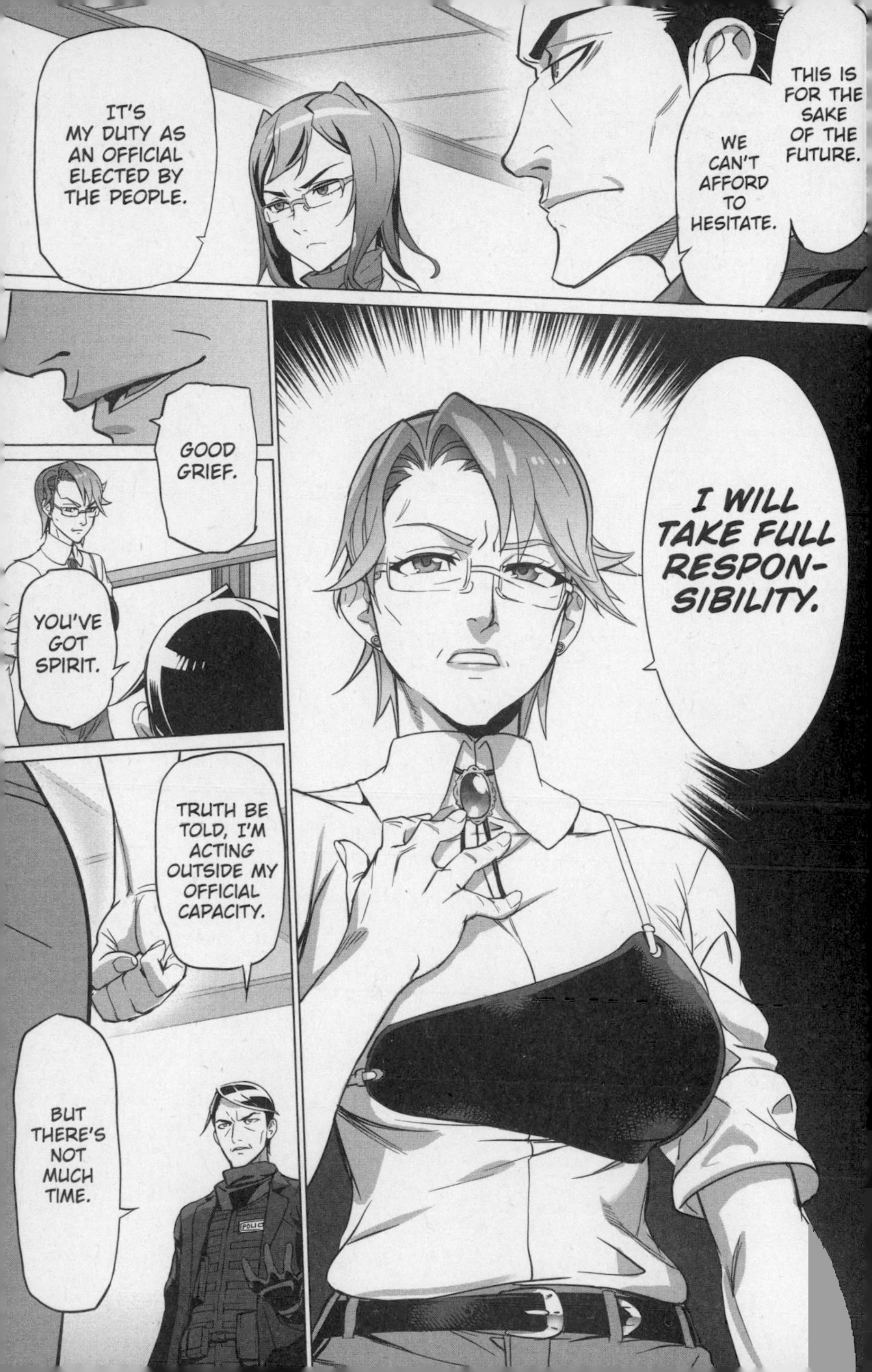
THIS IS FOR THE SAKE OF THE FUTURE.
WE CAN'T AFFORD TO HESITATE.
IT'S MY DUTY AS AN OFFICIAL ELECTED BY THE PEOPLE.
I WILL TAKE FULL RESPON-SIBILITY.
GOOD GRIEF.
YOU'VE GOT SPIRIT.
TRUTH BE TOLD, I'M ACTING OUTSIDE MY OFFICIAL CAPACITY.
BUT THERE'S NOT MUCH TIME.

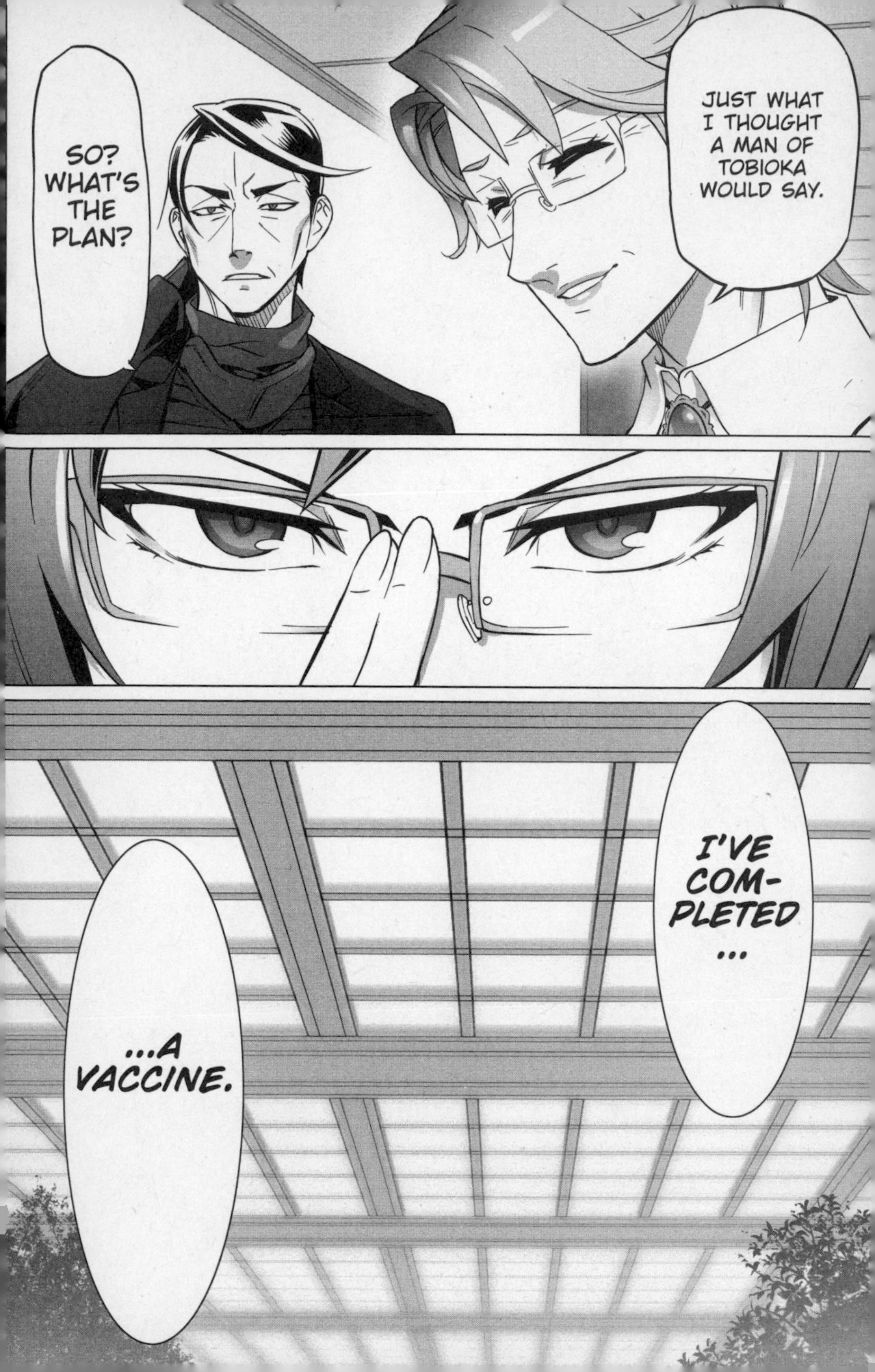
JUST WHAT I THOUGHT A MAN OF TOBIOKA WOULD SAY.
SO? WHAT'S THE PLAN?
I'VE COM-PLETED ...
...A VACCINE.

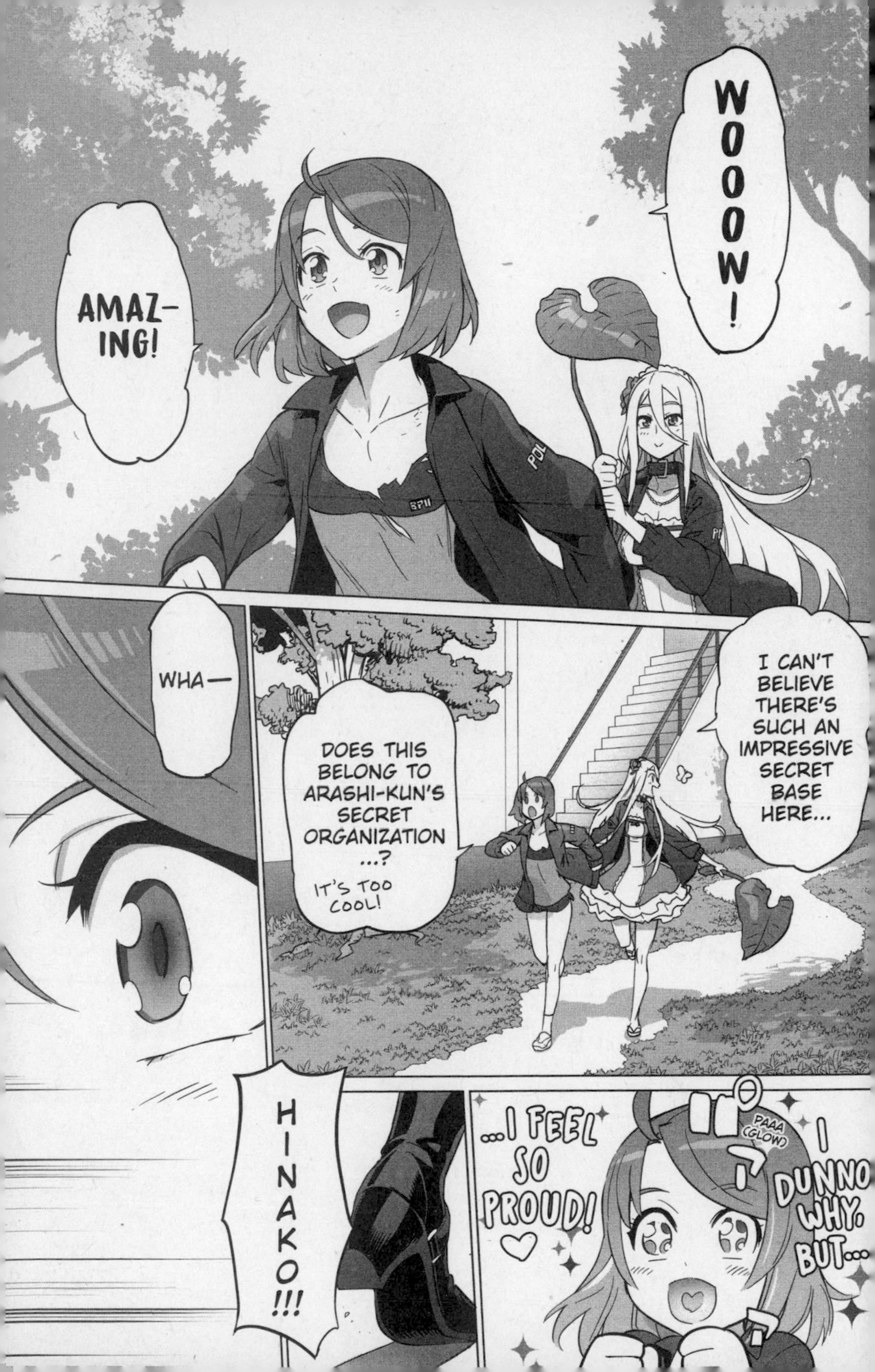
WOOOOW!
AMAZ-ING!
I CAN'T BELIEVE THERE'S SUCH AN IMPRESSIVE SECRET BASE HERE...
DOES THIS BELONG TO ARASHI-KUN'S SECRET ORGANIZATION ...?
IT'S TOO COOL!
WHA—
PAAA (GLOW)
I DUNNO WHY, BUT...
...I FEEL SO PROUD!
HINAKO!!!

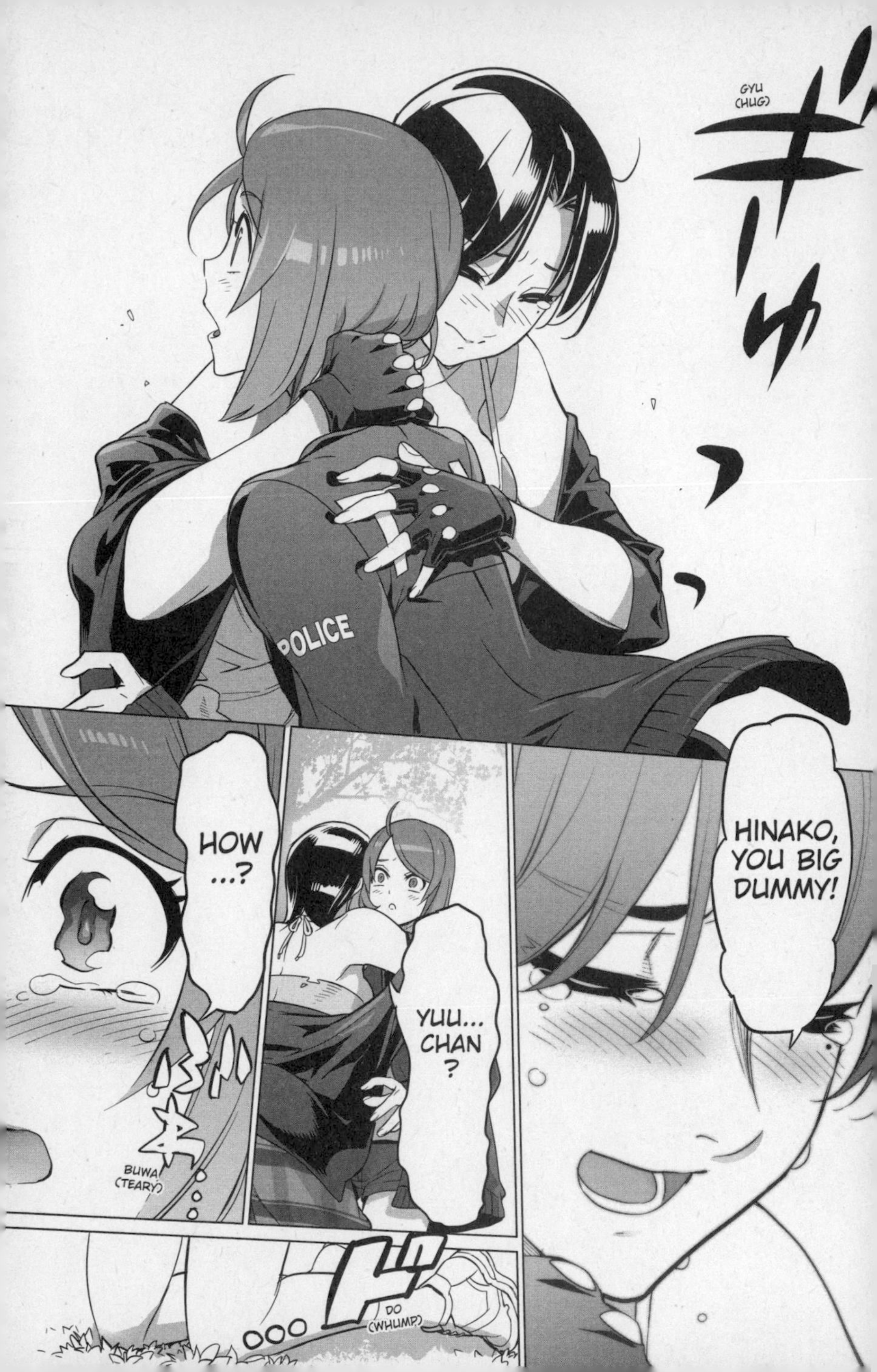
GYU (HUG)
HINAKO, YOU BIG DUMMY!
YUU... CHAN ?
HOW ...?
BUWA (TEARY)
DO (WHUMP)

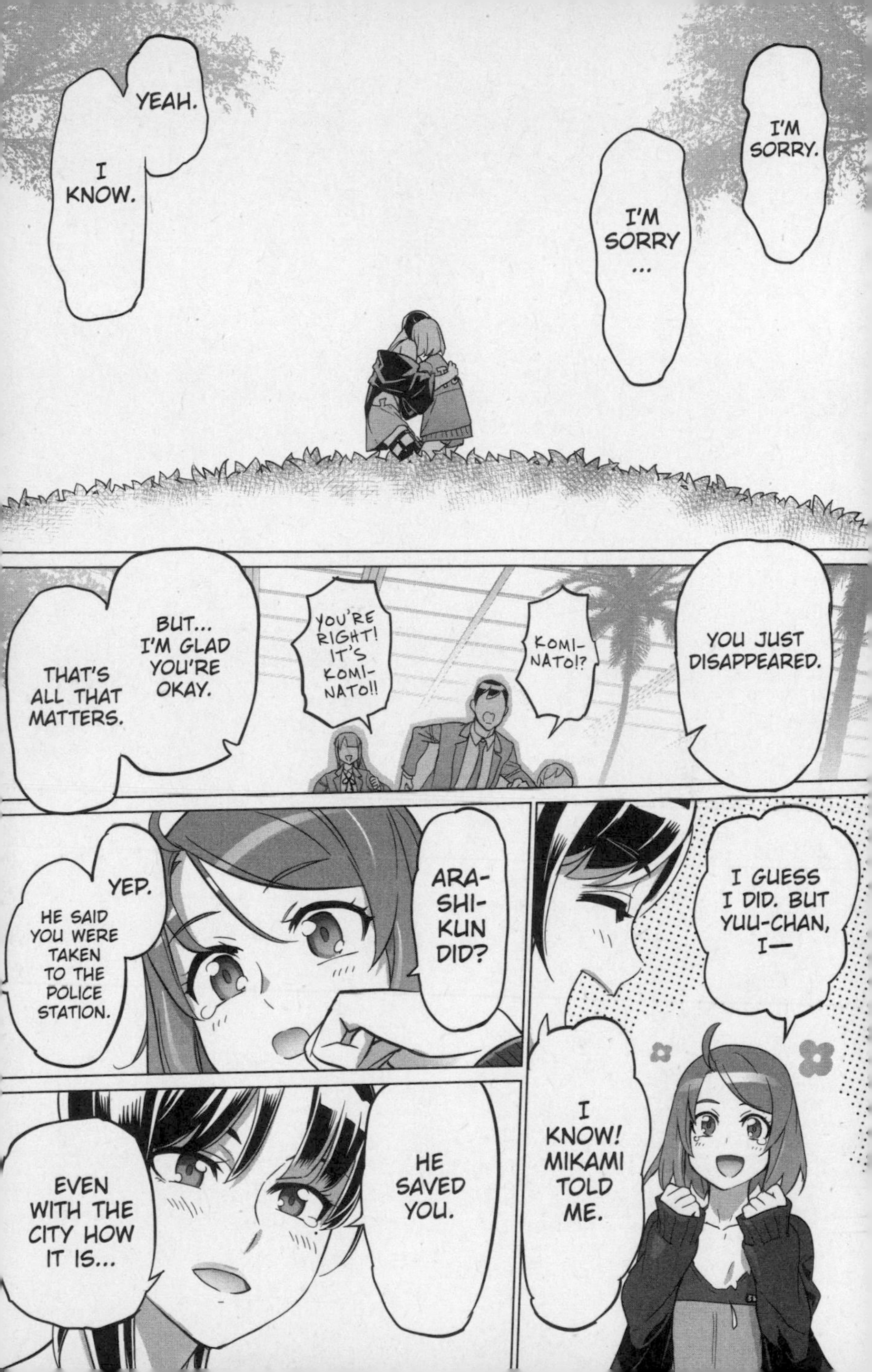
I'M SORRY.
I'M SORRY...
YEAH. I KNOW.
YOU JUST DISAPPEARED.
KOMI-NATO!?
YOU'RE RIGHT! IT'S KOMI-NATO!!
BUT... I'M GLAD YOU'RE OKAY. THAT'S ALL THAT MATTERS.
I GUESS I DID. BUT YUU-CHAN, I—
I KNOW! MIKAMI TOLD ME.
ARA-SHI-KUN DID?
YEP. HE SAID YOU WERE TAKEN TO THE POLICE STATION.
HE SAVED YOU.
EVEN WITH THE CITY HOW IT IS...

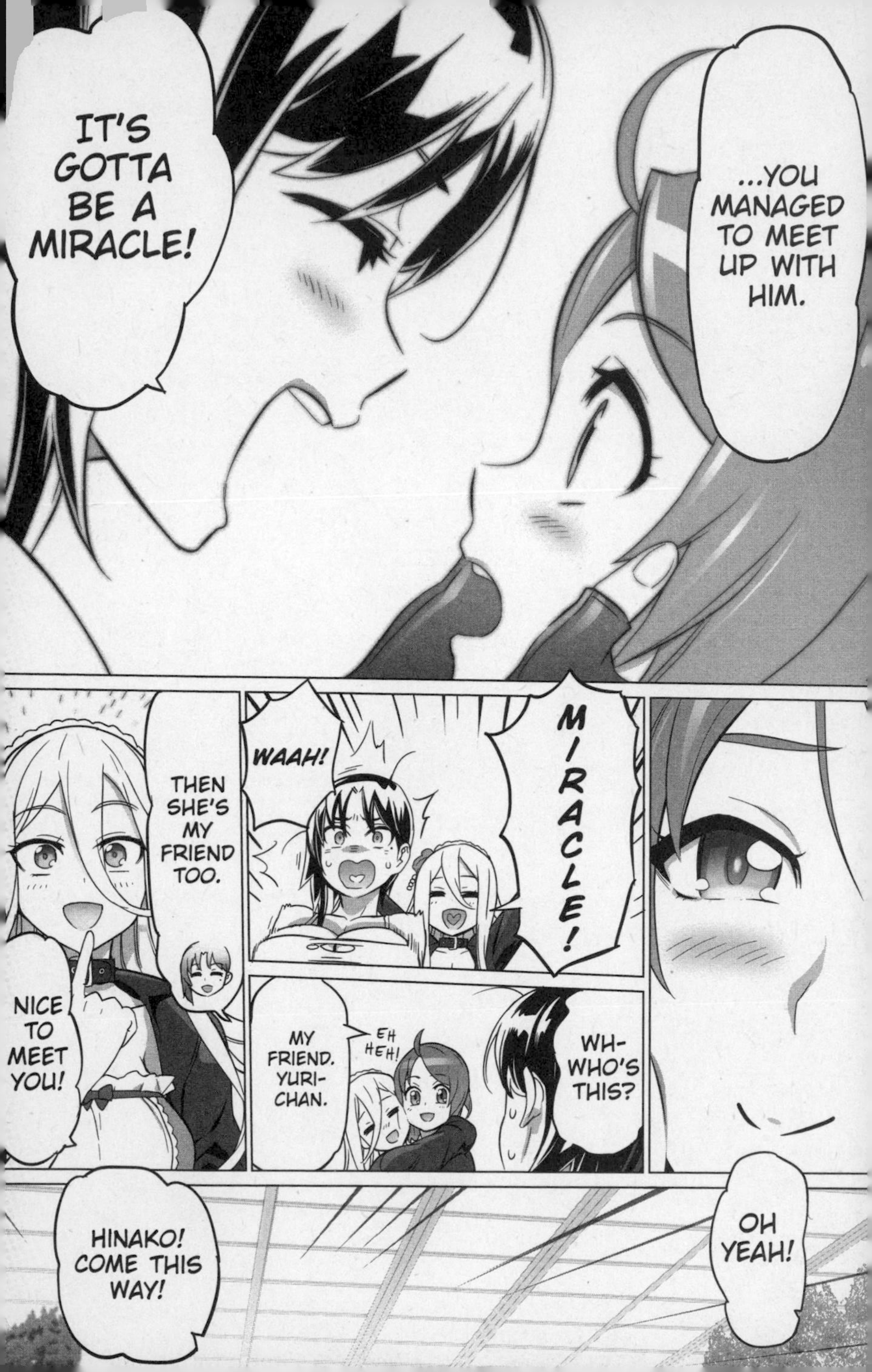
...YOU MANAGED TO MEET UP WITH HIM.
IT'S GOTTA BE A MIRACLE!
MIRACLE!
WAAH!
WH-WHO'S THIS?
EH HEH!
MY FRIEND. YURI-CHAN.
THEN SHE'S MY FRIEND TOO.
NICE TO MEET YOU!
OH YEAH!
HINAKO! COME THIS WAY!

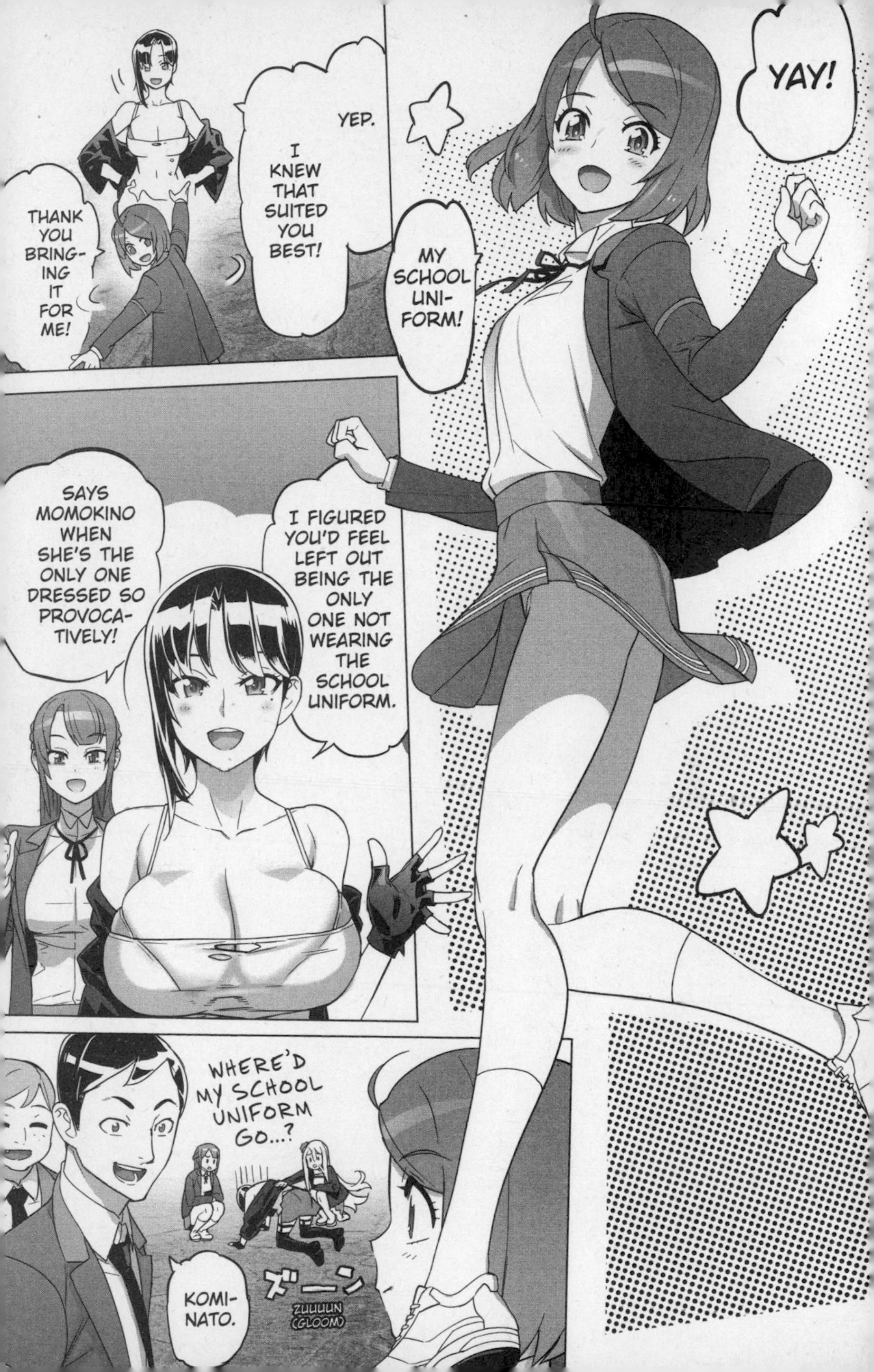
YAY!
MY SCHOOL UNIFORM!
YEP. I KNEW THAT SUITED YOU BEST!
THANK YOU BRINGING IT FOR ME!
I FIGURED YOU'D FEEL LEFT OUT BEING THE ONLY ONE NOT WEARING THE SCHOOL UNIFORM.
SAYS MOMOKINO WHEN SHE'S THE ONLY ONE DRESSED SO PROVOCATIVELY!
WHERE'D MY SCHOOL UNIFORM GO...?
ズーン
ZUUUUN (GLOOM)
KOMINATO.

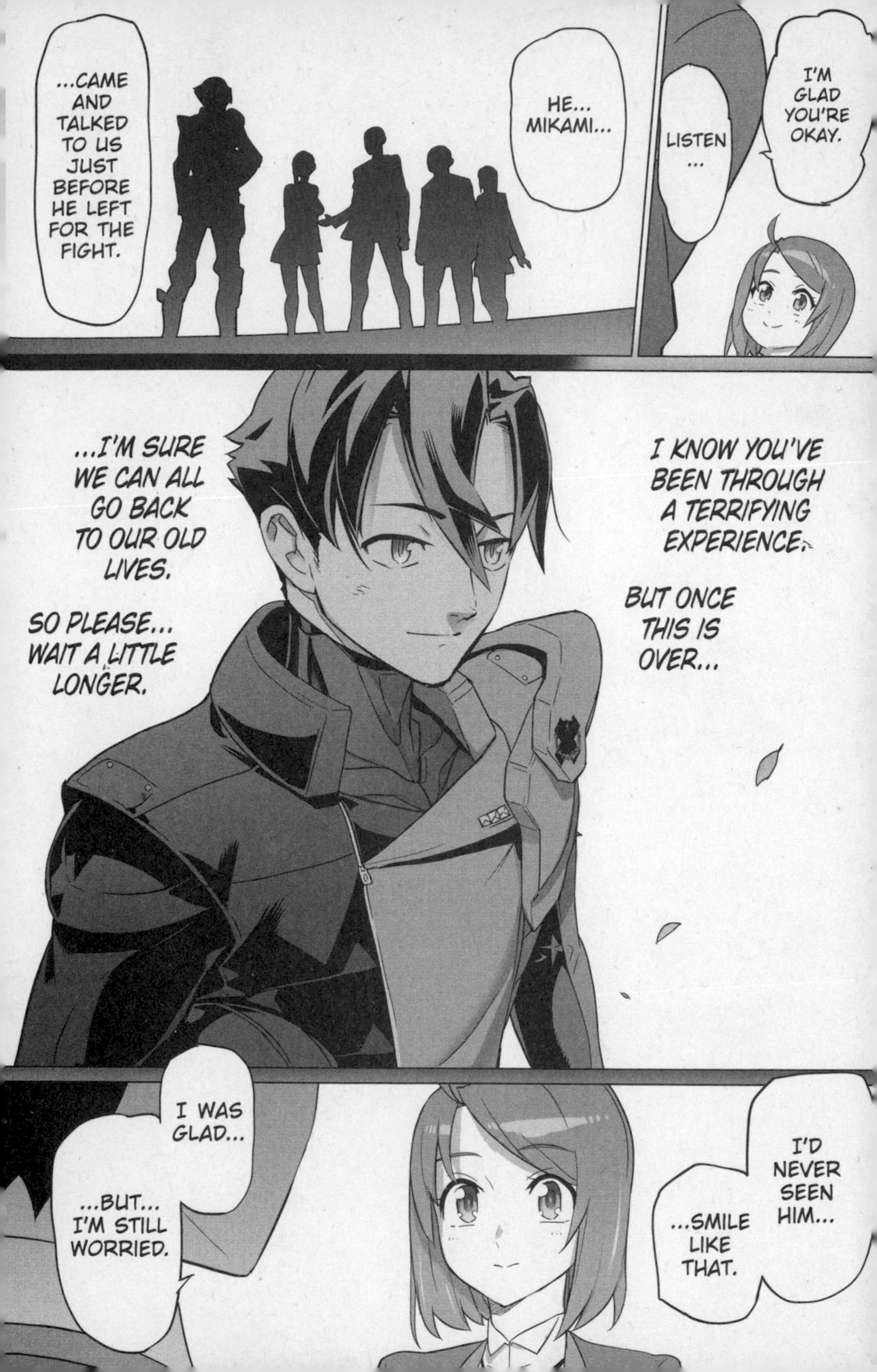
I'M GLAD YOU'RE OKAY.
LISTEN...
HE... MIKAMI...
...CAME AND TALKED TO US JUST BEFORE HE LEFT FOR THE FIGHT.
I KNOW YOU'VE BEEN THROUGH A TERRIFYING EXPERIENCE.
BUT ONCE THIS IS OVER...
...I'M SURE WE CAN ALL GO BACK TO OUR OLD LIVES.
SO PLEASE... WAIT A LITTLE LONGER.
I'D NEVER SEEN HIM...
...SMILE LIKE THAT.
I WAS GLAD...
...BUT... I'M STILL WORRIED.

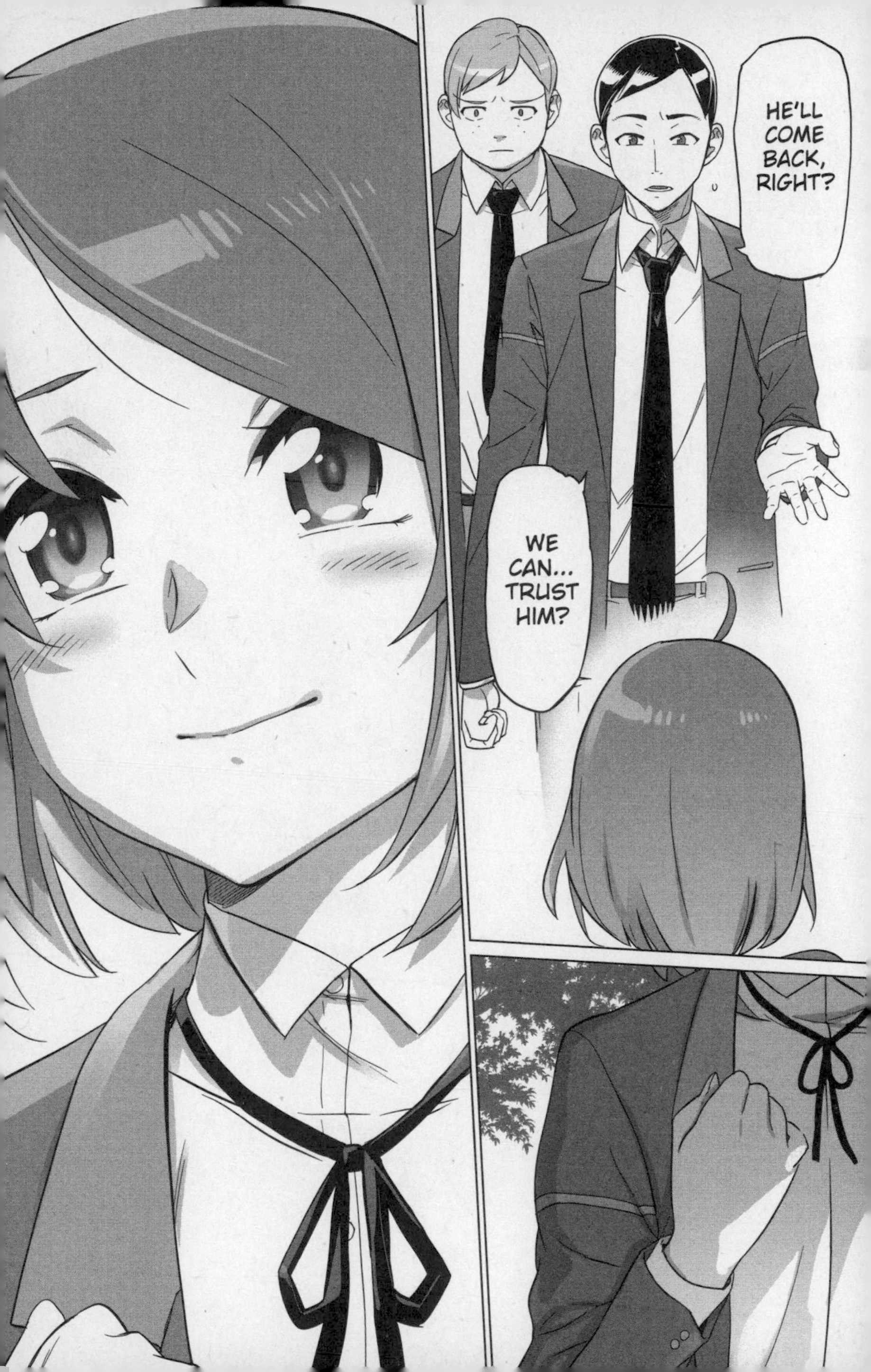
HE'LL COME BACK, RIGHT?
WE CAN... TRUST HIM?

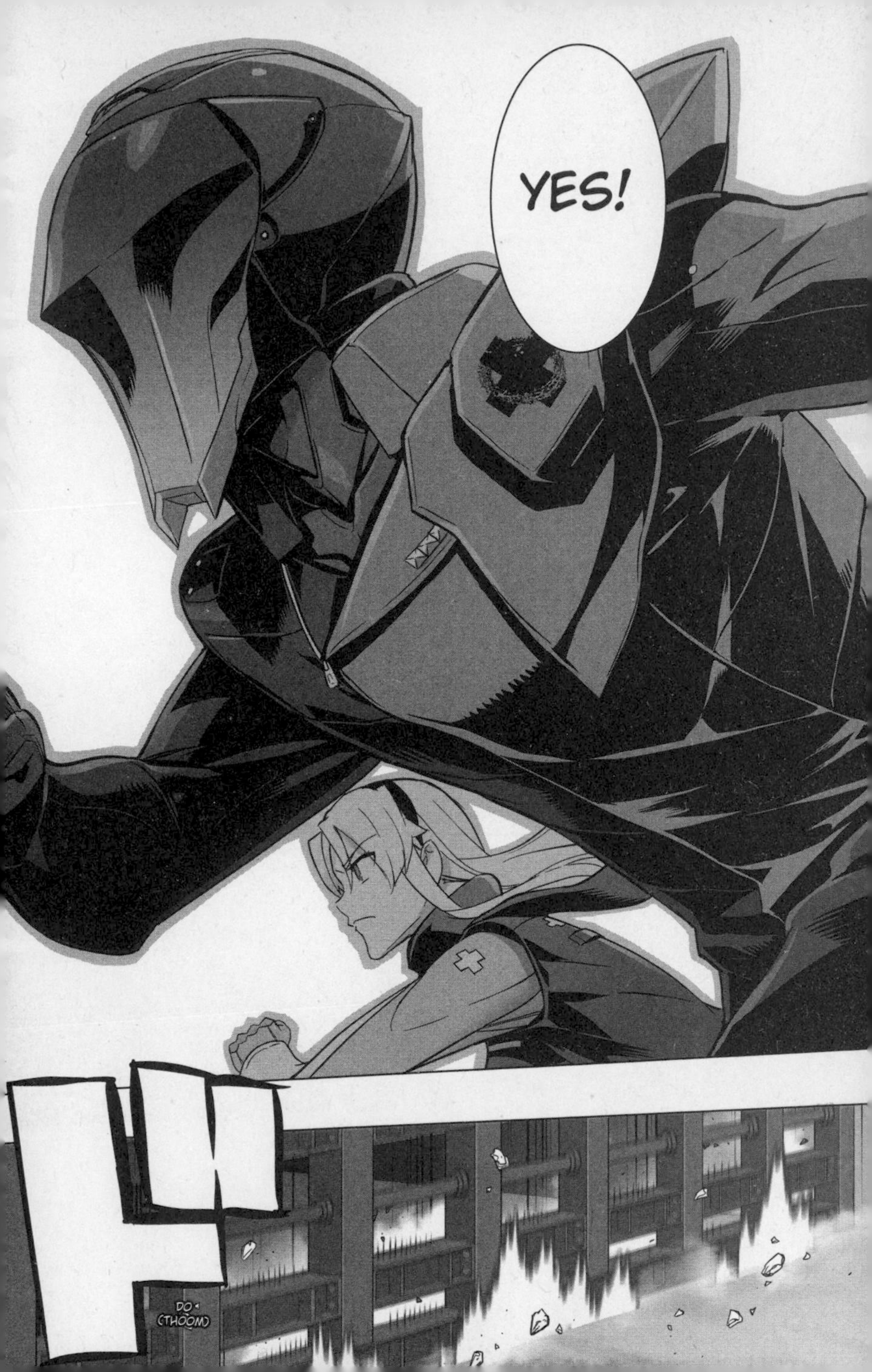
YES!
DO
(THOOM)

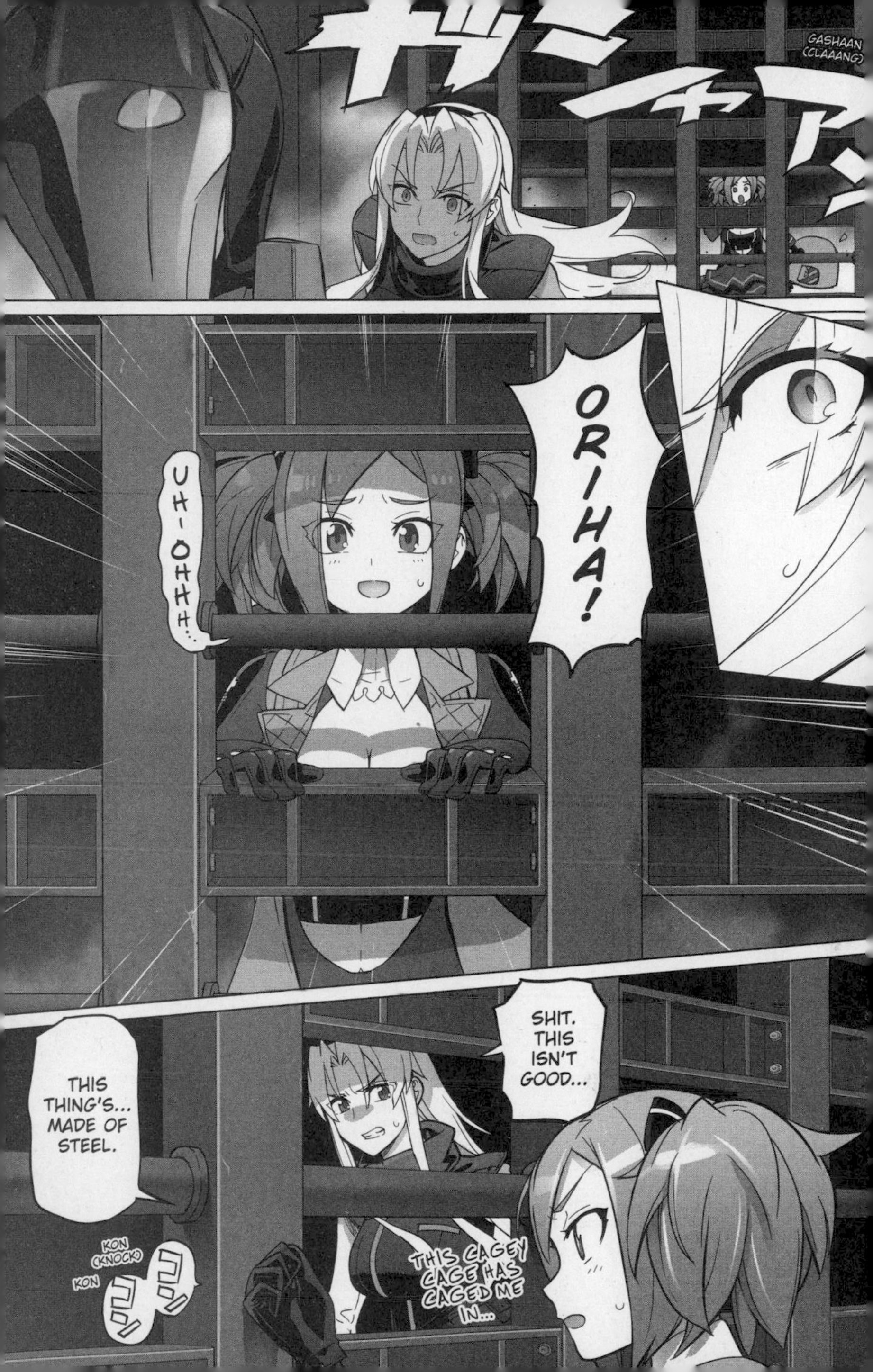
GASHAAN (CLAAANG)
ORIHA!
UH-OHHHH...
SHIT. THIS ISN'T GOOD...
THIS THING'S... MADE OF STEEL.
THIS CAGEY CAGE HAS CAGED ME IN...
KON (KNOCK) KON

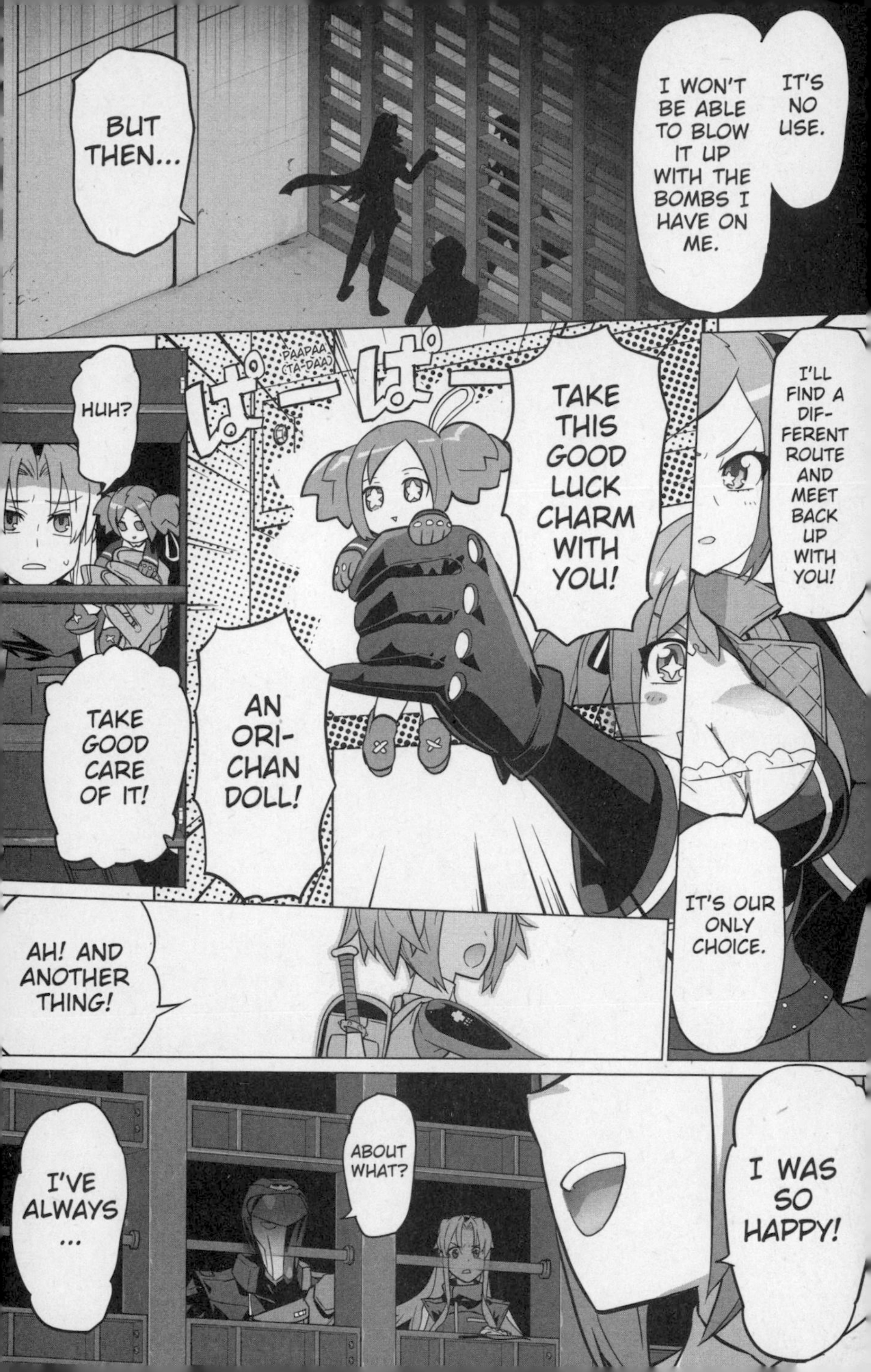

IT'S NO USE.
I WON'T BE ABLE TO BLOW IT UP WITH THE BOMBS I HAVE ON ME.
BUT THEN...
I'LL FIND A DIF-FERENT ROUTE AND MEET BACK UP WITH YOU!
IT'S OUR ONLY CHOICE.
ぱーぱー
PAAPAA (TA-DAA)
TAKE THIS GOOD LUCK CHARM WITH YOU!
AN ORI-CHAN DOLL!
TAKE GOOD CARE OF IT!
HUH?
AH! AND ANOTHER THING!
I WAS SO HAPPY!
ABOUT WHAT?
I'VE ALWAYS ...

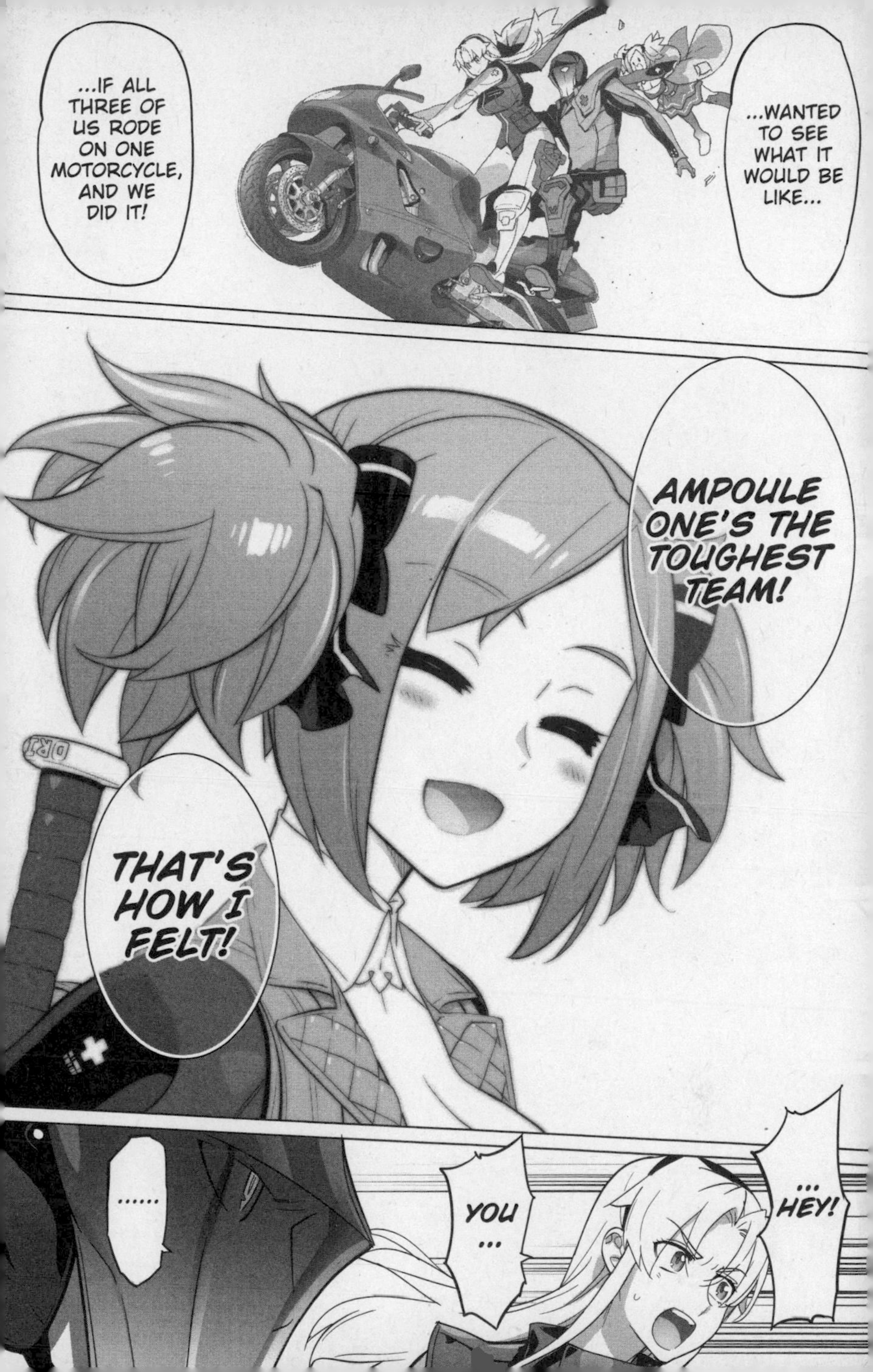
...WANTED TO SEE WHAT IT WOULD BE LIKE...
...IF ALL THREE OF US RODE ON ONE MOTORCYCLE, AND WE DID IT!
AMPOULE ONE'S THE TOUGHEST TEAM!
THAT'S HOW I FELT!
...HEY!
YOU ...
......

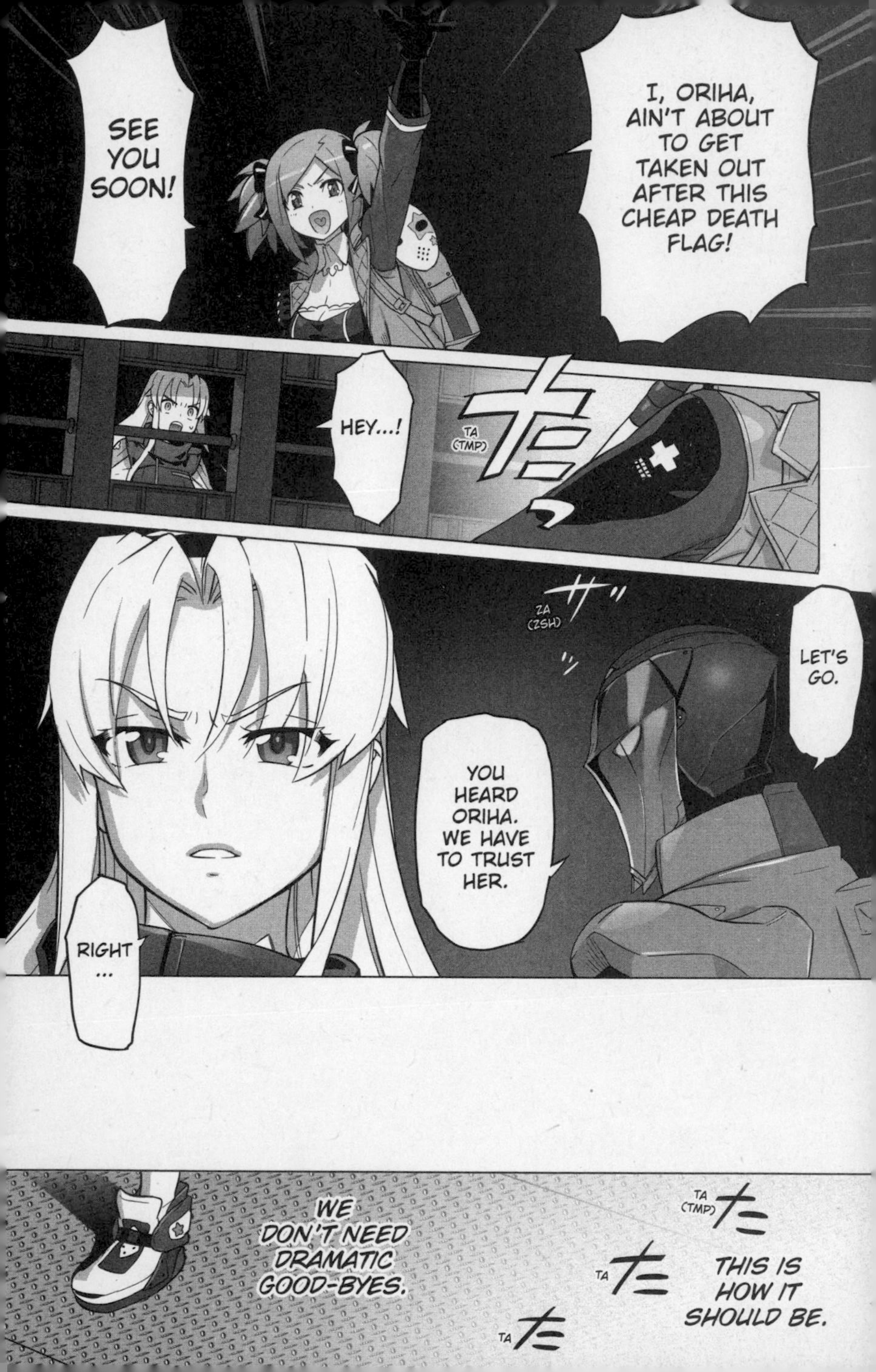
I, ORIHA, AIN'T ABOUT TO GET TAKEN OUT AFTER THIS CHEAP DEATH FLAG!
SEE YOU SOON!
TA (TMP)
HEY...!
ZA (ZSH)
LET'S GO.
YOU HEARD ORIHA. WE HAVE TO TRUST HER.
RIGHT ...
TA (TMP)
TA
THIS IS HOW IT SHOULD BE.
TA
WE DON'T NEED DRAMATIC GOOD-BYES.

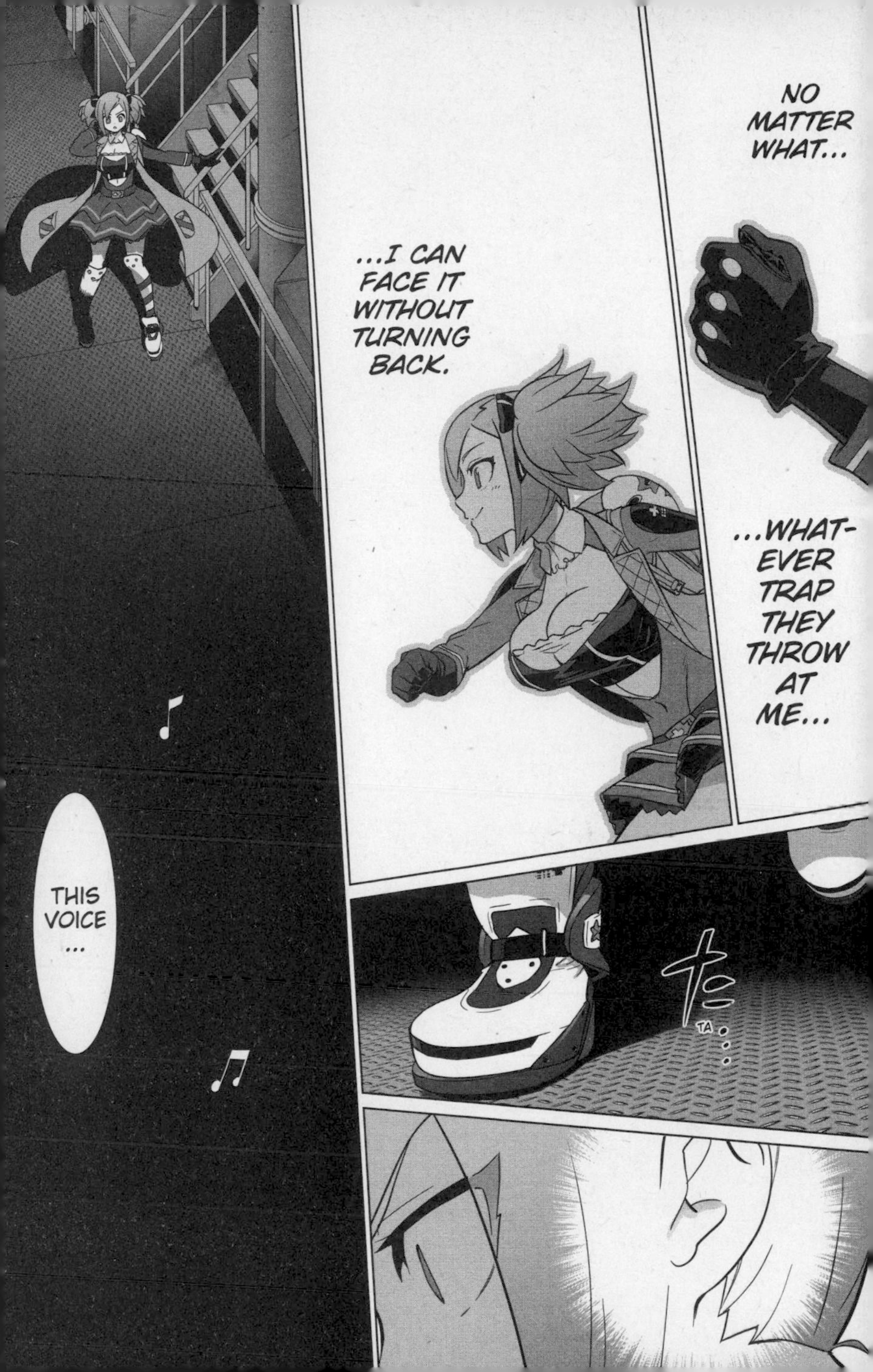
NO MATTER WHAT...
...WHAT-EVER TRAP THEY THROW AT ME...
...I CAN FACE IT WITHOUT TURNING BACK.
TA...
THIS VOICE...

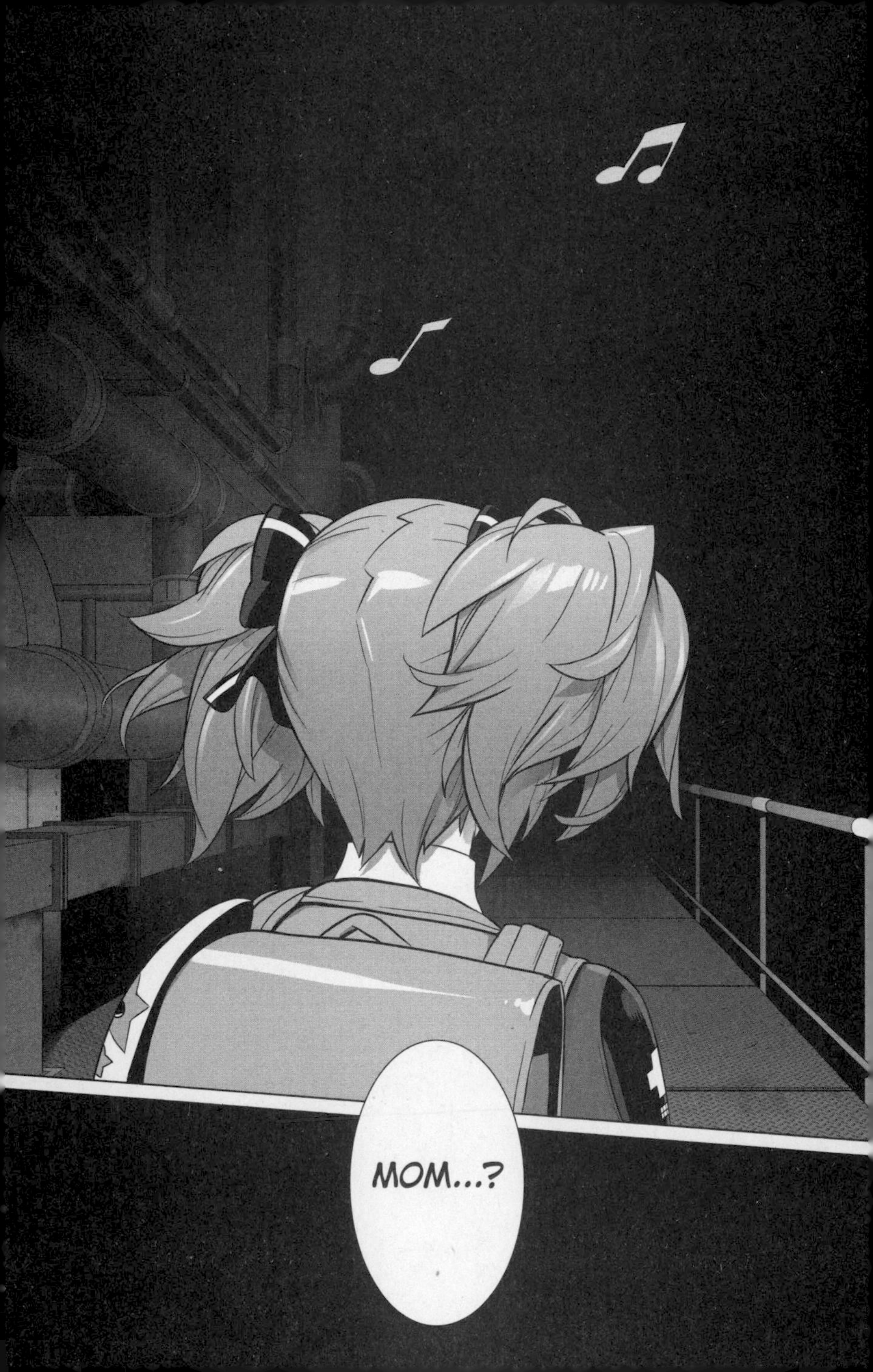
MOM...?

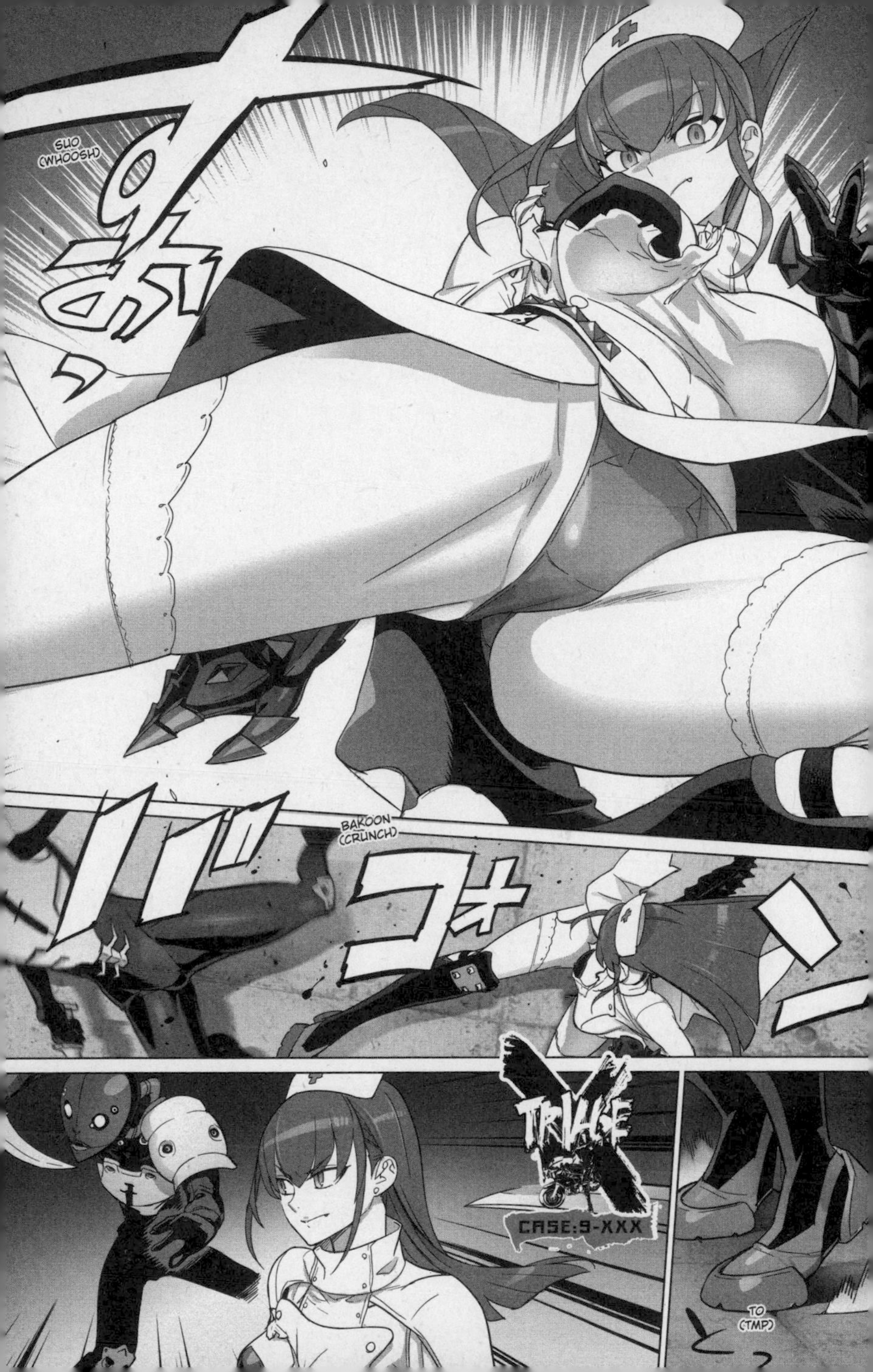
SUO (WHOOSH)
BAKOON (CRUNCH)
TO (TMP)
TRIAGE X
CASE:9-XXX

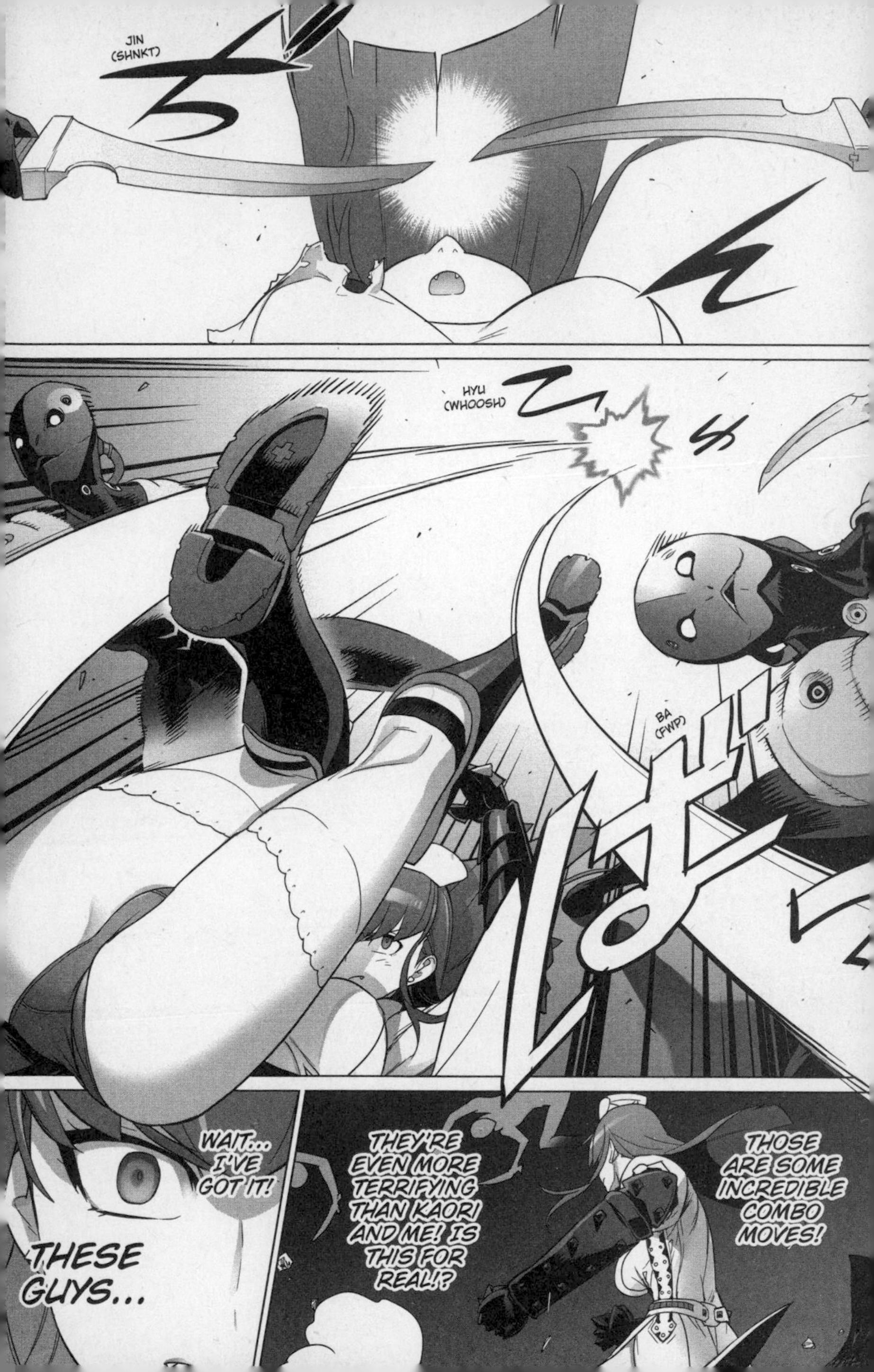
JIN (SHNKT)
HYU (WHOOSH)
BA (FWP)
THOSE ARE SOME INCREDIBLE COMBO MOVES!
THEY'RE EVEN MORE TERRIFYING THAN KAORI AND ME! IS THIS FOR REAL!?
WAIT... I'VE GOT IT!
THESE GUYS...

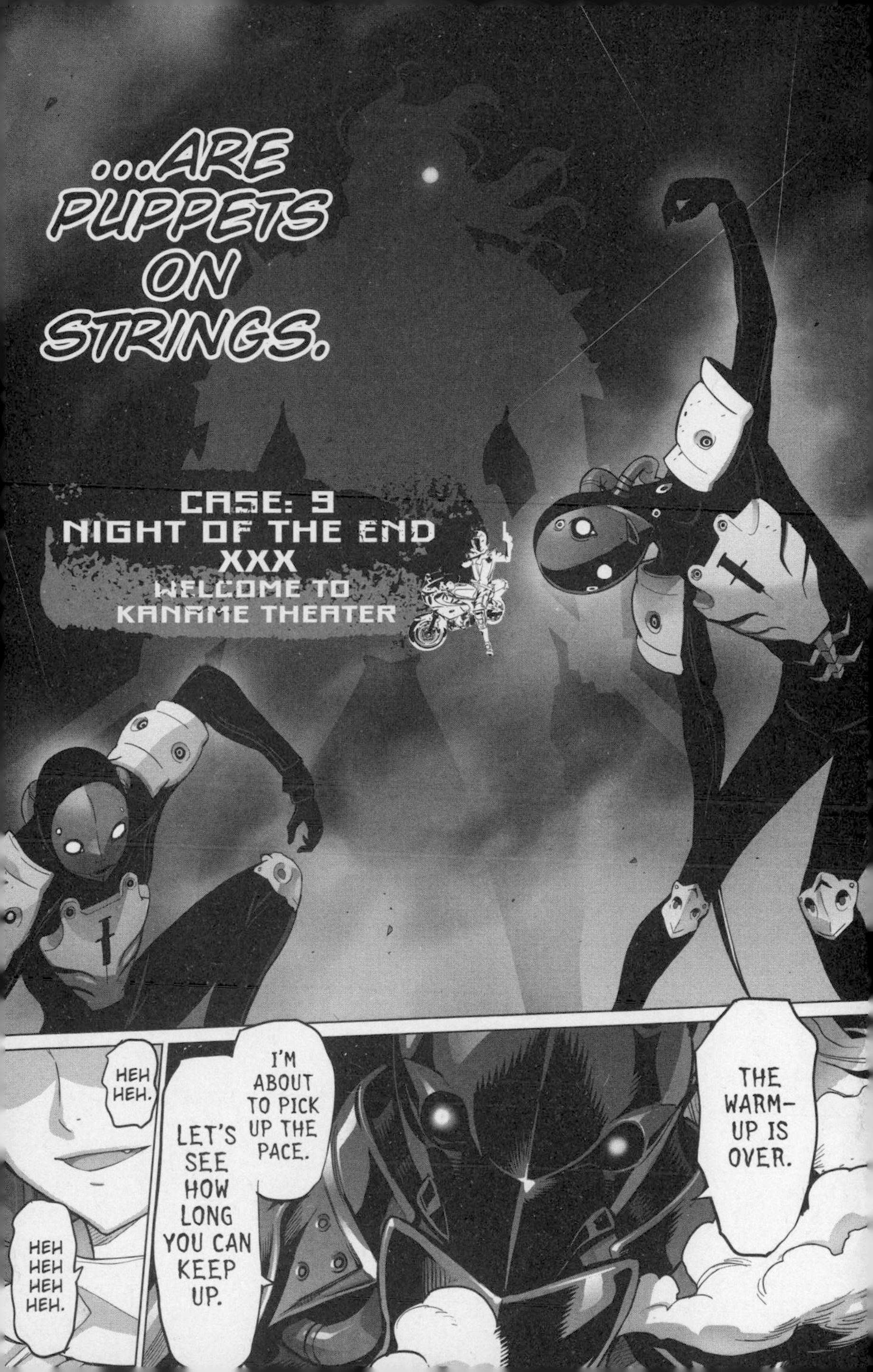
...ARE PUPPETS ON STRINGS.
CASE: 9
NIGHT OF THE END XXX
WELCOME TO KANAME THEATER
THE WARM-UP IS OVER.
I'M ABOUT TO PICK UP THE PACE.
LET'S SEE HOW LONG YOU CAN KEEP UP.
HEH HEH.
HEH HEH HEH HEH.

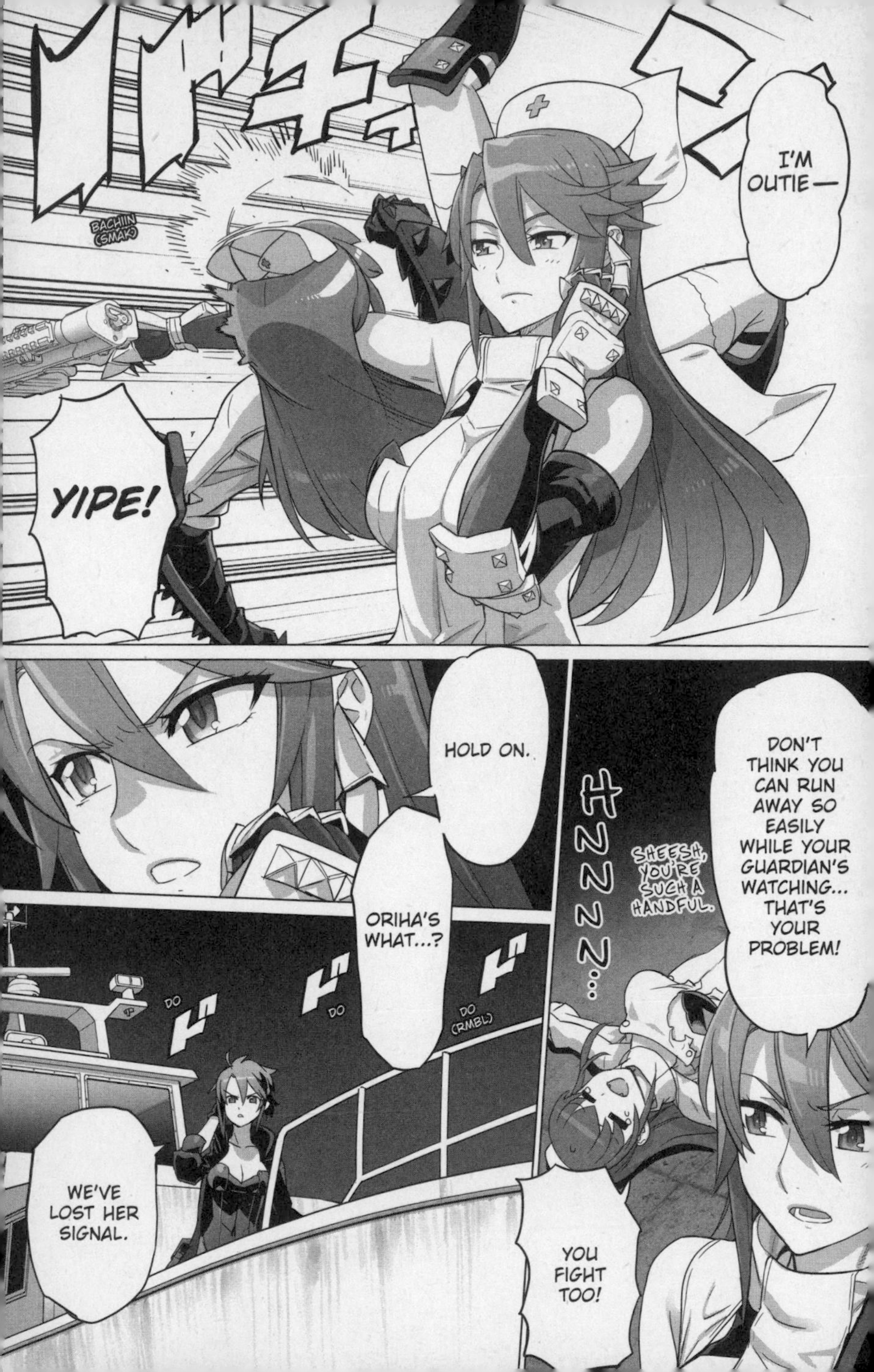
I'M OUTIE—
BACHIIN (SMAK)
YIPE!
DON'T THINK YOU CAN RUN AWAY SO EASILY WHILE YOUR GUARDIAN'S WATCHING... THAT'S YOUR PROBLEM!
HNNNNN...
SHEESH, YOU'RE SUCH A HANDFUL.
YOU FIGHT TOO!
HOLD ON.
ORIHA'S WHAT...?
DO
DO
DO (RMBL)
WE'VE LOST HER SIGNAL.

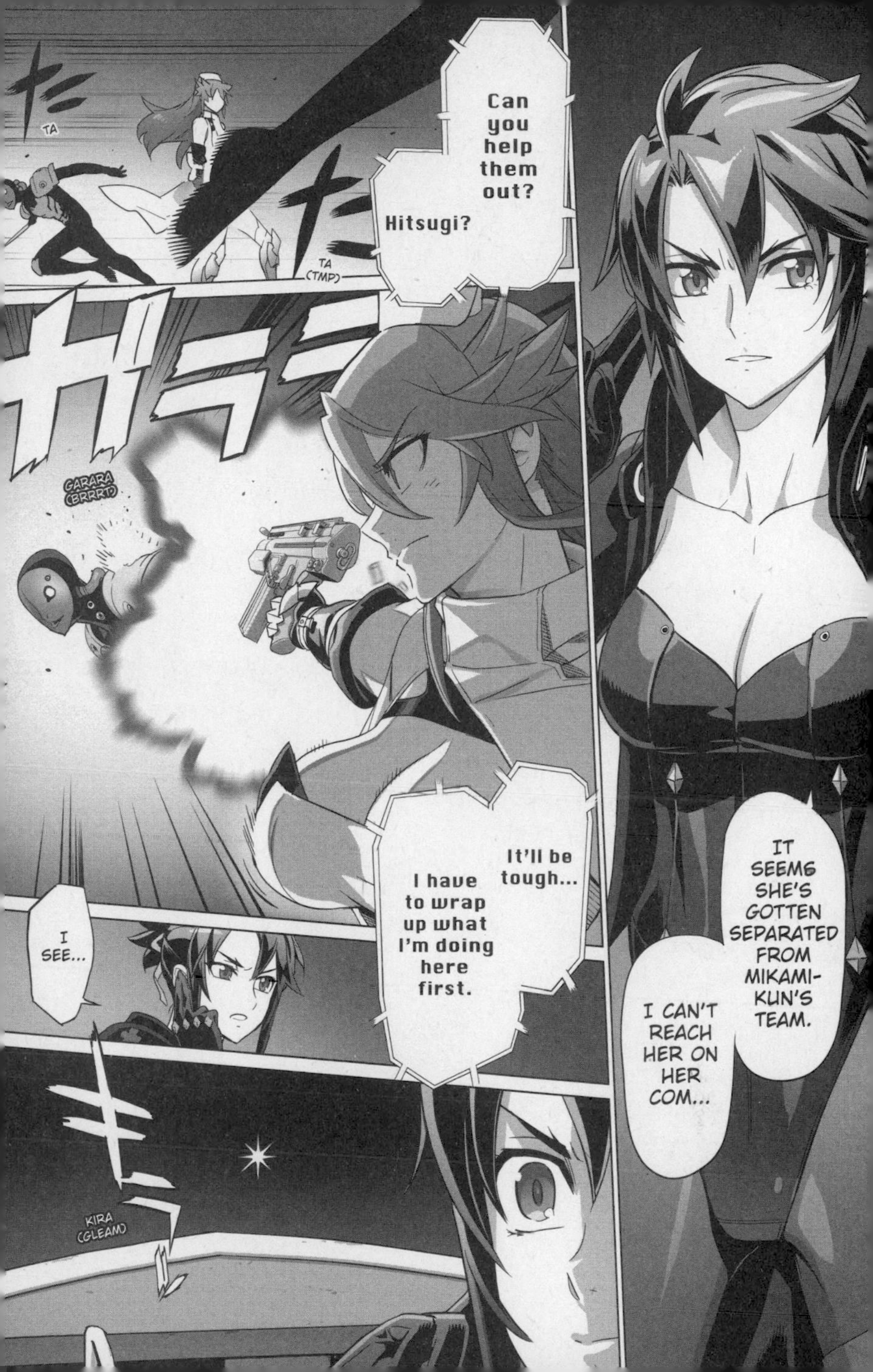
IT SEEMS SHE'S GOTTEN SEPARATED FROM MIKAMI-KUN'S TEAM.
I CAN'T REACH HER ON HER COM...
TA
TA (TMP)
Can you help them out?
Hitsugi?
GARARA (BRRRT)
It'll be tough...
I have to wrap up what I'm doing here first.
I SEE...
KIRA (GLEAM)

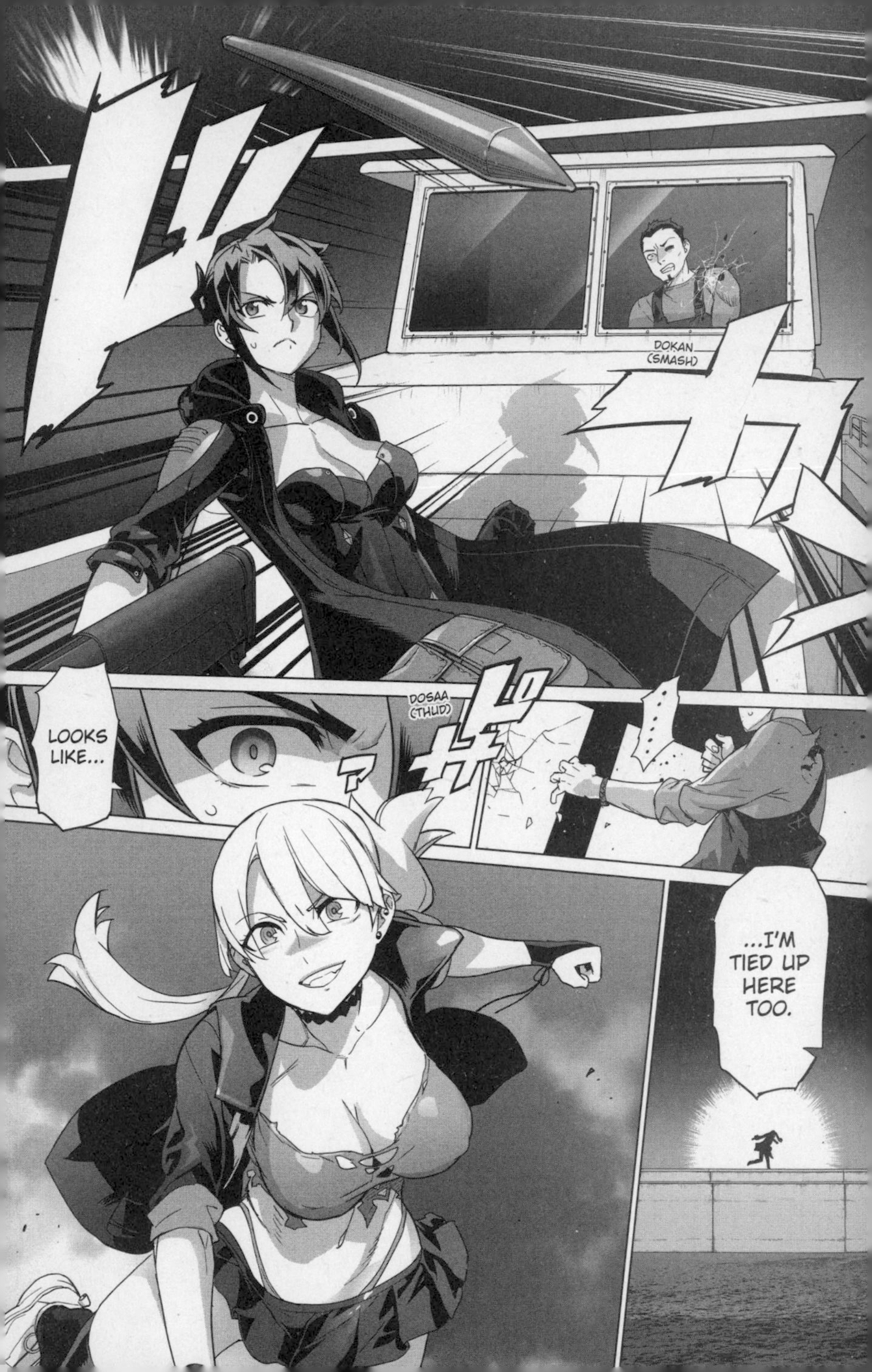
DOKAN (SMASH)
DOSAA (THUD)
LOOKS LIKE...
...I'M TIED UP HERE TOO.

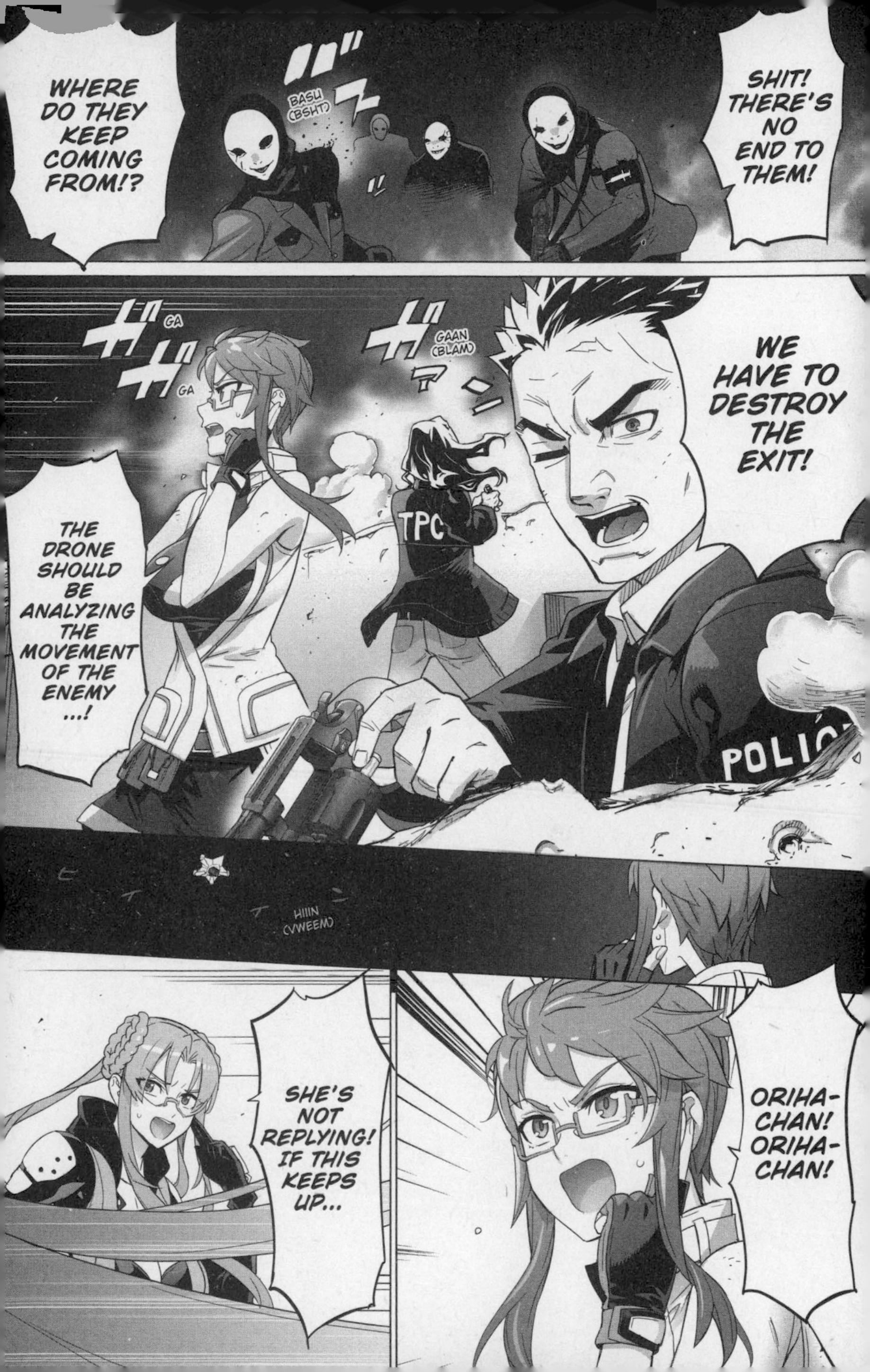
SHIT! THERE'S NO END TO THEM!
BASU (BSHT)
WHERE DO THEY KEEP COMING FROM!?
WE HAVE TO DESTROY THE EXIT!
GAAN (BLAM)
GA
GA
THE DRONE SHOULD BE ANALYZING THE MOVEMENT OF THE ENEMY ...!
TPC
POLIC
HIIIN (VWEEM)
ORIHA-CHAN! ORIHA-CHAN!
SHE'S NOT REPLYING! IF THIS KEEPS UP...

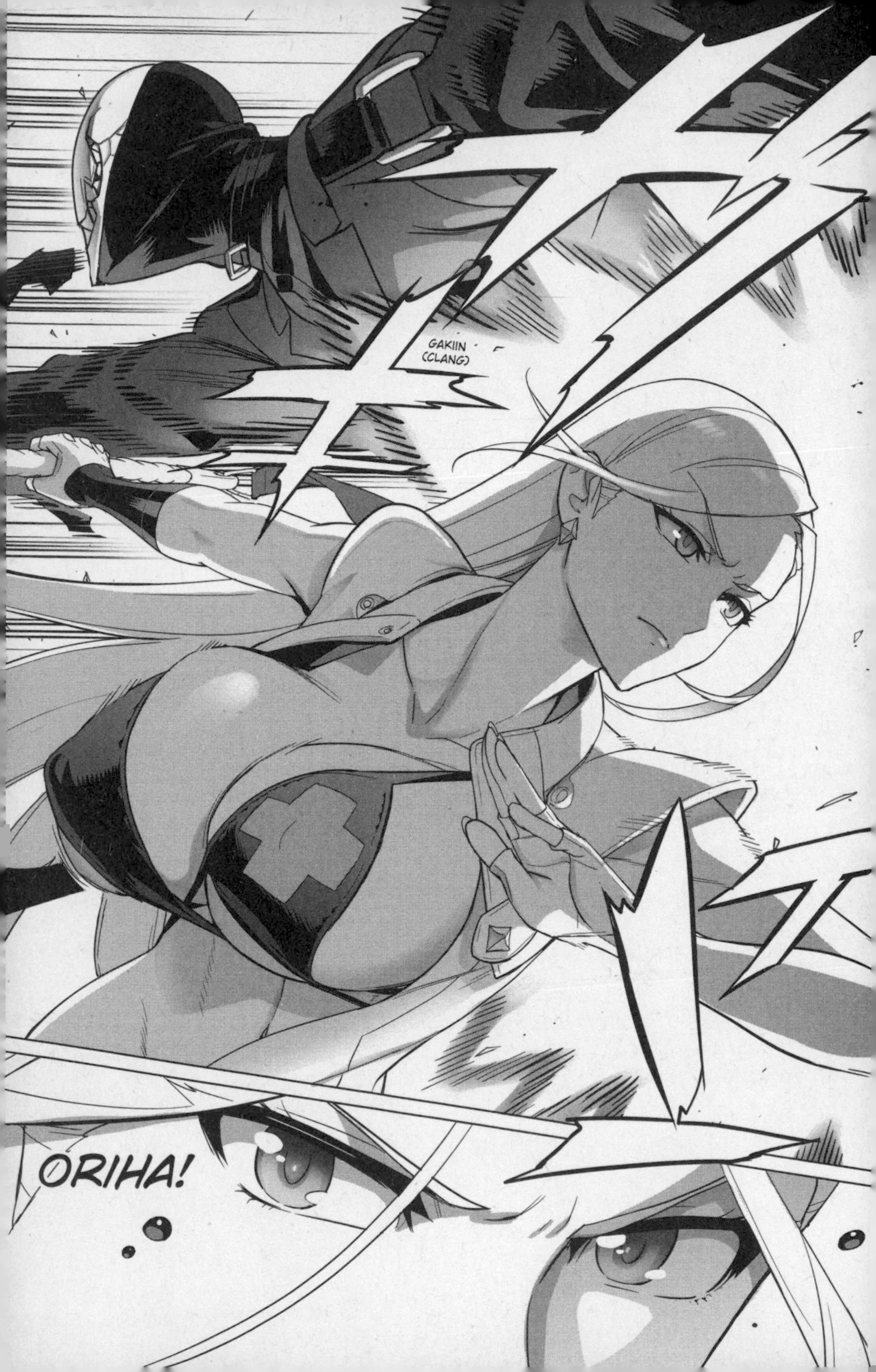
GAKIIN
(CLANG)
ORIHA!

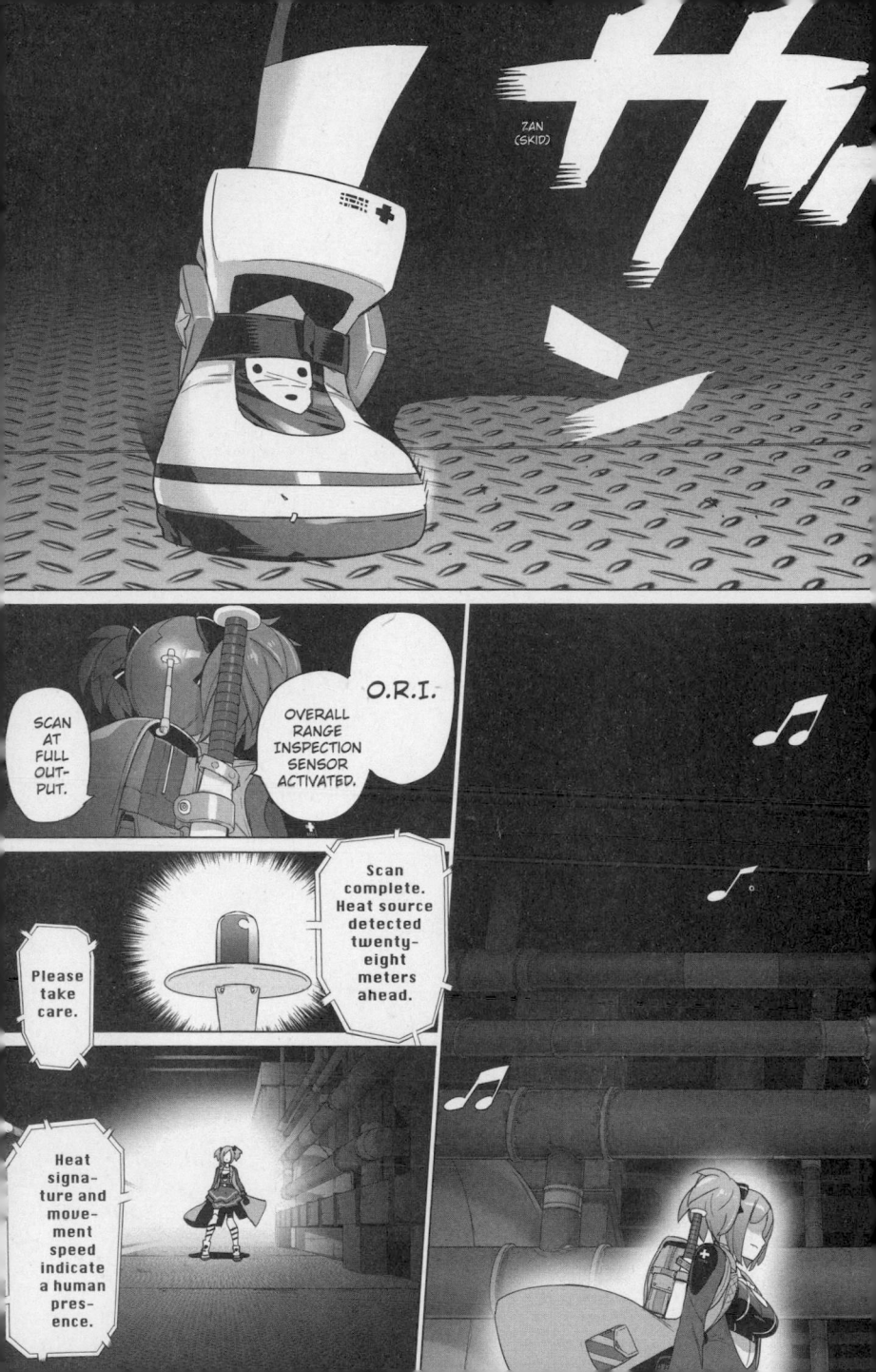

ZAN
(SKID)

O.R.I.

OVERALL
RANGE
INSPECTION
SENSOR
ACTIVATED.

SCAN
AT
FULL
OUT-
PUT.

Scan
complete.
Heat source
detected
twenty-
eight
meters
ahead.

Please
take
care.

Heat
signa-
ture and
move-
ment
speed
indicate
a human
pres-
ence.

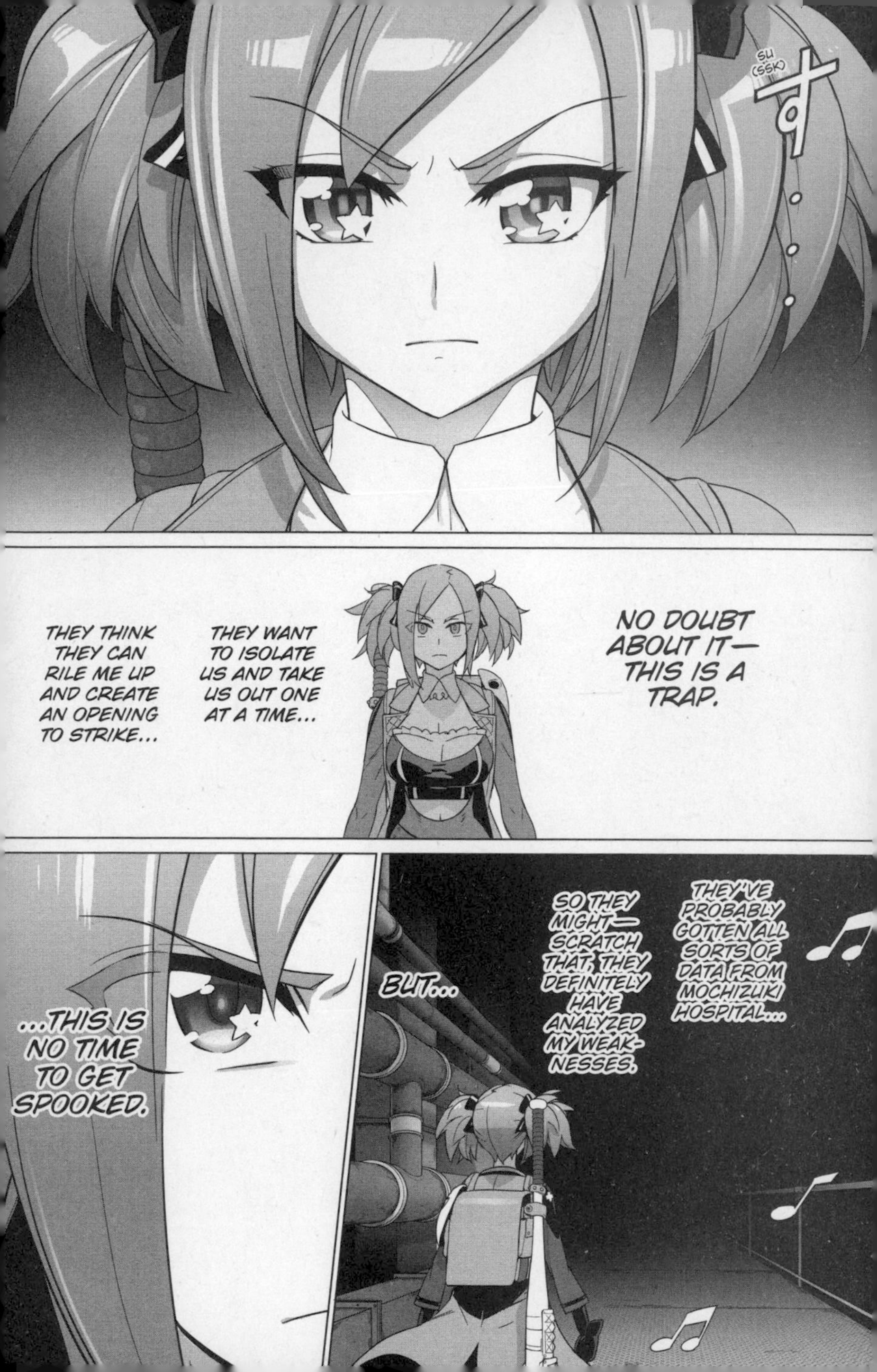
SU (SSK)
す
NO DOUBT ABOUT IT— THIS IS A TRAP.
THEY WANT TO ISOLATE US AND TAKE US OUT ONE AT A TIME...
THEY THINK THEY CAN RILE ME UP AND CREATE AN OPENING TO STRIKE...
THEY'VE PROBABLY GOTTEN ALL SORTS OF DATA FROM MOCHIZUKI HOSPITAL...
SO THEY MIGHT— SCRATCH THAT, THEY DEFINITELY HAVE ANALYZED MY WEAK-NESSES.
BUT...
...THIS IS NO TIME TO GET SPOOKED.

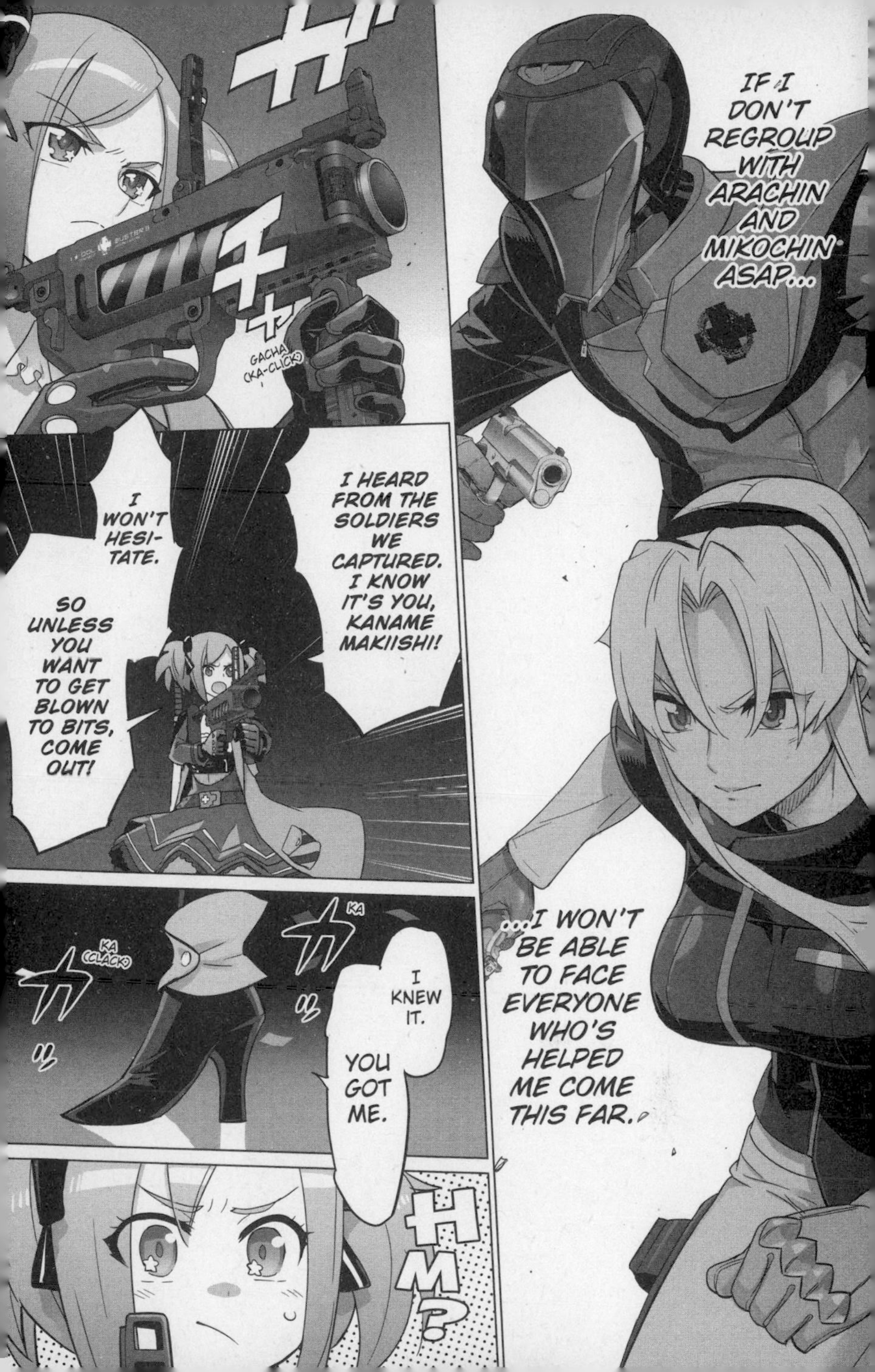

IF I DON'T REGROUP WITH ARACHIN AND MIKOCHIN ASAP...
...I WON'T BE ABLE TO FACE EVERYONE WHO'S HELPED ME COME THIS FAR.
GACHA (KA-CLICK)
I HEARD FROM THE SOLDIERS WE CAPTURED. I KNOW IT'S YOU, KANAME MAKIISHI!
I WON'T HESI-TATE.
SO UNLESS YOU WANT TO GET BLOWN TO BITS, COME OUT!
KA
KA (CLACK)
I KNEW IT.
YOU GOT ME.
HM?

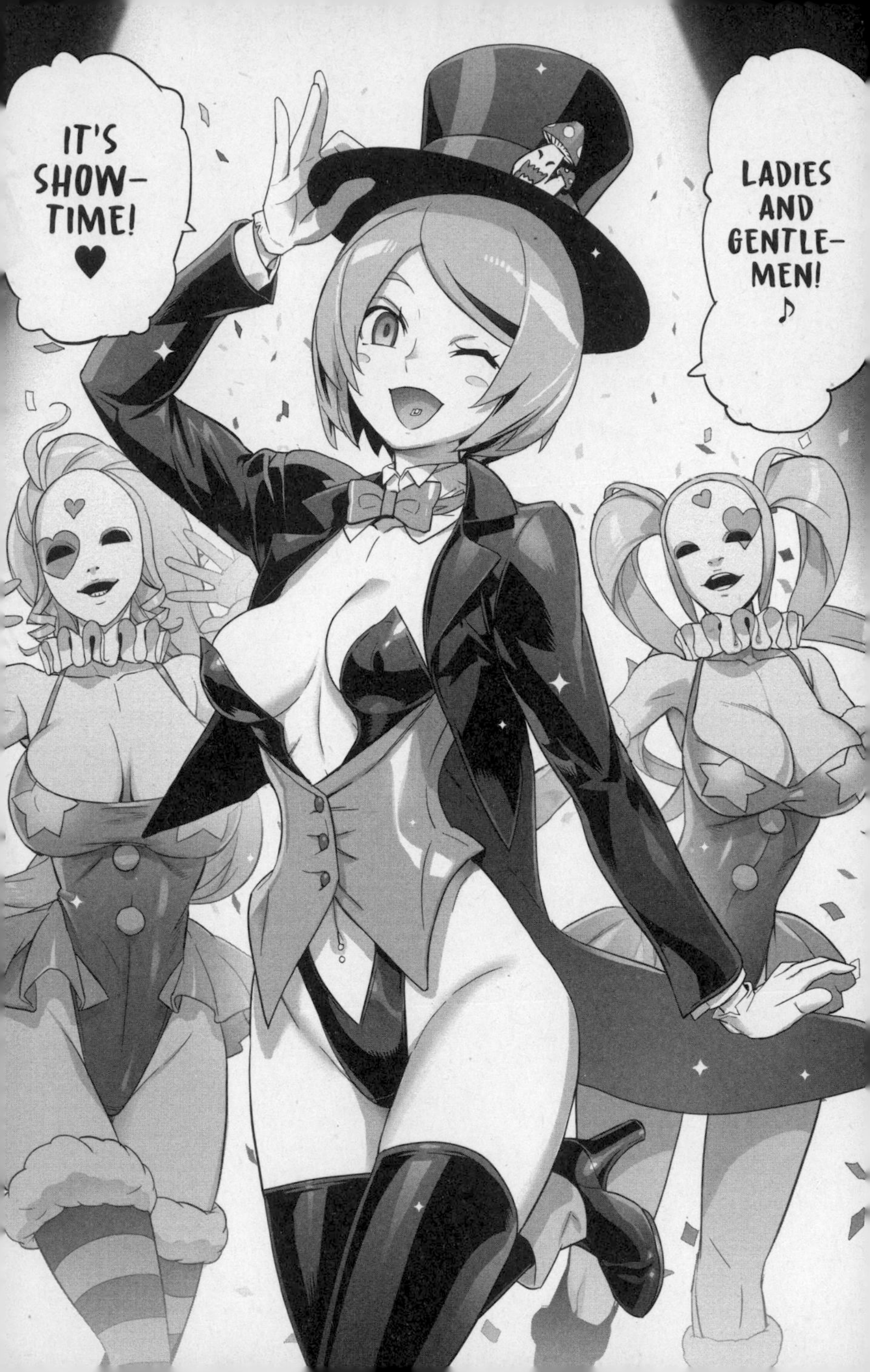
LADIES AND GENTLE-MEN! ♪
IT'S SHOW-TIME! ♥

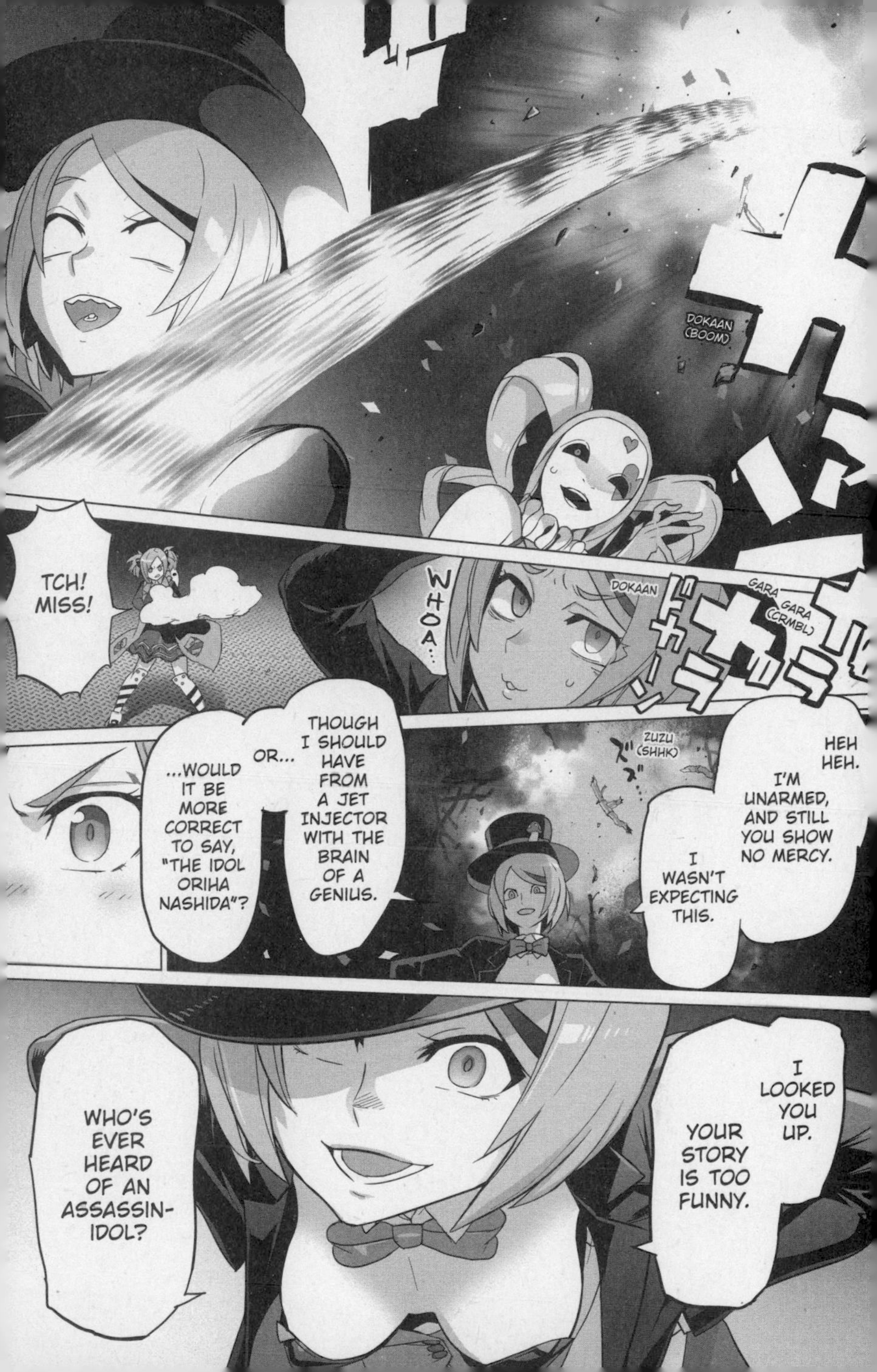
DOKAAN (BOOM)
DOKAAN
GARA GARA (CRMBL)
WHOA...
TCH! MISS!
HEH HEH.
I'M UNARMED, AND STILL YOU SHOW NO MERCY.
I WASN'T EXPECTING THIS.
ZUZU (SHHK)
THOUGH I SHOULD HAVE FROM A JET INJECTOR WITH THE BRAIN OF A GENIUS.
OR...
...WOULD IT BE MORE CORRECT TO SAY, "THE IDOL ORIHA NASHIDA"?
I LOOKED YOU UP.
YOUR STORY IS TOO FUNNY.
WHO'S EVER HEARD OF AN ASSASSIN-IDOL?

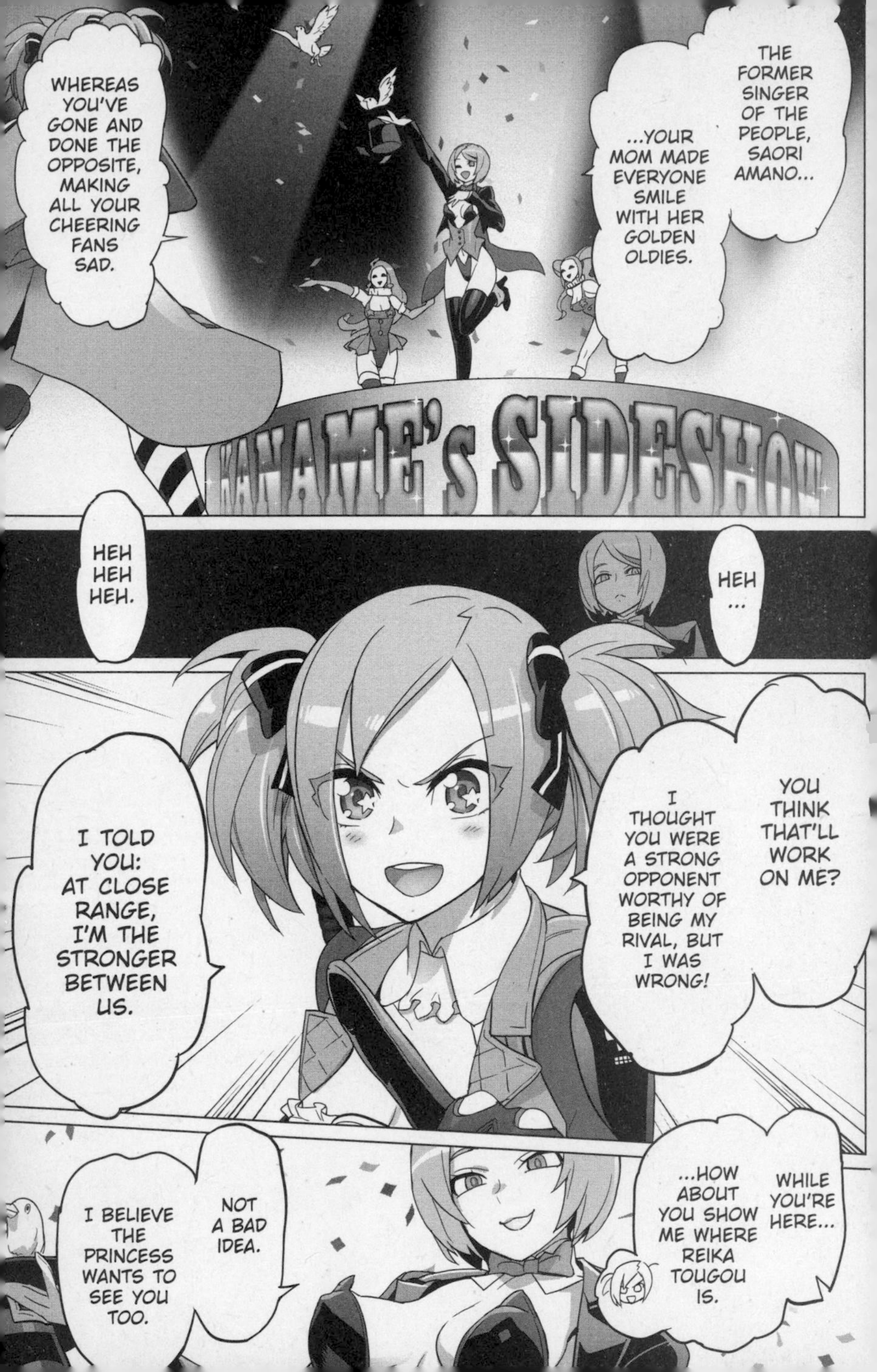
THE FORMER SINGER OF THE PEOPLE, SAORI AMANO...
...YOUR MOM MADE EVERYONE SMILE WITH HER GOLDEN OLDIES.
WHEREAS YOU'VE GONE AND DONE THE OPPOSITE, MAKING ALL YOUR CHEERING FANS SAD.
KANAME'S SIDESHOW
HEH ...
HEH HEH HEH.
YOU THINK THAT'LL WORK ON ME?
I THOUGHT YOU WERE A STRONG OPPONENT WORTHY OF BEING MY RIVAL, BUT I WAS WRONG!
I TOLD YOU: AT CLOSE RANGE, I'M THE STRONGER BETWEEN US.
WHILE YOU'RE HERE...
...HOW ABOUT YOU SHOW ME WHERE REIKA TOUGOU IS.
NOT A BAD IDEA.
I BELIEVE THE PRINCESS WANTS TO SEE YOU TOO.

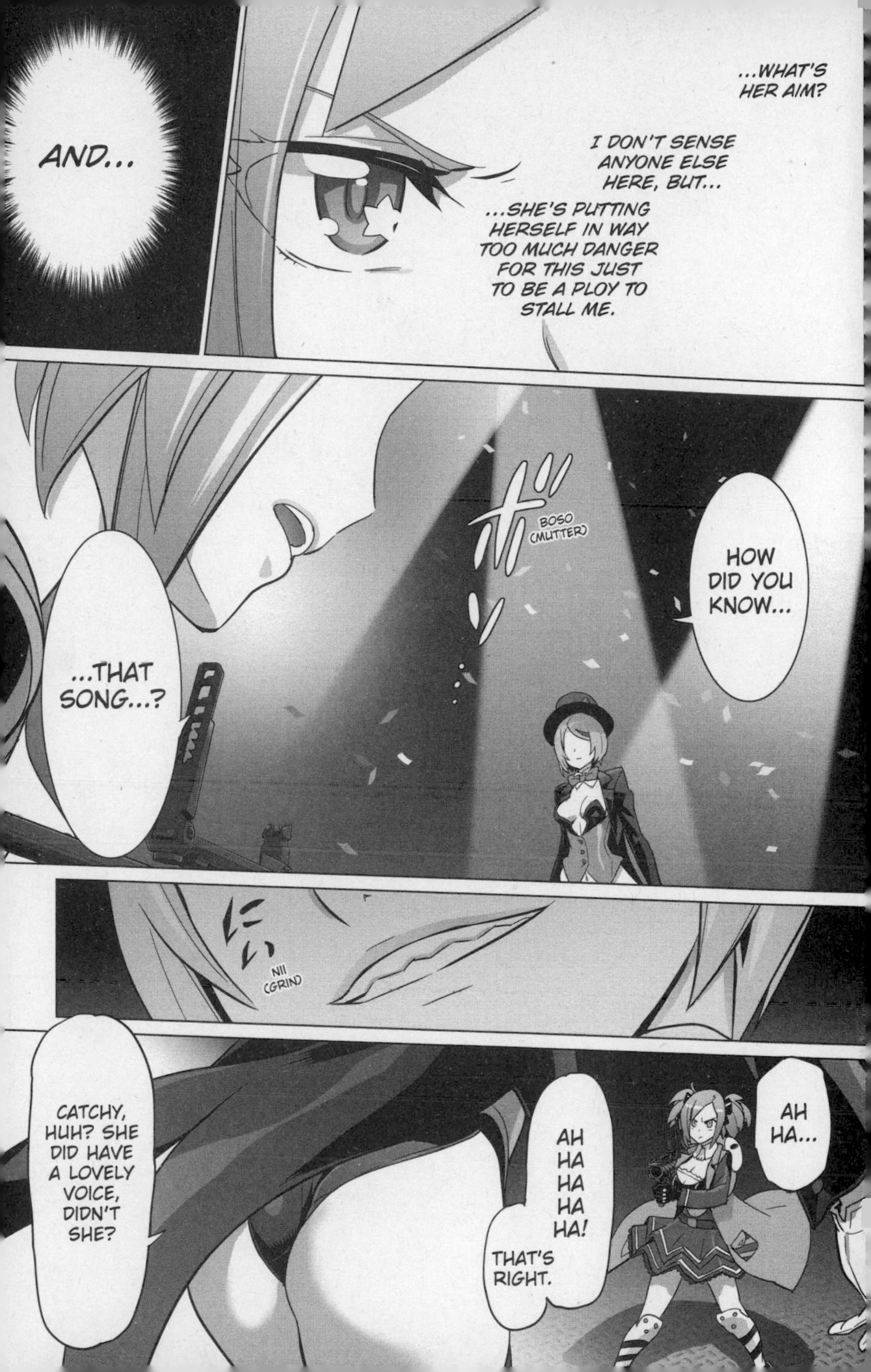
...WHAT'S HER AIM?
I DON'T SENSE ANYONE ELSE HERE, BUT...
...SHE'S PUTTING HERSELF IN WAY TOO MUCH DANGER FOR THIS JUST TO BE A PLOY TO STALL ME.
AND...
HOW DID YOU KNOW...
BOSO (MUTTER)
...THAT SONG...?
NII (GRIN)
AH HA...
AH HA HA HA HA!
THAT'S RIGHT.
CATCHY, HUH? SHE DID HAVE A LOVELY VOICE, DIDN'T SHE?

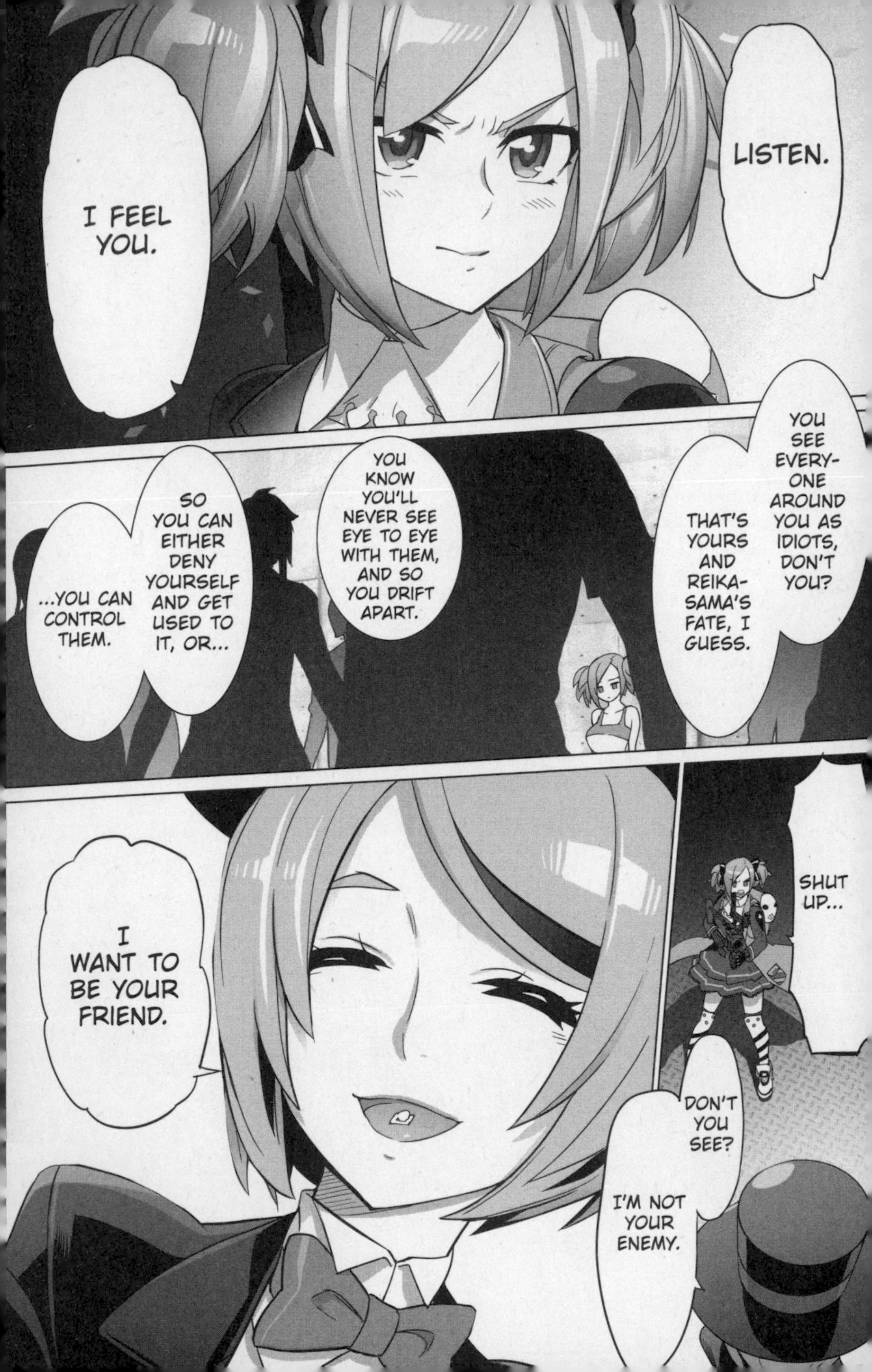
LISTEN.
I FEEL YOU.
YOU SEE EVERY-ONE AROUND YOU AS IDIOTS, DON'T YOU?
THAT'S YOURS AND REIKA-SAMA'S FATE, I GUESS.
YOU KNOW YOU'LL NEVER SEE EYE TO EYE WITH THEM, AND SO YOU DRIFT APART.
SO YOU CAN EITHER DENY YOURSELF AND GET USED TO IT, OR...
...YOU CAN CONTROL THEM.
SHUT UP...
DON'T YOU SEE?
I'M NOT YOUR ENEMY.
I WANT TO BE YOUR FRIEND.

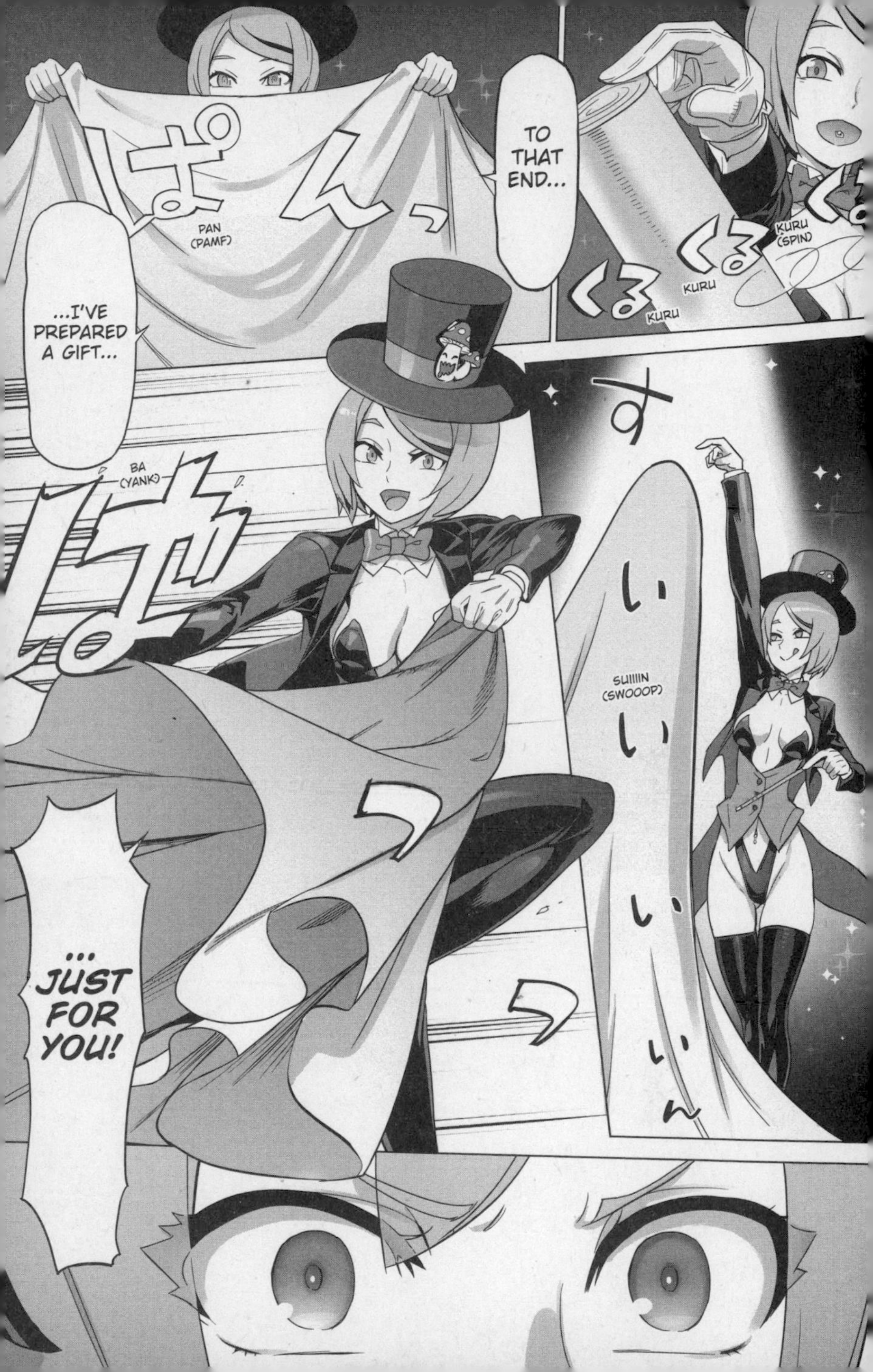
TO THAT END...
KURU (SPIN)
KURU
KURU
PAN (PAMF)
...I'VE PREPARED A GIFT...
SUIIIIN (SWOOOP)
BA (YANK)
...JUST FOR YOU!

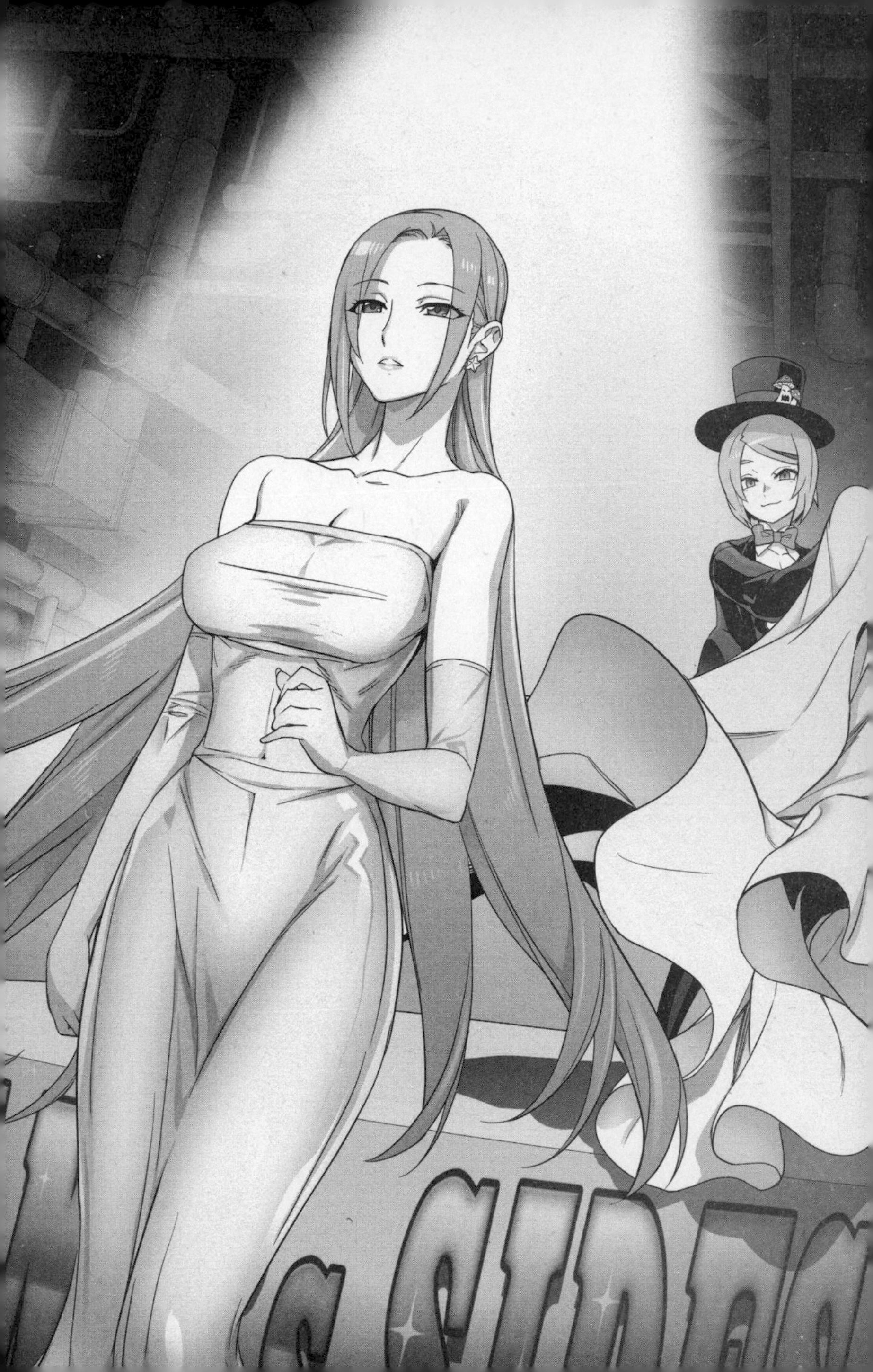

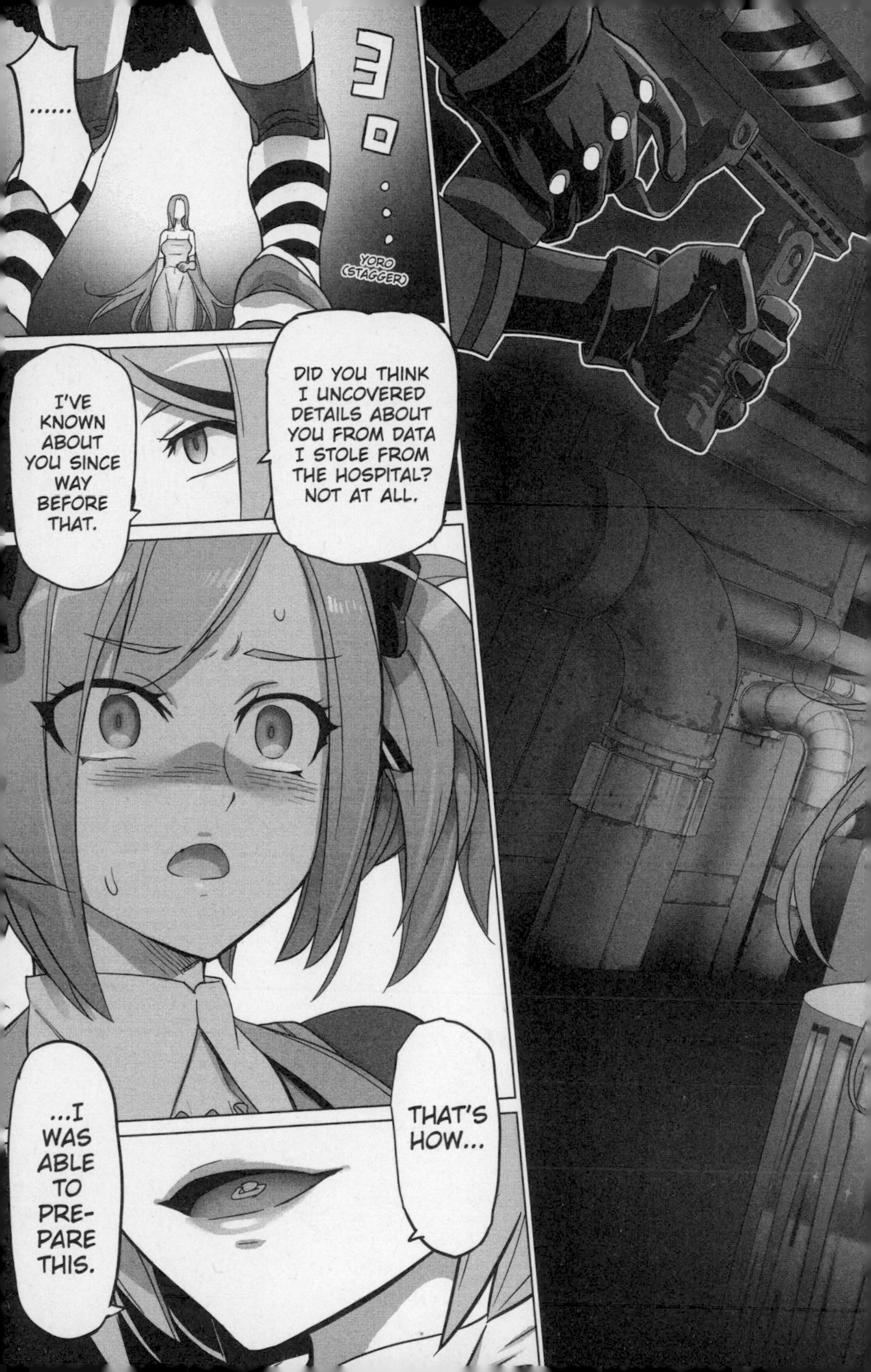
......
YORO (STAGGER)
DID YOU THINK I UNCOVERED DETAILS ABOUT YOU FROM DATA I STOLE FROM THE HOSPITAL? NOT AT ALL.
I'VE KNOWN ABOUT YOU SINCE WAY BEFORE THAT.
THAT'S HOW...
...I WAS ABLE TO PREPARE THIS.

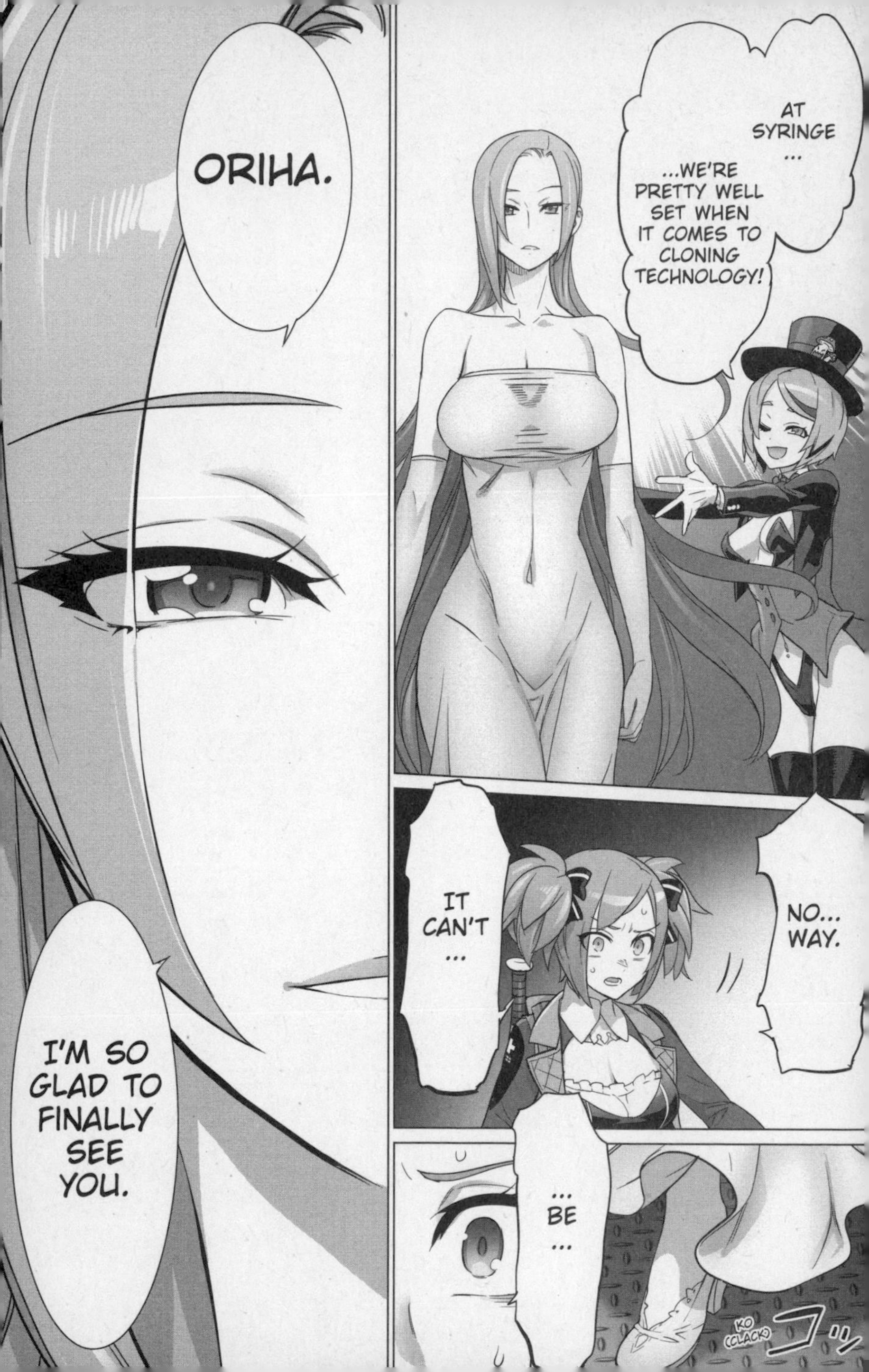
AT SYRINGE ...
...WE'RE PRETTY WELL SET WHEN IT COMES TO CLONING TECHNOLOGY!
NO... WAY.
IT CAN'T ...
... BE ...
KO (CLACK)
ORIHA.
I'M SO GLAD TO FINALLY SEE YOU.

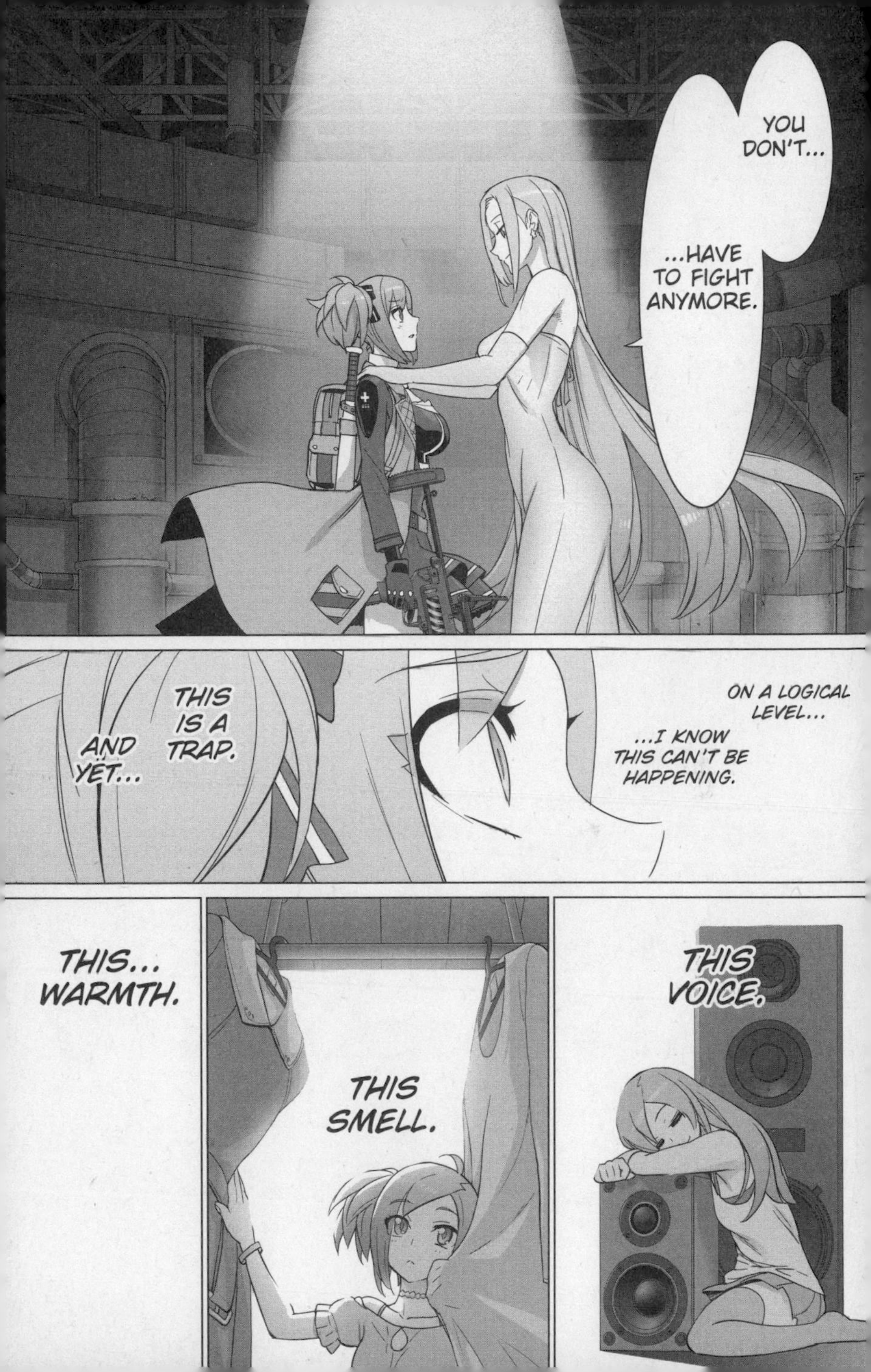
YOU DON'T...
...HAVE TO FIGHT ANYMORE.
ON A LOGICAL LEVEL...
...I KNOW THIS CAN'T BE HAPPENING.
THIS IS A TRAP.
AND YET...
THIS VOICE.
THIS SMELL.
THIS... WARMTH.

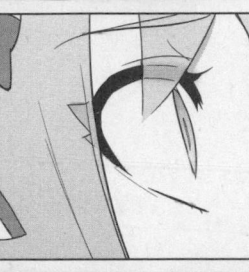

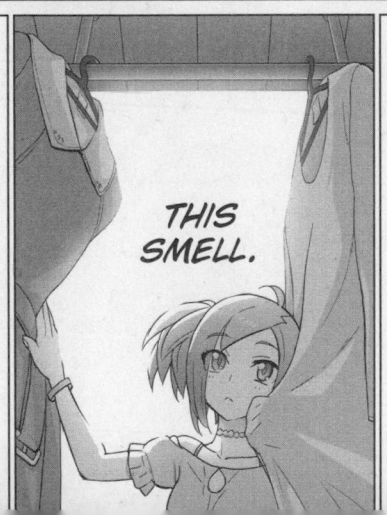

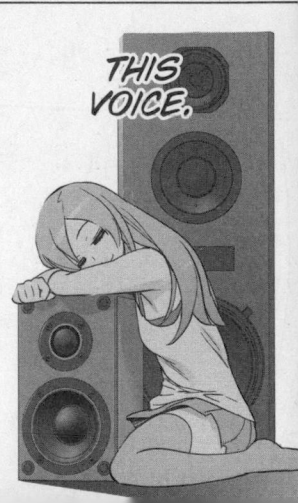

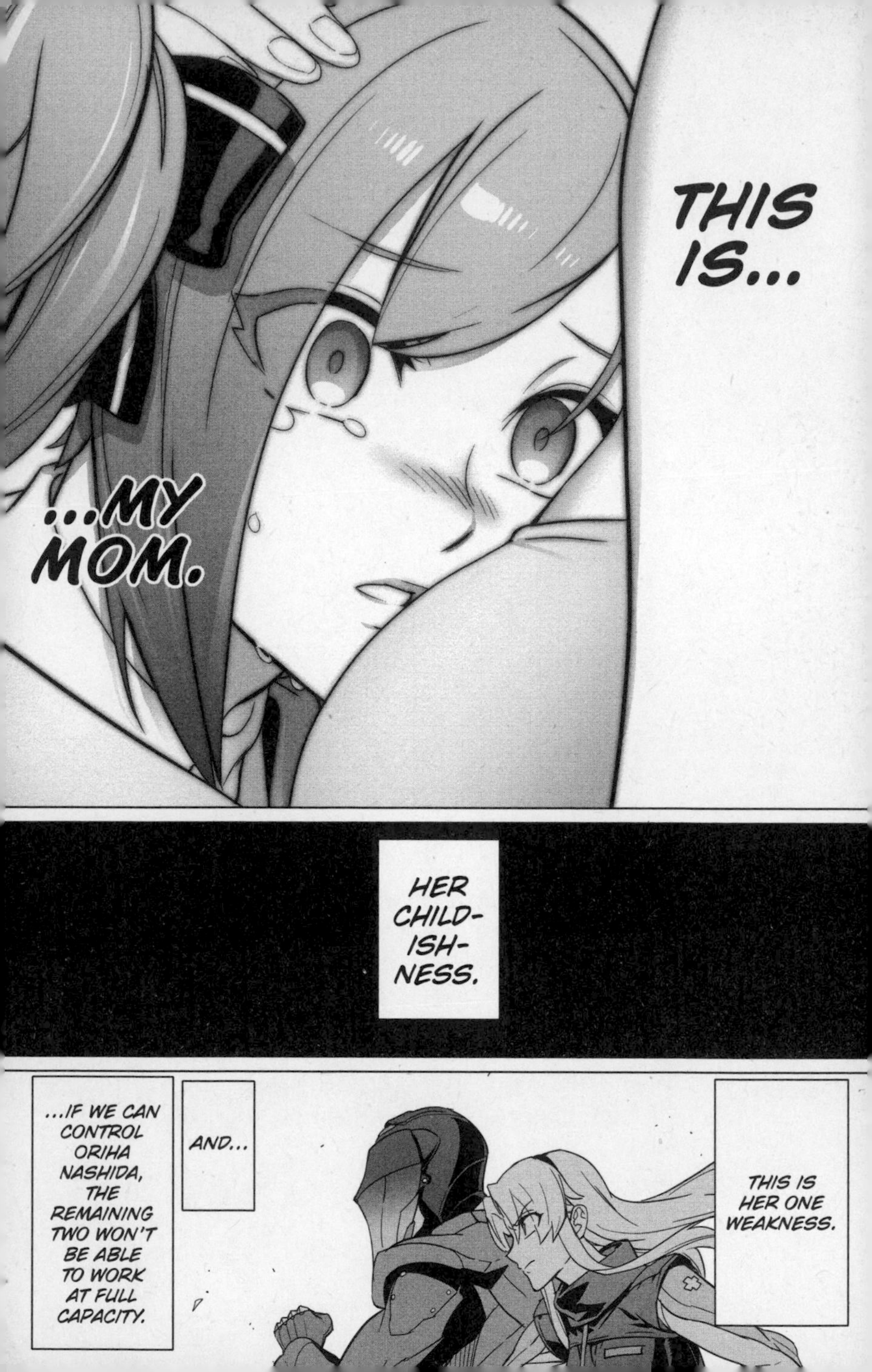
THIS IS...
...MY MOM.
HER CHILDISHNESS.
THIS IS HER ONE WEAKNESS.
AND...
...IF WE CAN CONTROL ORIHA NASHIDA, THE REMAINING TWO WON'T BE ABLE TO WORK AT FULL CAPACITY.

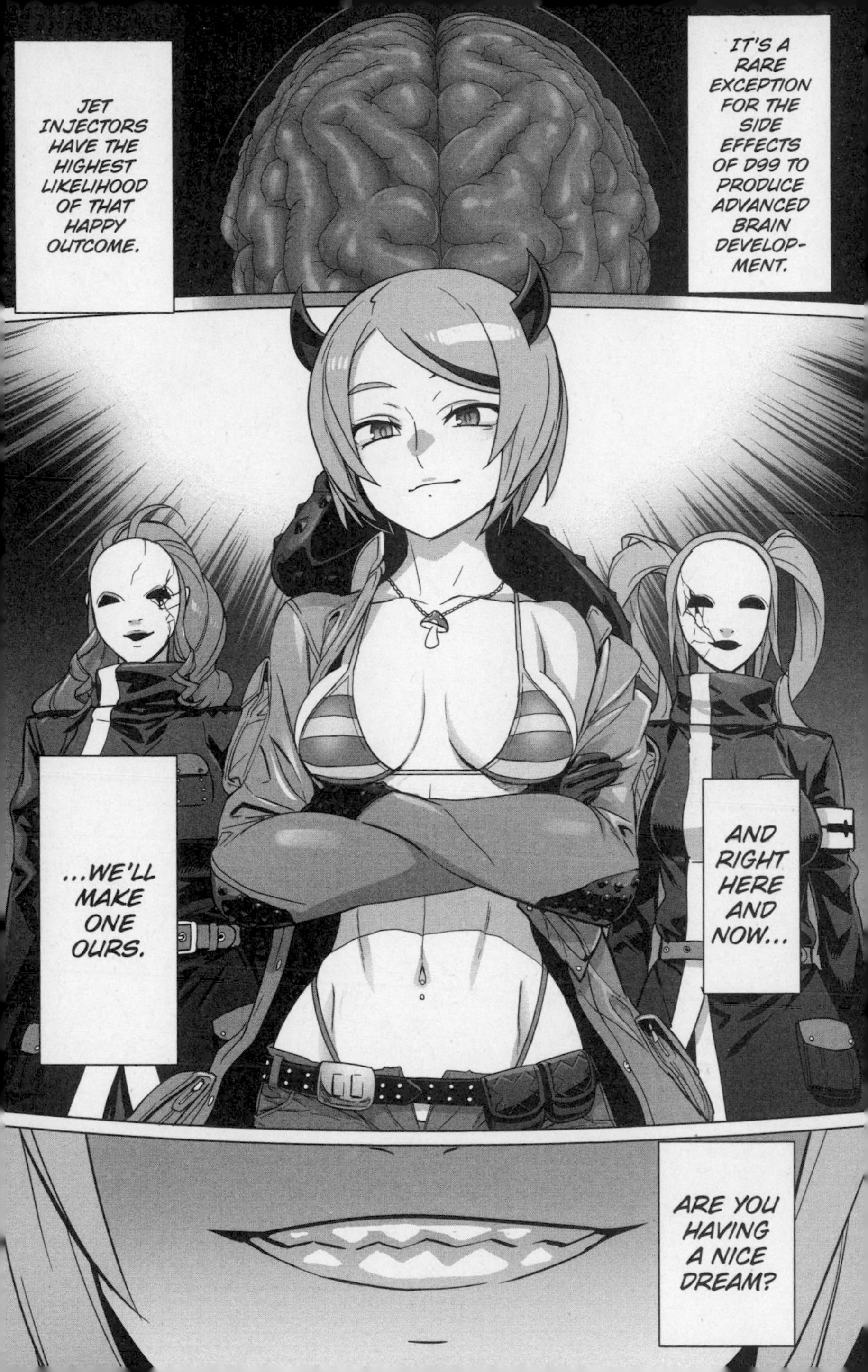
IT'S A RARE EXCEPTION FOR THE SIDE EFFECTS OF D99 TO PRODUCE ADVANCED BRAIN DEVELOP-MENT.
JET INJECTORS HAVE THE HIGHEST LIKELIHOOD OF THAT HAPPY OUTCOME.
AND RIGHT HERE AND NOW...
...WE'LL MAKE ONE OURS.
ARE YOU HAVING A NICE DREAM?

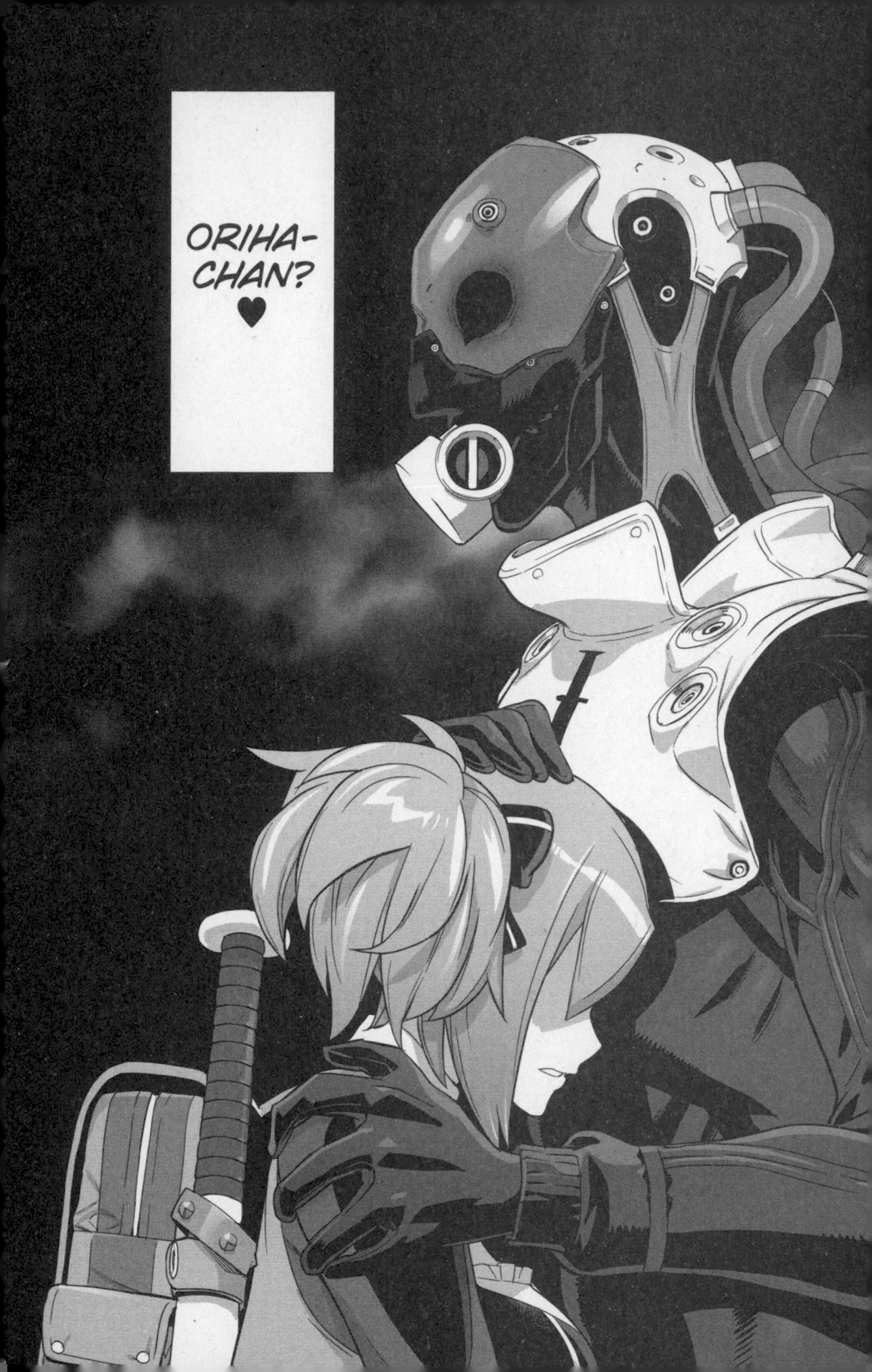
ORIHA-
CHAN?
♥

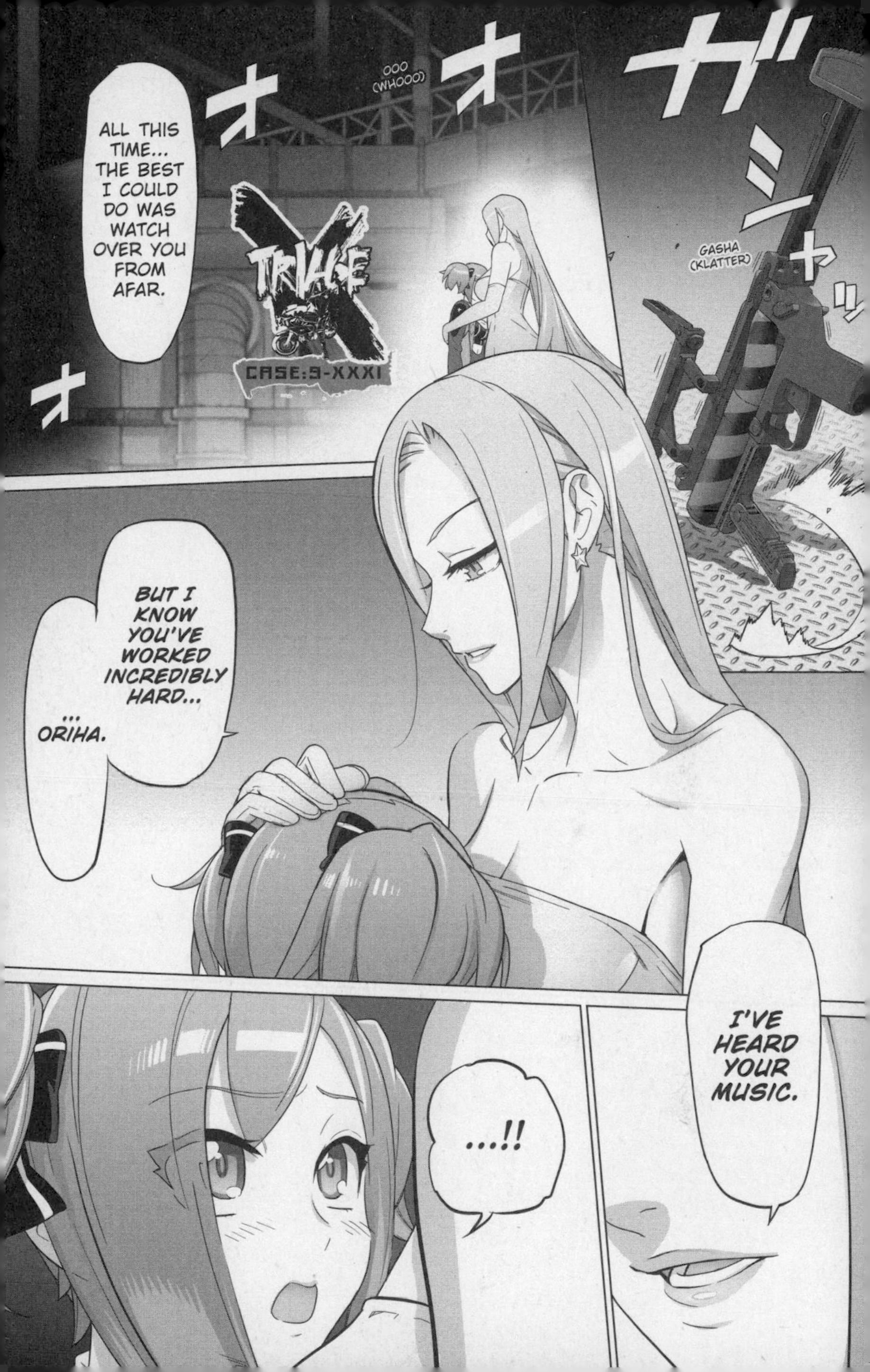
GASHA (KLATTER)
OOO (WHOOO)
ALL THIS TIME... THE BEST I COULD DO WAS WATCH OVER YOU FROM AFAR.
TRIAGE X
CASE:9-XXXI
BUT I KNOW YOU'VE WORKED INCREDIBLY HARD...
... ORIHA.
I'VE HEARD YOUR MUSIC.
...!!

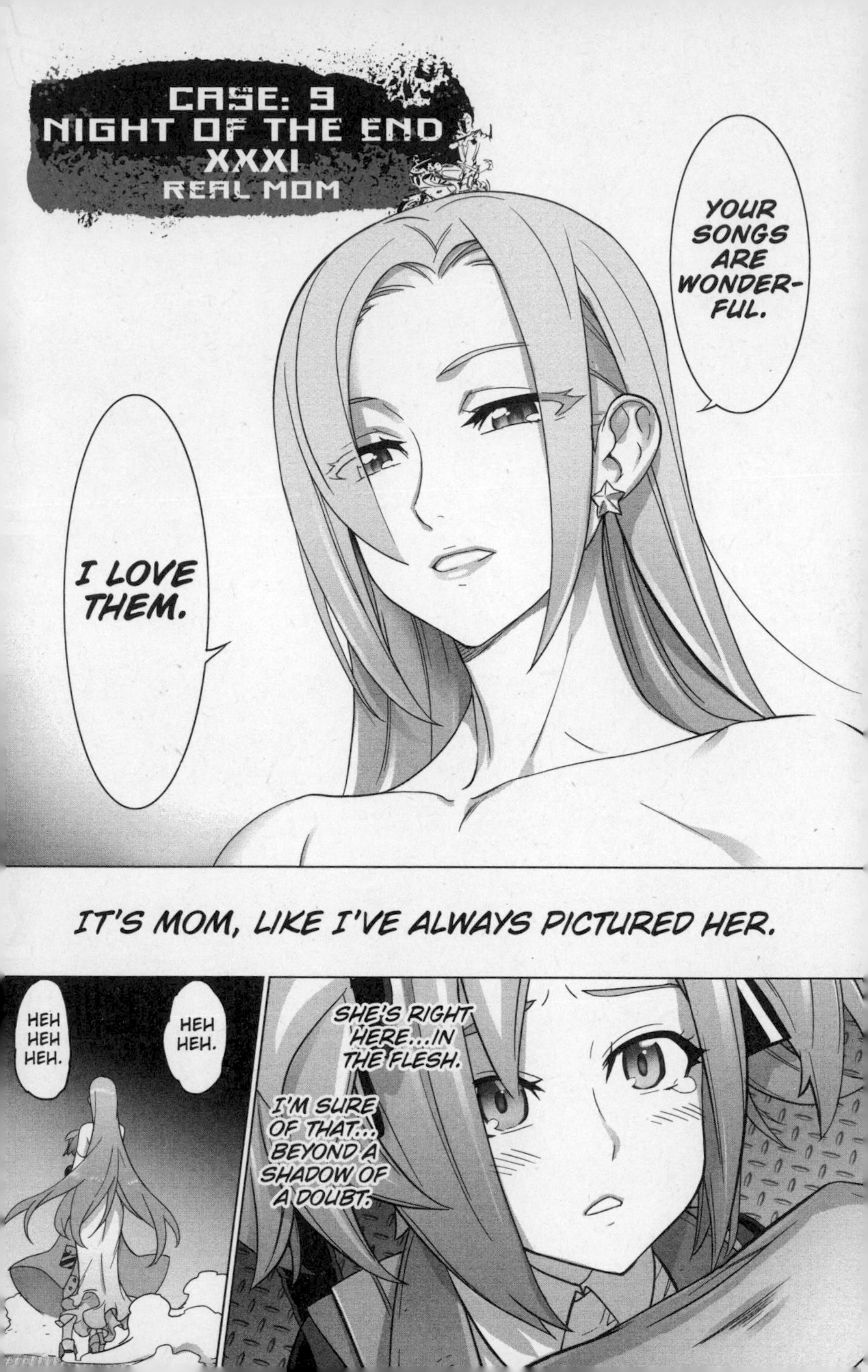
CASE: 9
NIGHT OF THE END
XXXI
REAL MOM
YOUR SONGS ARE WONDERFUL.
I LOVE THEM.
IT'S MOM, LIKE I'VE ALWAYS PICTURED HER.
SHE'S RIGHT HERE...IN THE FLESH.
I'M SURE OF THAT... BEYOND A SHADOW OF A DOUBT.
HEH HEH.
HEH HEH HEH.

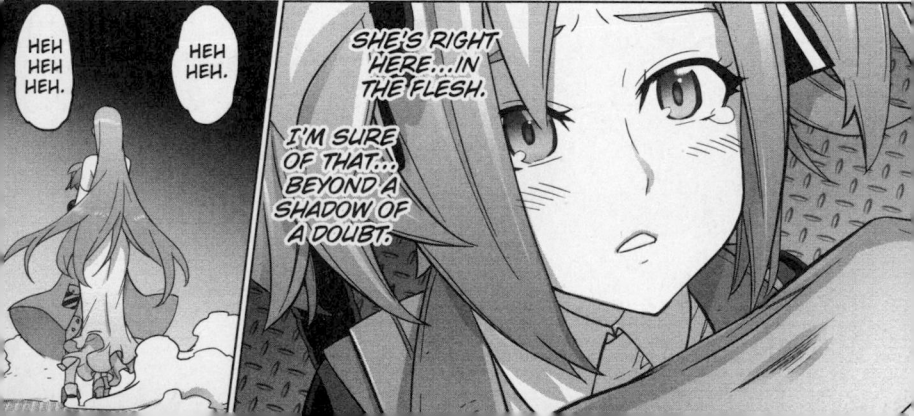

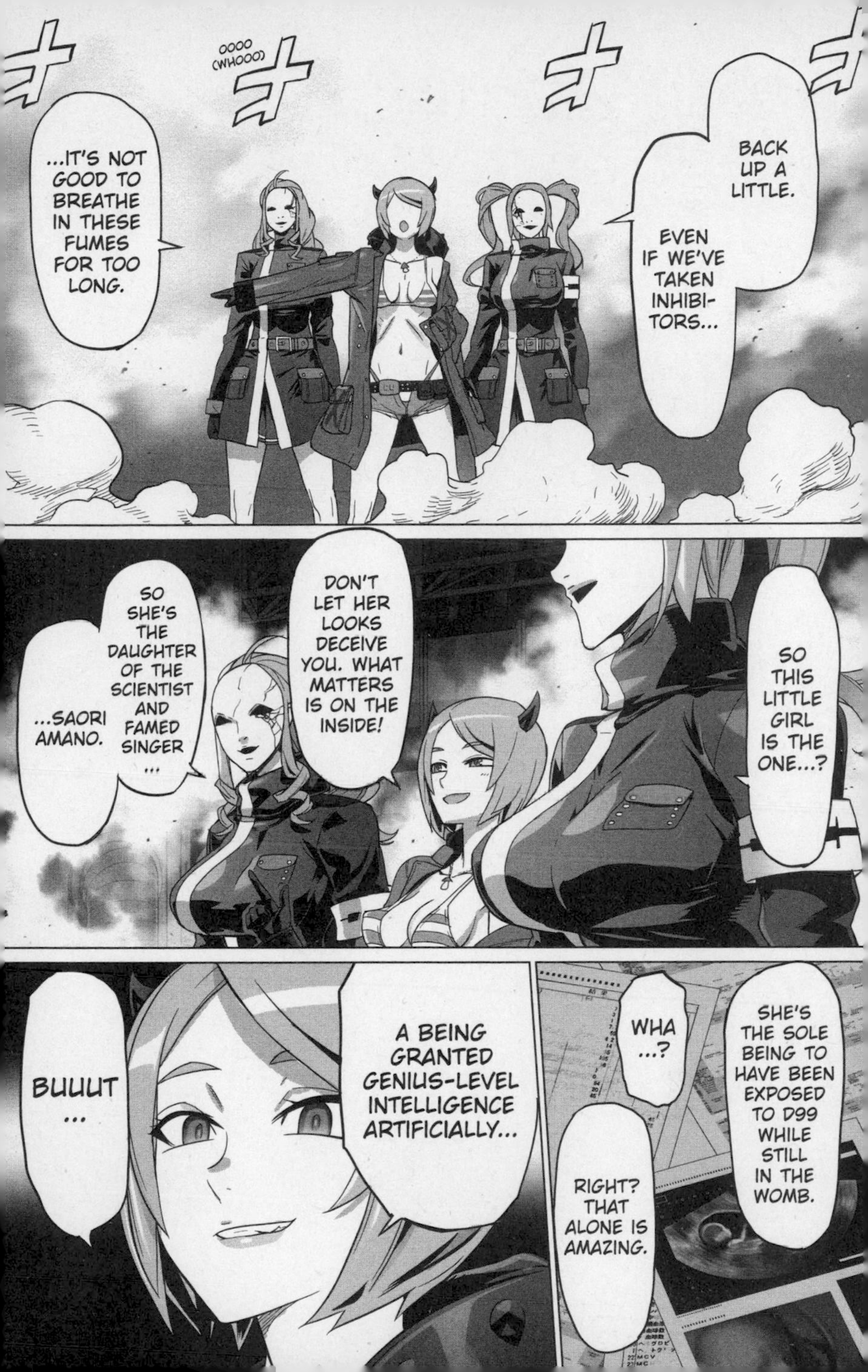
オ
オ
OOOO (WHOOO)
オ
オ
BACK UP A LITTLE.
EVEN IF WE'VE TAKEN INHIBITORS...
...IT'S NOT GOOD TO BREATHE IN THESE FUMES FOR TOO LONG.
SO THIS LITTLE GIRL IS THE ONE...?
DON'T LET HER LOOKS DECEIVE YOU. WHAT MATTERS IS ON THE INSIDE!
SO SHE'S THE DAUGHTER OF THE SCIENTIST AND FAMED SINGER...
...SAORI AMANO.
SHE'S THE SOLE BEING TO HAVE BEEN EXPOSED TO D99 WHILE STILL IN THE WOMB.
WHA...?
RIGHT? THAT ALONE IS AMAZING.
A BEING GRANTED GENIUS-LEVEL INTELLIGENCE ARTIFICIALLY...
BUUUT...

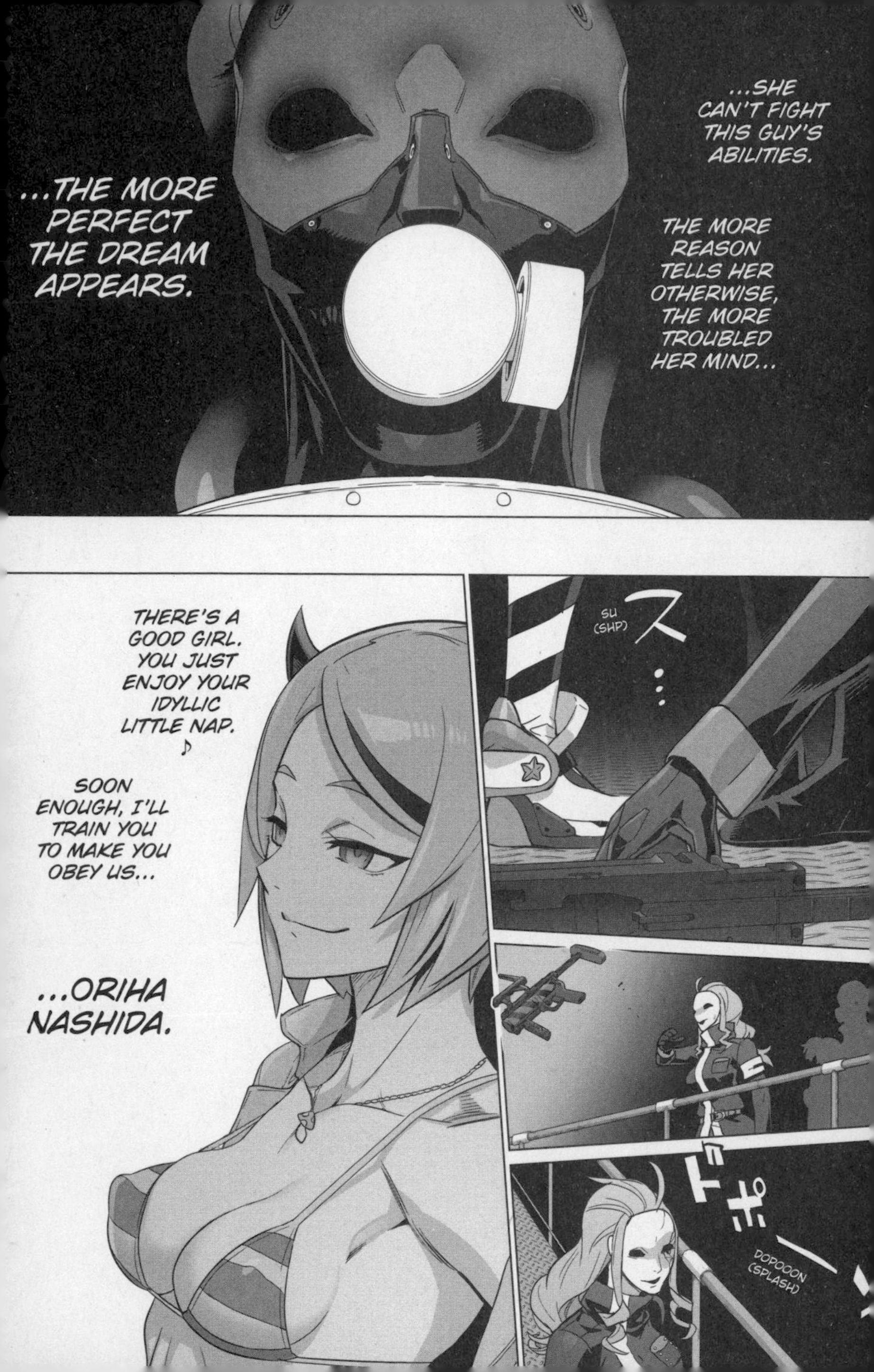
...SHE CAN'T FIGHT THIS GUY'S ABILITIES.
THE MORE REASON TELLS HER OTHERWISE, THE MORE TROUBLED HER MIND...
...THE MORE PERFECT THE DREAM APPEARS.
ス
SU (SHP)
...
ドポーン
DOPOOON (SPLASH)
THERE'S A GOOD GIRL. YOU JUST ENJOY YOUR IDYLLIC LITTLE NAP. ♪
SOON ENOUGH, I'LL TRAIN YOU TO MAKE YOU OBEY US...
...ORIHA NASHIDA.

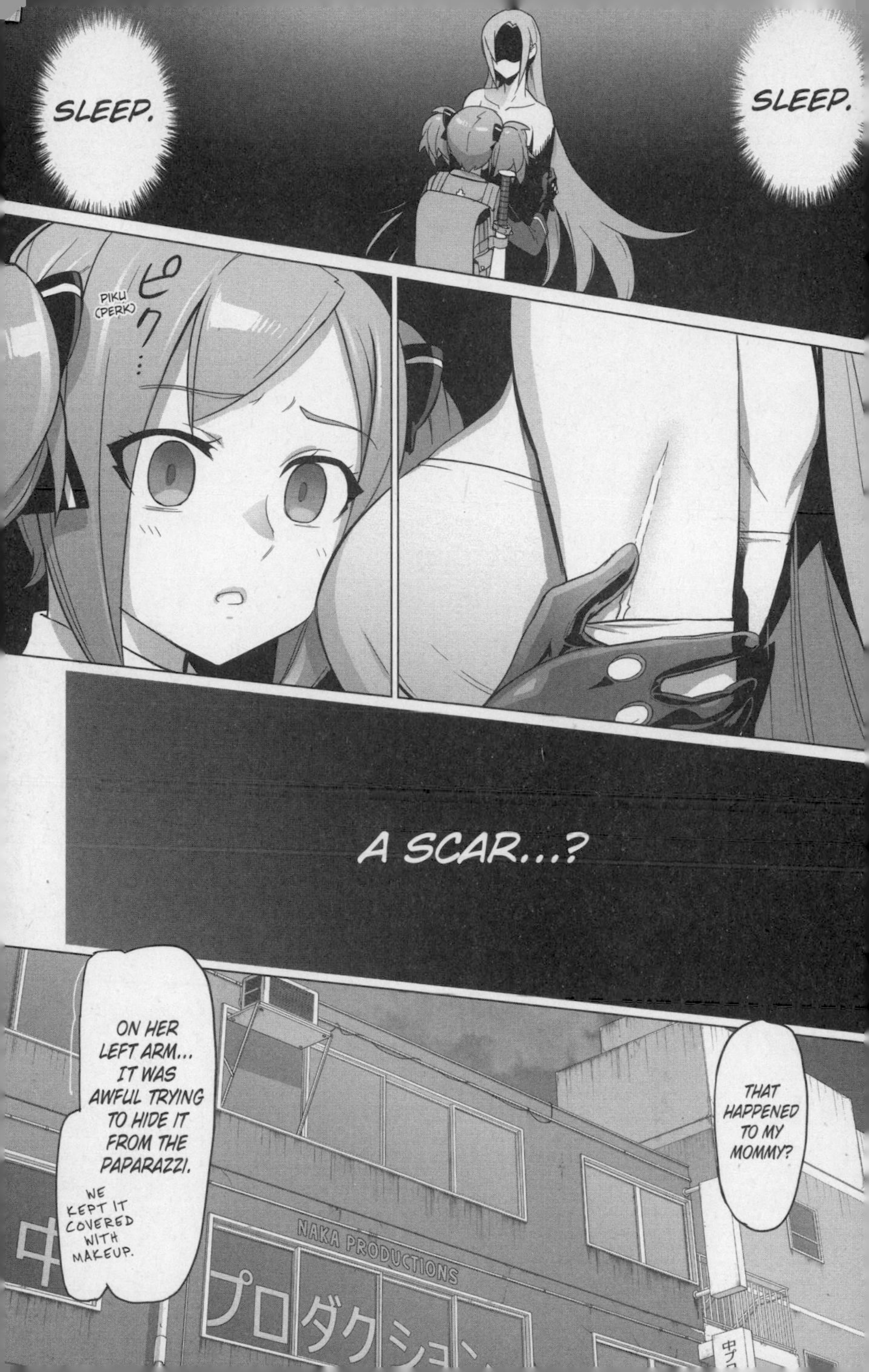
SLEEP.
SLEEP.
ピク…
PIKU (PERK)
A SCAR...?
THAT HAPPENED TO MY MOMMY?
ON HER LEFT ARM... IT WAS AWFUL TRYING TO HIDE IT FROM THE PAPARAZZI.
WE KEPT IT COVERED WITH MAKEUP.
NAKA PRODUCTIONS
中プロダクション

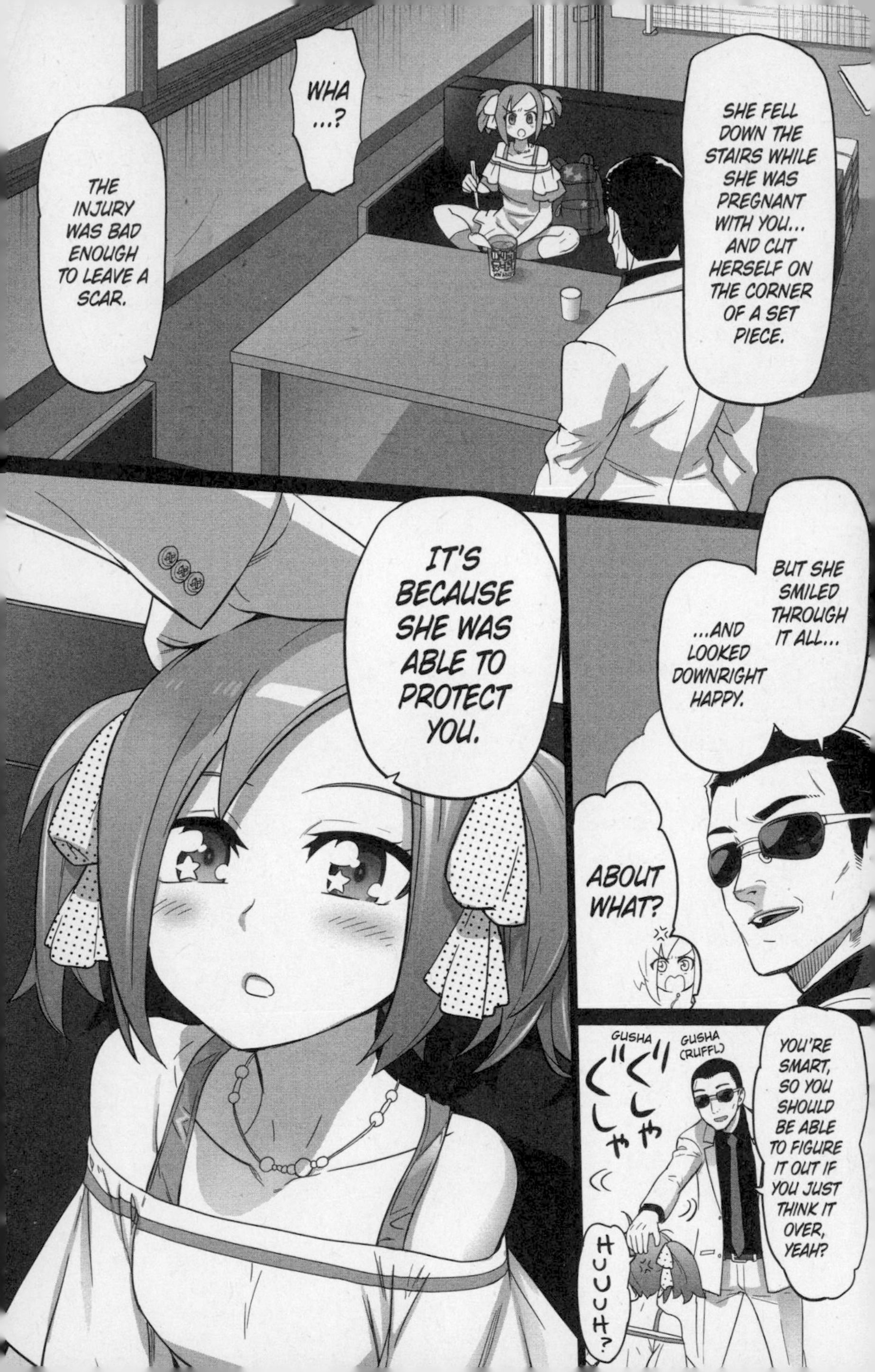
SHE FELL DOWN THE STAIRS WHILE SHE WAS PREGNANT WITH YOU... AND CUT HERSELF ON THE CORNER OF A SET PIECE.
WHA ...?
THE INJURY WAS BAD ENOUGH TO LEAVE A SCAR.
BUT SHE SMILED THROUGH IT ALL...
...AND LOOKED DOWNRIGHT HAPPY.
ABOUT WHAT?
GUSHA
GUSHA (RUFFL)
ぐしゃぐしゃ
YOU'RE SMART, SO YOU SHOULD BE ABLE TO FIGURE IT OUT IF YOU JUST THINK IT OVER, YEAH?
HUUUH?
IT'S BECAUSE SHE WAS ABLE TO PROTECT YOU.

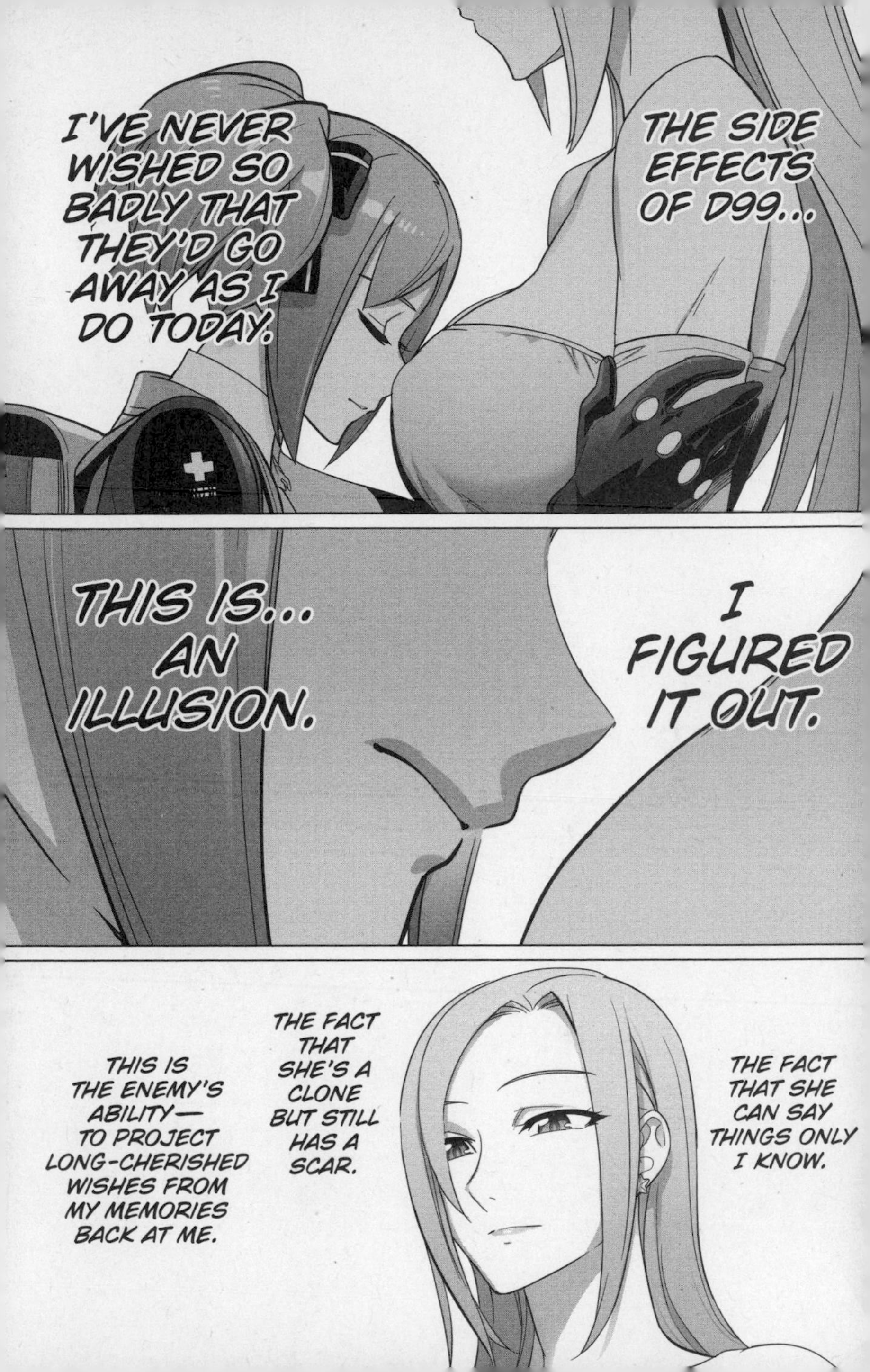
THE SIDE EFFECTS OF D99...
I'VE NEVER WISHED SO BADLY THAT THEY'D GO AWAY AS I DO TODAY.
I FIGURED IT OUT.
THIS IS... AN ILLUSION.
THE FACT THAT SHE CAN SAY THINGS ONLY I KNOW.
THE FACT THAT SHE'S A CLONE BUT STILL HAS A SCAR.
THIS IS THE ENEMY'S ABILITY— TO PROJECT LONG-CHERISHED WISHES FROM MY MEMORIES BACK AT ME.

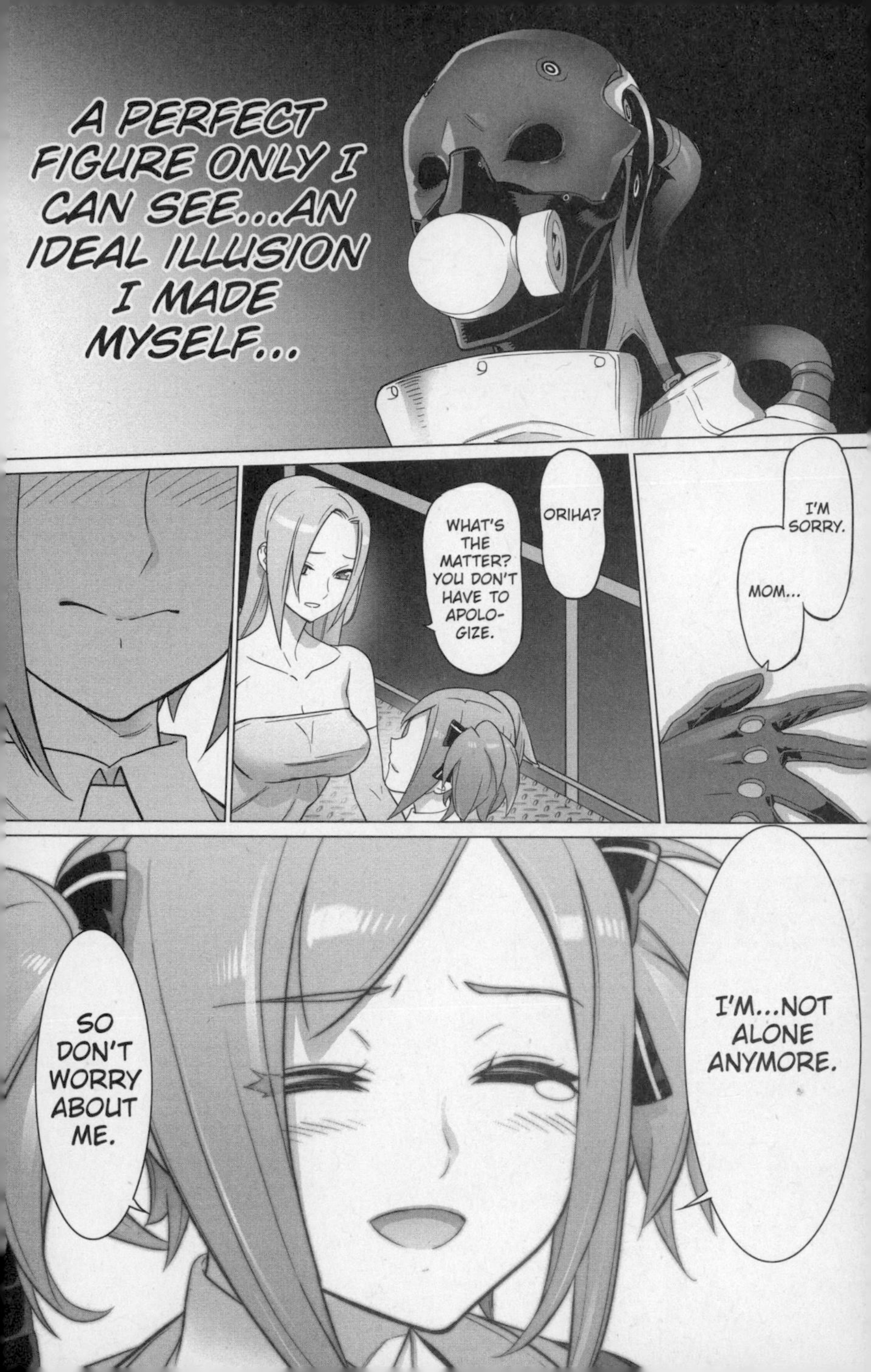
A PERFECT FIGURE ONLY I CAN SEE...AN IDEAL ILLUSION I MADE MYSELF...
I'M SORRY.
MOM...
ORIHA?
WHAT'S THE MATTER? YOU DON'T HAVE TO APOLOGIZE.
I'M...NOT ALONE ANYMORE.
SO DON'T WORRY ABOUT ME.

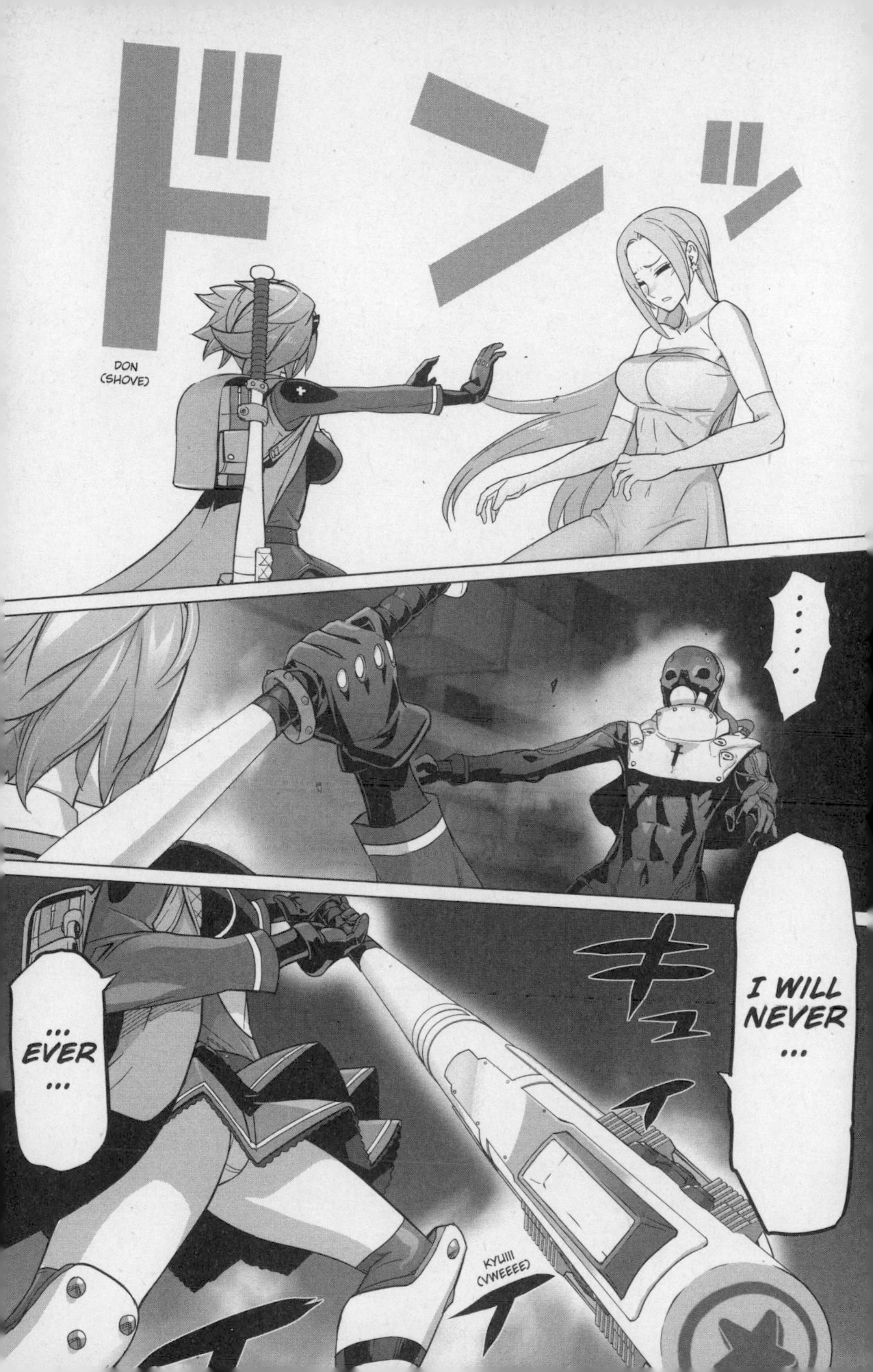
ドン
DON (SHOVE)
......
I WILL NEVER ...
KYUIII (VWEEEE)
... EVER ...

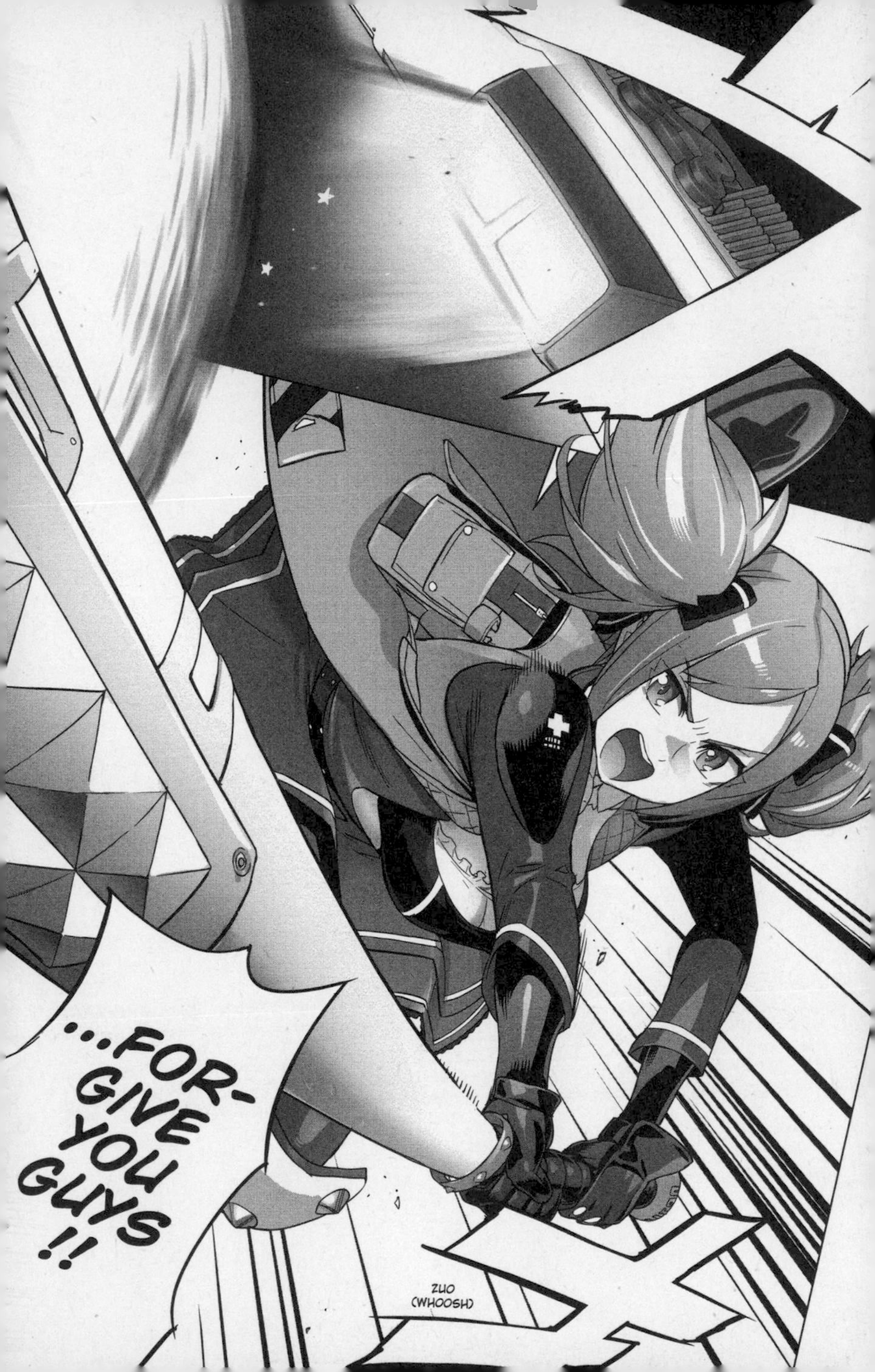
...FOR-
GIVE
YOU
GUYS
!!
ZUO
(WHOOSH)

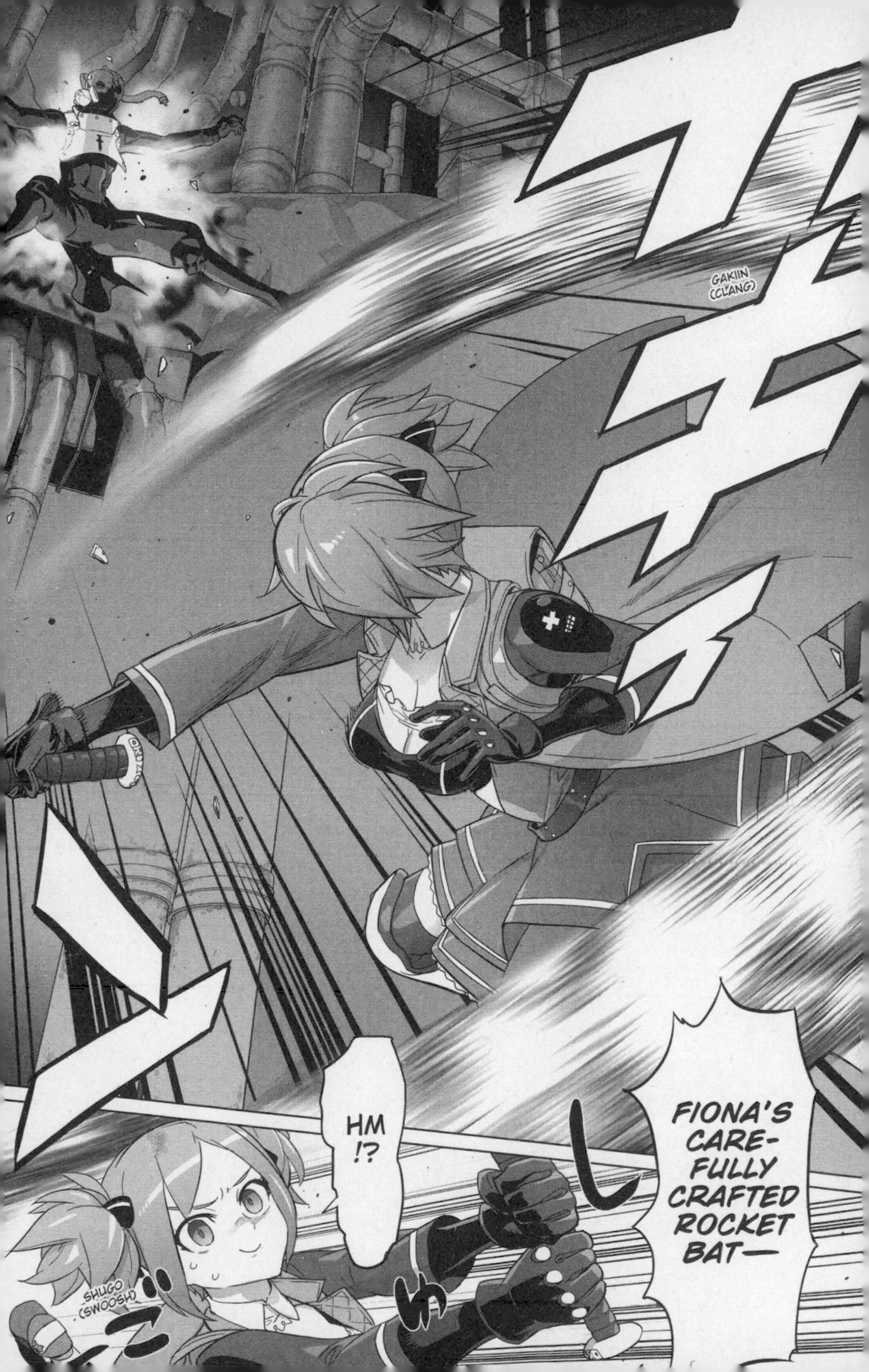
GAKIIN (CLANG)
FIONA'S CARE-FULLY CRAFTED ROCKET BAT—
HM !?
SHUGO (SWOOSH)

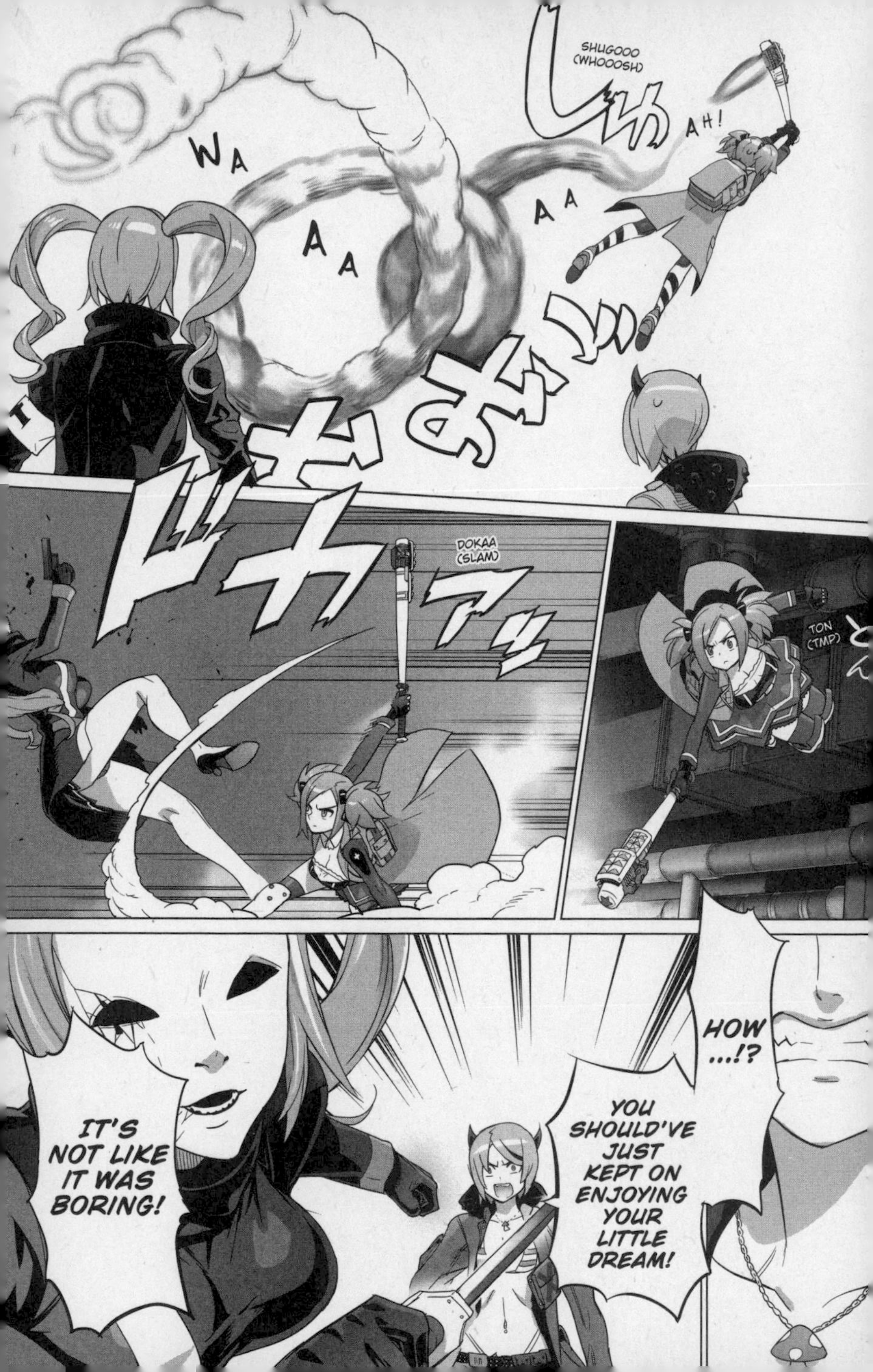
SHUGOOO (WHOOOSH)
WA A A A A A
AH!
TON (TMP)
DOKAA (SLAM)
HOW ...!?
YOU SHOULD'VE JUST KEPT ON ENJOYING YOUR LITTLE DREAM!
IT'S NOT LIKE IT WAS BORING!

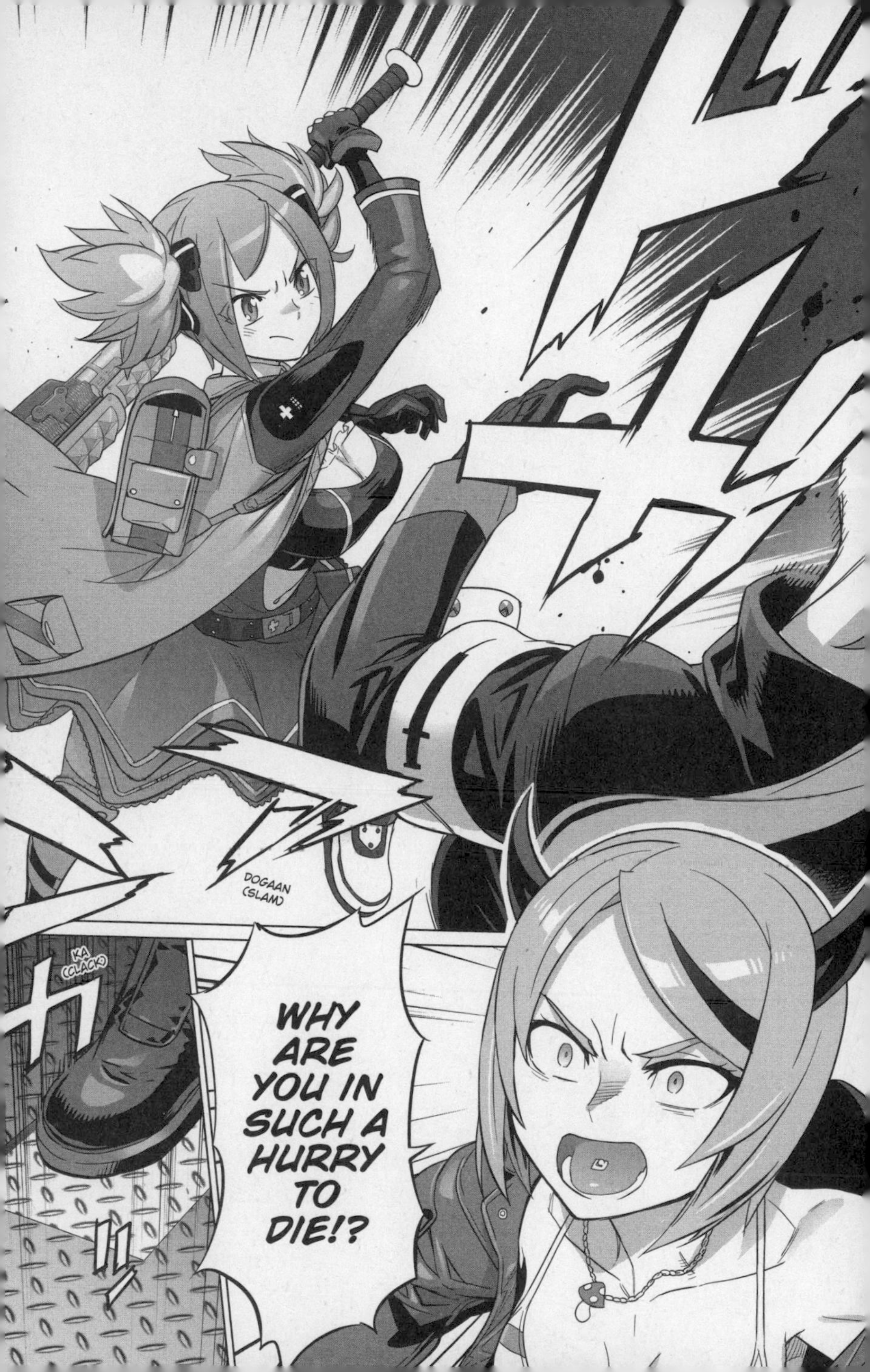
DOGAAN
(SLAM)
KA
(CLACK)
WHY ARE YOU IN SUCH A HURRY TO DIE!?

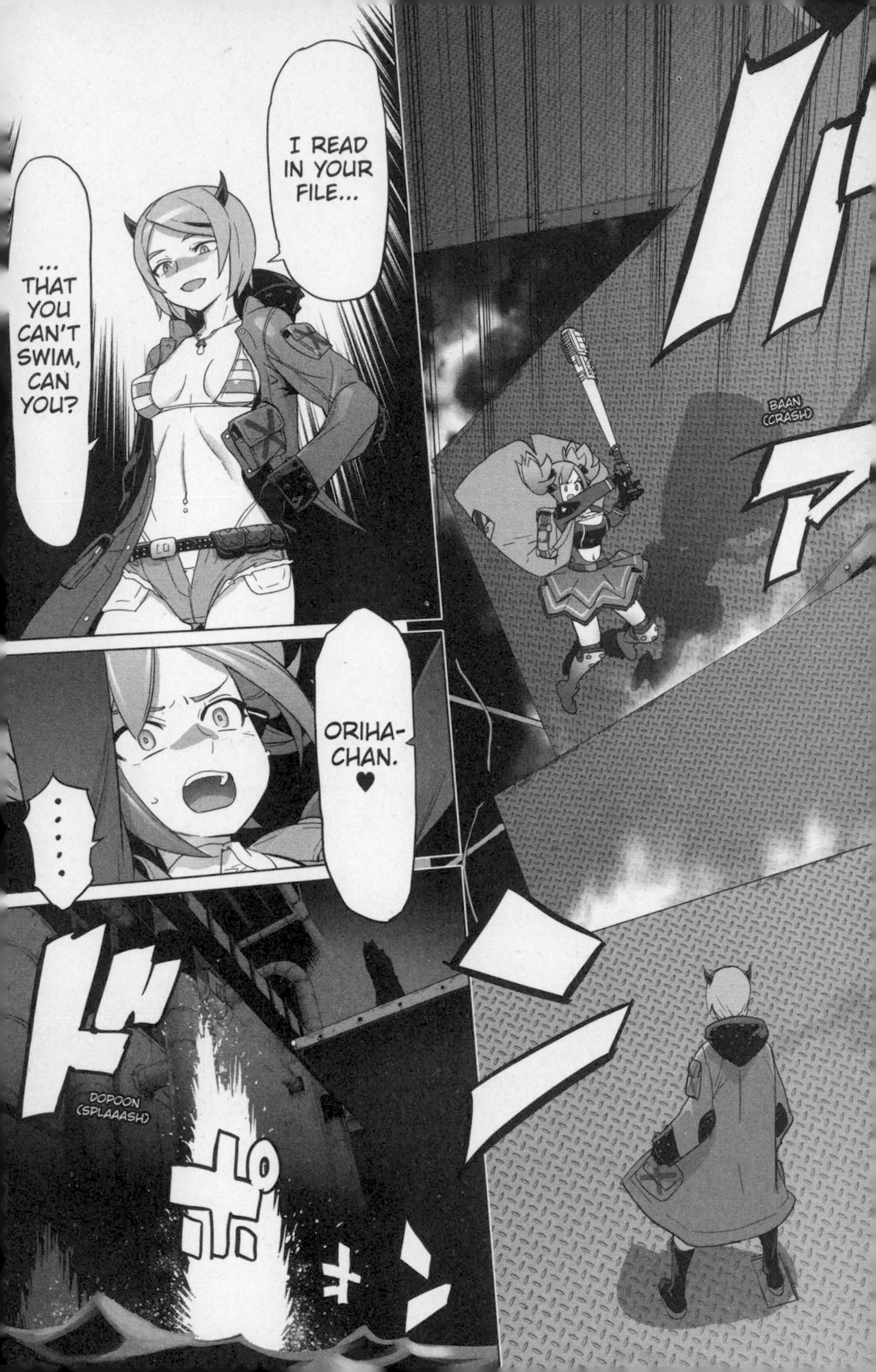
BAAN (CRASH)
I READ IN YOUR FILE...
...THAT YOU CAN'T SWIM, CAN YOU?
ORIHA-CHAN. ♥
......
DOPOON (SPLAAASH)

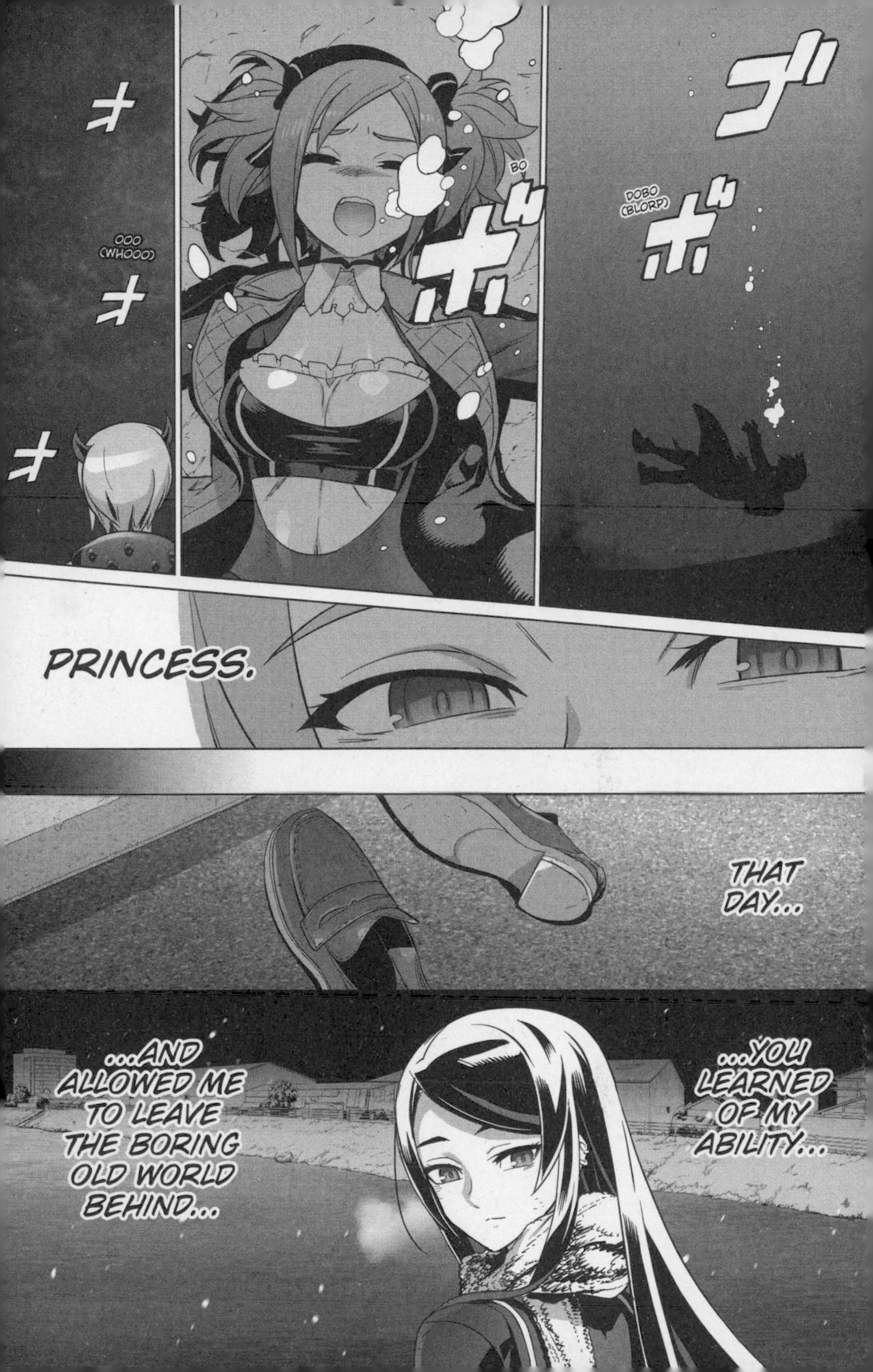
ゴボ
DOBO (BLORP)
ボ
BO
オオオ
OOO (WHOOO)
PRINCESS.
THAT DAY...
...YOU LEARNED OF MY ABILITY...
...AND ALLOWED ME TO LEAVE THE BORING OLD WORLD BEHIND...

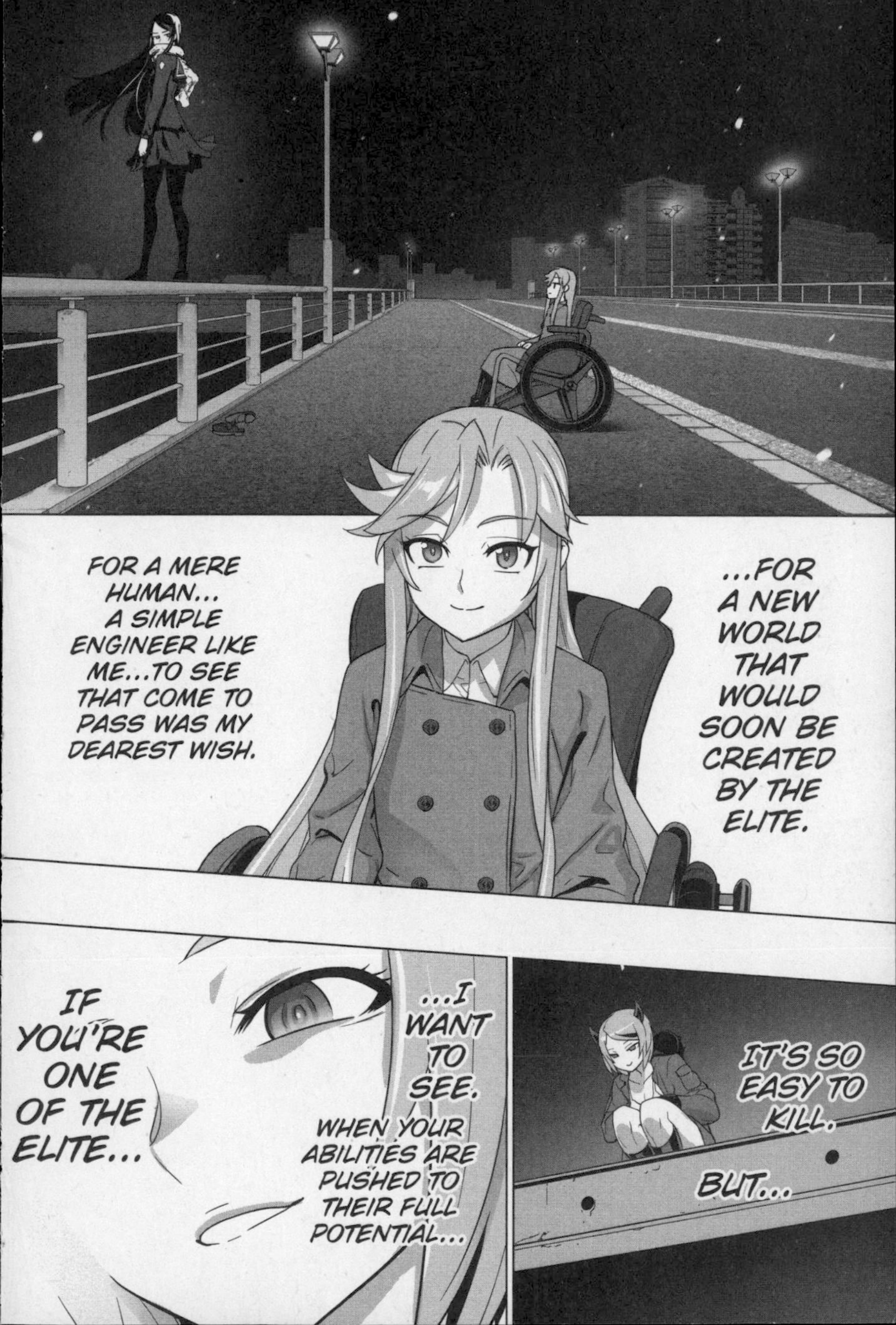
...FOR A NEW WORLD THAT WOULD SOON BE CREATED BY THE ELITE.
FOR A MERE HUMAN... A SIMPLE ENGINEER LIKE ME...TO SEE THAT COME TO PASS WAS MY DEAREST WISH.
IT'S SO EASY TO KILL.
BUT...
IF YOU'RE ONE OF THE ELITE...
...I WANT TO SEE.
WHEN YOUR ABILITIES ARE PUSHED TO THEIR FULL POTENTIAL...

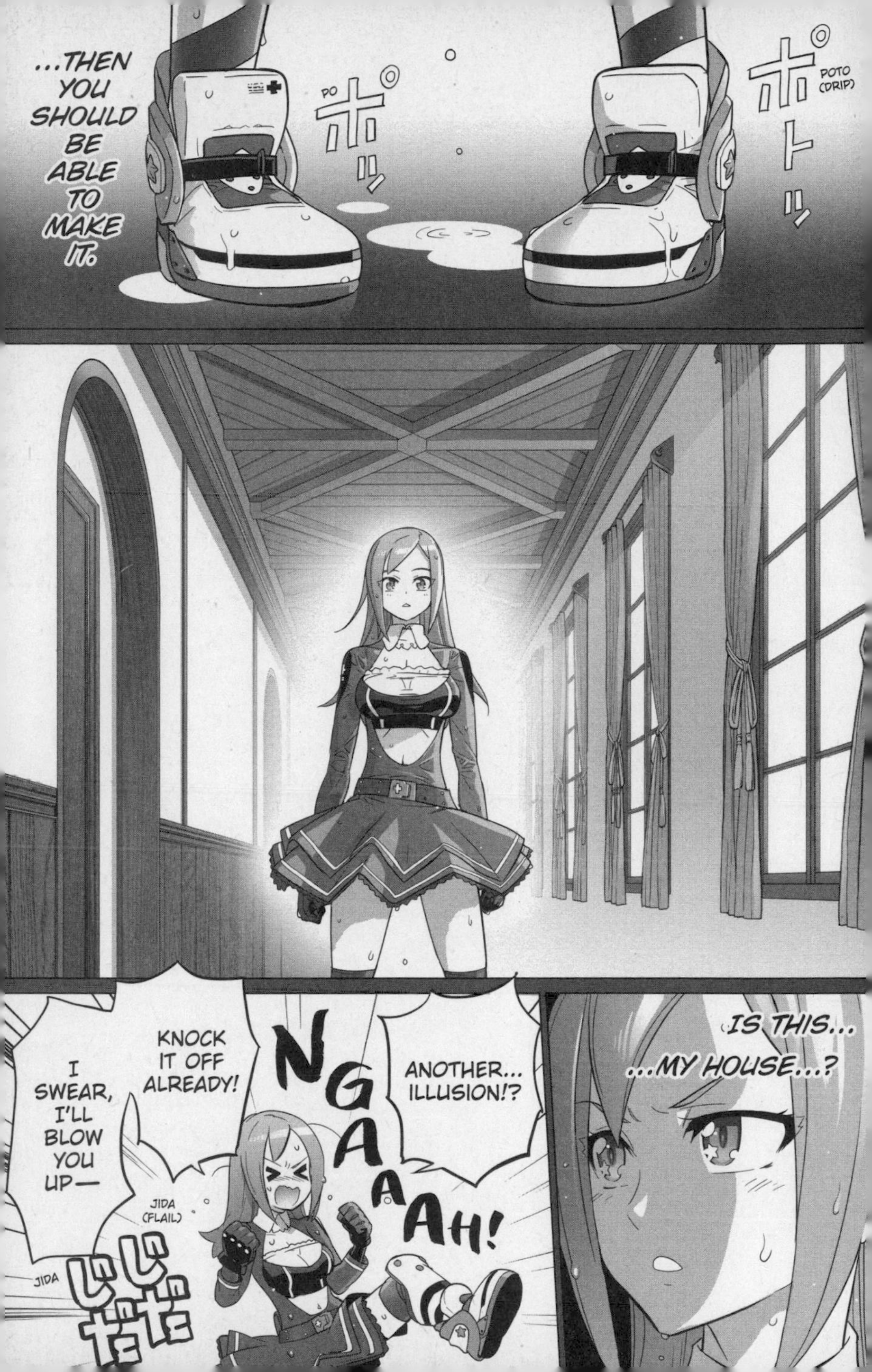
ポトッ
POTO (DRIP)
ポッ
PO
...THEN YOU SHOULD BE ABLE TO MAKE IT.
IS THIS... ...MY HOUSE...?
ANOTHER... ILLUSION!?
NGAAAAH!
KNOCK IT OFF ALREADY!
I SWEAR, I'LL BLOW YOU UP—
JIDA (FLAIL)
じたばた
JIDA

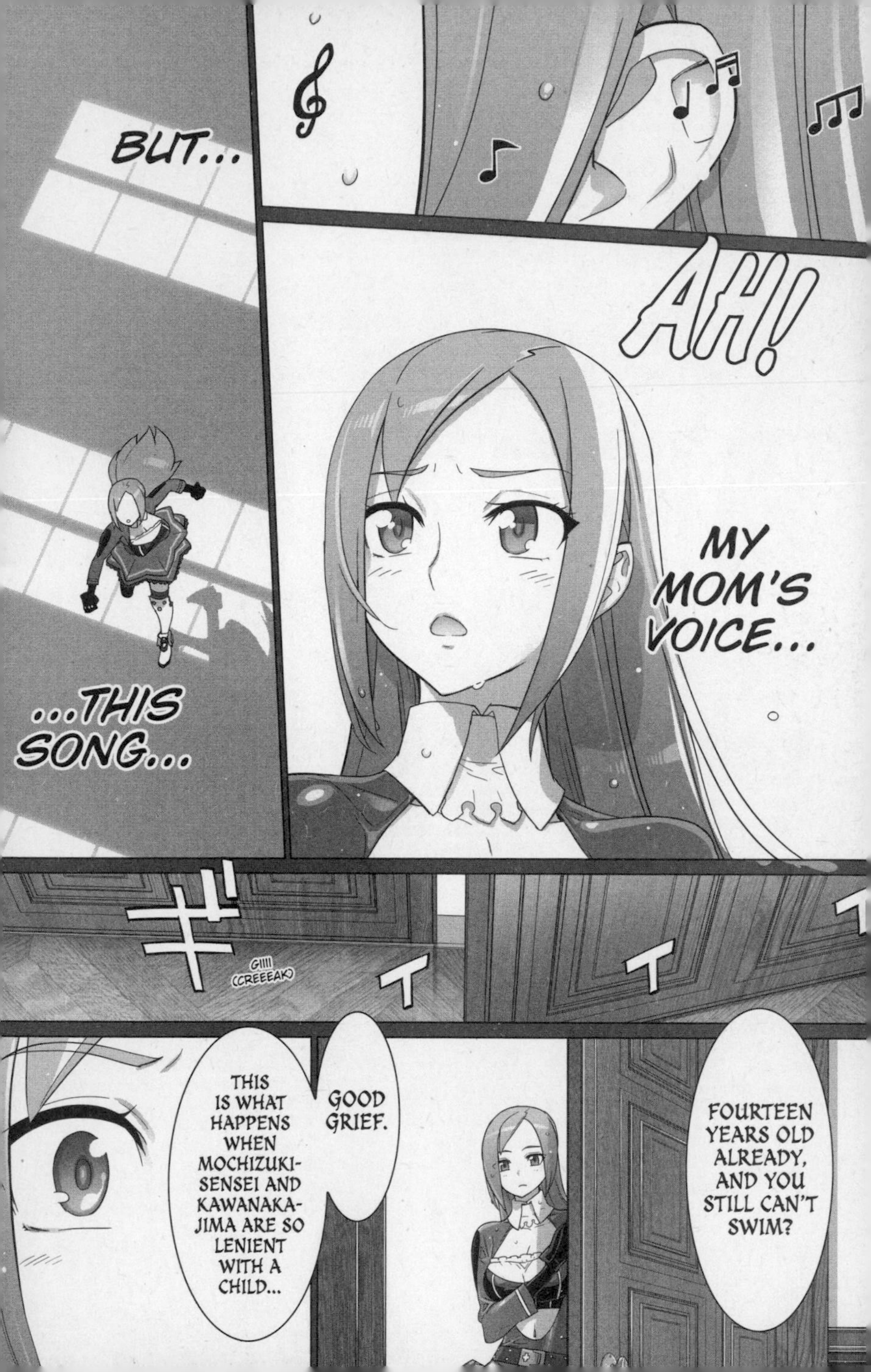
AH!
MY MOM'S VOICE...
BUT...
...THIS SONG...
GIIII (CREEEAK)
FOURTEEN YEARS OLD ALREADY, AND YOU STILL CAN'T SWIM?
GOOD GRIEF.
THIS IS WHAT HAPPENS WHEN MOCHIZUKI-SENSEI AND KAWANAKAJIMA ARE SO LENIENT WITH A CHILD...

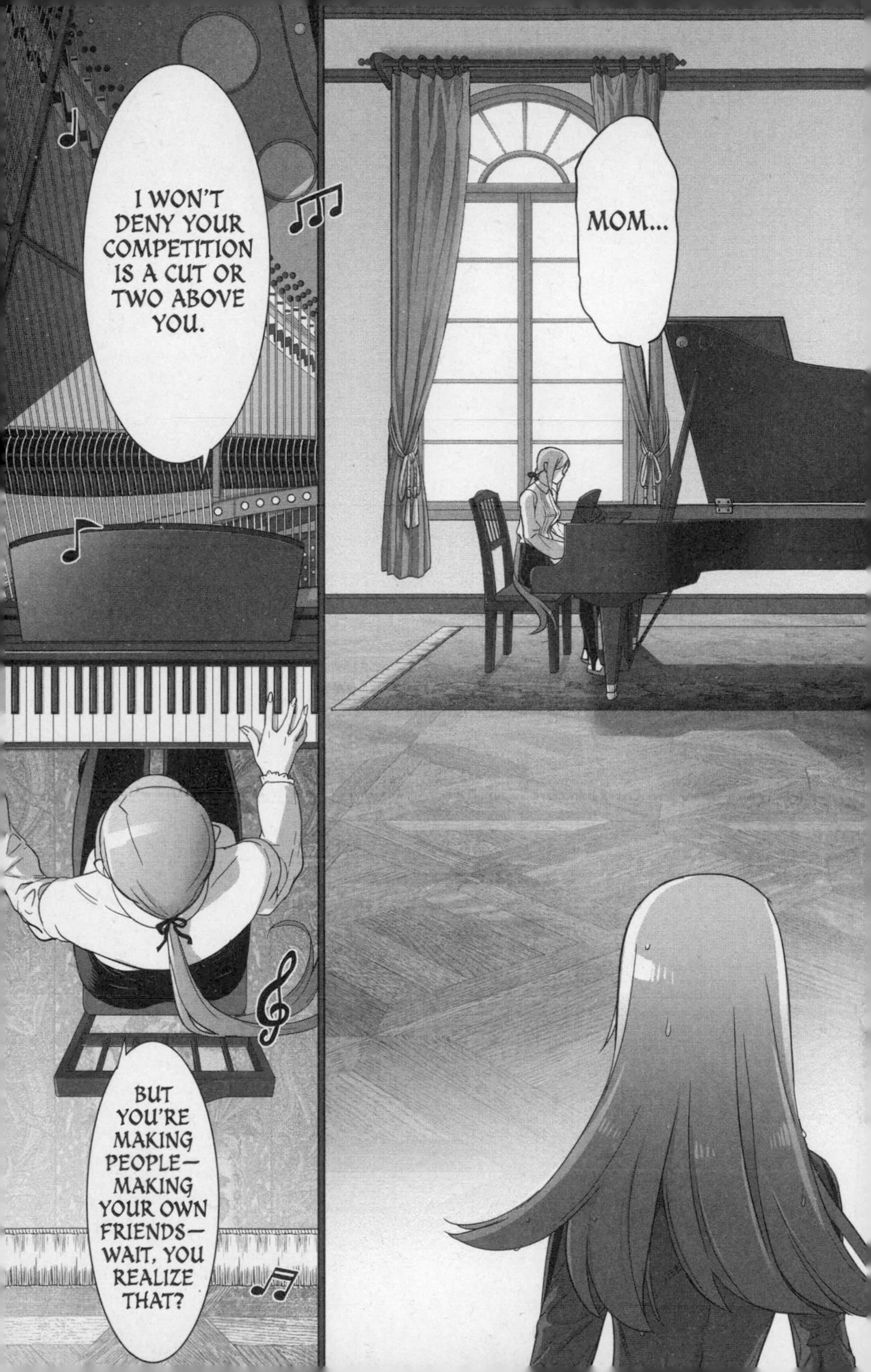
MOM...
I WON'T DENY YOUR COMPETITION IS A CUT OR TWO ABOVE YOU.
BUT YOU'RE MAKING PEOPLE— MAKING YOUR OWN FRIENDS— WAIT, YOU REALIZE THAT?

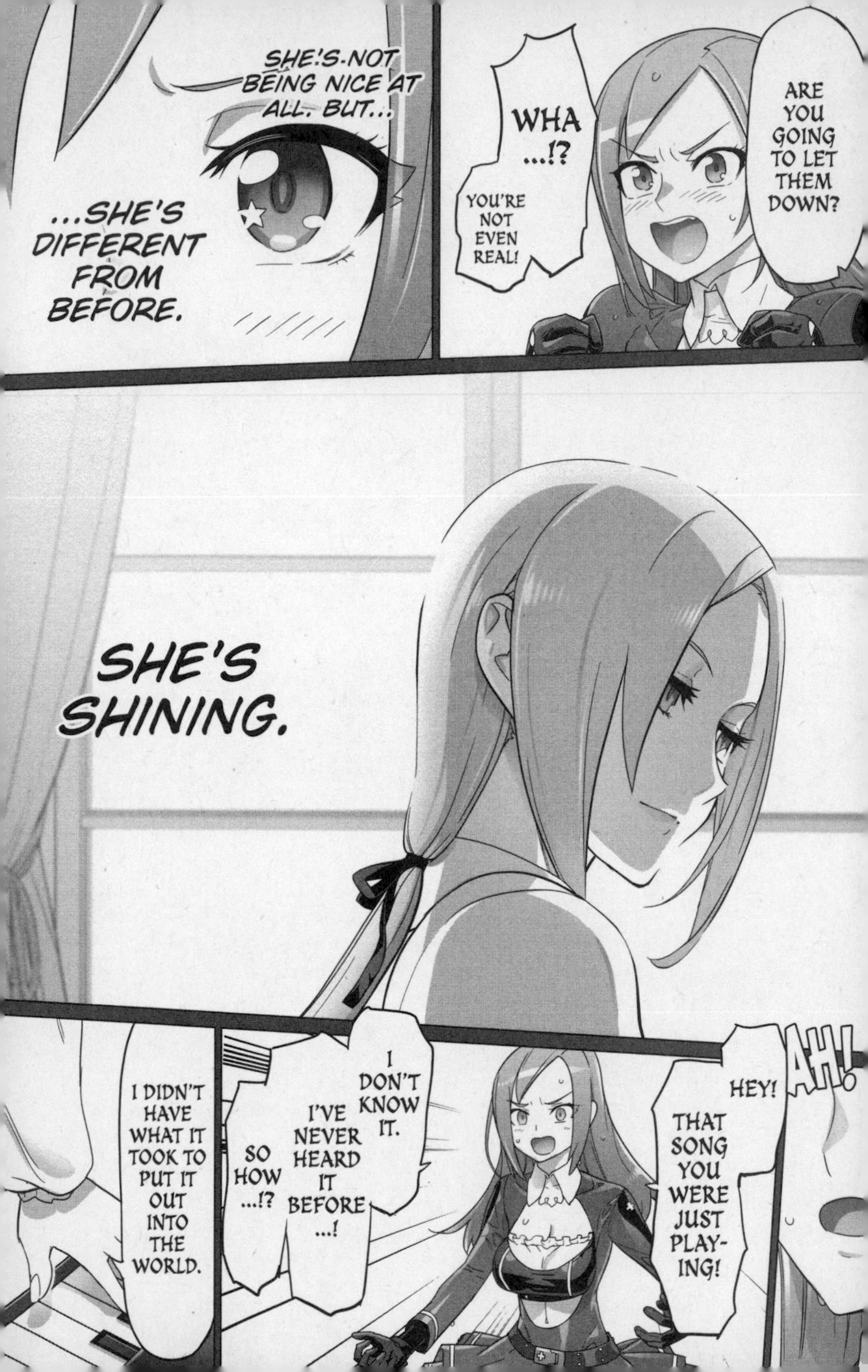
ARE YOU GOING TO LET THEM DOWN?
WHA ...!?
YOU'RE NOT EVEN REAL!
SHE'S NOT BEING NICE AT ALL. BUT...
...SHE'S DIFFERENT FROM BEFORE.
SHE'S SHINING.
AH!
HEY!
THAT SONG YOU WERE JUST PLAY-ING!
I DON'T KNOW IT.
I'VE NEVER HEARD IT BEFORE ...!
SO HOW ...!?
I DIDN'T HAVE WHAT IT TOOK TO PUT IT OUT INTO THE WORLD.

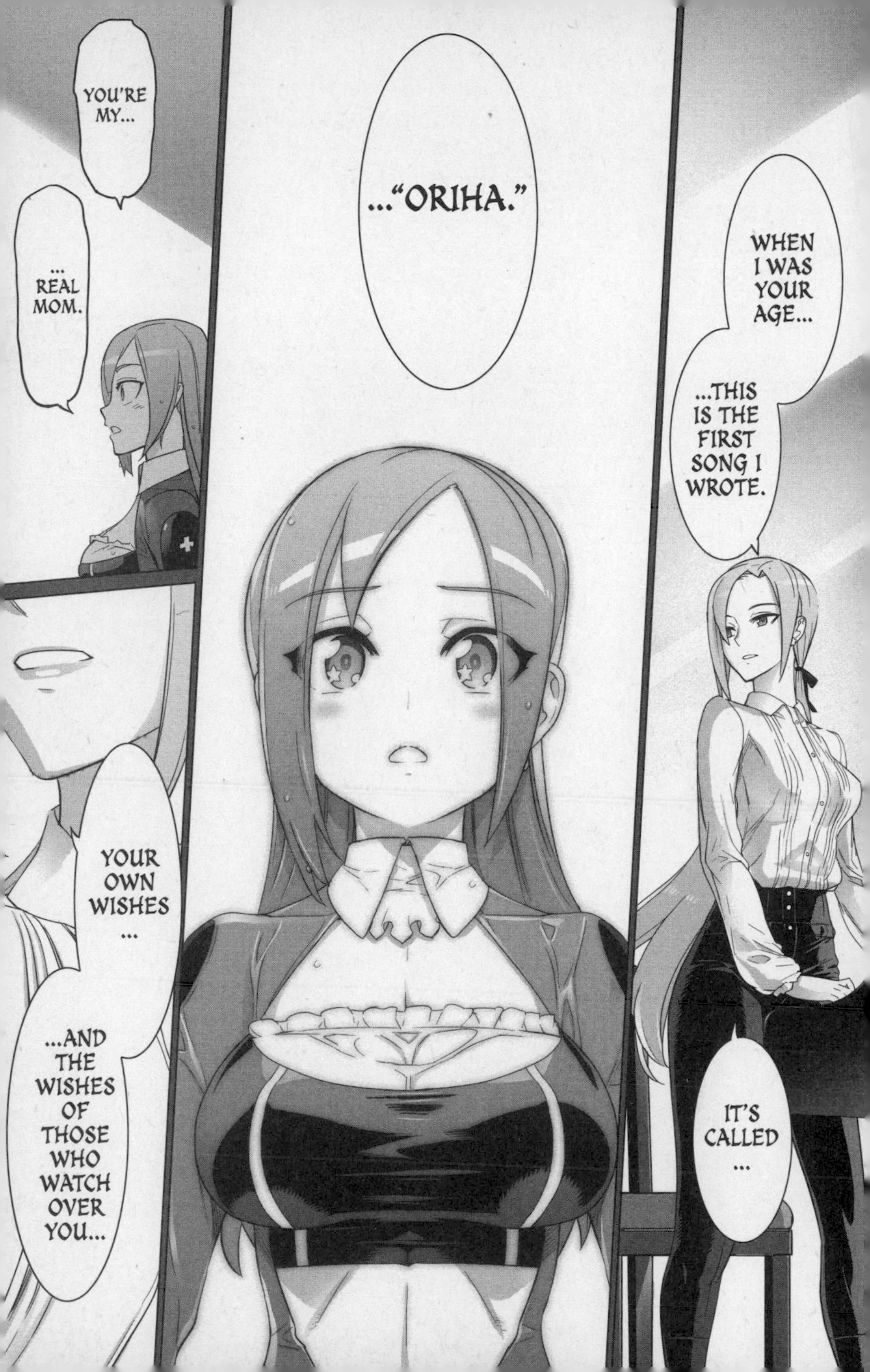
WHEN I WAS YOUR AGE...
...THIS IS THE FIRST SONG I WROTE.
IT'S CALLED...
..."ORIHA."
YOU'RE MY...
...REAL MOM.
YOUR OWN WISHES...
...AND THE WISHES OF THOSE WHO WATCH OVER YOU...

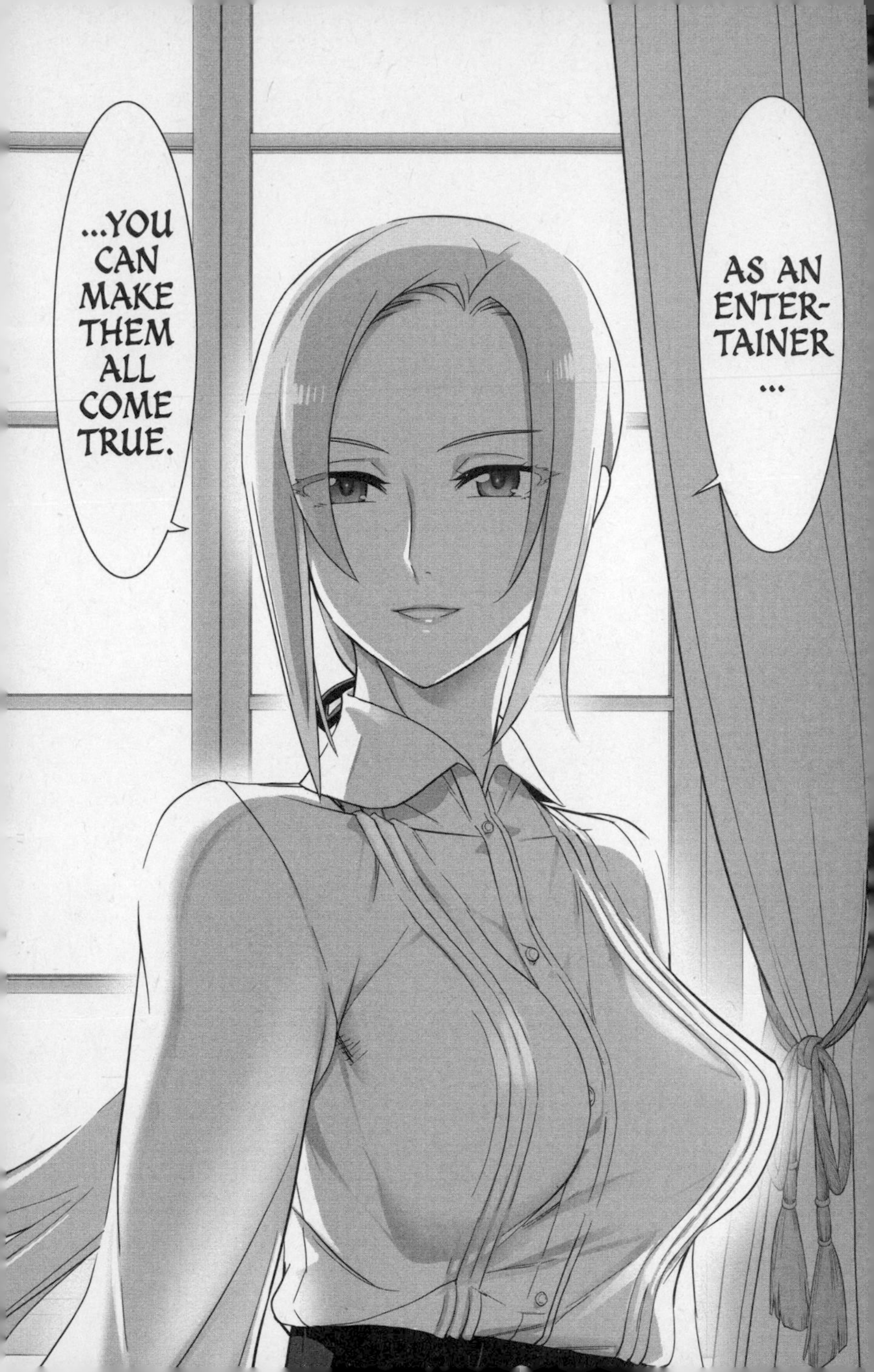
AS AN ENTER-TAINER ...
...YOU CAN MAKE THEM ALL COME TRUE.

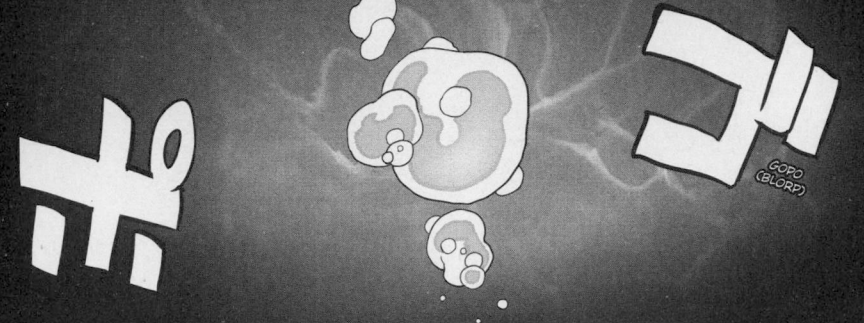

GOPO
(BLORP)

THE BUBBLES ARE RISING IN SLOW MOTION.

HUH...?

IS THIS...

...MY COGNITIVE ABILITY SURPASSING THE BOUNDARIES OF THIS WORLD?

BUT WITH THIS...

I WONDER IF THIS IS A BONUS ABILITY FROM D99.

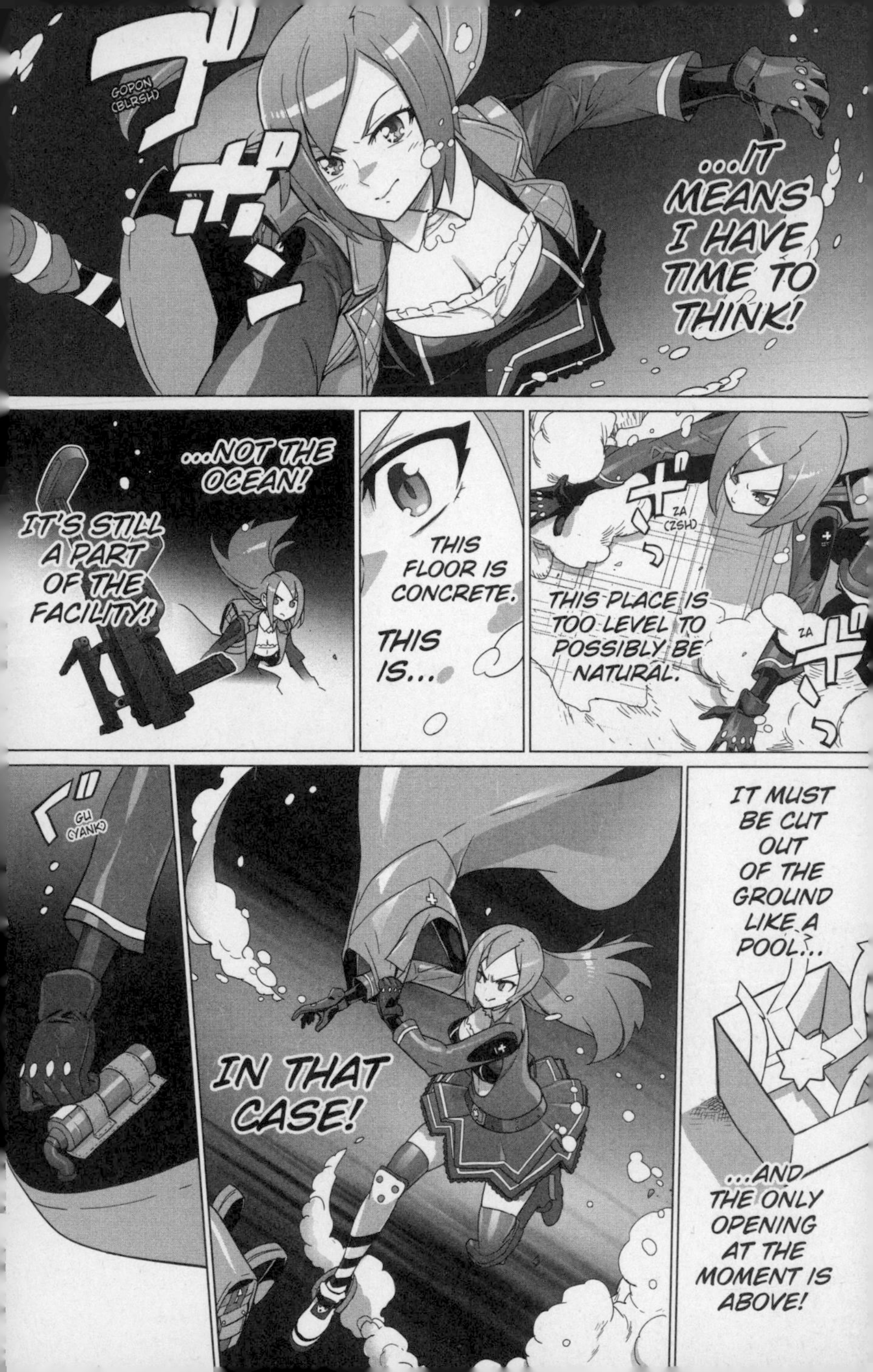
GOPON (BLRSH)
...IT MEANS I HAVE TIME TO THINK!
ZA (ZSH)
THIS PLACE IS TOO LEVEL TO POSSIBLY BE NATURAL.
ZA
THIS FLOOR IS CONCRETE.
THIS IS...
...NOT THE OCEAN!
IT'S STILL A PART OF THE FACILITY!
IT MUST BE CUT OUT OF THE GROUND LIKE A POOL...
...AND THE ONLY OPENING AT THE MOMENT IS ABOVE!
IN THAT CASE!
GU (YANK)

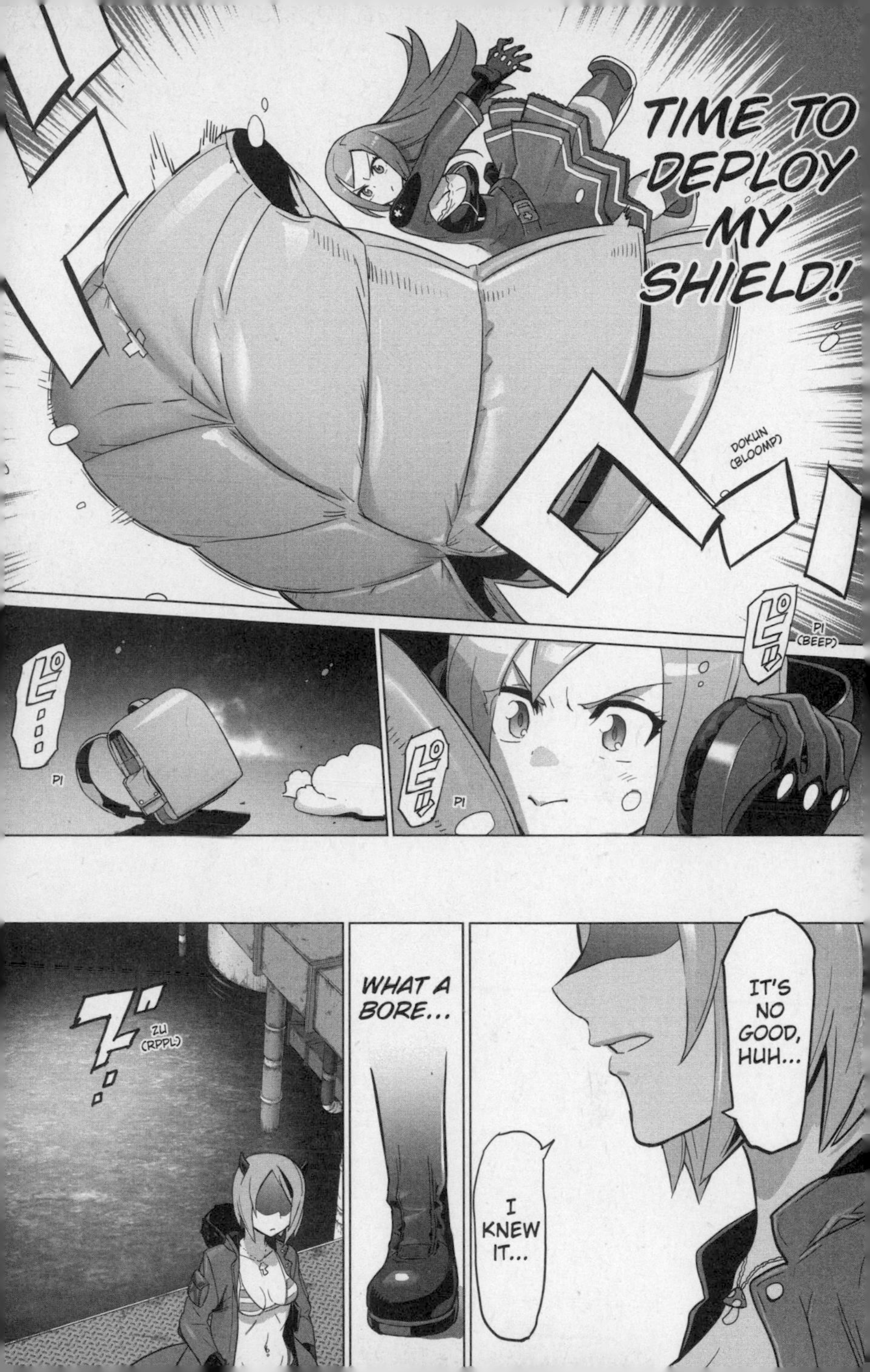
TIME TO DEPLOY MY SHIELD!
DOKUN (BLOOMP)
PI (BEEP)
PI
PI
IT'S NO GOOD, HUH...
I KNEW IT...
WHAT A BORE...
ZU (RPPL)

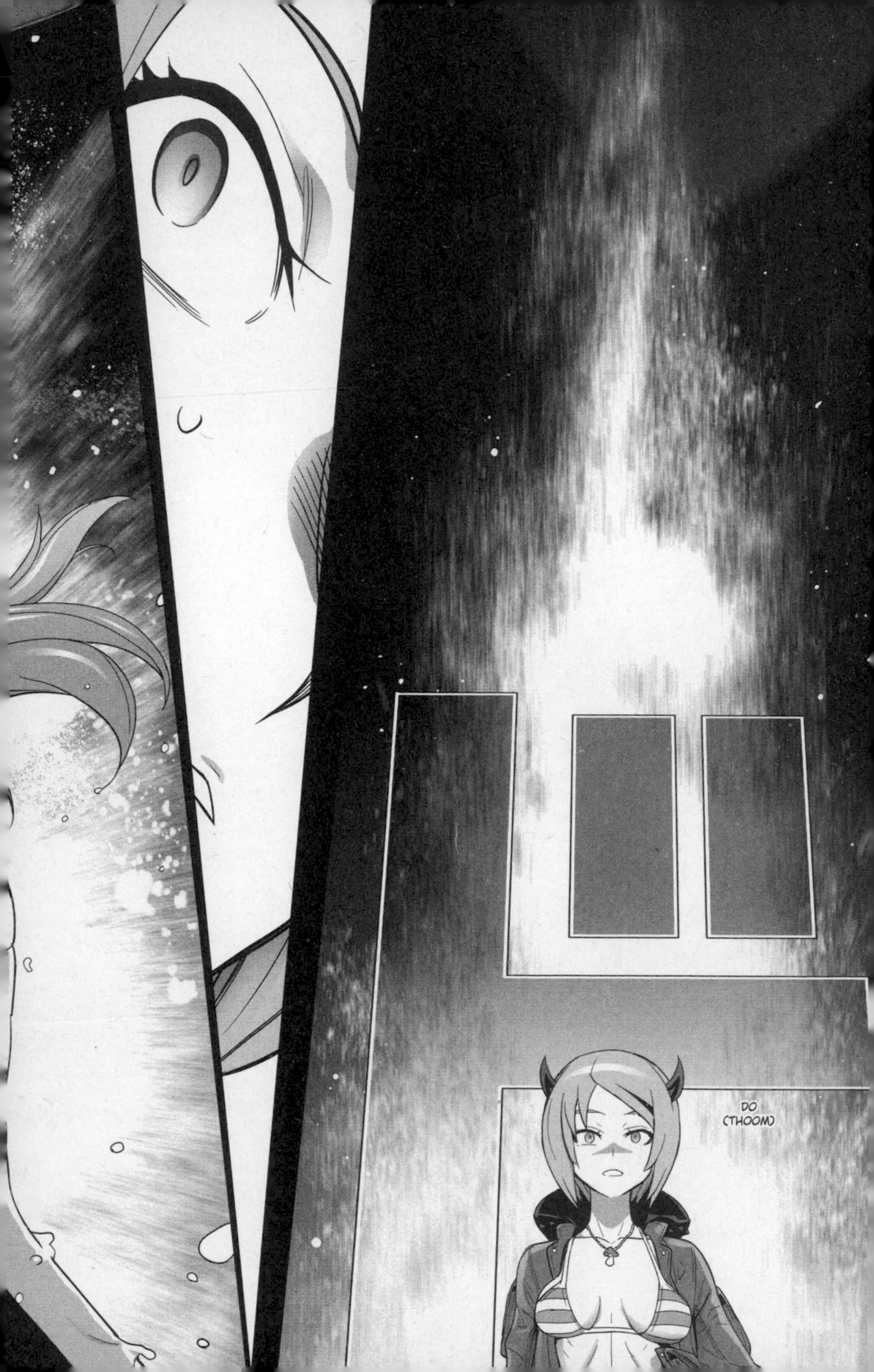
DO
(THOOM)

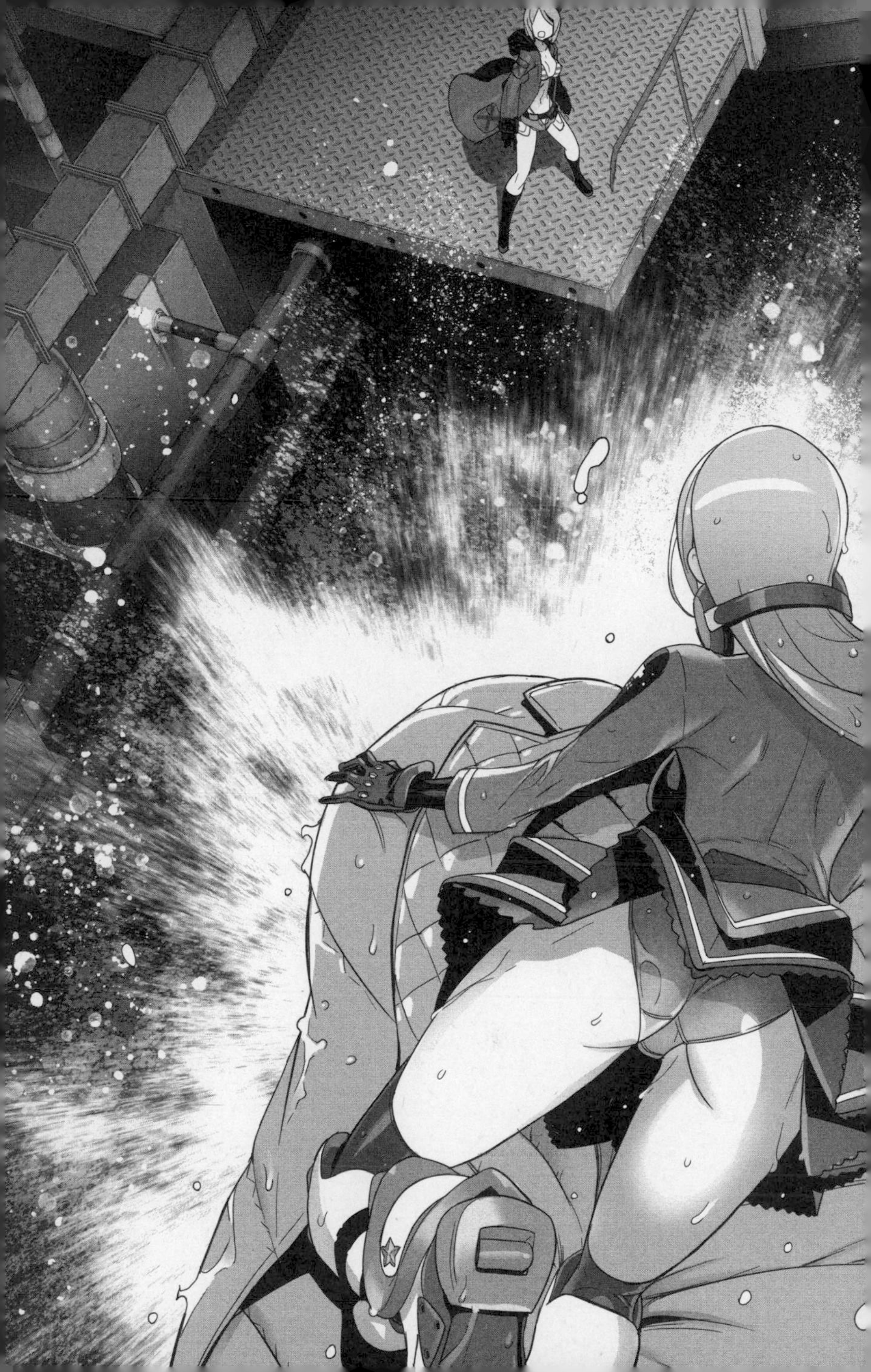
!

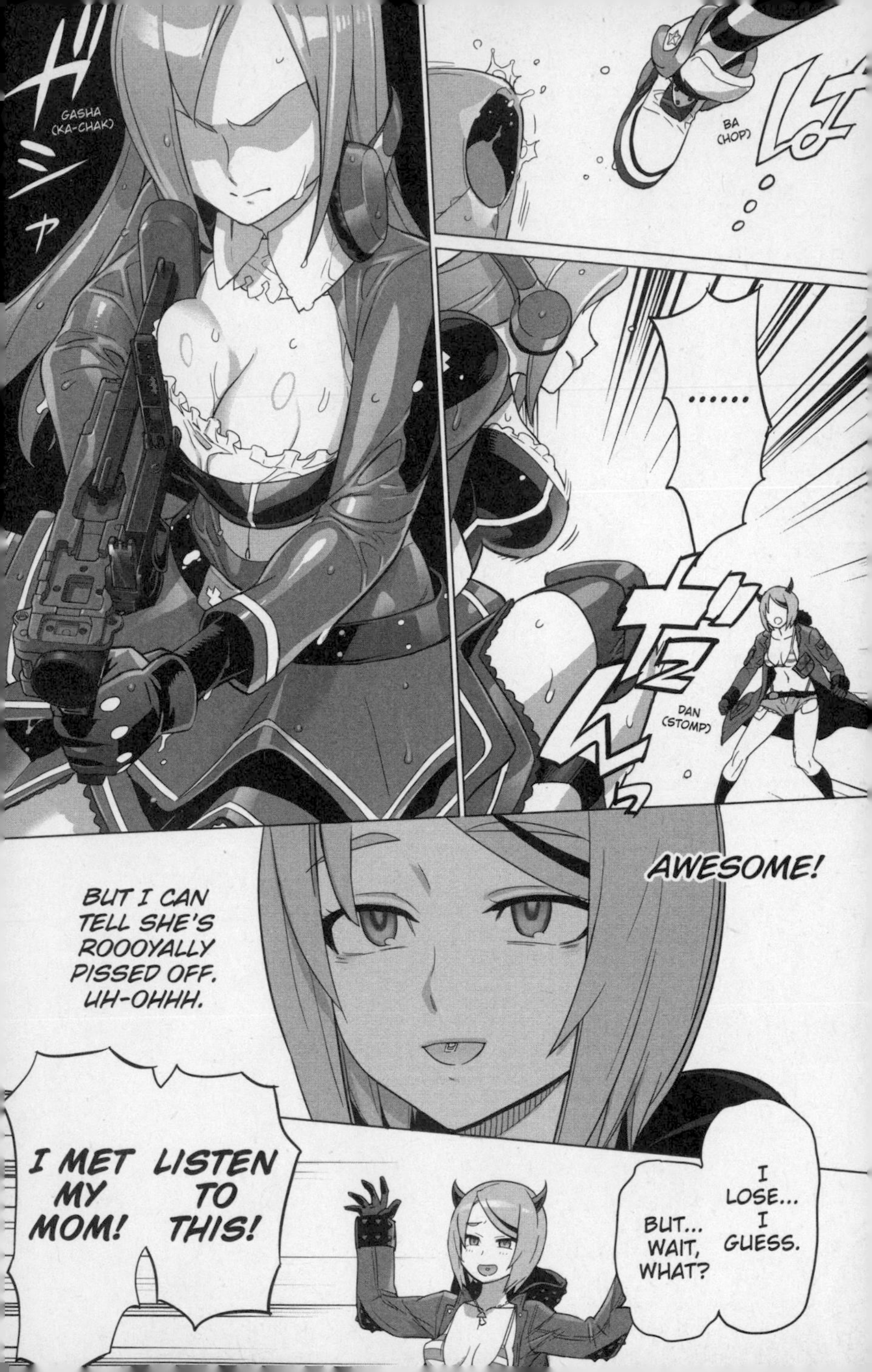
BA
(HOP)
......
DAN
(STOMP)
GASHA
(KA-CHAK)
AWESOME!
BUT I CAN TELL SHE'S ROOOYALLY PISSED OFF. UH-OHHH.
I LOSE... I GUESS.
BUT... WAIT, WHAT?
LISTEN TO THIS!
I MET MY MOM!

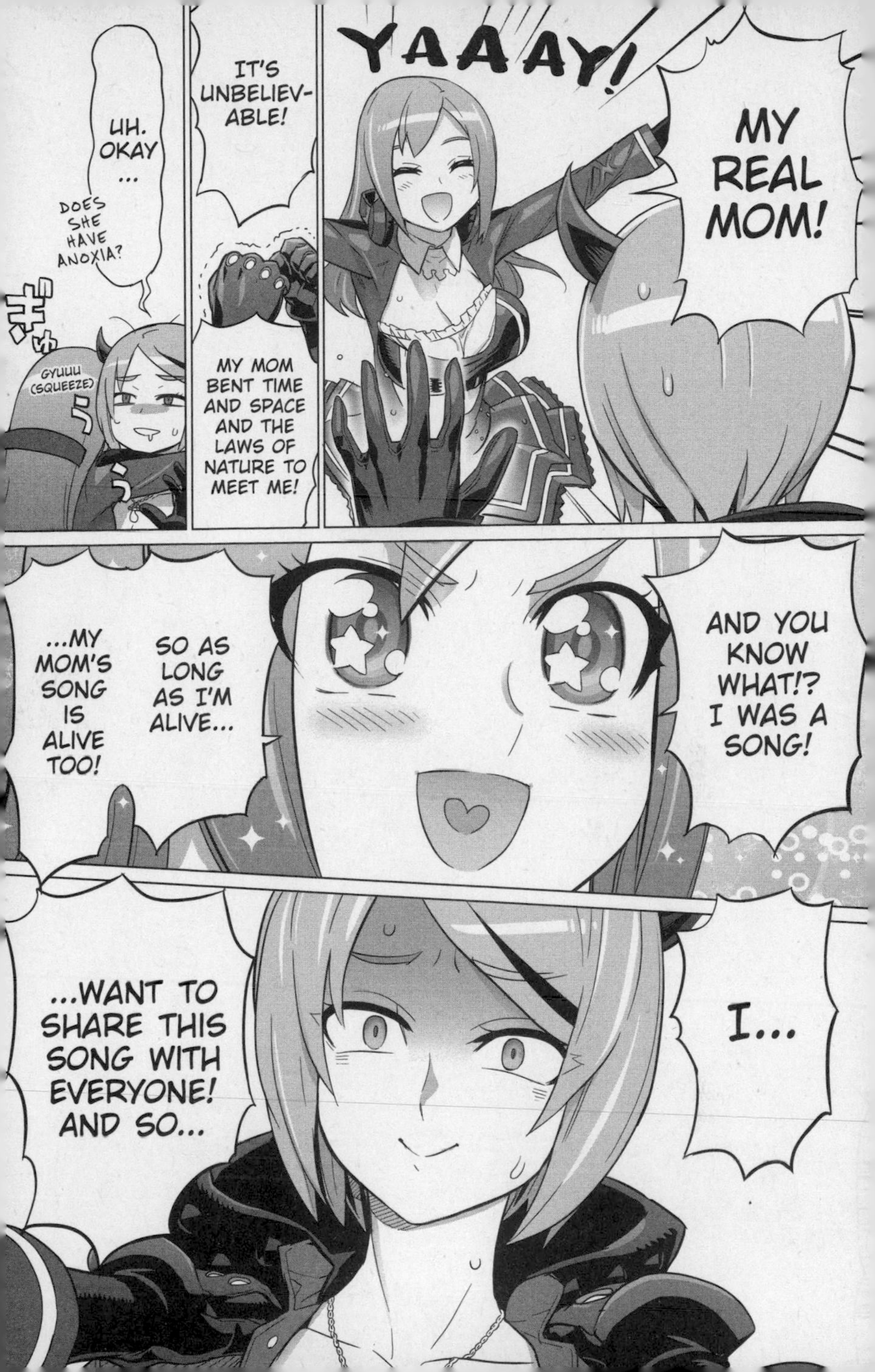
YAAAY!
MY REAL MOM!
IT'S UNBELIEV-ABLE!
MY MOM BENT TIME AND SPACE AND THE LAWS OF NATURE TO MEET ME!
UH. OKAY ...
DOES SHE HAVE ANOXIA?
GYUUU (SQUEEZE)
AND YOU KNOW WHAT!? I WAS A SONG!
SO AS LONG AS I'M ALIVE...
...MY MOM'S SONG IS ALIVE TOO!
I...
...WANT TO SHARE THIS SONG WITH EVERYONE! AND SO...

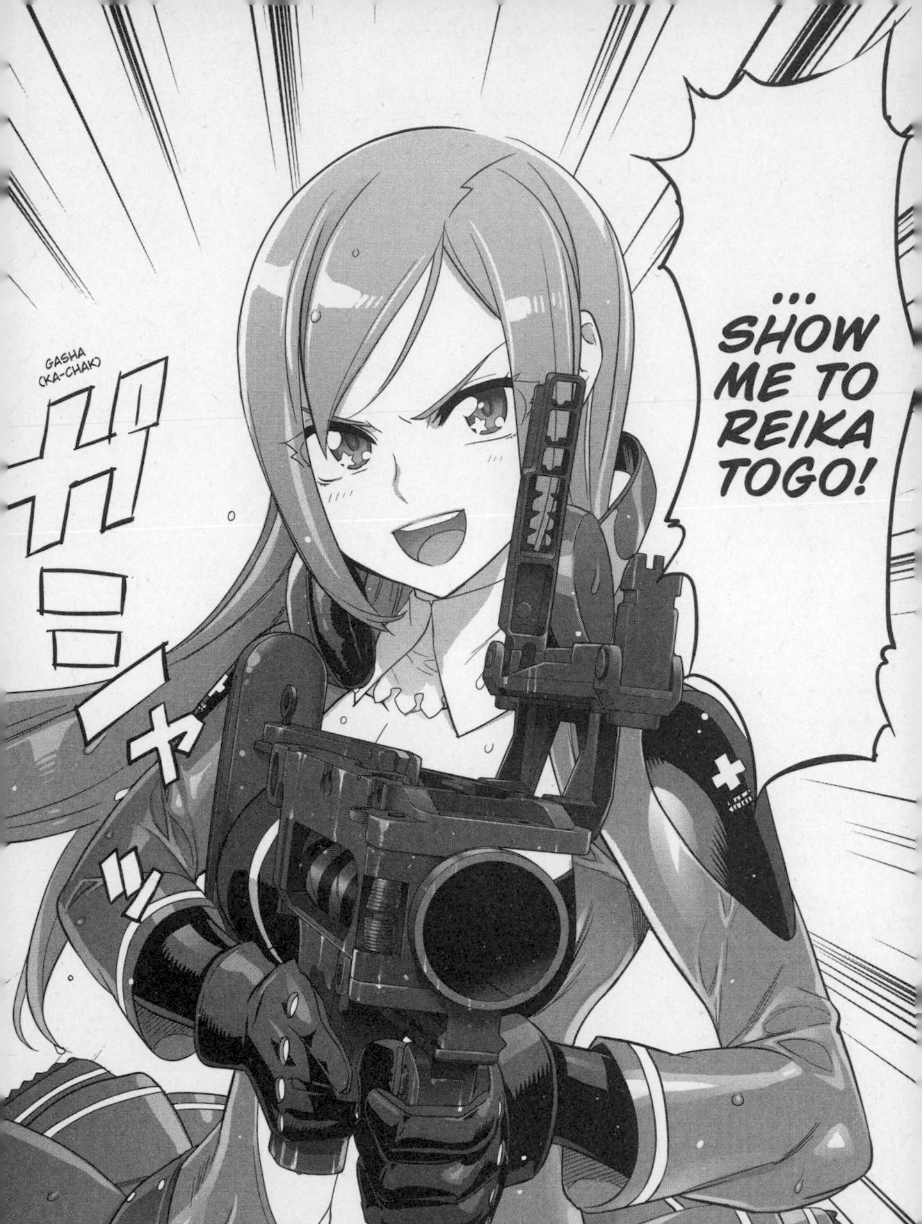
...SHOW ME TO REIKA TOGO!
GASHA (KA-CHAK)
ガシャ
ガローン

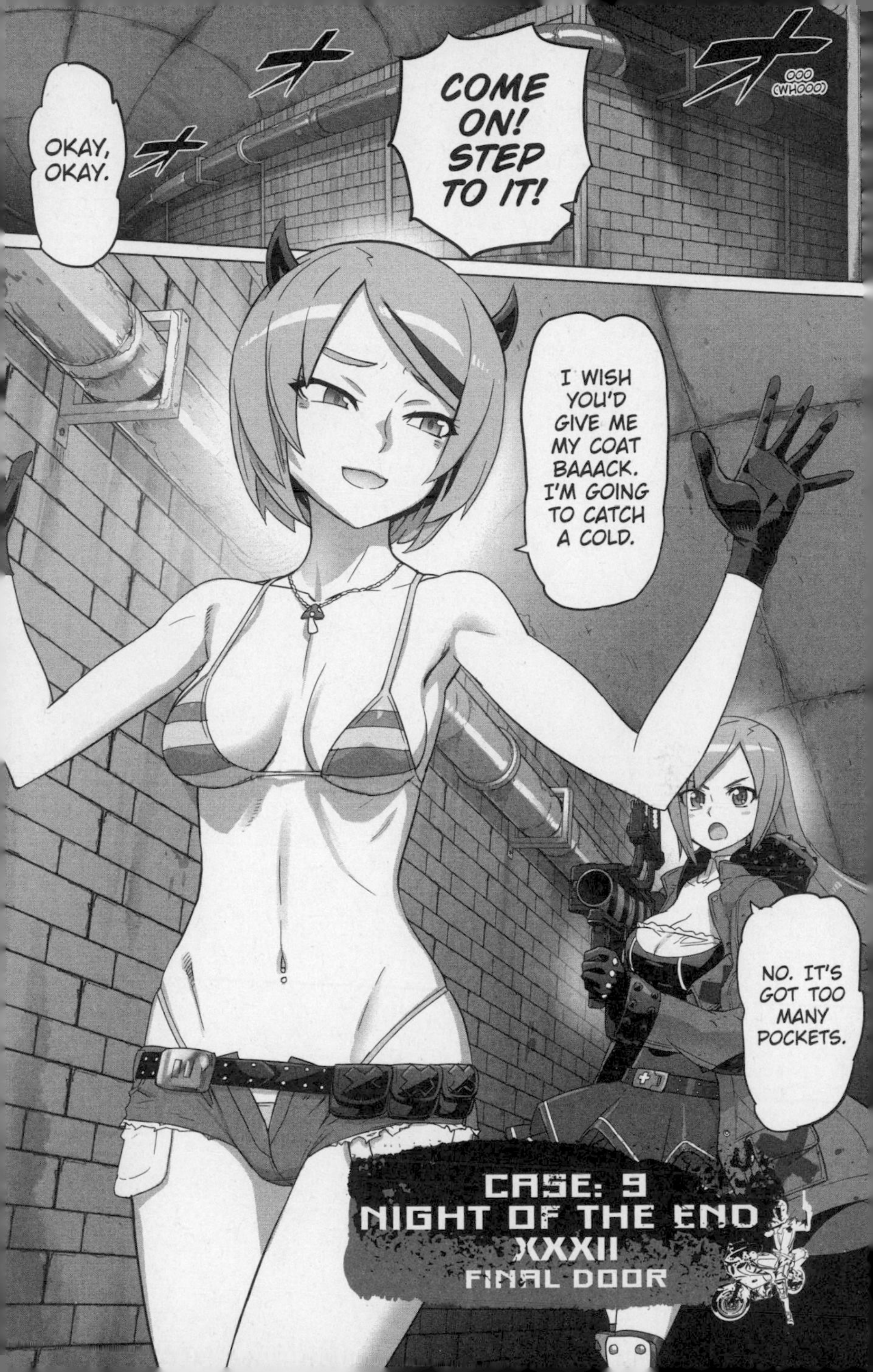
OOO (WHOOO)
COME ON! STEP TO IT!
OKAY, OKAY.
I WISH YOU'D GIVE ME MY COAT BAAACK. I'M GOING TO CATCH A COLD.
NO. IT'S GOT TOO MANY POCKETS.
CASE: 9
NIGHT OF THE END
XXXII
FINAL DOOR

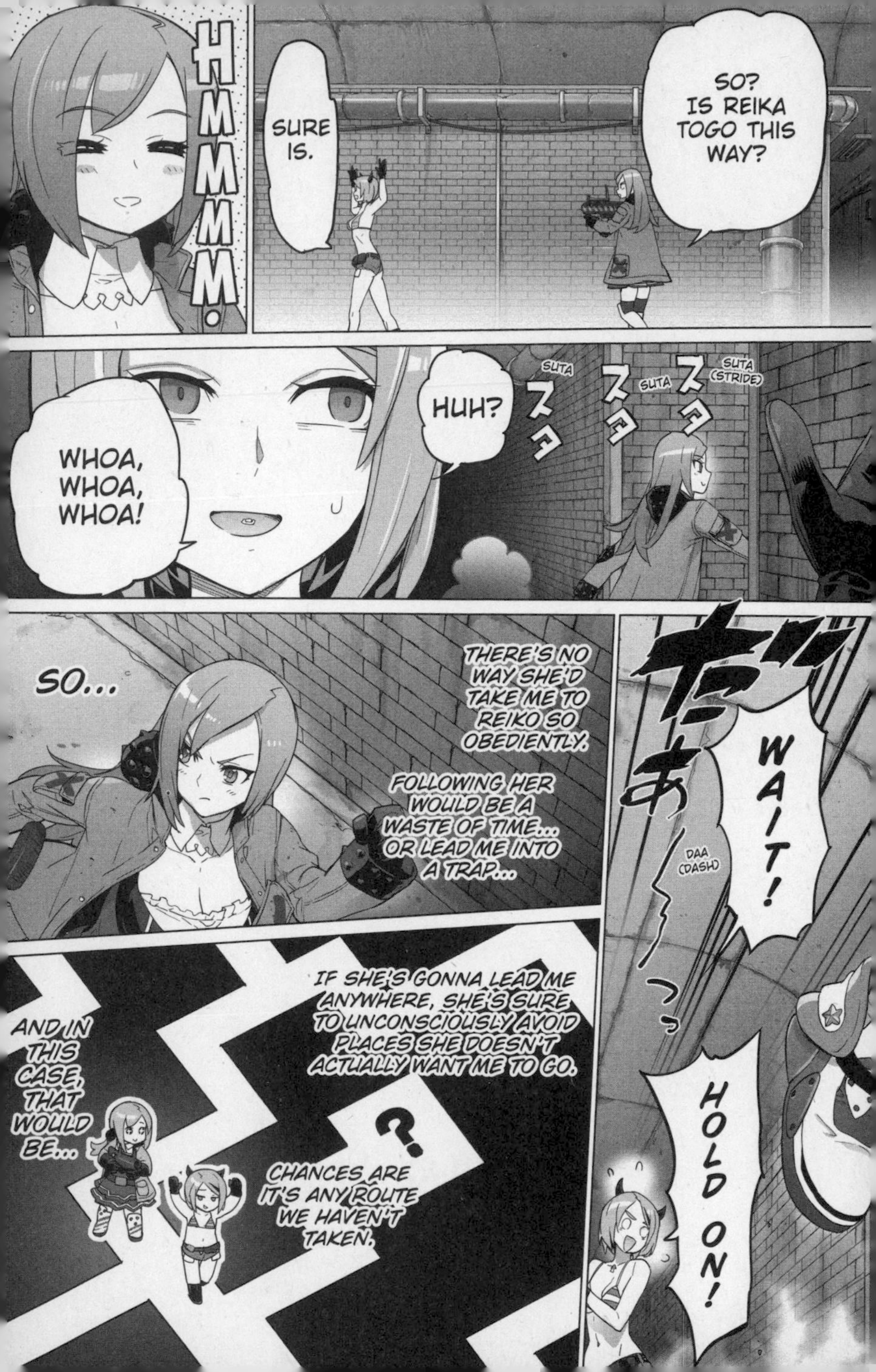
SO? IS REIKA TOGO THIS WAY?
SURE IS.
HMMMM.
SUTA (STRIDE)
SUTA
SUTA
HUH?
WHOA, WHOA, WHOA!
WAIT!
DAA (DASH)
HOLD ON!
SO...
THERE'S NO WAY SHE'D TAKE ME TO REIKO SO OBEDIENTLY.
FOLLOWING HER WOULD BE A WASTE OF TIME... OR LEAD ME INTO A TRAP...
IF SHE'S GONNA LEAD ME ANYWHERE, SHE'S SURE TO UNCONSCIOUSLY AVOID PLACES SHE DOESN'T ACTUALLY WANT ME TO GO.
AND IN THIS CASE, THAT WOULD BE...
?
CHANCES ARE IT'S ANY ROUTE WE HAVEN'T TAKEN.

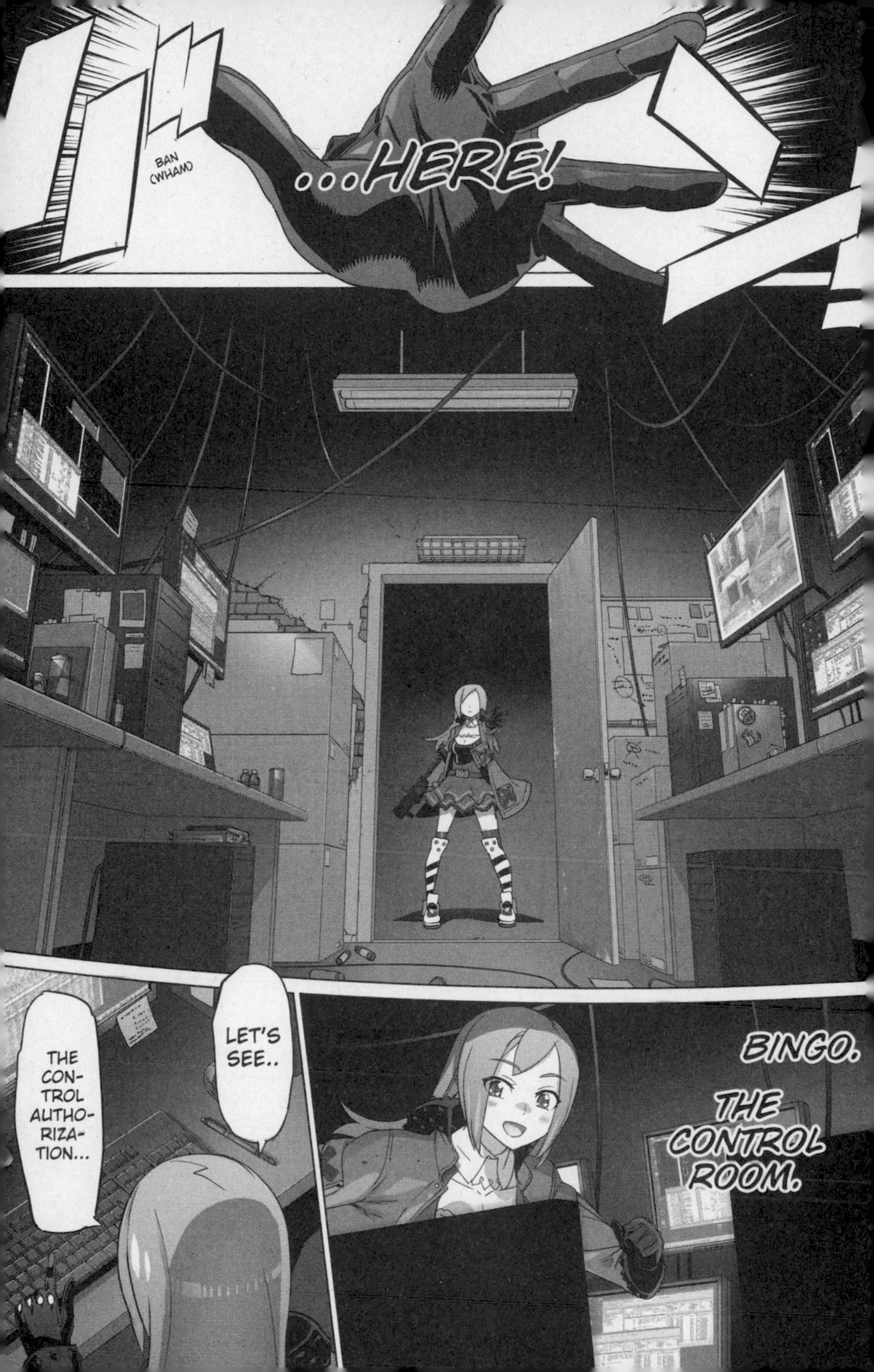
...HERE!
BAN (WHAM)
BINGO.
THE CONTROL ROOM.
LET'S SEE..
THE CONTROL AUTHORIZATION...

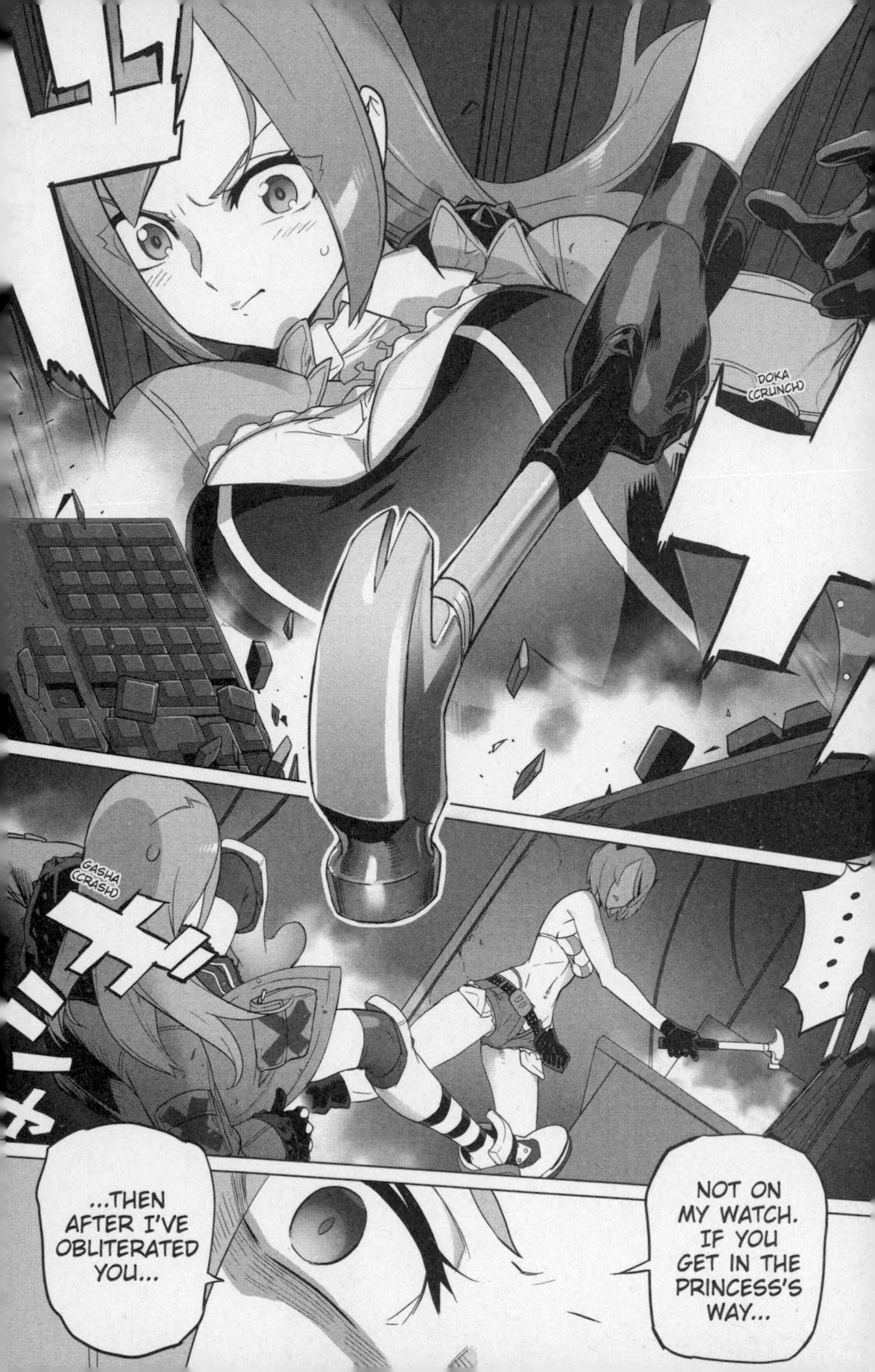
DOKA (CRUNCH)
GASHA (CRASH)
NOT ON MY WATCH. IF YOU GET IN THE PRINCESS'S WAY...
...THEN AFTER I'VE OBLITERATED YOU...

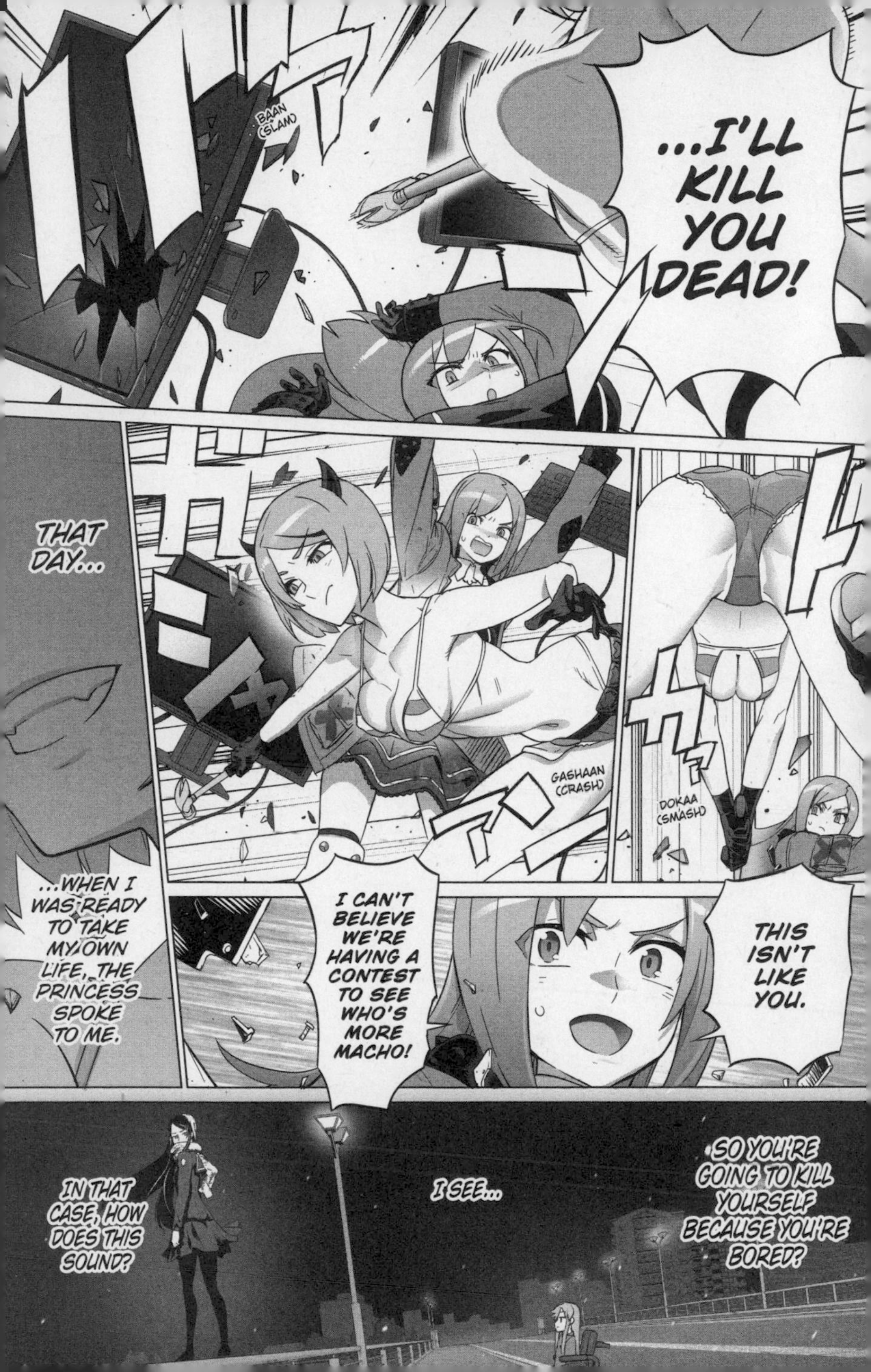
...I'LL KILL YOU DEAD!
BAAN (SLAM)
DOKAA (SMASH)
GASHAAN (CRASH)
THAT DAY...
THIS ISN'T LIKE YOU.
I CAN'T BELIEVE WE'RE HAVING A CONTEST TO SEE WHO'S MORE MACHO!
...WHEN I WAS READY TO TAKE MY OWN LIFE, THE PRINCESS SPOKE TO ME.
SO YOU'RE GOING TO KILL YOURSELF BECAUSE YOU'RE BORED?
I SEE...
IN THAT CASE, HOW DOES THIS SOUND?

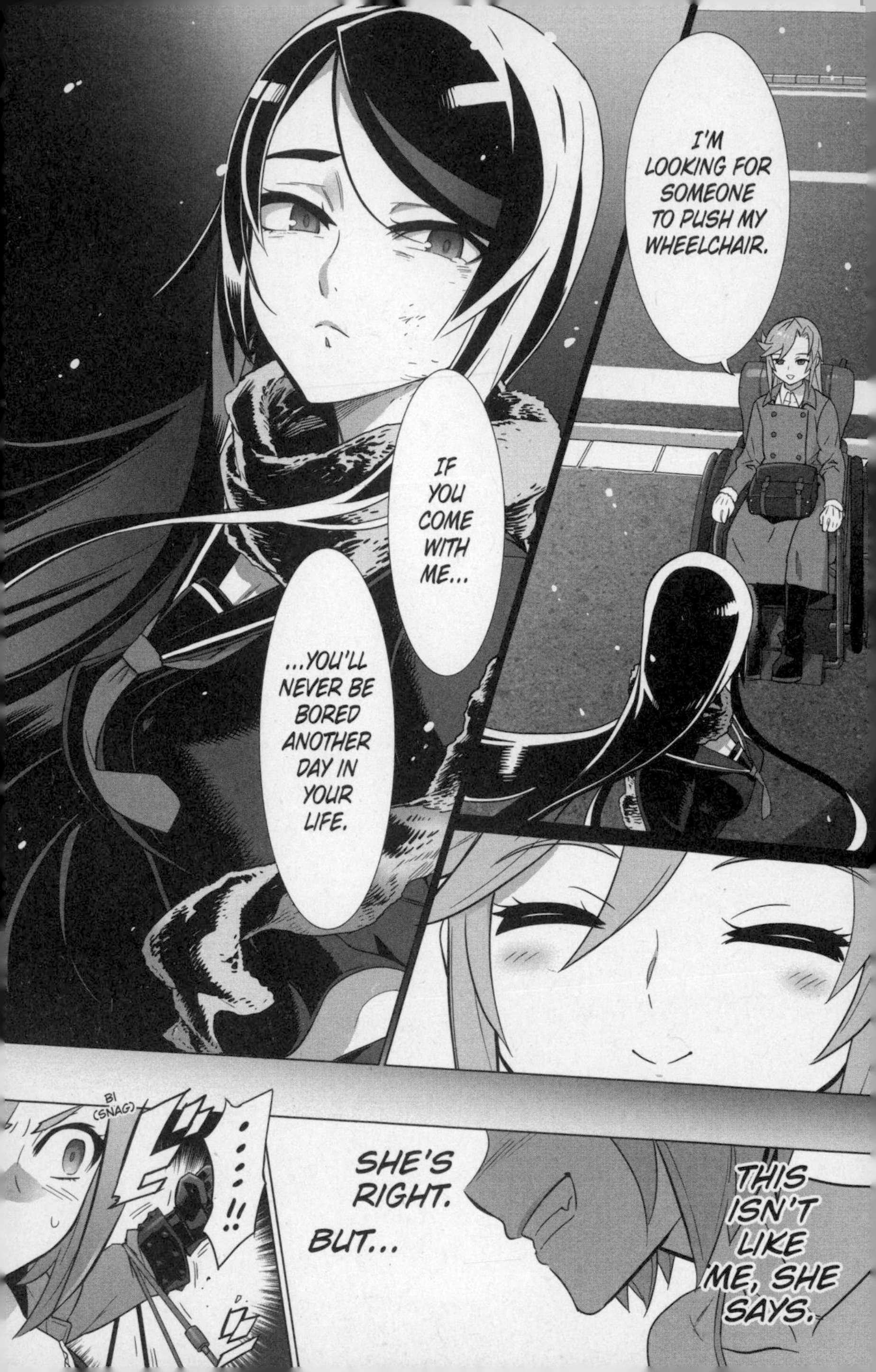
I'M LOOKING FOR SOMEONE TO PUSH MY WHEELCHAIR.
IF YOU COME WITH ME...
...YOU'LL NEVER BE BORED ANOTHER DAY IN YOUR LIFE.
THIS ISN'T LIKE ME, SHE SAYS.
SHE'S RIGHT.
BUT...
......!!
BI (SNAG)

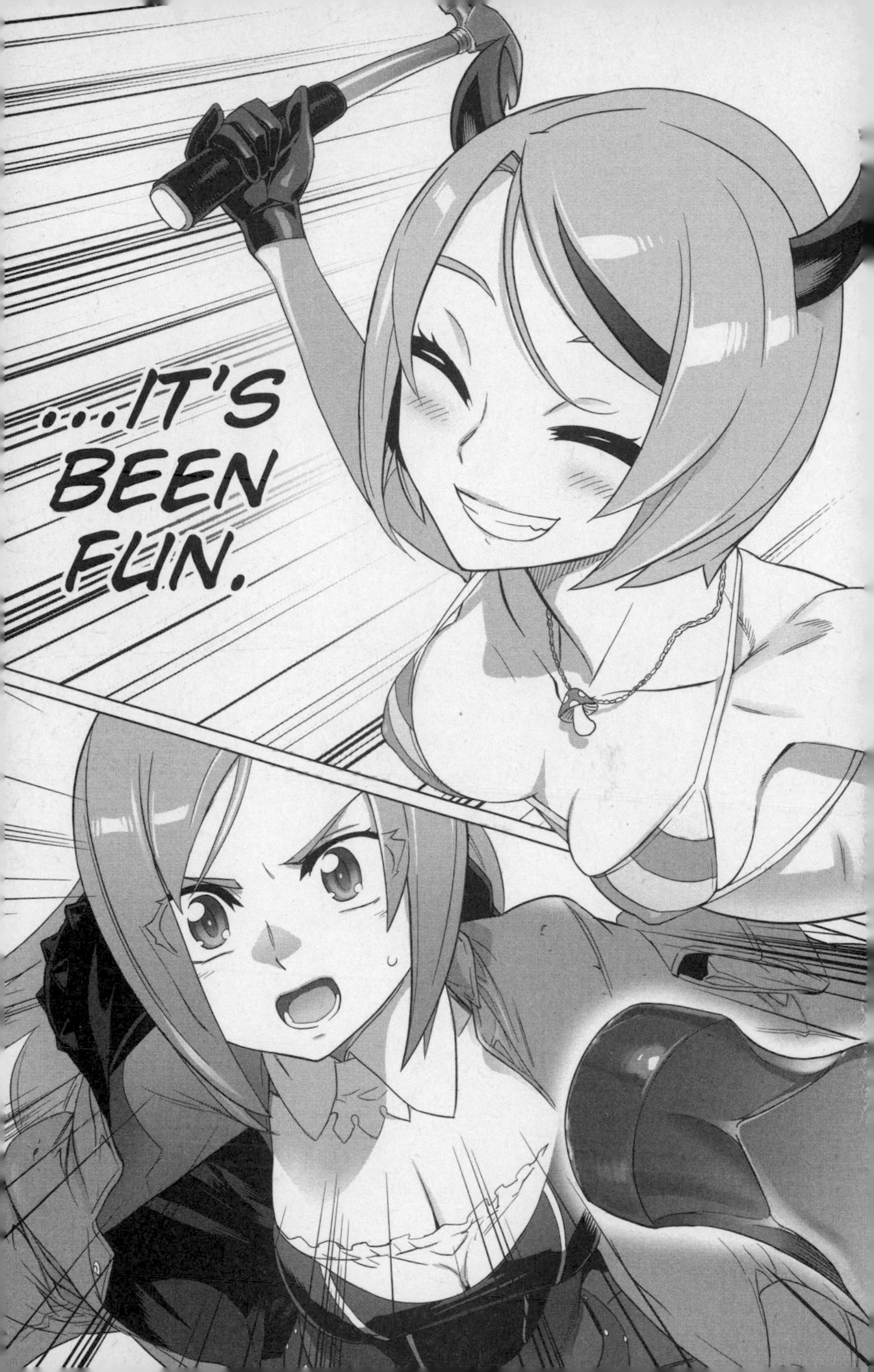
...IT'S BEEN FUN.

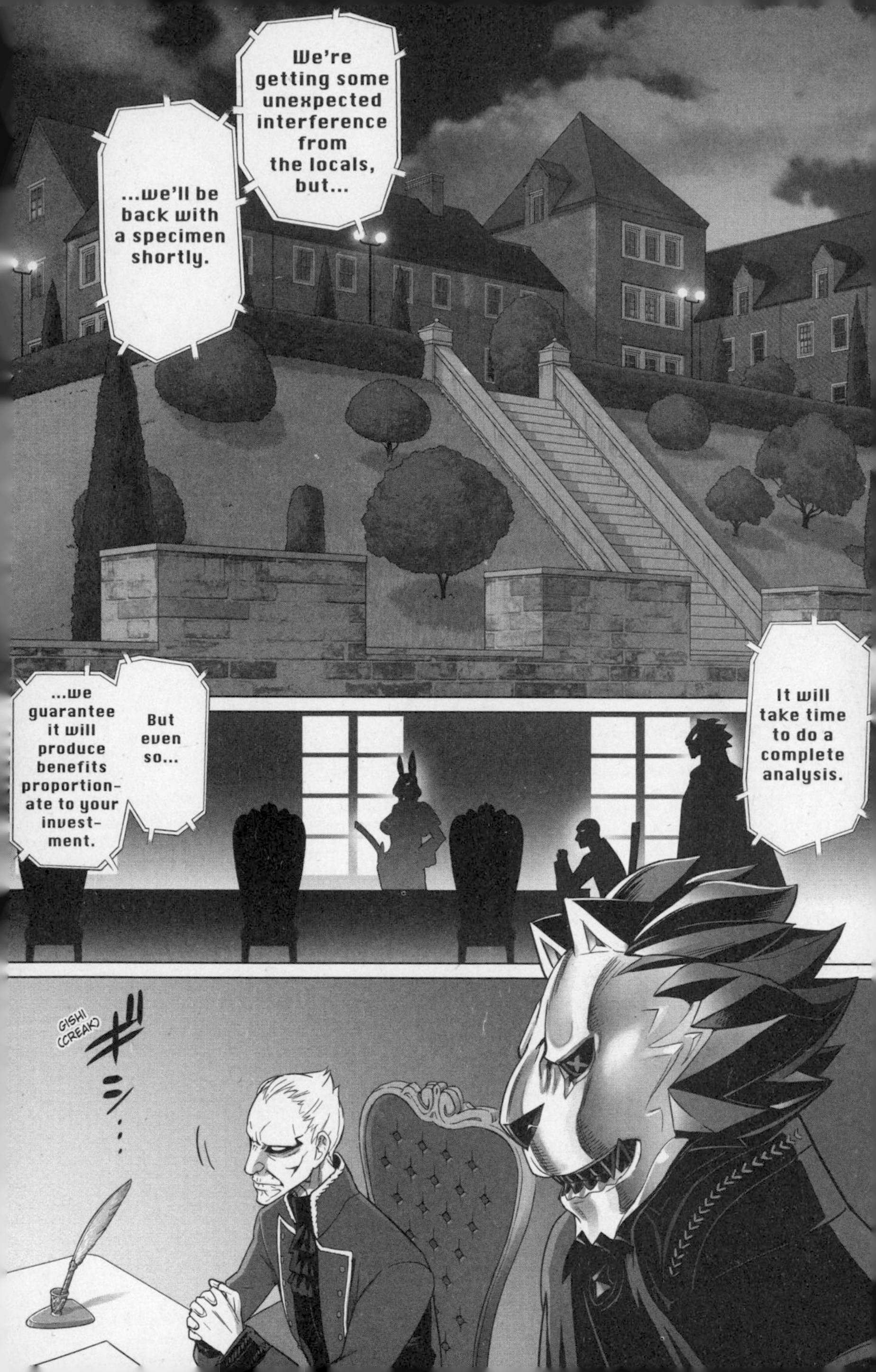
We're getting some unexpected interference from the locals, but...
...we'll be back with a specimen shortly.
It will take time to do a complete analysis.
But even so...
...we guarantee it will produce benefits proportion-ate to your invest-ment.
GISHI (CREAK)

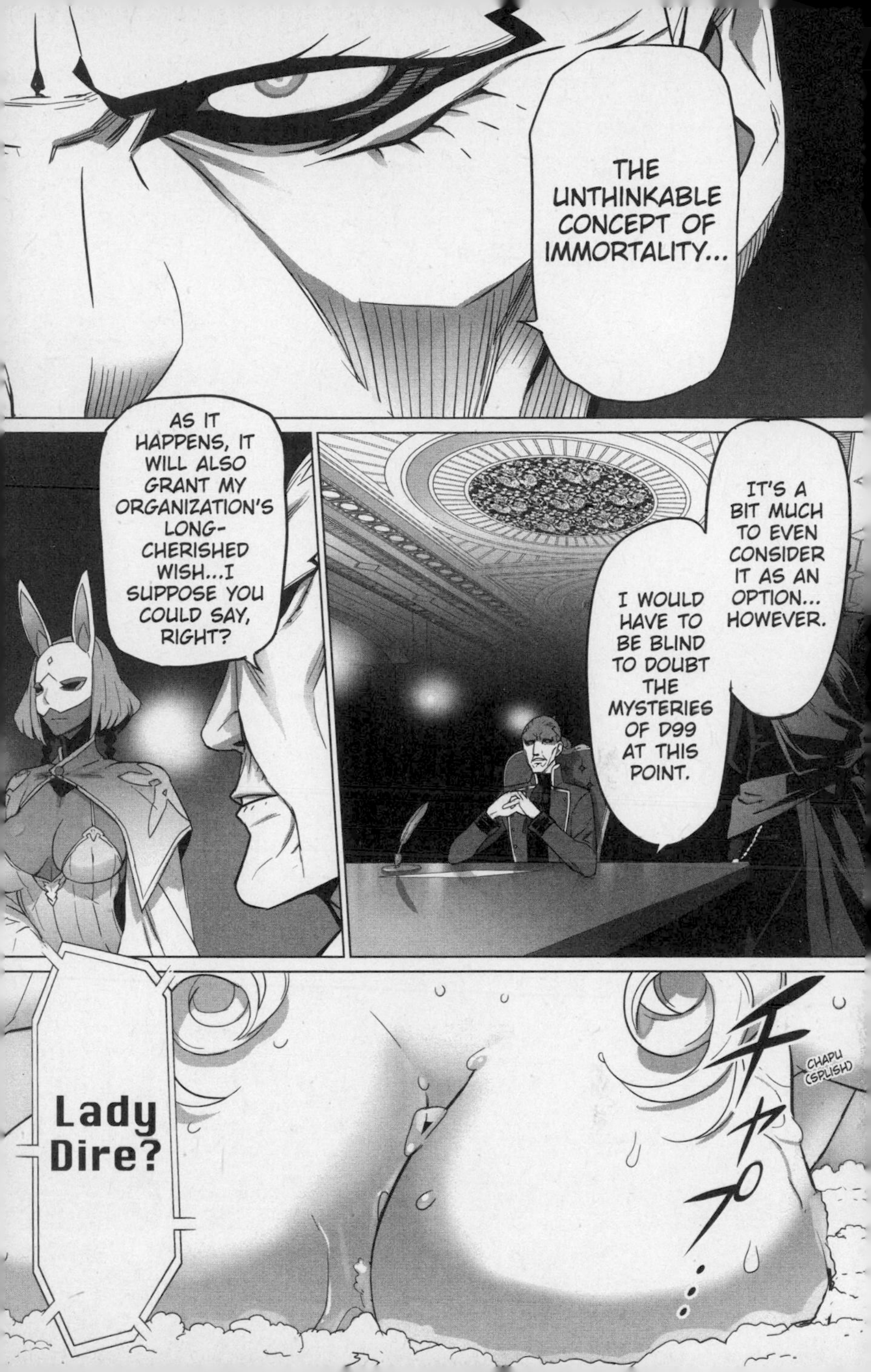
THE UNTHINKABLE CONCEPT OF IMMORTALITY...
IT'S A BIT MUCH TO EVEN CONSIDER IT AS AN OPTION... HOWEVER.
I WOULD HAVE TO BE BLIND TO DOUBT THE MYSTERIES OF D99 AT THIS POINT.
AS IT HAPPENS, IT WILL ALSO GRANT MY ORGANIZATION'S LONG-CHERISHED WISH...I SUPPOSE YOU COULD SAY, RIGHT?
CHAPU (SPLISH)
Lady Dire?

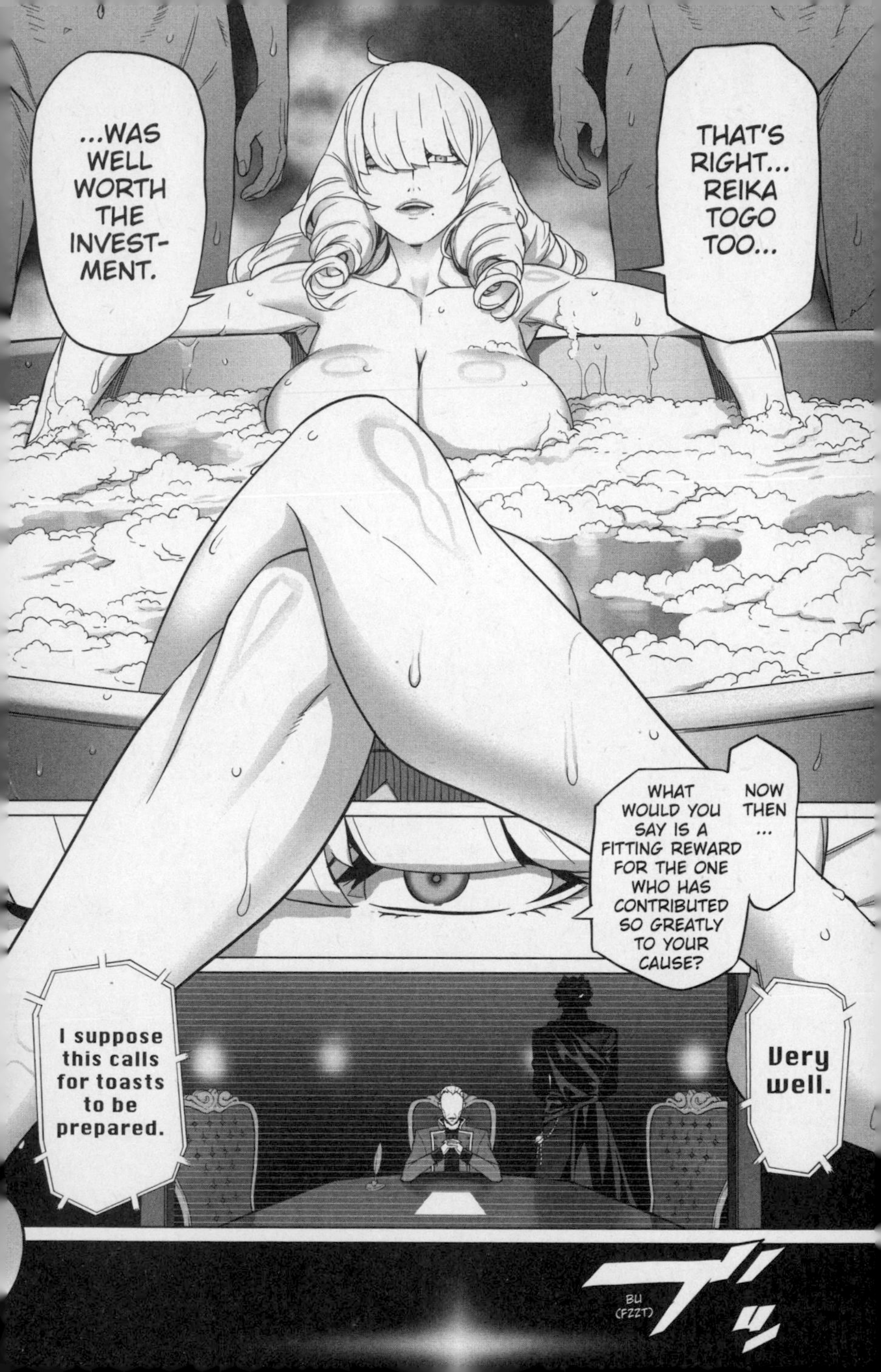
THAT'S RIGHT... REIKA TOGO TOO...
...WAS WELL WORTH THE INVEST-MENT.
NOW THEN ...
WHAT WOULD YOU SAY IS A FITTING REWARD FOR THE ONE WHO HAS CONTRIBUTED SO GREATLY TO YOUR CAUSE?
Very well.
I suppose this calls for toasts to be prepared.
BU (FZZT)

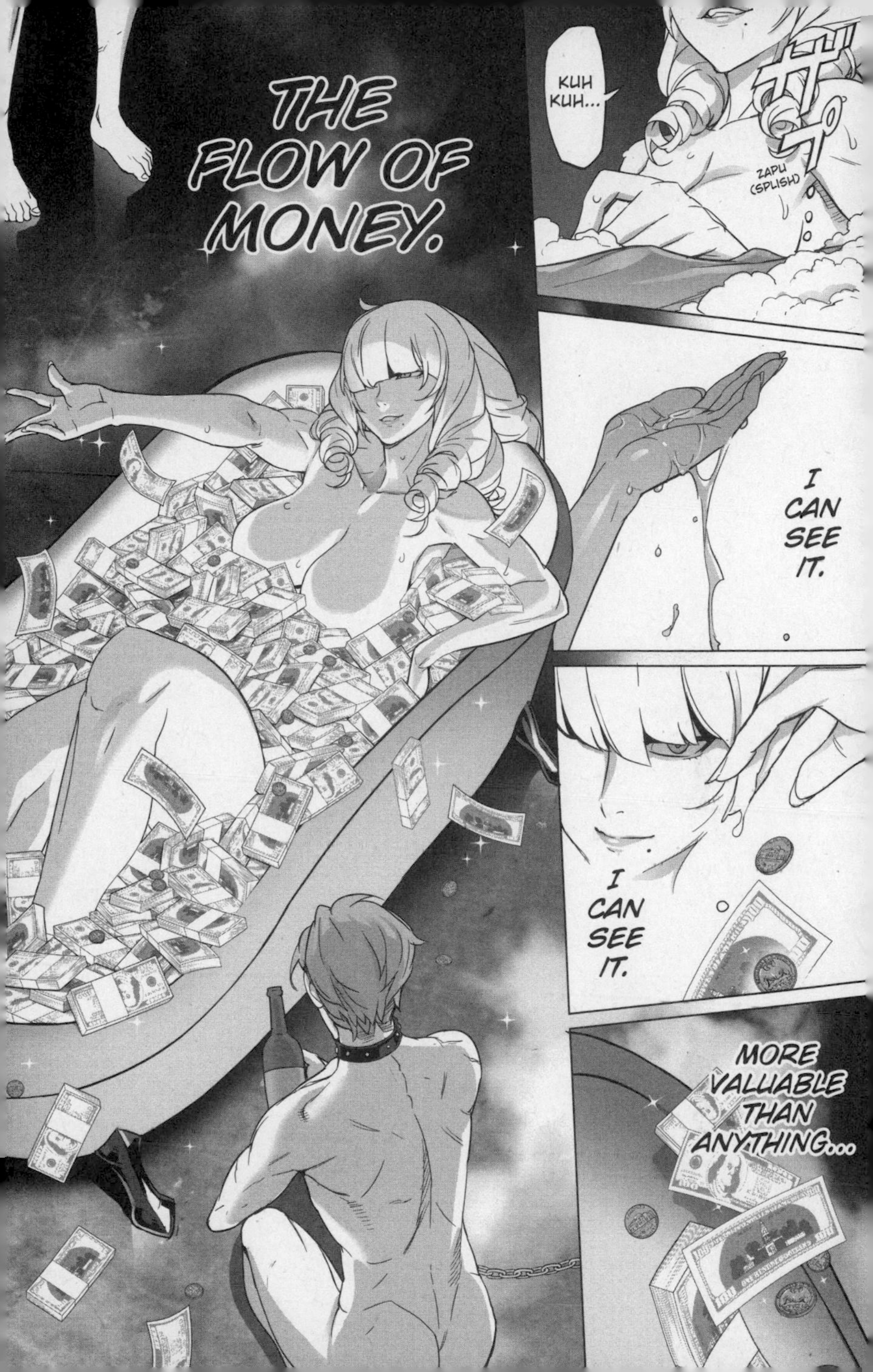

KUH KUH...
ZAPU (SPLISH)
I CAN SEE IT.
I CAN SEE IT.
MORE VALUABLE THAN ANYTHING...
THE FLOW OF MONEY.

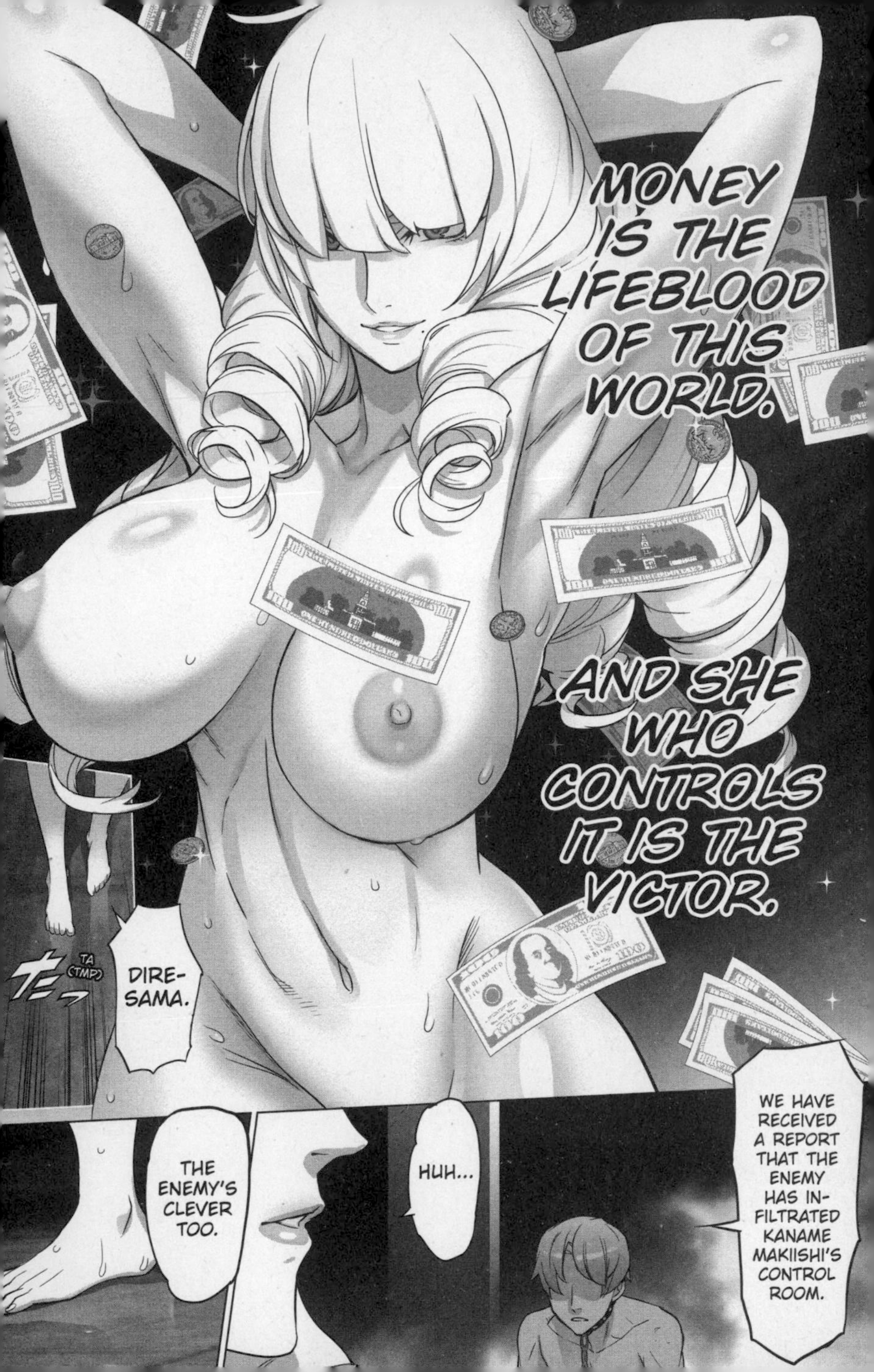
MONEY IS THE LIFEBLOOD OF THIS WORLD.
AND SHE WHO CONTROLS IT IS THE VICTOR.
TA (TMP)
DIRE-SAMA.
WE HAVE RECEIVED A REPORT THAT THE ENEMY HAS IN-FILTRATED KANAME MAKIISHI'S CONTROL ROOM.
HUH...
THE ENEMY'S CLEVER TOO.

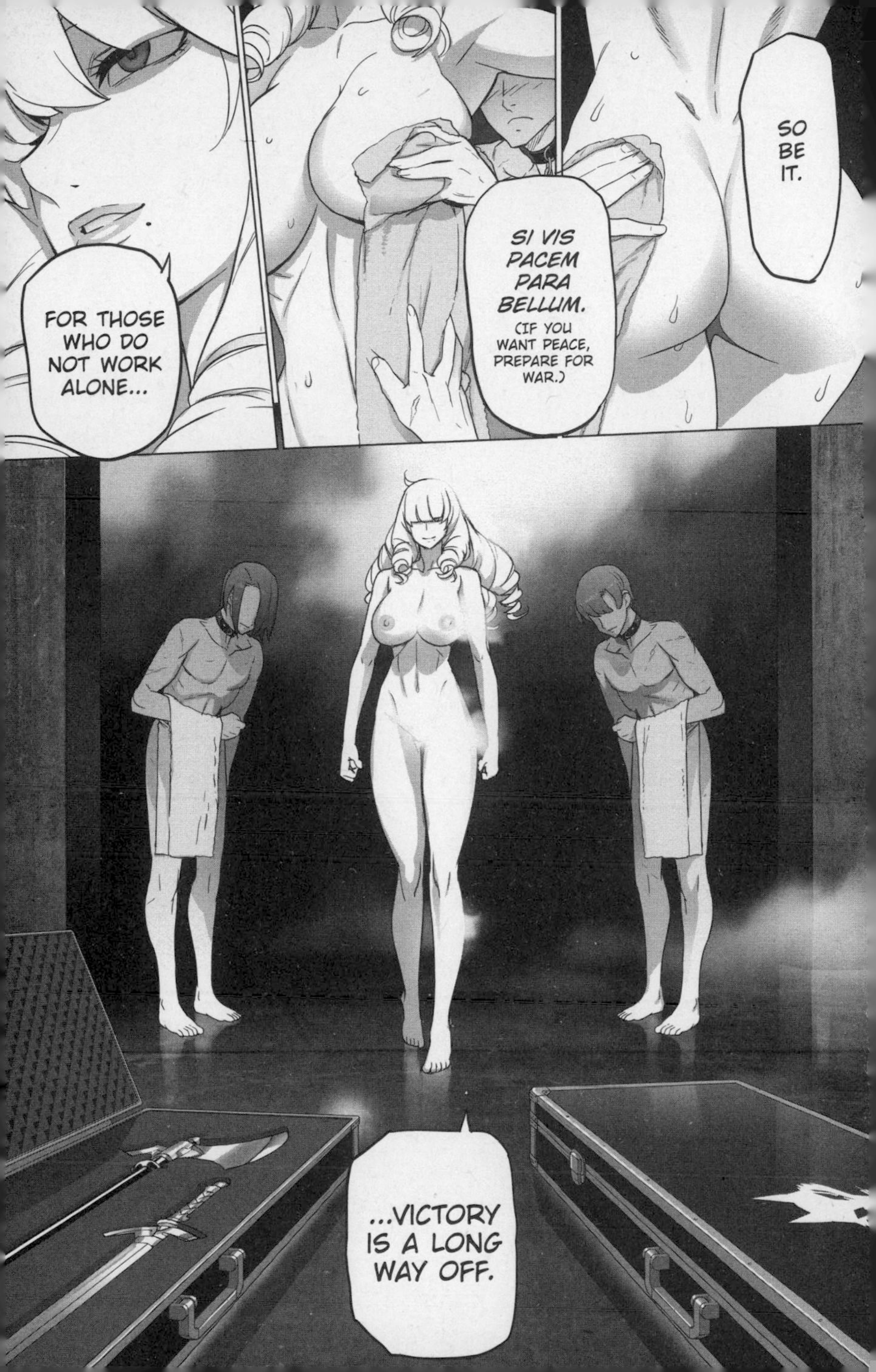
SO BE IT.
SI VIS PACEM PARA BELLUM.
(IF YOU WANT PEACE, PREPARE FOR WAR.)
FOR THOSE WHO DO NOT WORK ALONE...
...VICTORY IS A LONG WAY OFF.

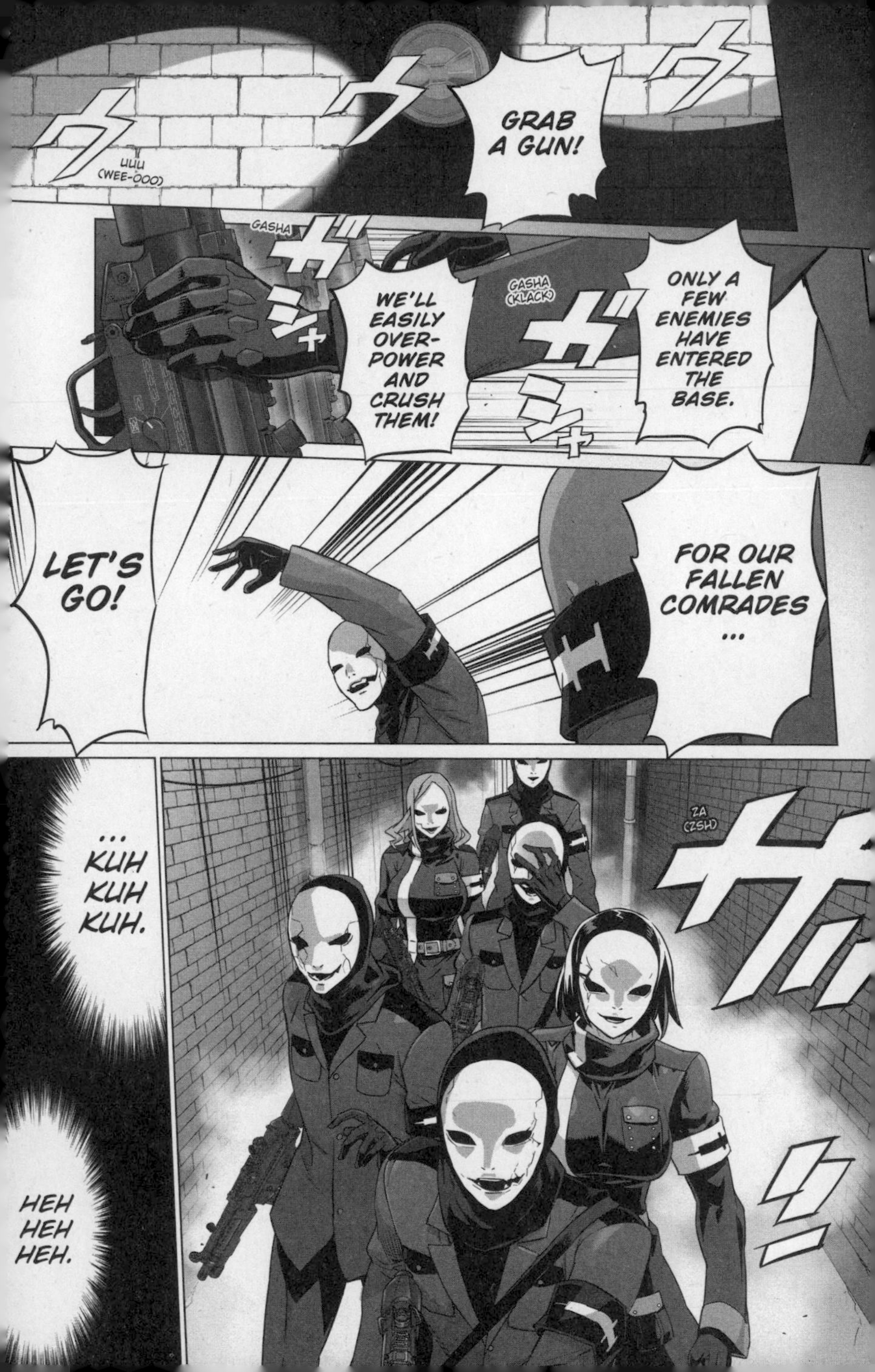
ウ
GRAB A GUN!
ウ
ウ
UUU (WEE-OOO)
ONLY A FEW ENEMIES HAVE ENTERED THE BASE.
GASHA (KLACK)
ガシャ
WE'LL EASILY OVER-POWER AND CRUSH THEM!
GASHA
ガシャ
FOR OUR FALLEN COMRADES ...
LET'S GO!
ZA (ZSH)
!
... KUH KUH KUH.
HEH HEH HEH.

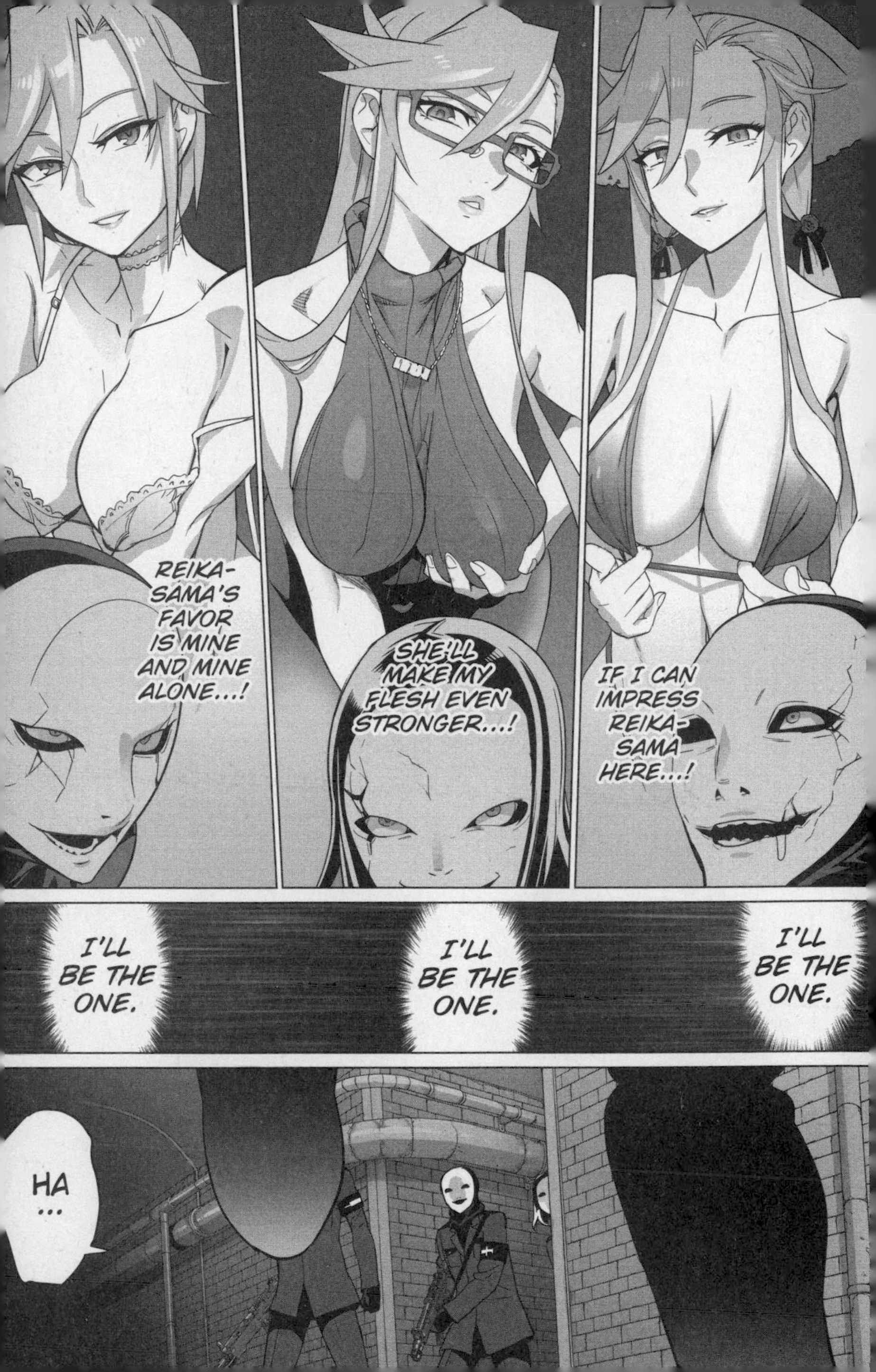
IF I CAN IMPRESS REIKA-SAMA HERE...!
SHE'LL MAKE MY FLESH EVEN STRONGER...!
REIKA-SAMA'S FAVOR IS MINE AND MINE ALONE...!
I'LL BE THE ONE.
I'LL BE THE ONE.
I'LL BE THE ONE.
HA...

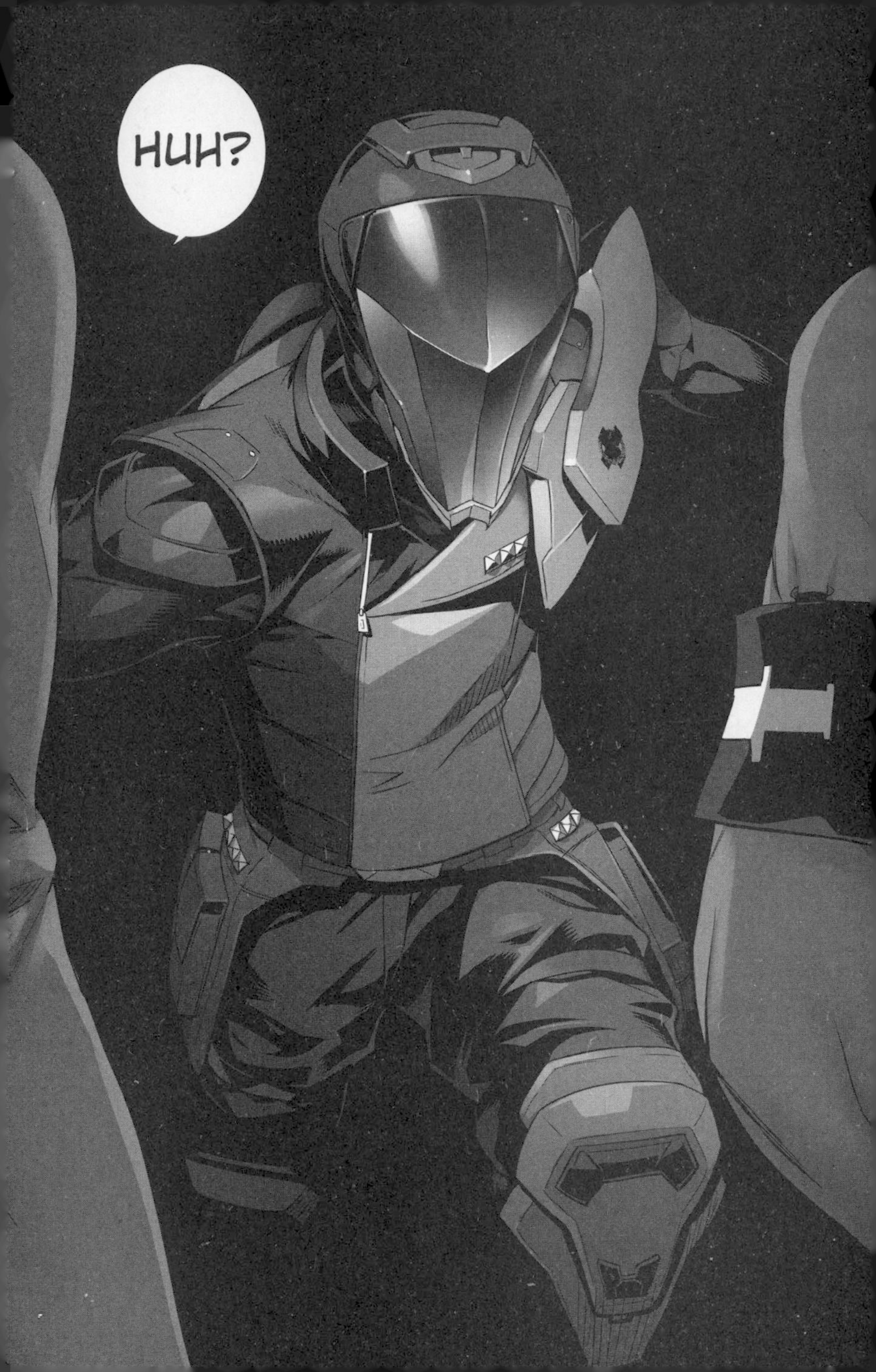
HUH?

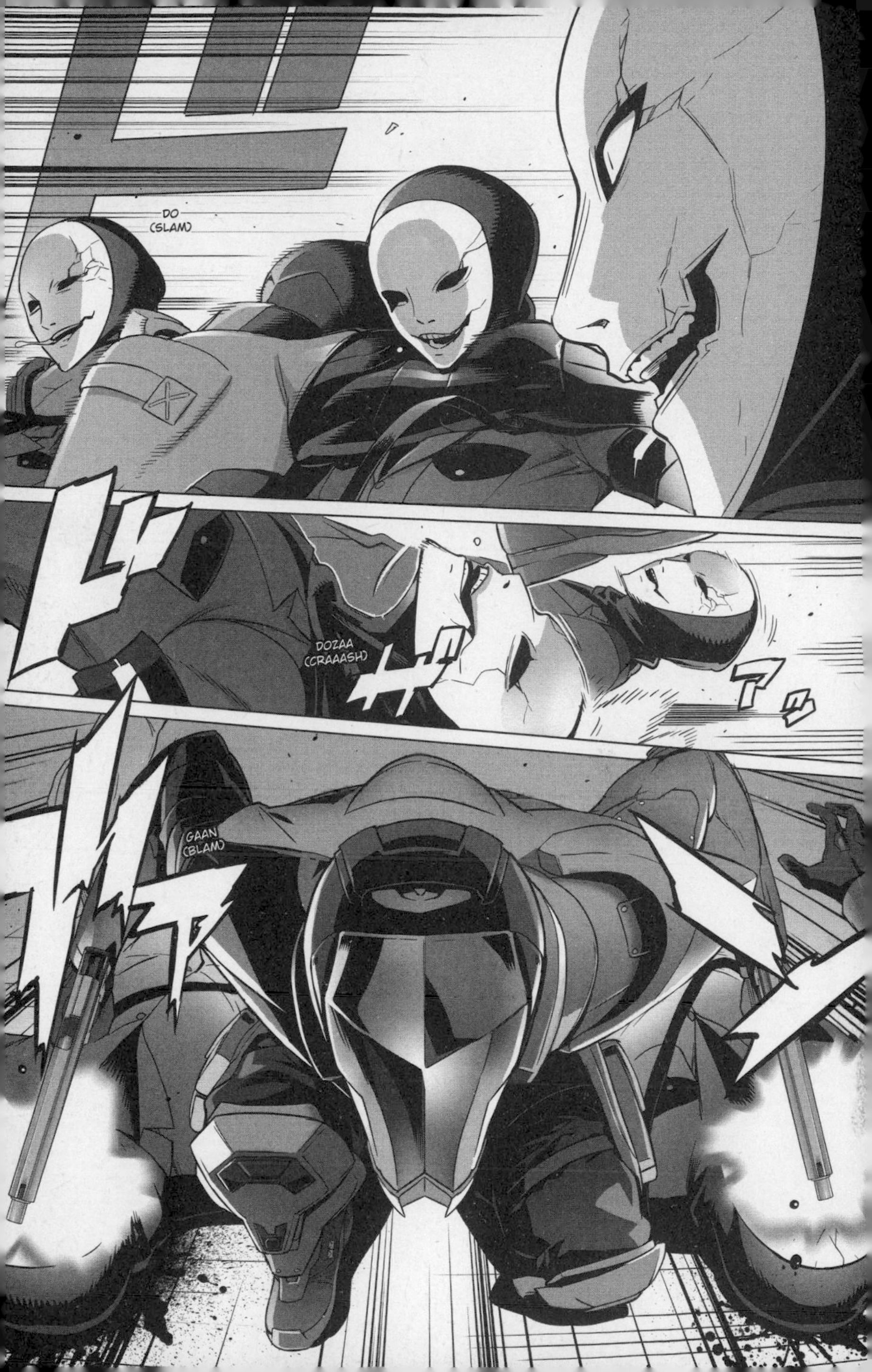
DO
(SLAM)
DOZAA
(CRAAASH)
GAAN
(BLAM)

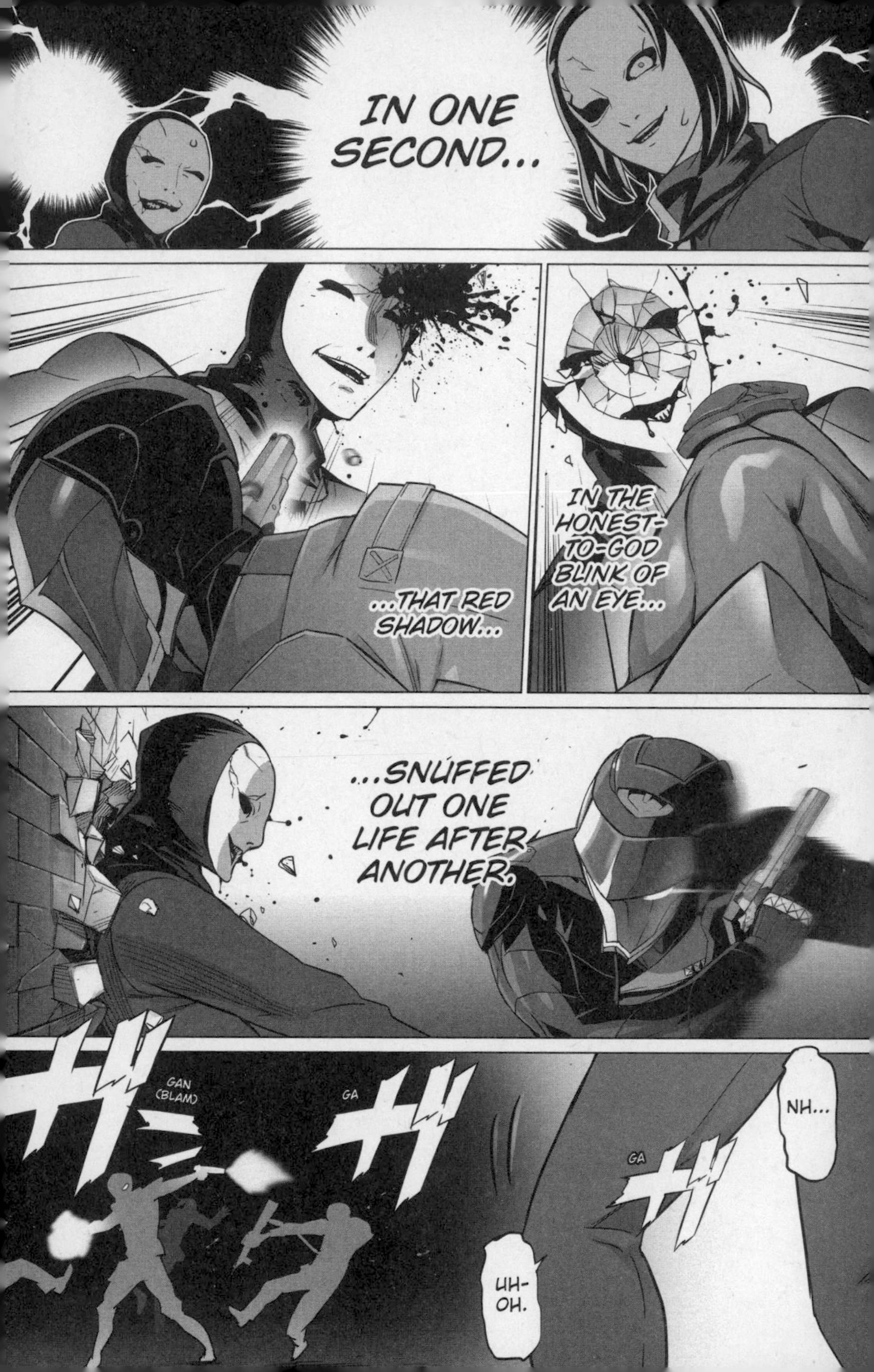
IN ONE SECOND...
IN THE HONEST-TO-GOD BLINK OF AN EYE...
...THAT RED SHADOW...
...SNUFFED OUT ONE LIFE AFTER ANOTHER.
NH...
GA
GA
GAN (BLAM)
UH-OH.

...LIKE A MACHINE,

...PRECISELY...

ACCURATELY...

DOGAA (SMASH)

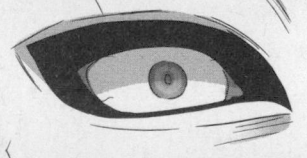

JUST
LIKE...

HE'S
LIKE...

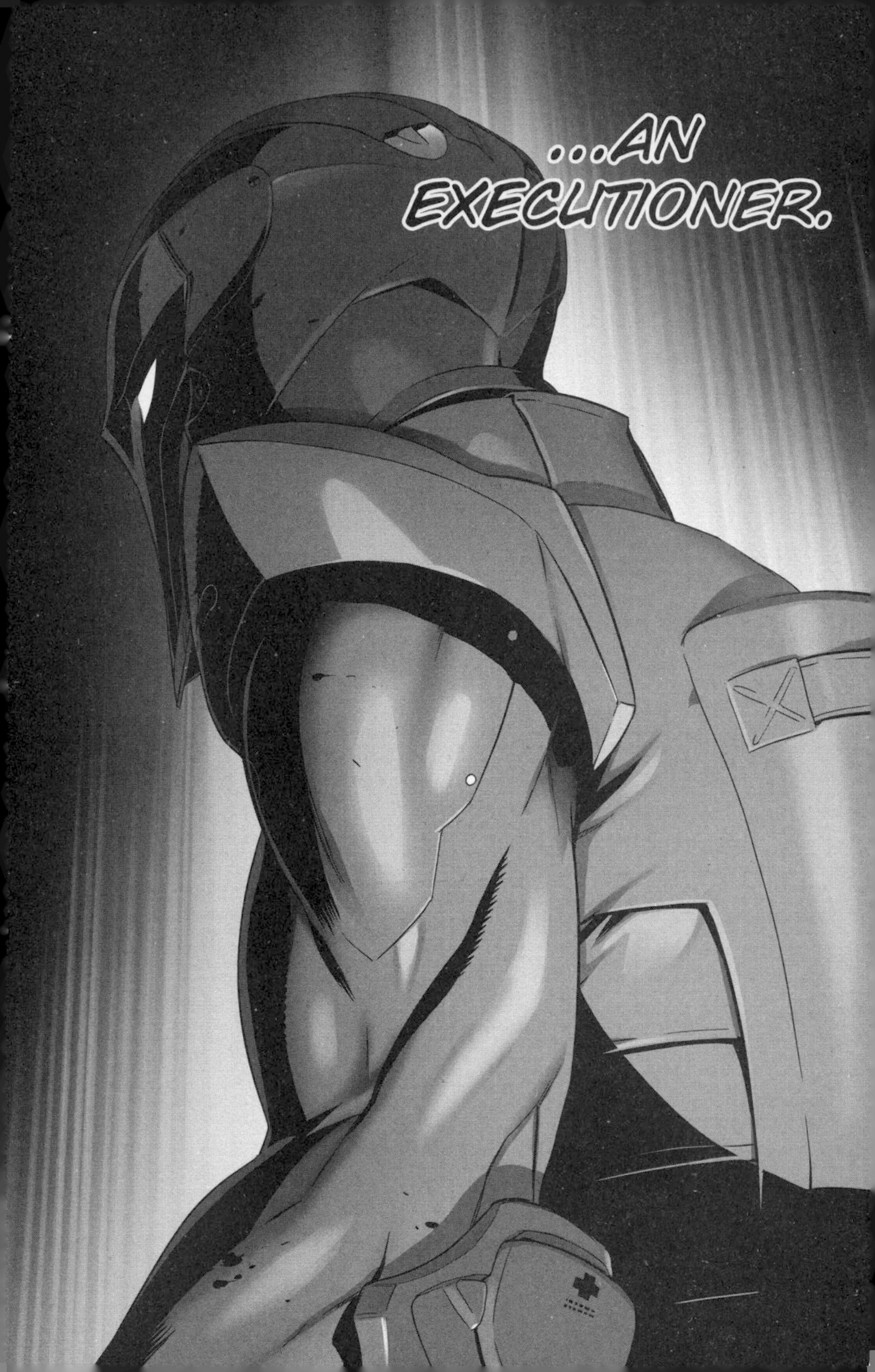
...AN EXECUTIONER.

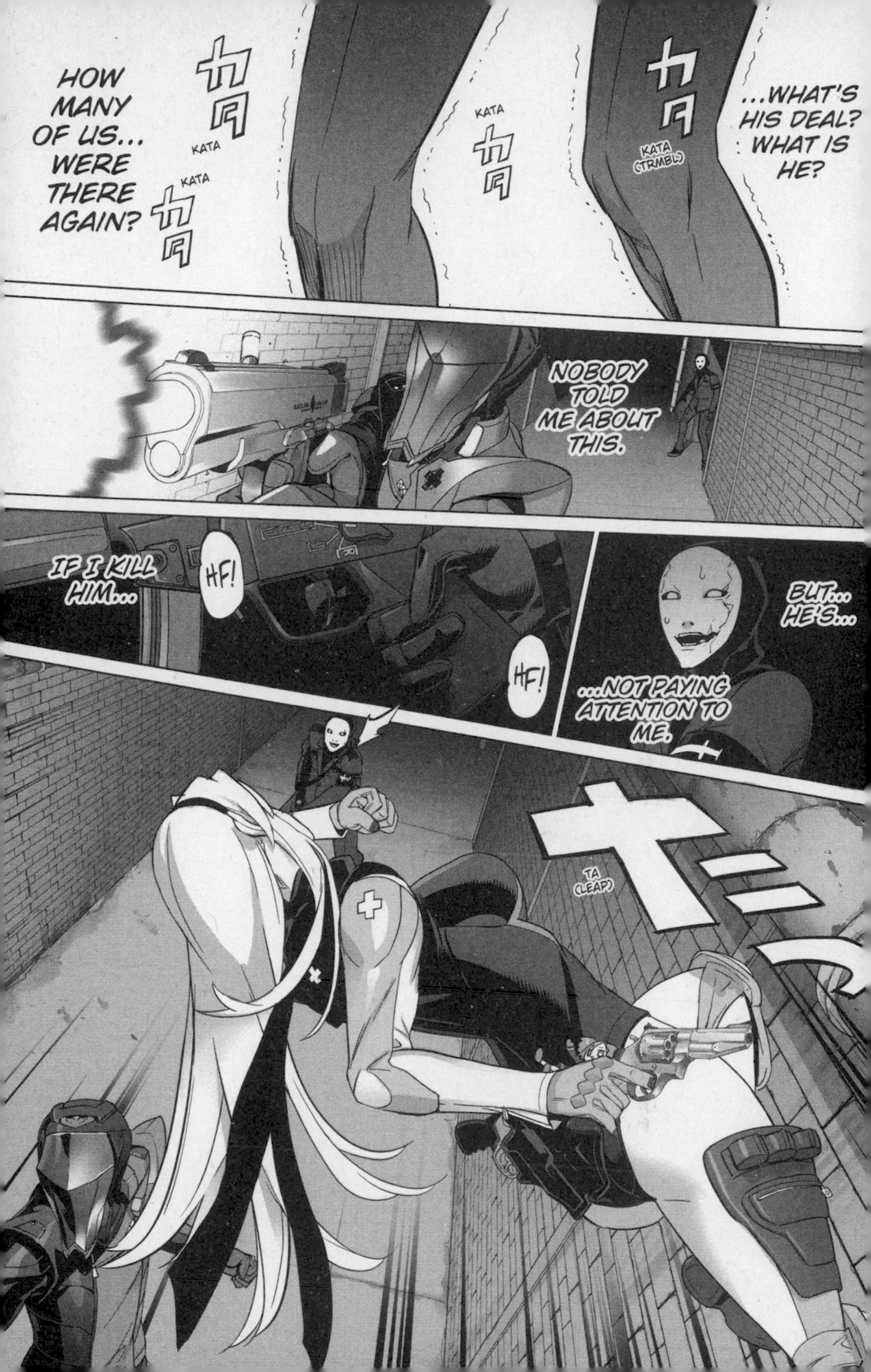
...WHAT'S HIS DEAL? WHAT IS HE?
KATA (TRMBL)
KATA
HOW MANY OF US... WERE THERE AGAIN?
KATA
KATA
NOBODY TOLD ME ABOUT THIS.
BUT... HE'S...
...NOT PAYING ATTENTION TO ME.
HF!
HF!
IF I KILL HIM...
TA (LEAP)

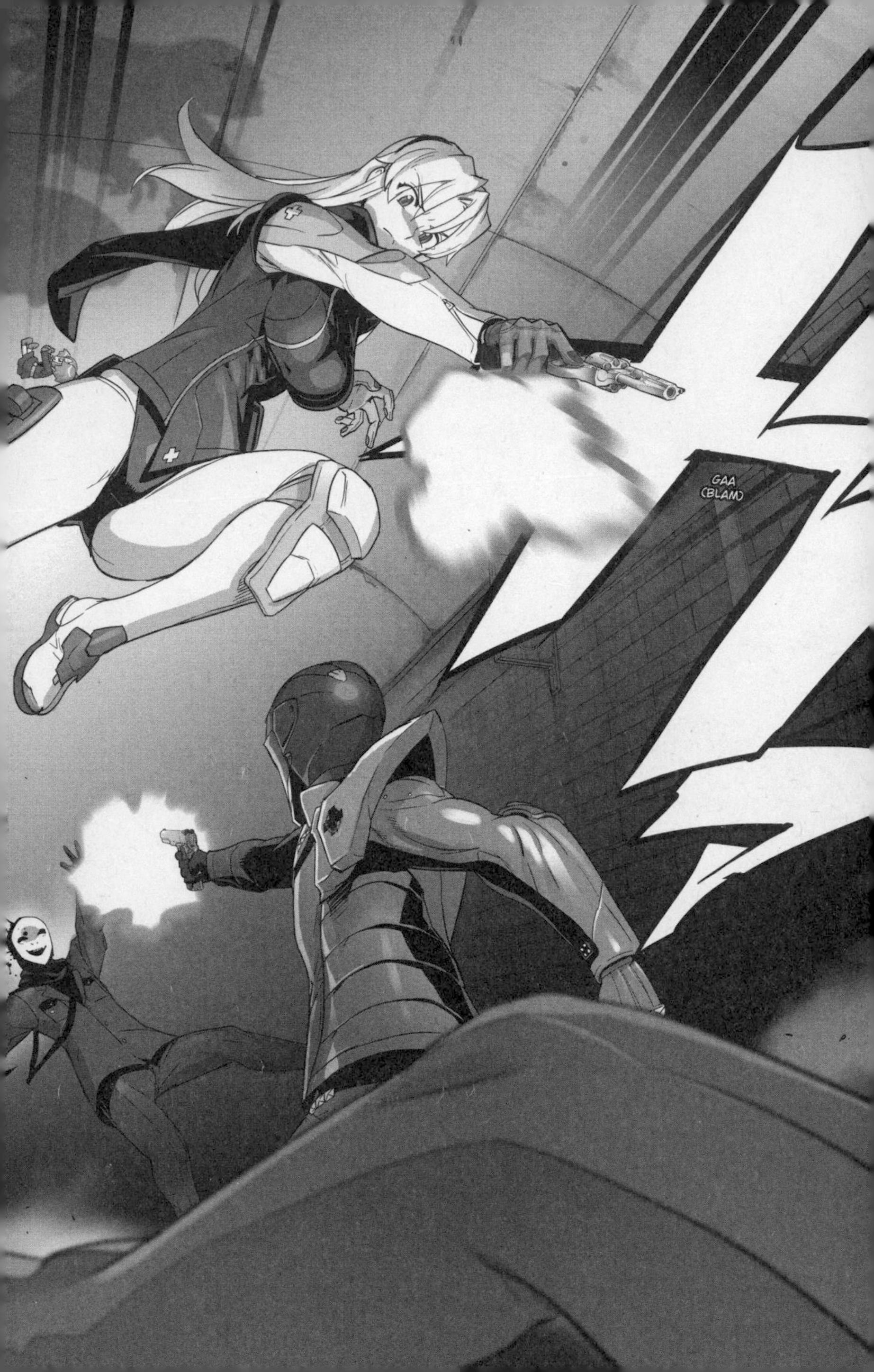
GAA
(BLAM)

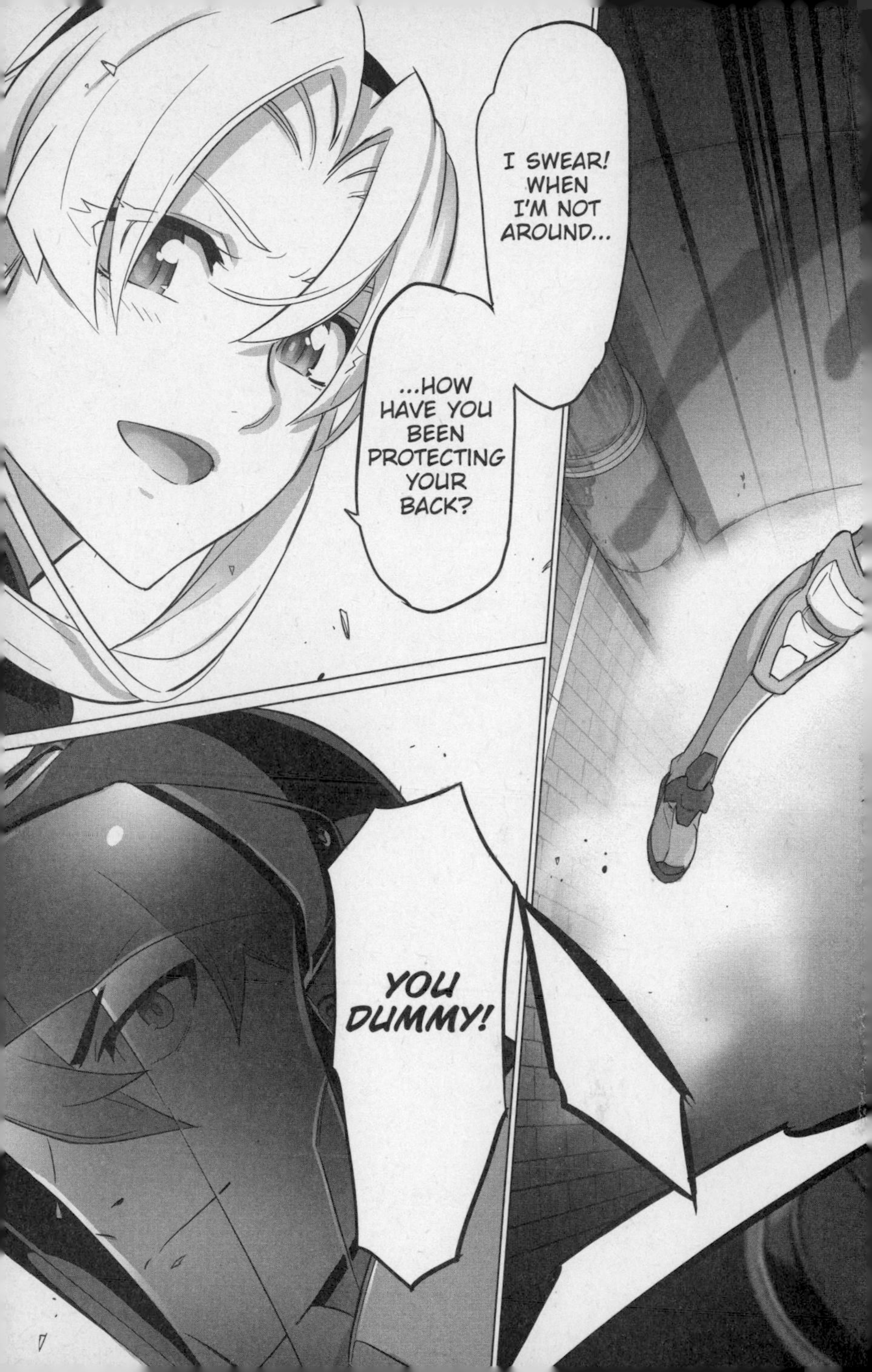
I SWEAR! WHEN I'M NOT AROUND...
...HOW HAVE YOU BEEN PROTECTING YOUR BACK?
YOU DUMMY!

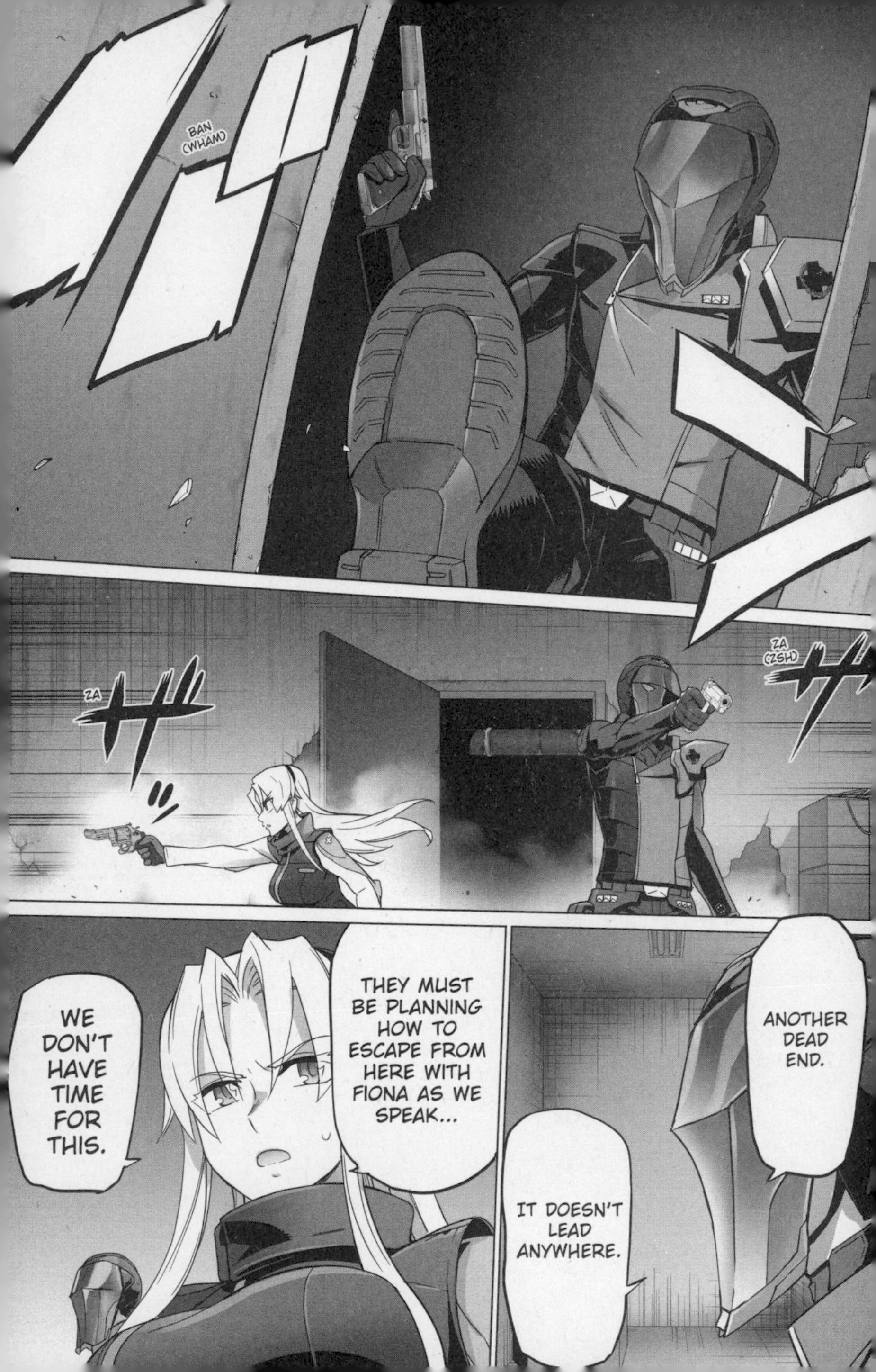
BAN (WHAM)
ZA (ZSH)
ZA
ANOTHER DEAD END.
IT DOESN'T LEAD ANYWHERE.
THEY MUST BE PLANNING HOW TO ESCAPE FROM HERE WITH FIONA AS WE SPEAK...
WE DON'T HAVE TIME FOR THIS.

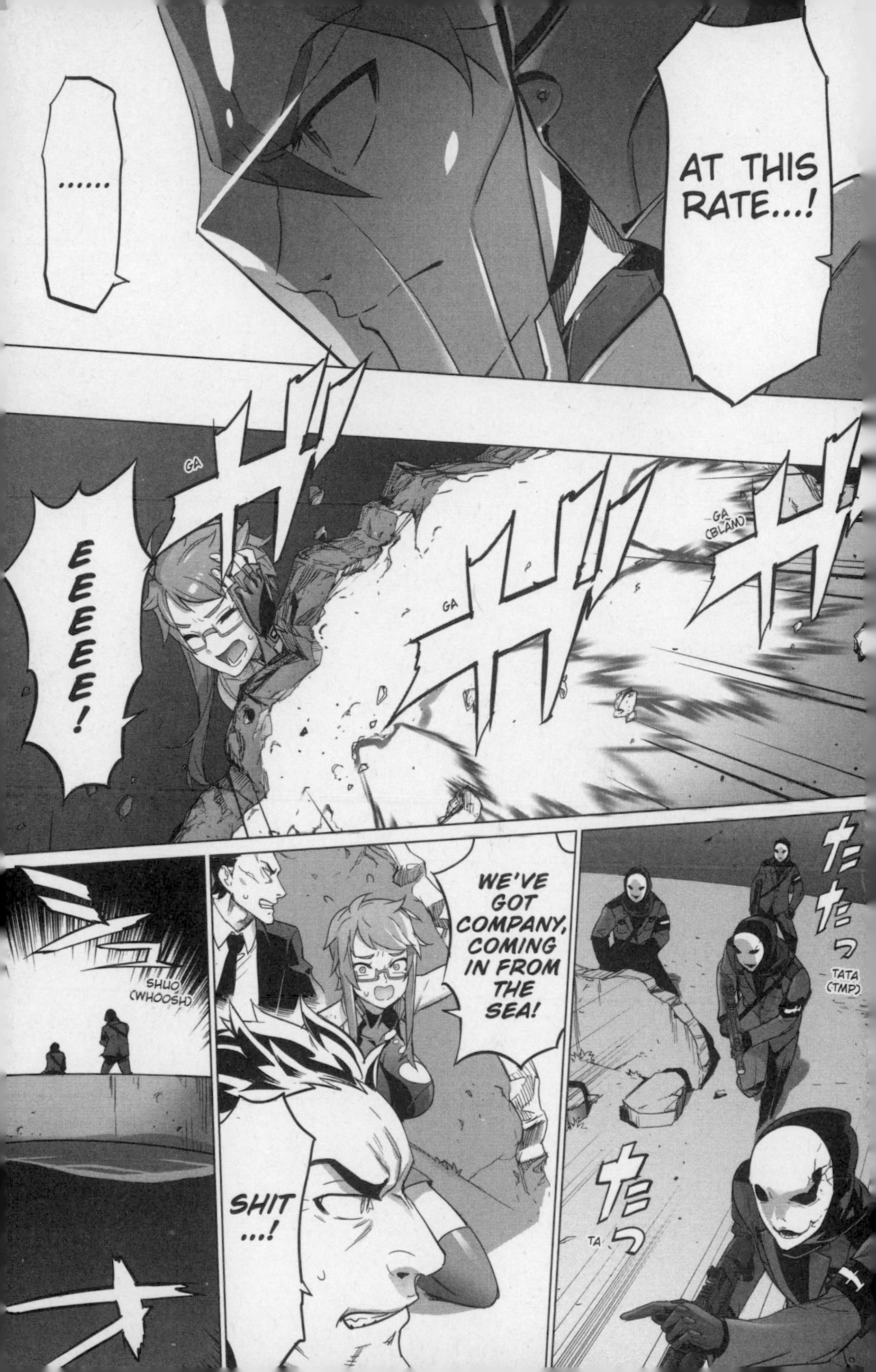
AT THIS RATE...!
......
GA
GA (BLAM)
GA
EEEEEE!
TATA (TMP)
TA
WE'VE GOT COMPANY, COMING IN FROM THE SEA!
SHIT ...!
SHUO (WHOOSH)

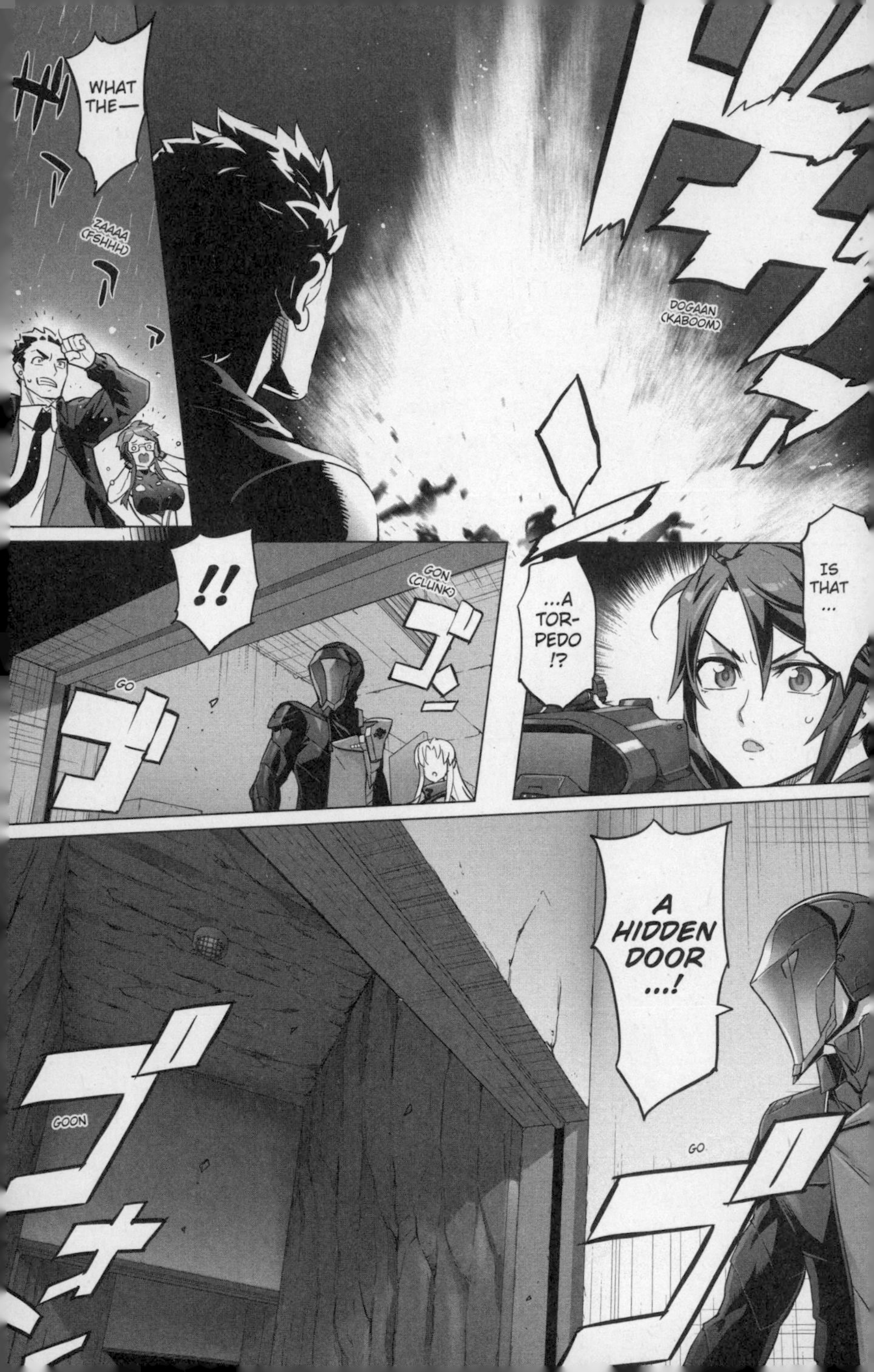
DOGAAN (KABOOM)
WHAT THE—
ZAAAA (FSHHH)
IS THAT ...
...A TOR-PEDO !?
!!
GON (CLUNK)
GO
A HIDDEN DOOR ...!
GO
GOON

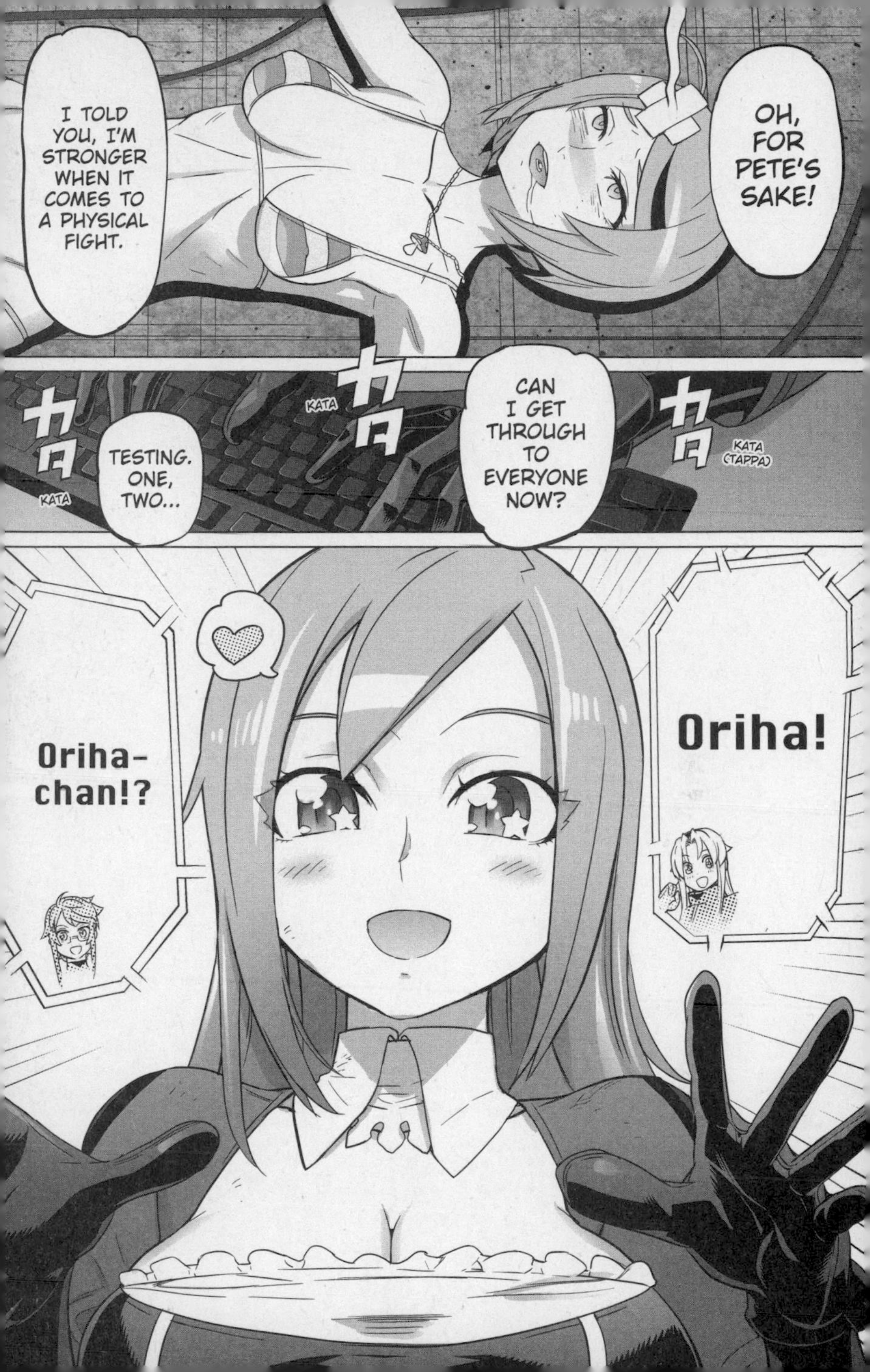
OH, FOR PETE'S SAKE!
I TOLD YOU, I'M STRONGER WHEN IT COMES TO A PHYSICAL FIGHT.
KATA (TAPPA)
CAN I GET THROUGH TO EVERYONE NOW?
KATA
TESTING. ONE, TWO...
KATA
Oriha!
Oriha-chan!?

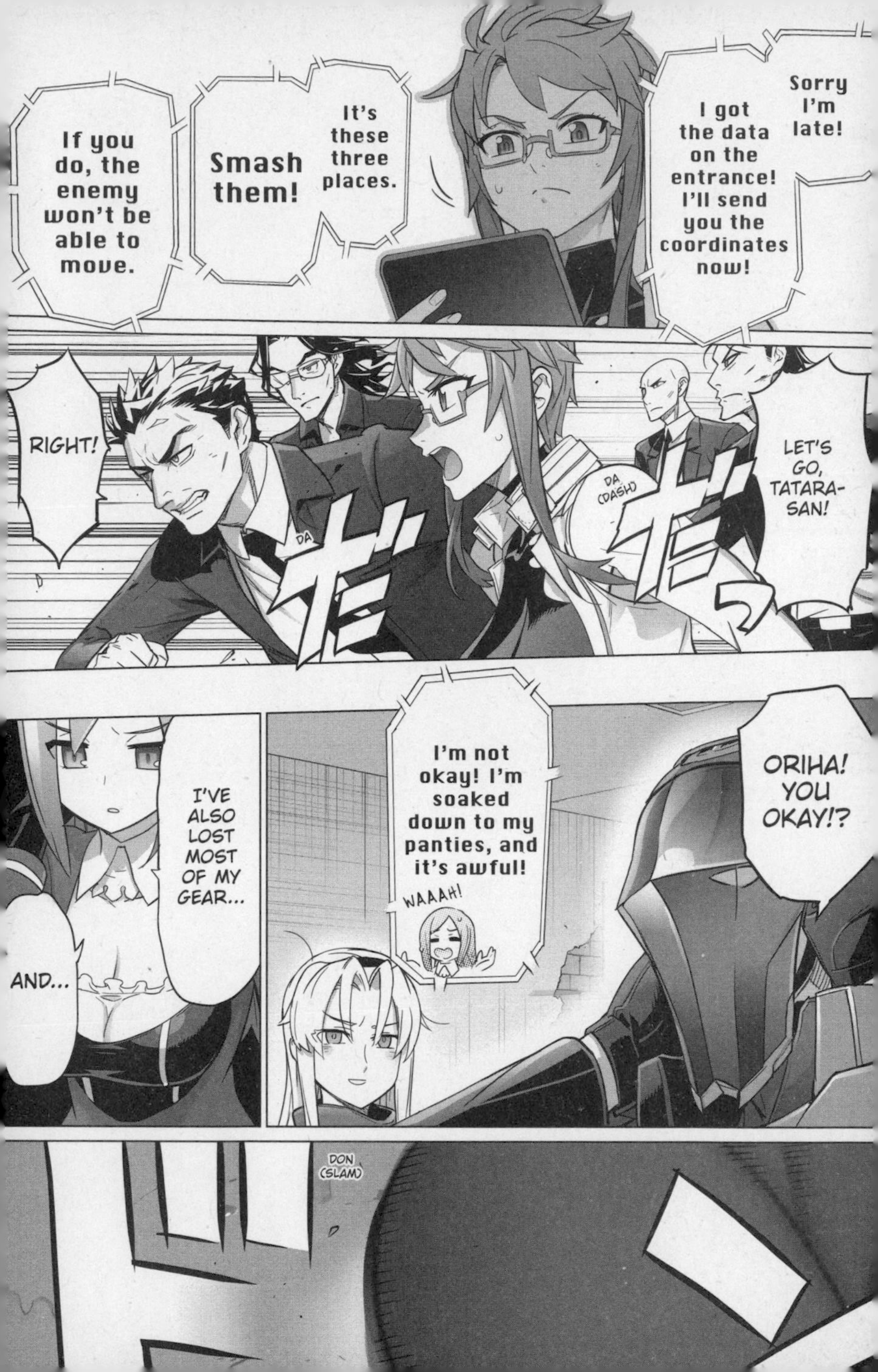
Sorry I'm late!
I got the data on the entrance! I'll send you the coordinates now!
It's these three places.
Smash them!
If you do, the enemy won't be able to move.
LET'S GO, TATARA-SAN!
DA (DASH)
DA
RIGHT!
ORIHA! YOU OKAY!?
I'm not okay! I'm soaked down to my panties, and it's awful!
WAAAH!
I'VE ALSO LOST MOST OF MY GEAR...
AND...
DON (SLAM)

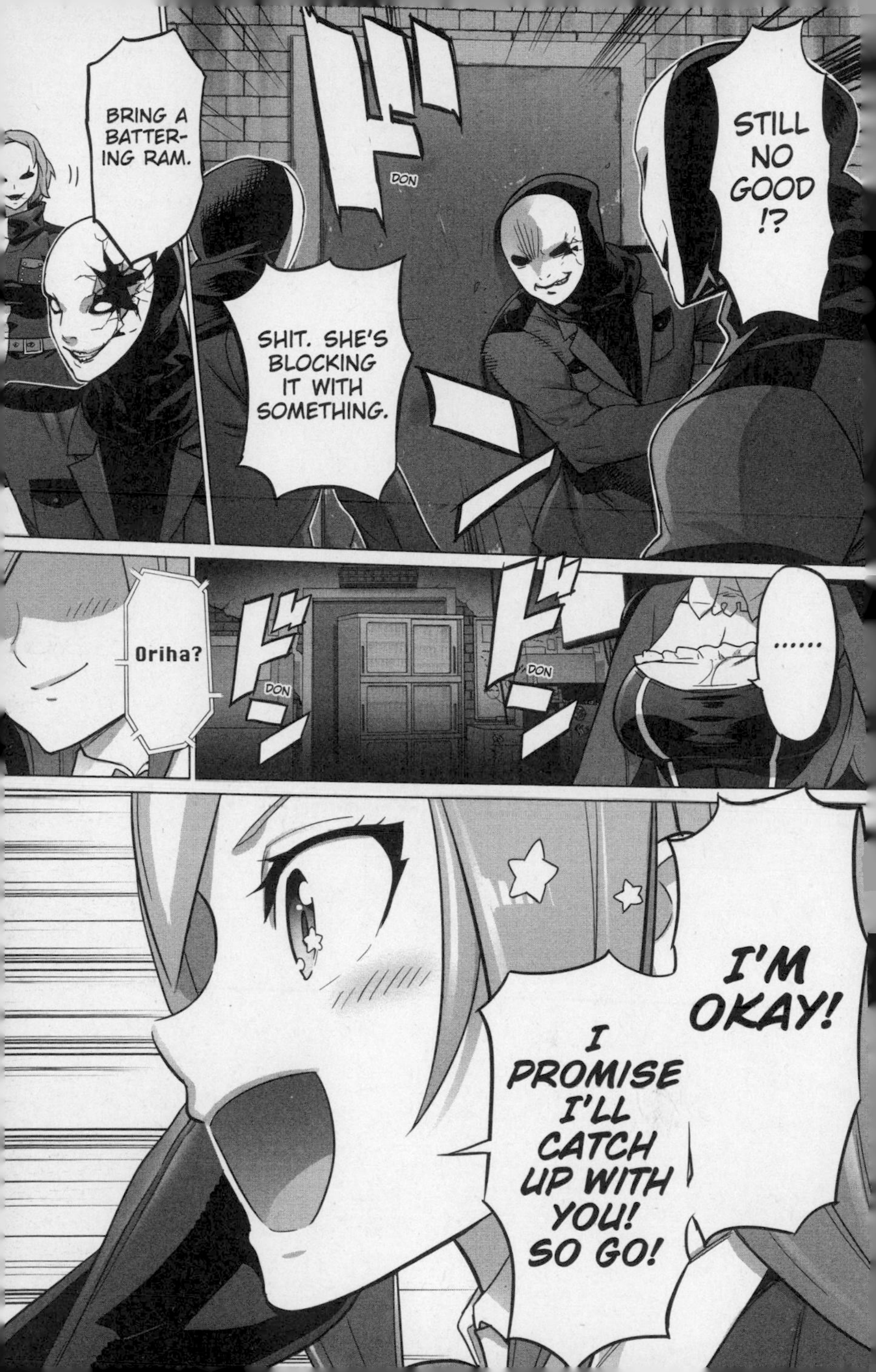
STILL NO GOOD !?
DON
SHIT. SHE'S BLOCKING IT WITH SOMETHING.
BRING A BATTERING RAM.
......
DON
DON
Oriha?
I'M OKAY!
I PROMISE I'LL CATCH UP WITH YOU! SO GO!

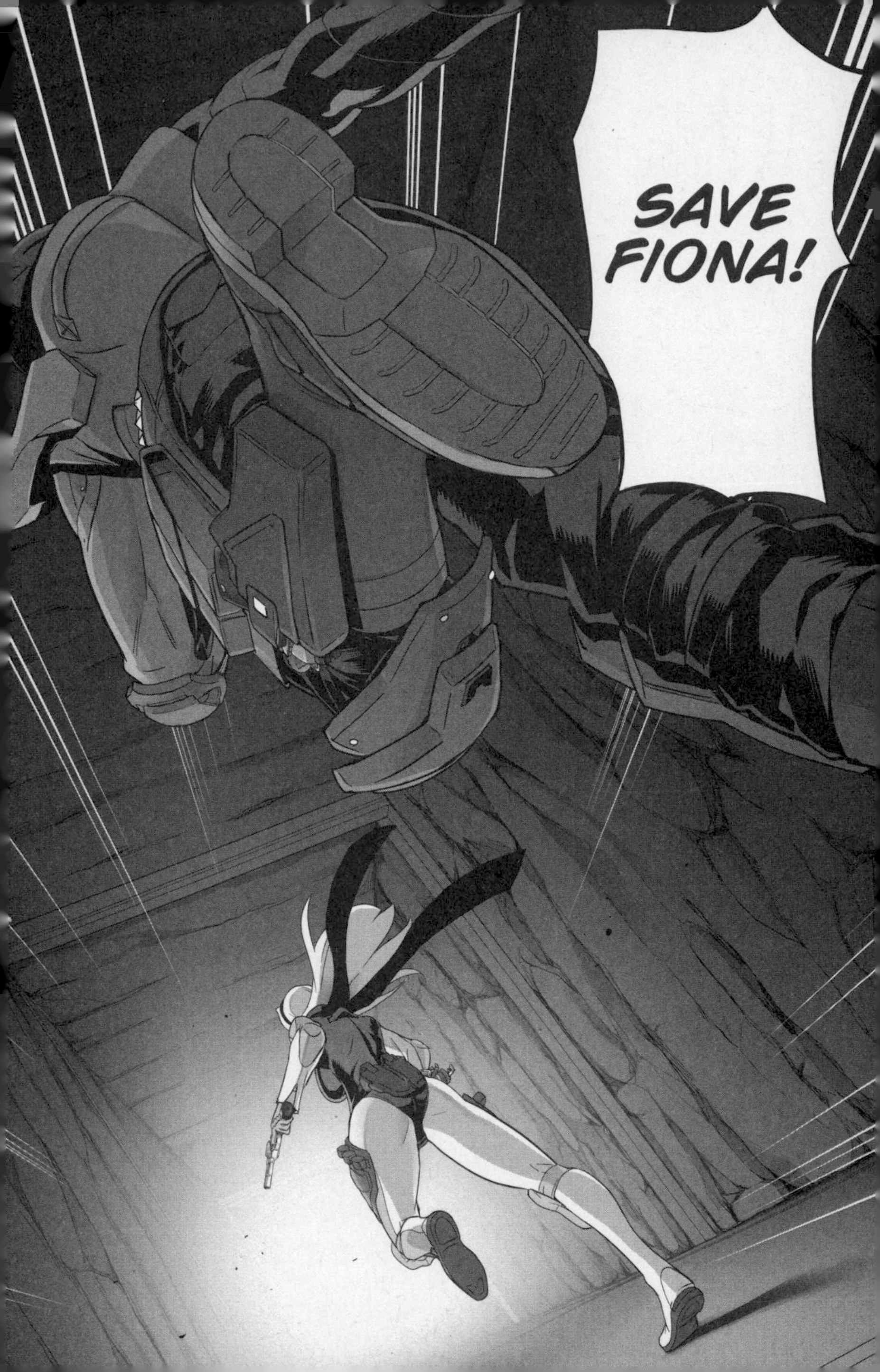
SAVE FIONA!

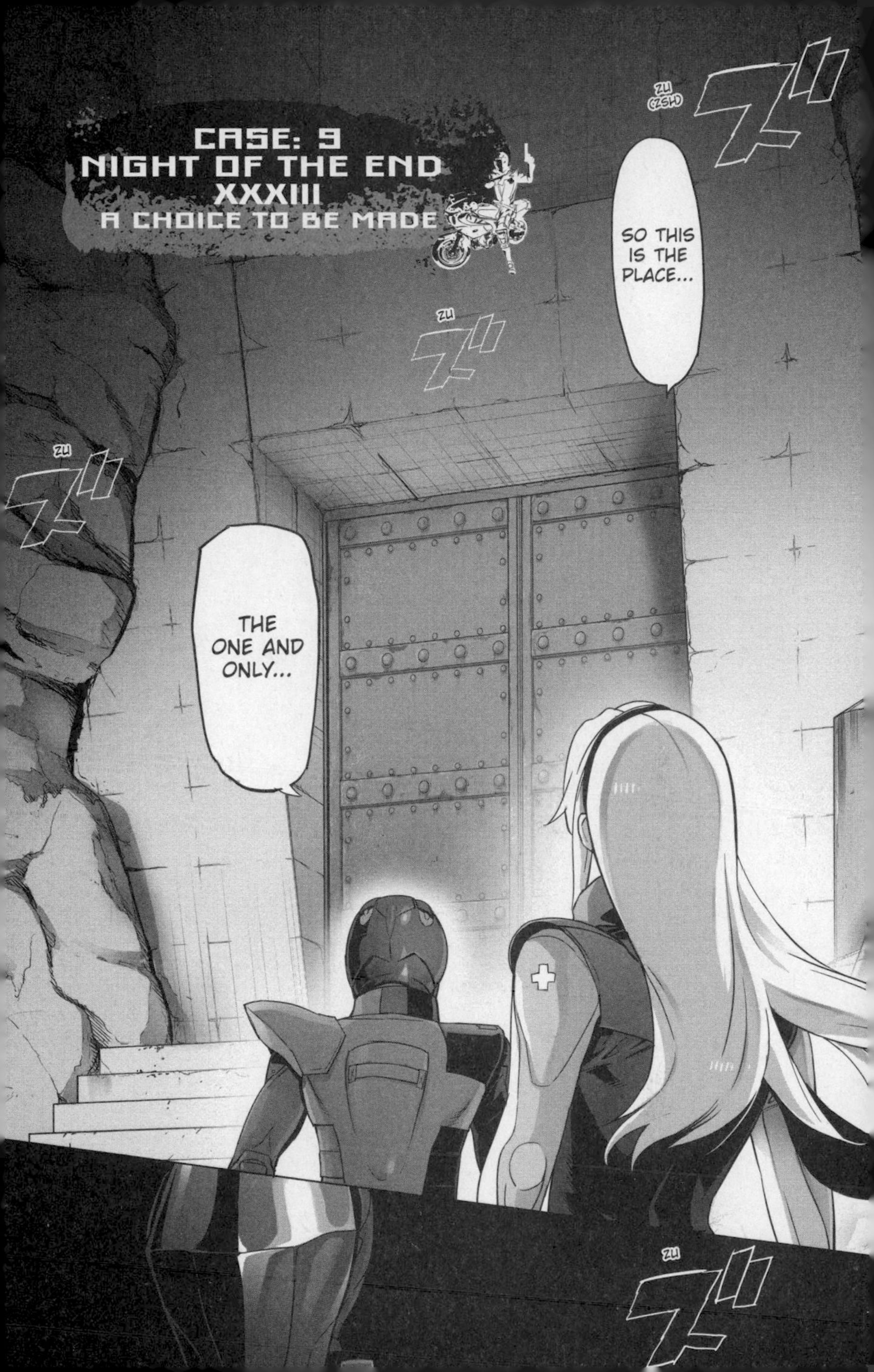
CASE: 9
NIGHT OF THE END
XXXIII
A CHOICE TO BE MADE
ZU (ZSH)
SO THIS IS THE PLACE...
ZU
ZU
THE ONE AND ONLY...
ZU

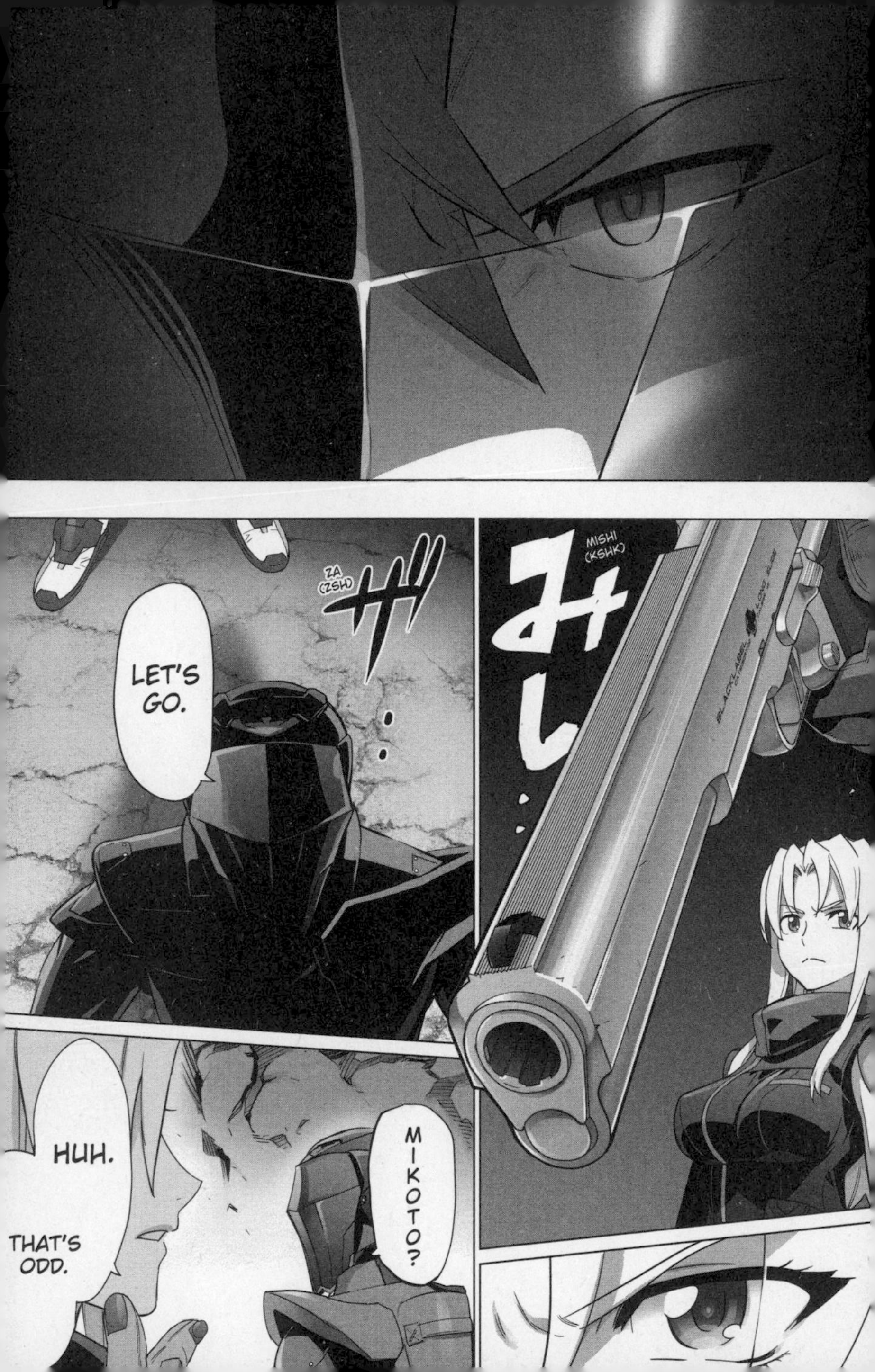
MISHI (KSHK)
みし…
ZA (ZSH)
ザッ
LET'S GO.
…
MIKOTO?
HUH.
THAT'S ODD.

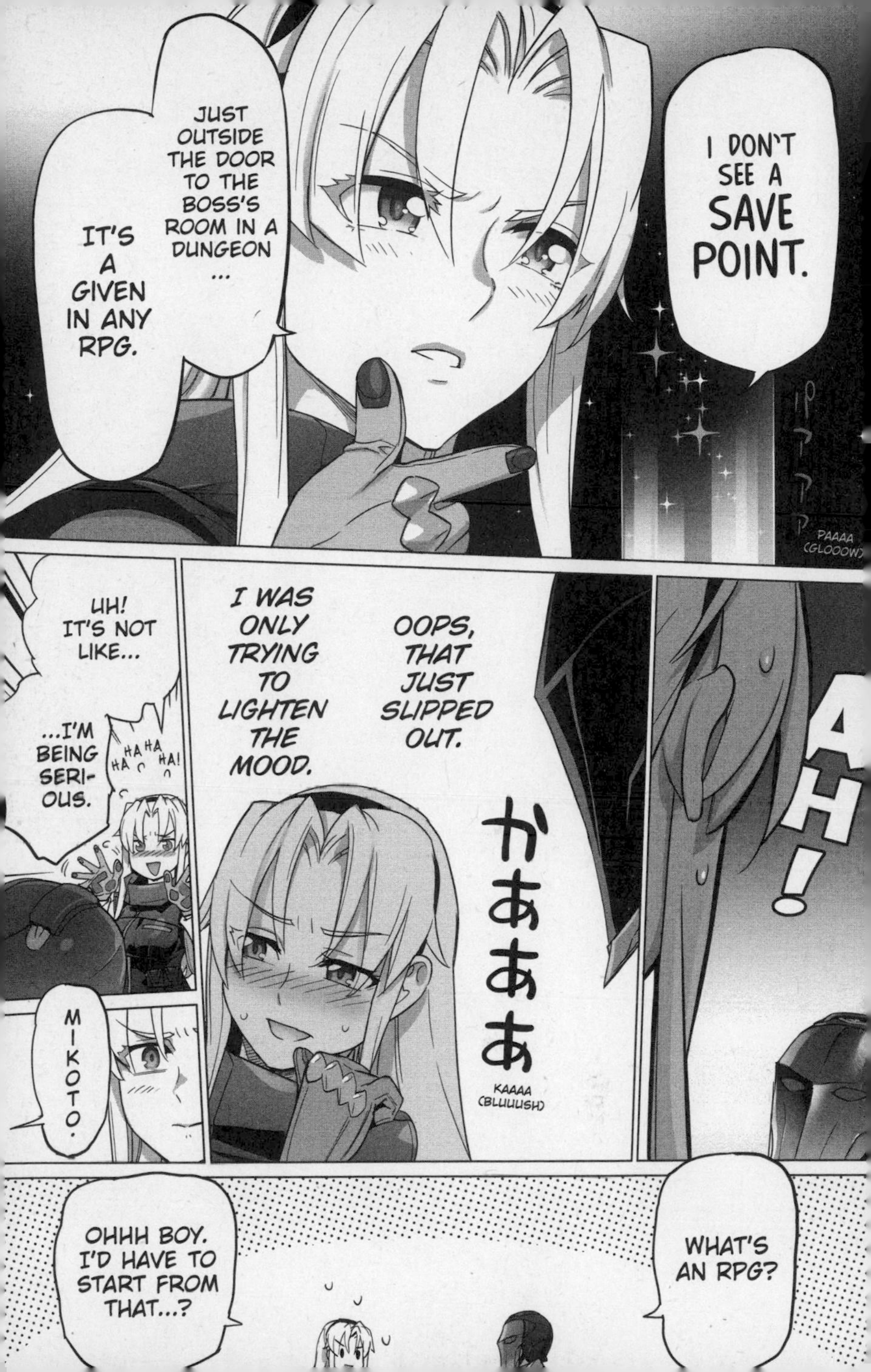
I DON'T SEE A SAVE POINT.
JUST OUTSIDE THE DOOR TO THE BOSS'S ROOM IN A DUNGEON ...
IT'S A GIVEN IN ANY RPG.
パァーァ
PAAAA (GLOOOW)
AH!
OOPS, THAT JUST SLIPPED OUT.
I WAS ONLY TRYING TO LIGHTEN THE MOOD.
かあああ
KAAAA (BLUUUSH)
UH! IT'S NOT LIKE...
...I'M BEING SERI-OUS.
HA HA HA HA!
MIKOTO.
WHAT'S AN RPG?
OHHH BOY. I'D HAVE TO START FROM THAT...?

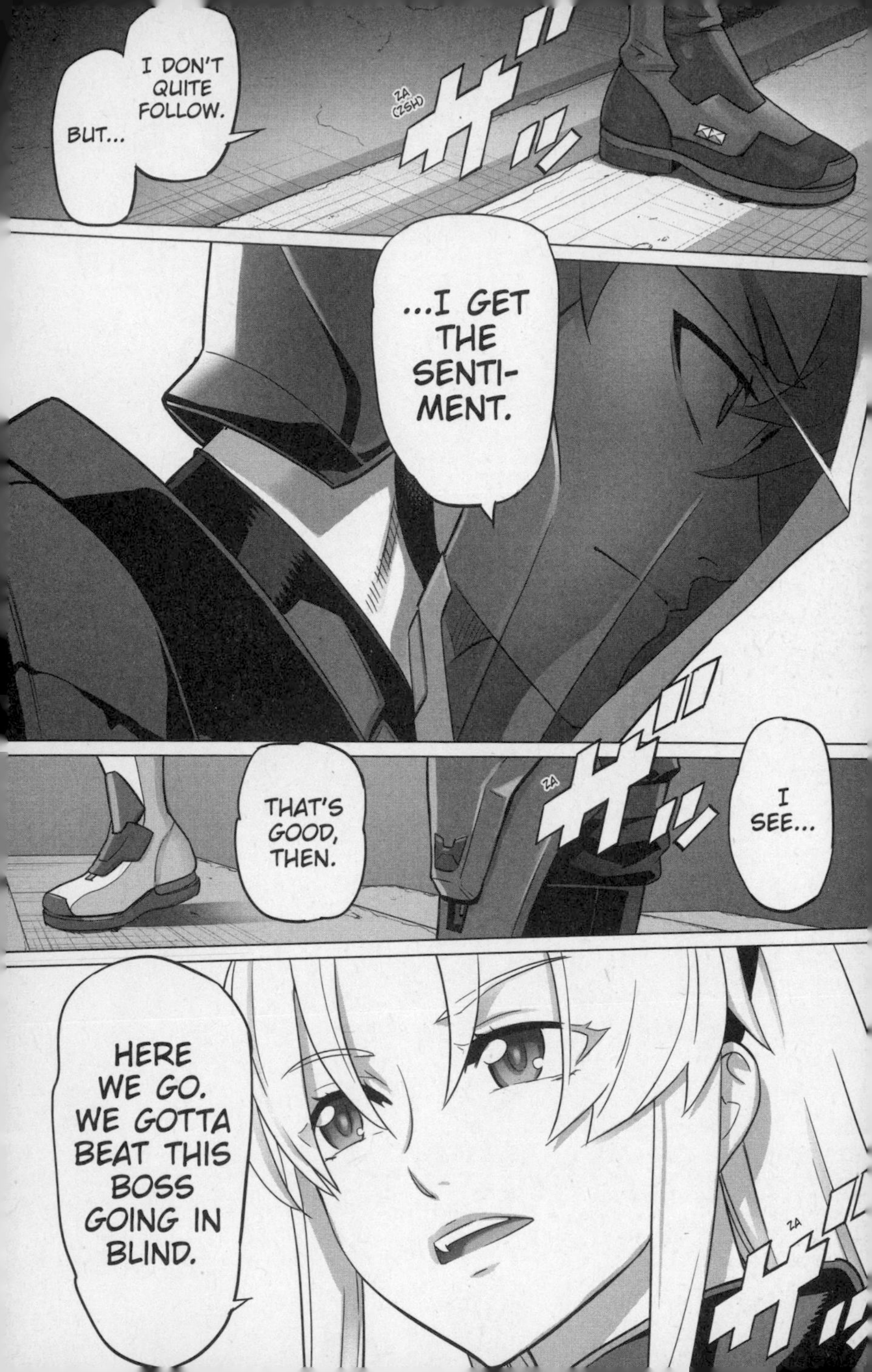
ZA (ZSH)
I DON'T QUITE FOLLOW. BUT...
...I GET THE SENTIMENT.
I SEE...
ZA
THAT'S GOOD, THEN.
ZA
HERE WE GO. WE GOTTA BEAT THIS BOSS GOING IN BLIND.

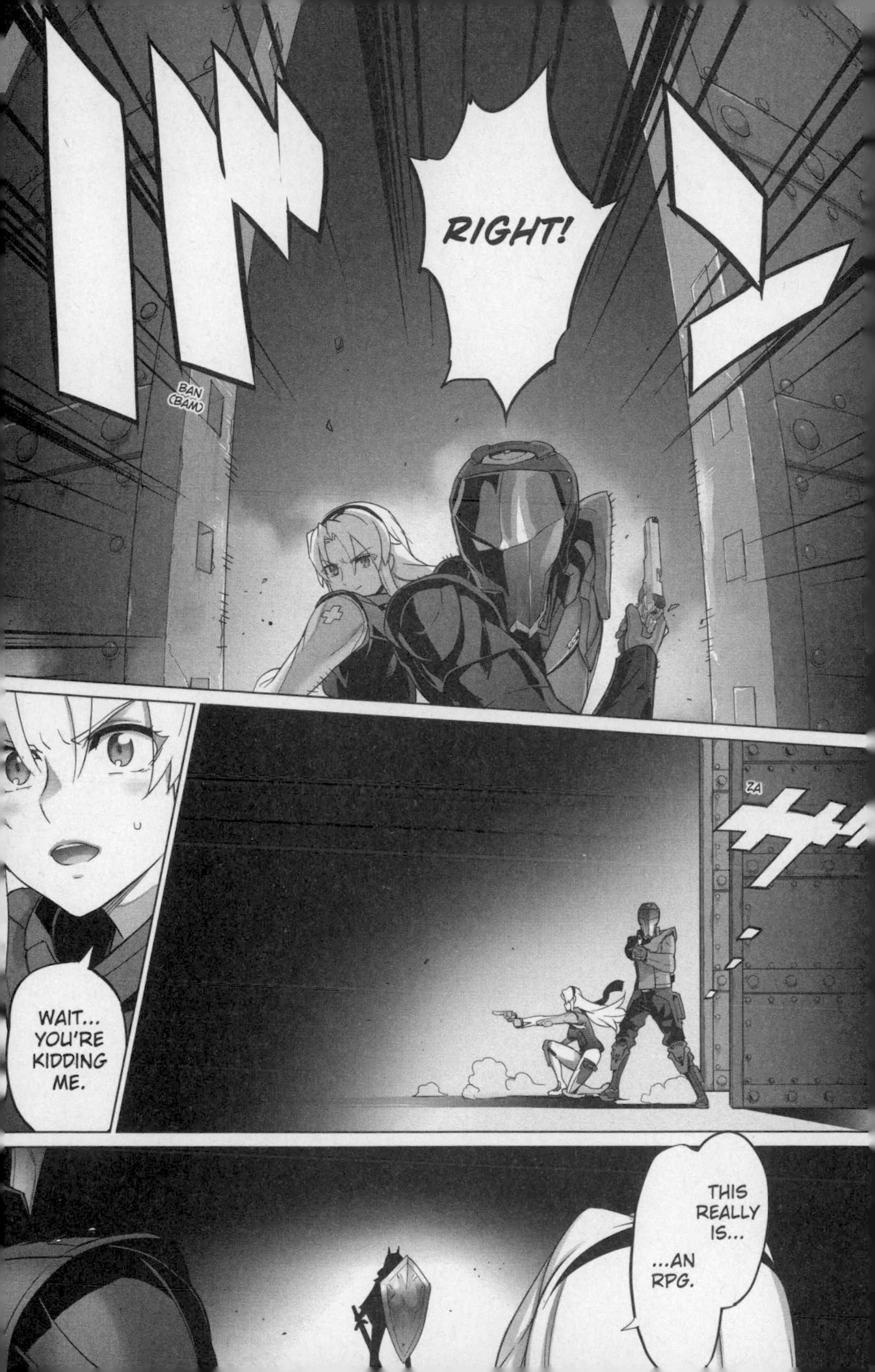
RIGHT!
BAN (BAM)
ZA
WAIT... YOU'RE KIDDING ME.
THIS REALLY IS...
...AN RPG.

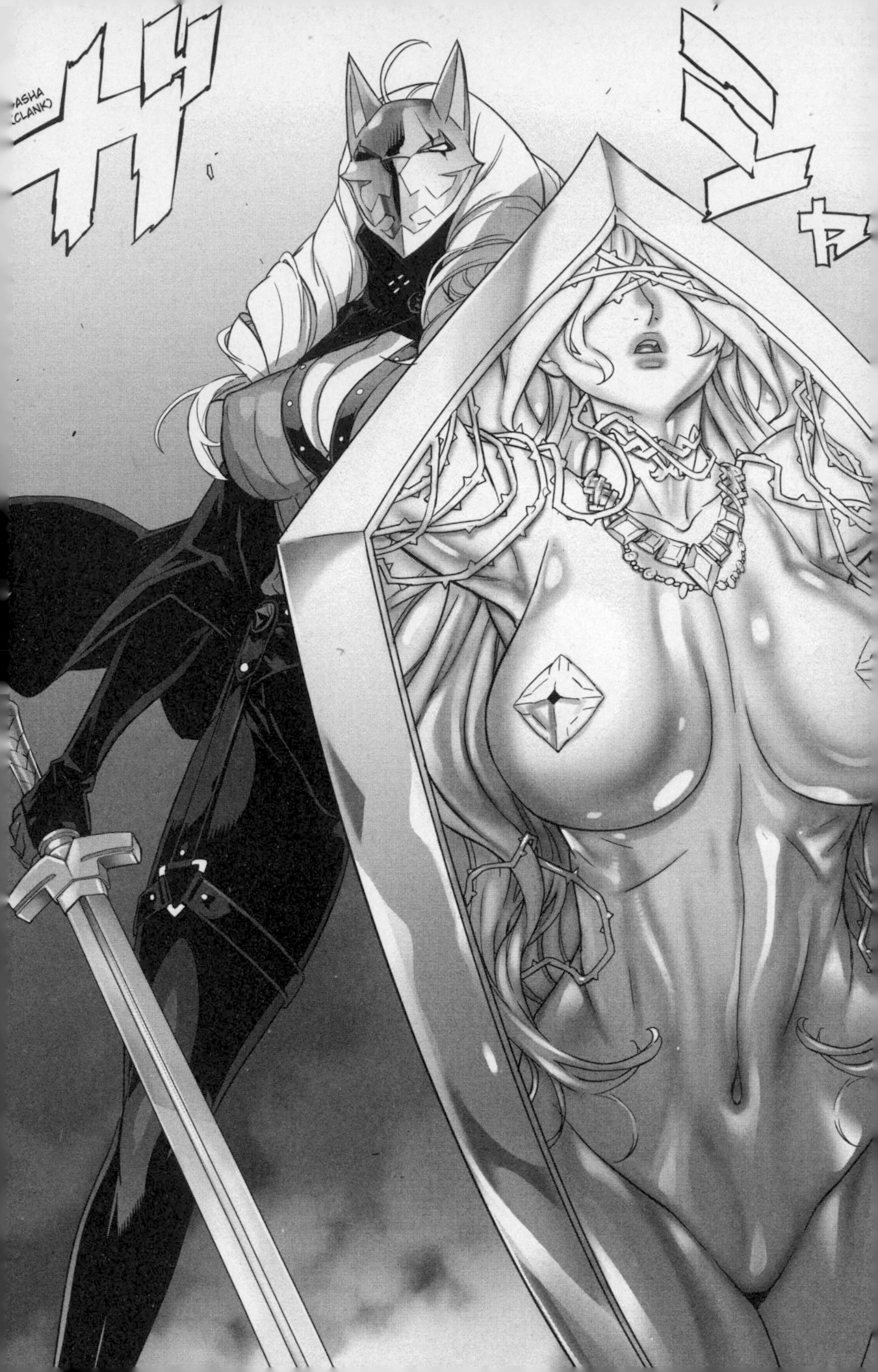
ガシャ
ASHA
(CLANK)

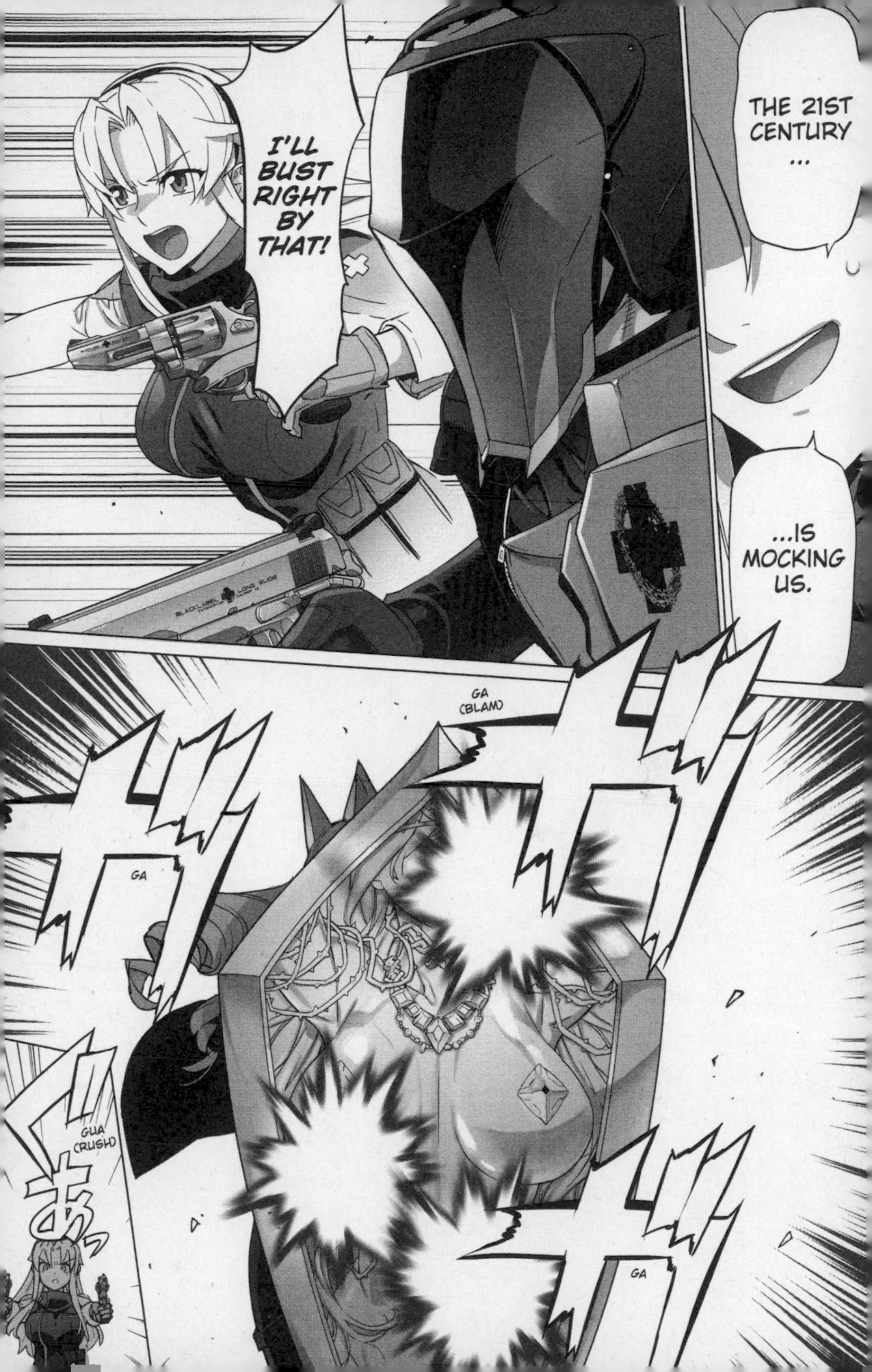
THE 21ST CENTURY ...
...IS MOCKING US.
I'LL BUST RIGHT BY THAT!
GA (BLAM)
GA
GA
GUA (RUSH)
あっ

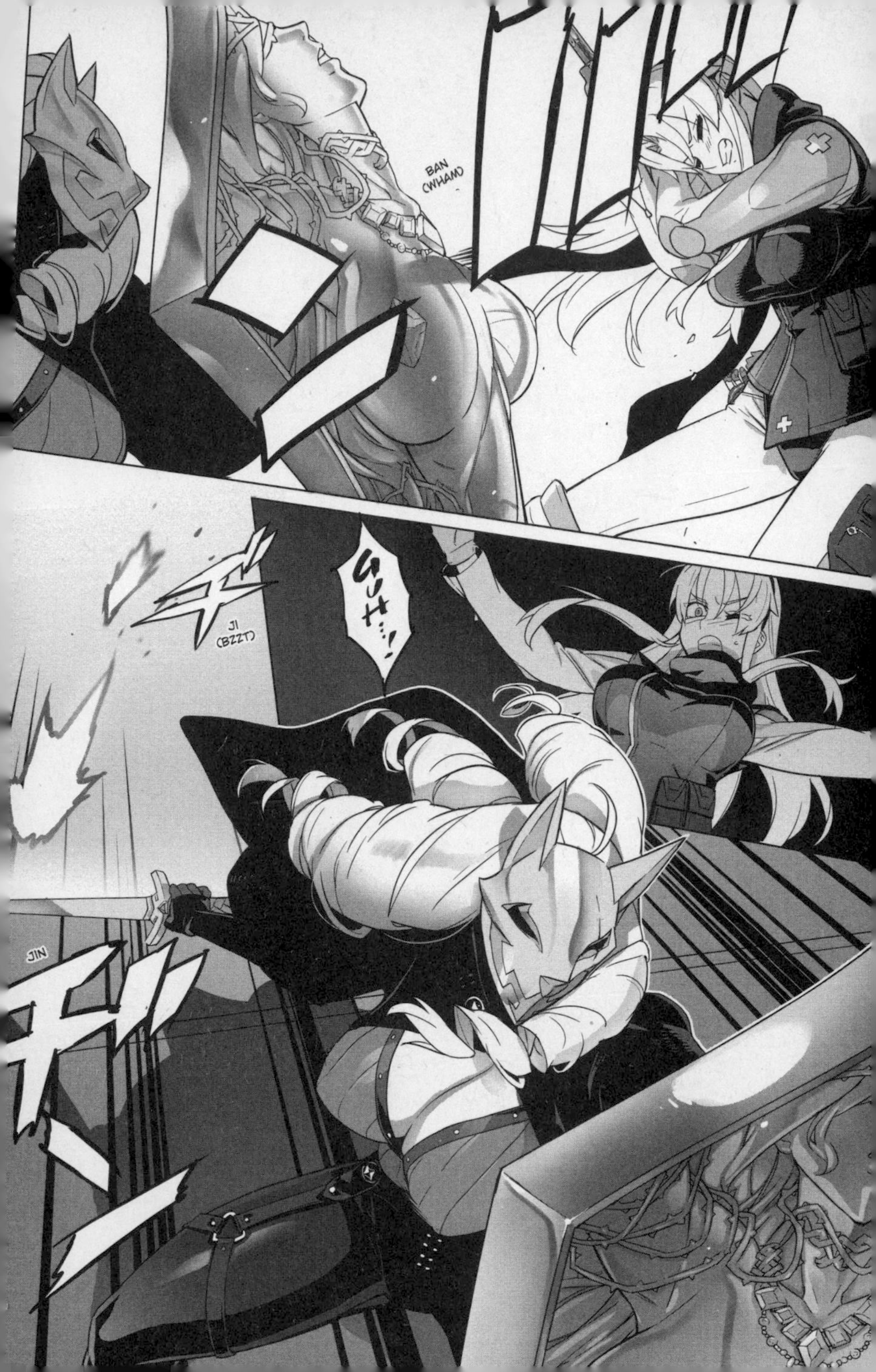
BAN
(WHAM)
UGH...!
JI
(BZZT)
JIN

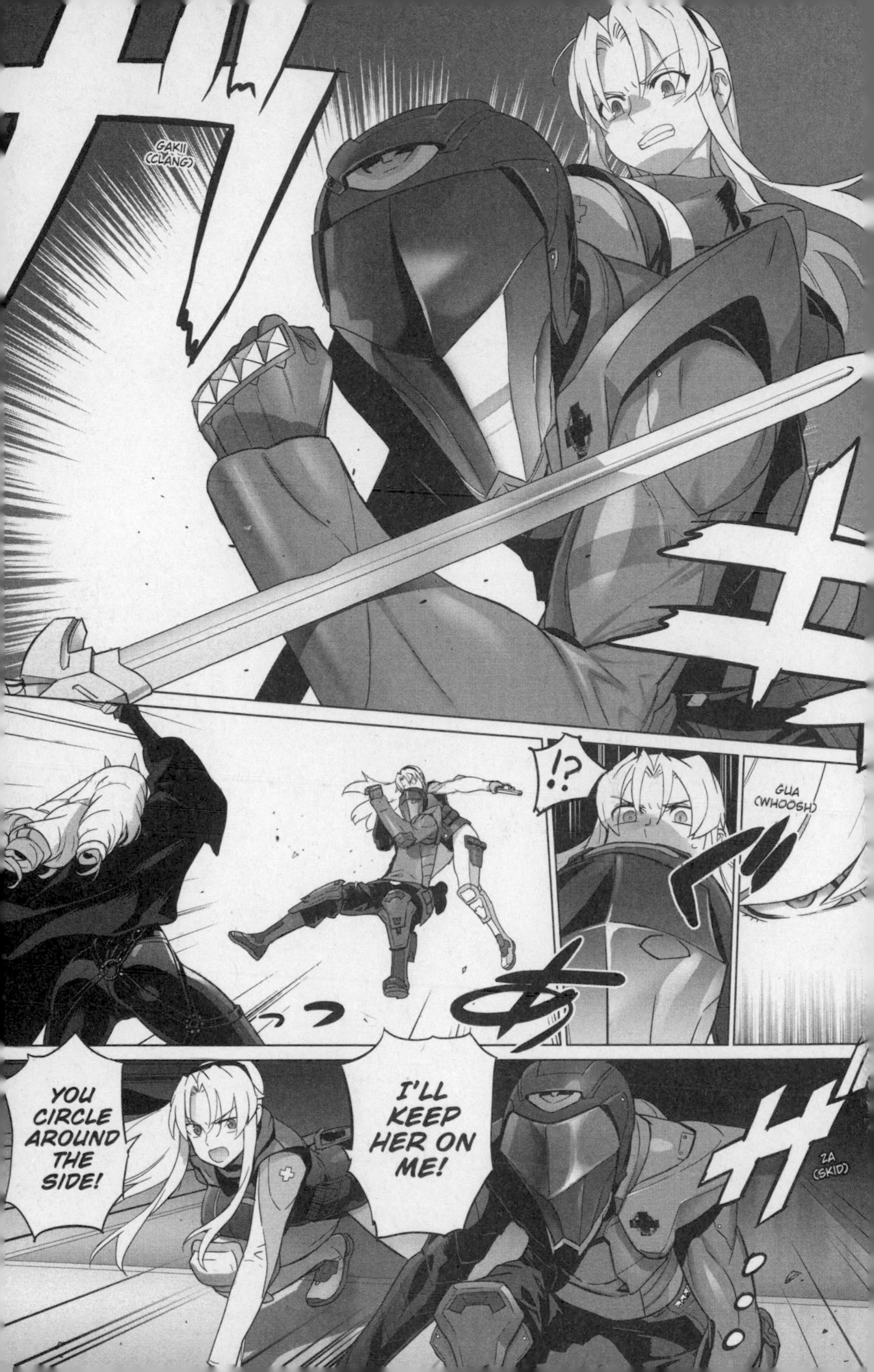
GAKII (CLANG)
!?
GUA (WHOOSH)
ZA (SKID)
I'LL KEEP HER ON ME!
YOU CIRCLE AROUND THE SIDE!

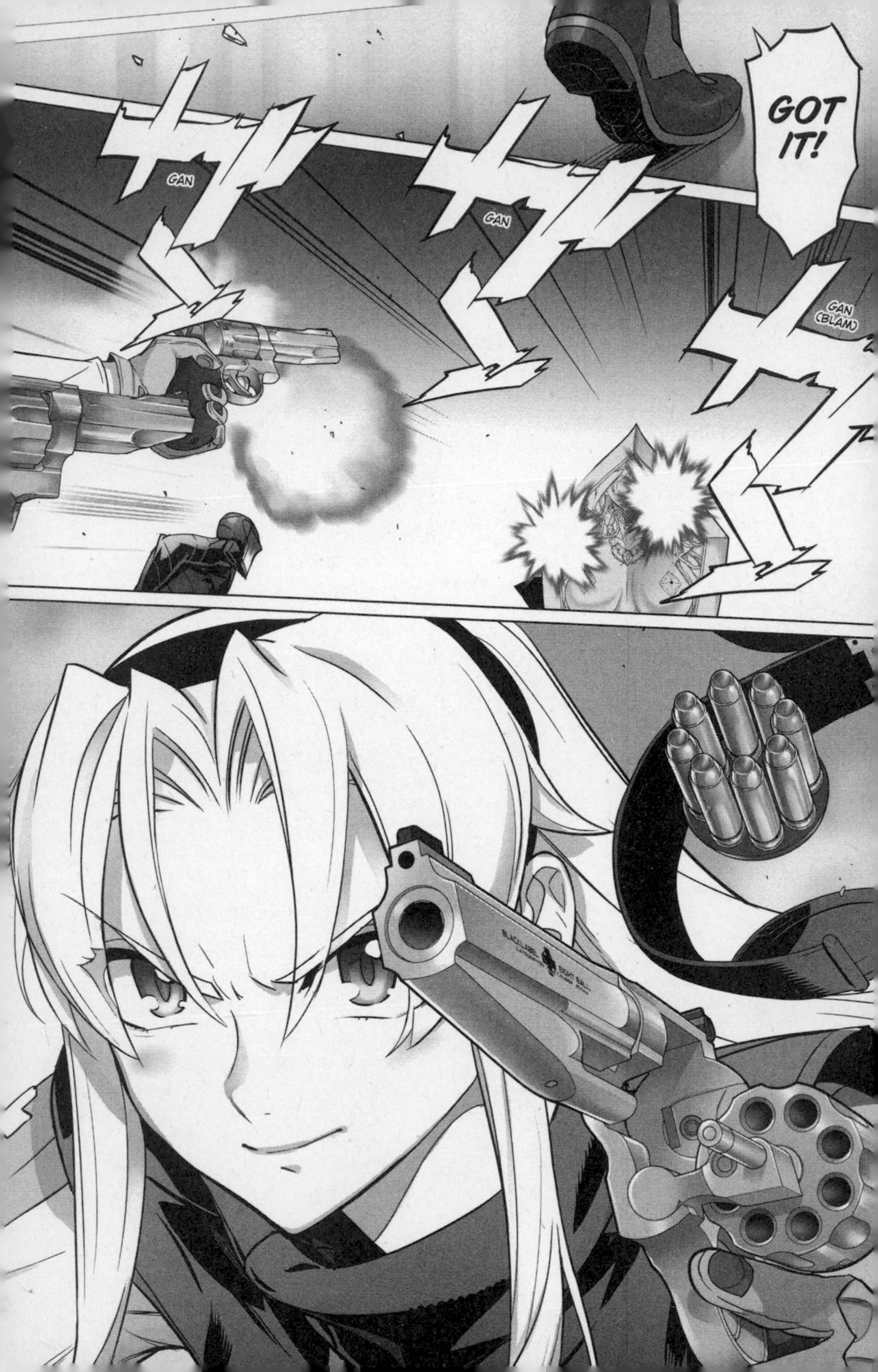
GOT IT!
GAN (BLAM)
GAN
GAN

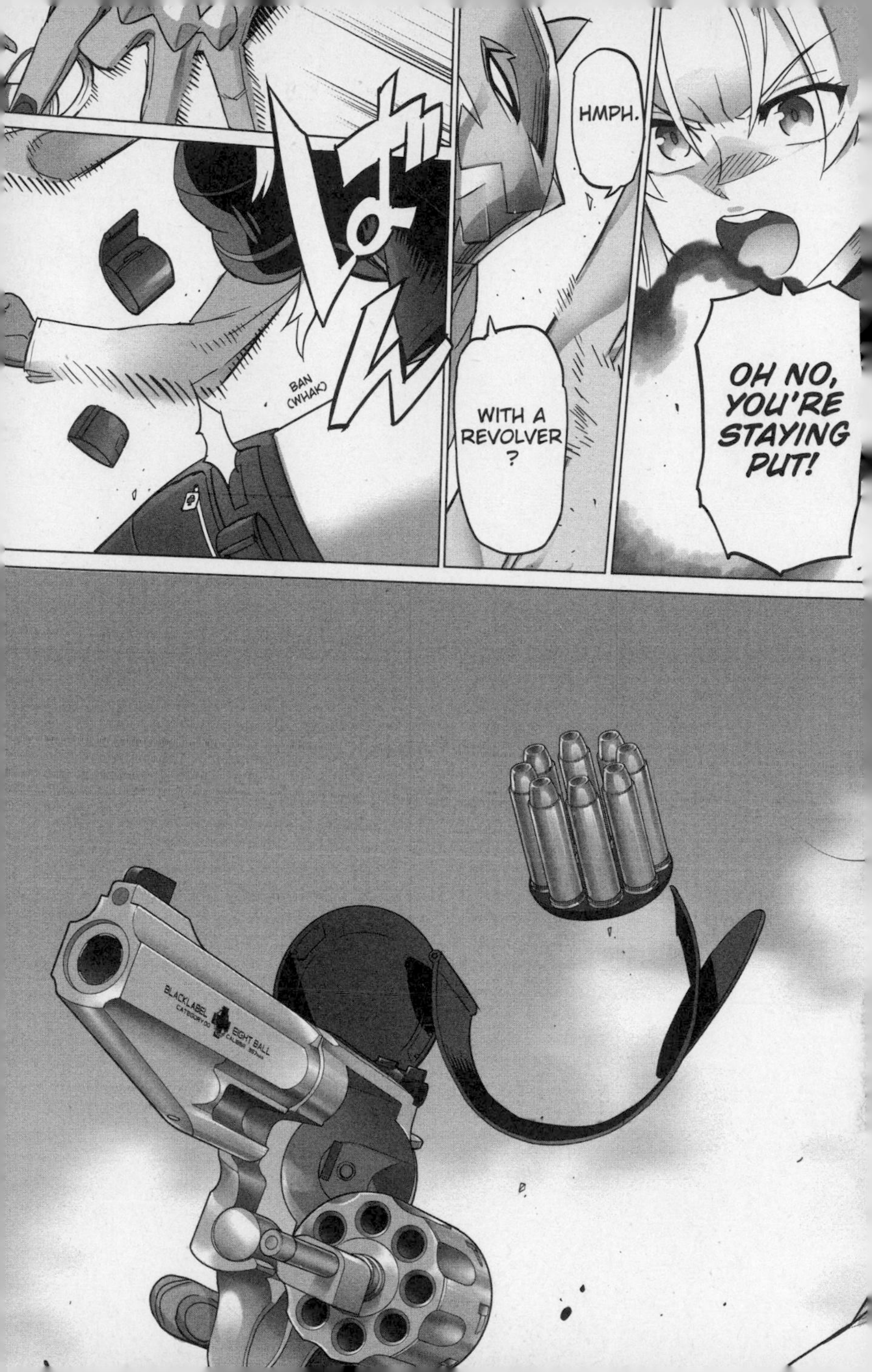
OH NO, YOU'RE STAYING PUT!
HMPH.
WITH A REVOLVER?
BAN (WHAK)
BLACKLABEL
EIGHT BALL

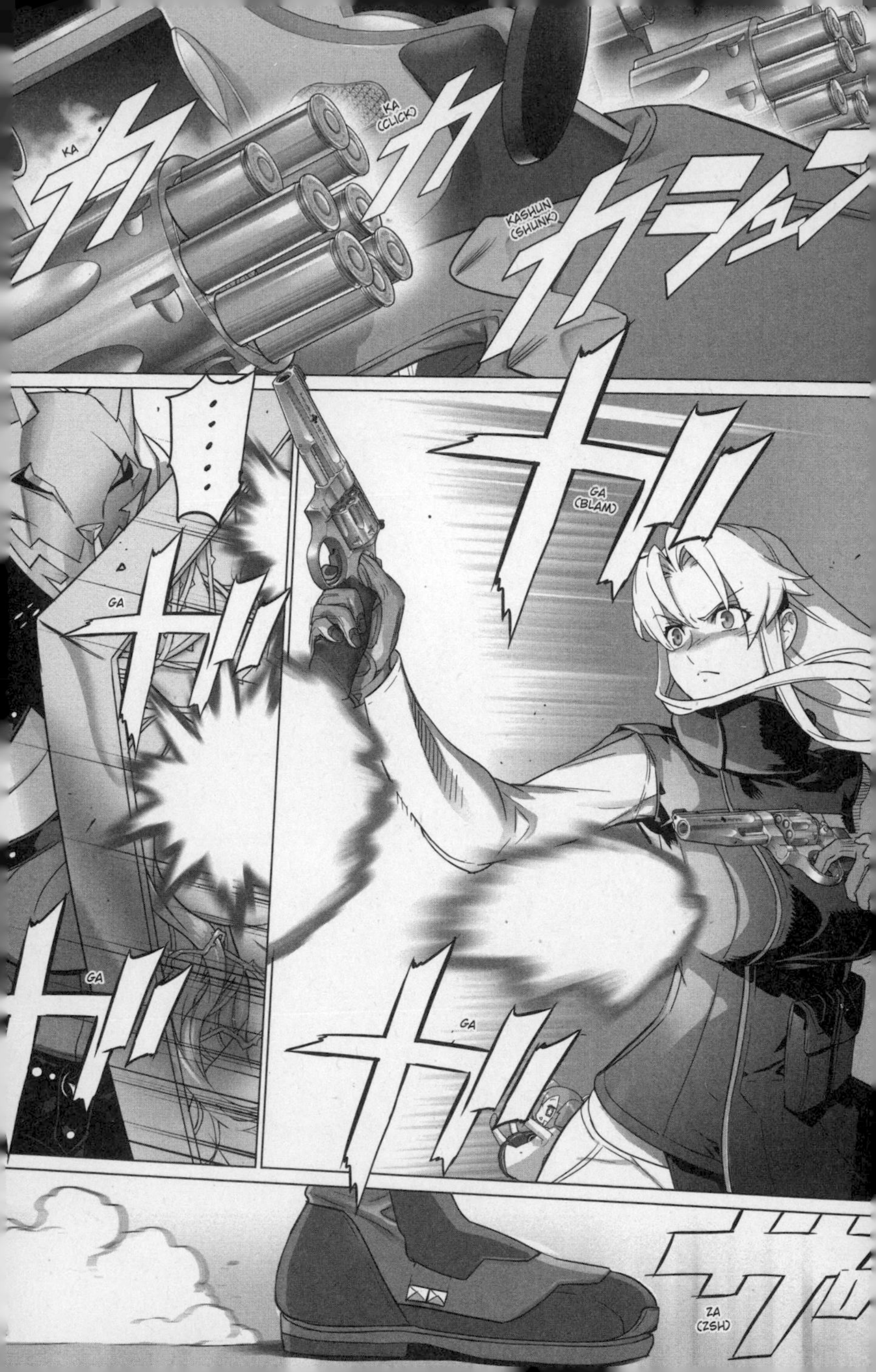
KA
KA (CLICK)
KASHUN (SHUNK)
GA (BLAM)
GA
GA
GA
ZA (ZSH)

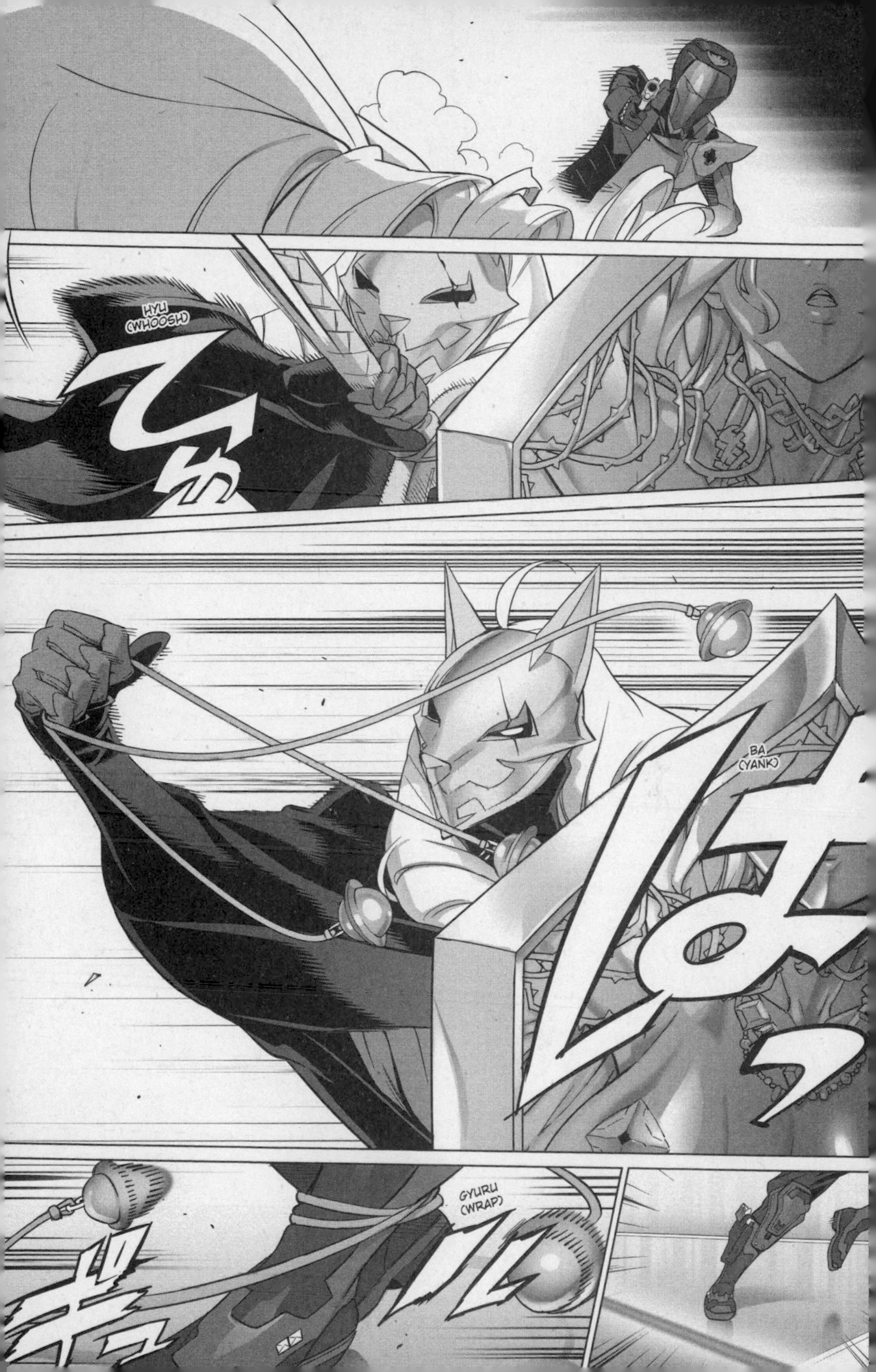
HYU
(WHOOSH)
BA
(YANK)
GYURU
(WRAP)

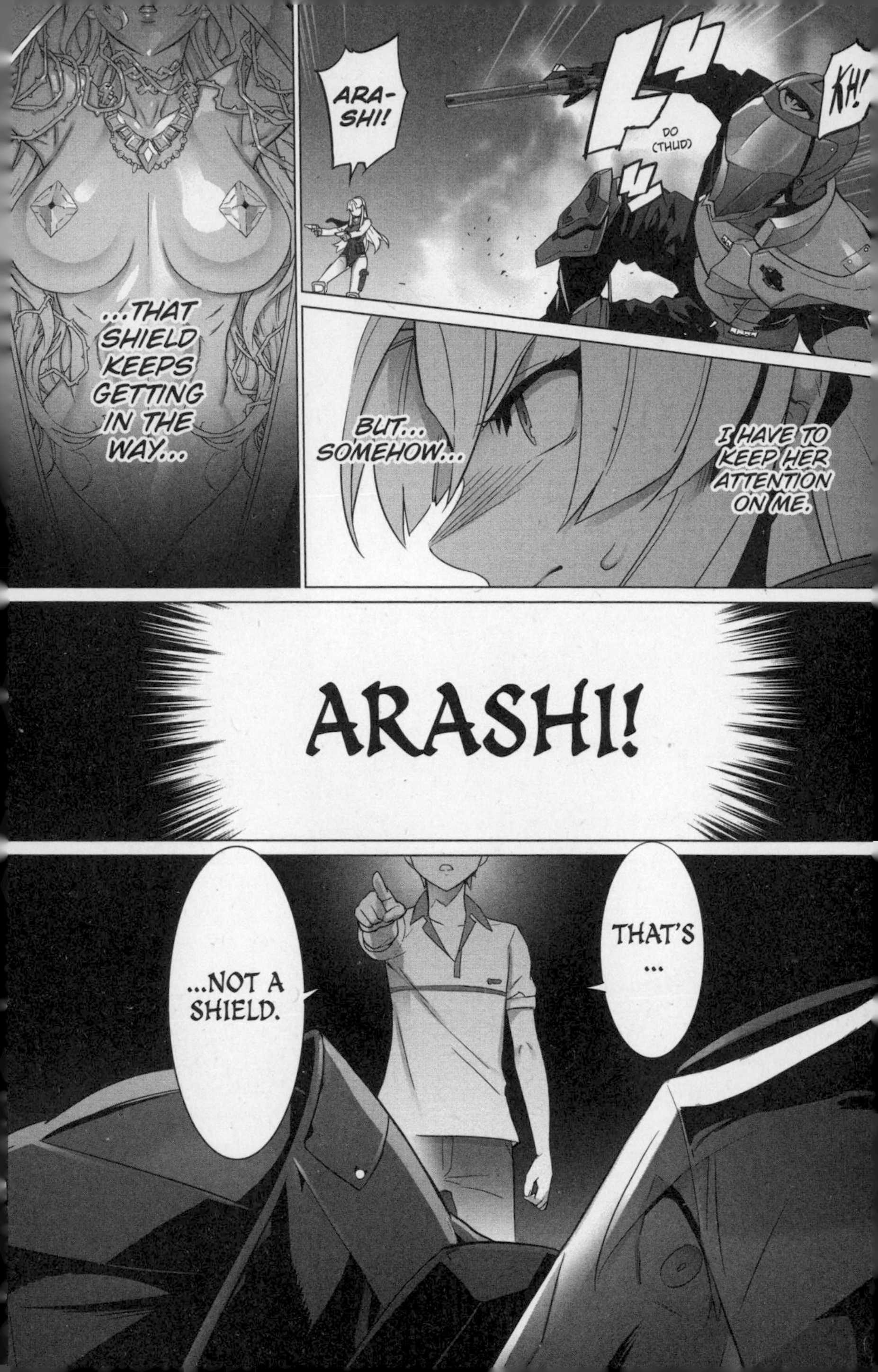
KH!
DO (THUD)
ARA-SHI!
I HAVE TO KEEP HER ATTENTION ON ME.
BUT... SOMEHOW...
...THAT SHIELD KEEPS GETTING IN THE WAY...
ARASHI!
THAT'S ...
...NOT A SHIELD.

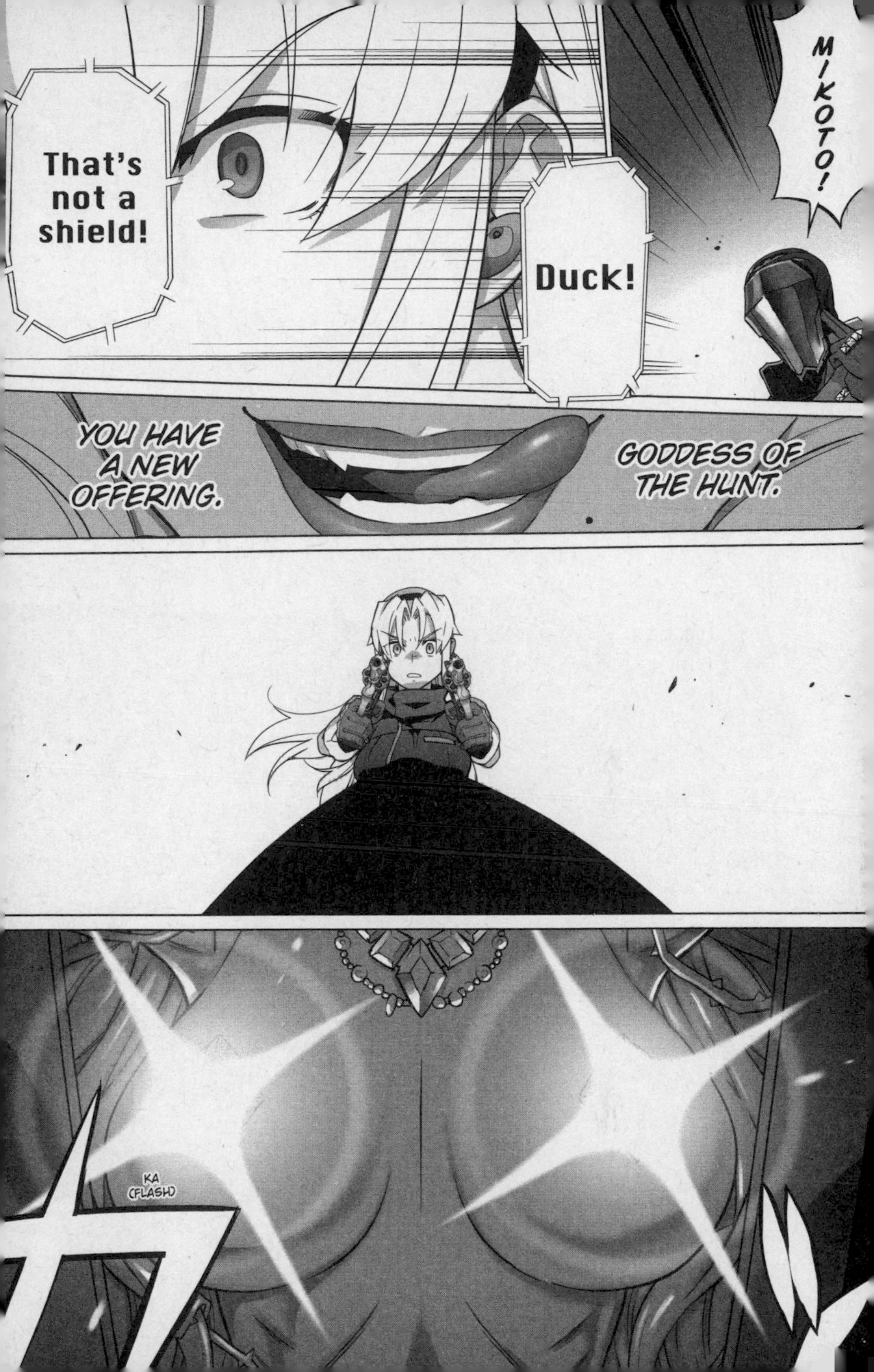
MIKOTO!
Duck!
That's not a shield!
YOU HAVE A NEW OFFERING.
GODDESS OF THE HUNT.
KA (FLASH)

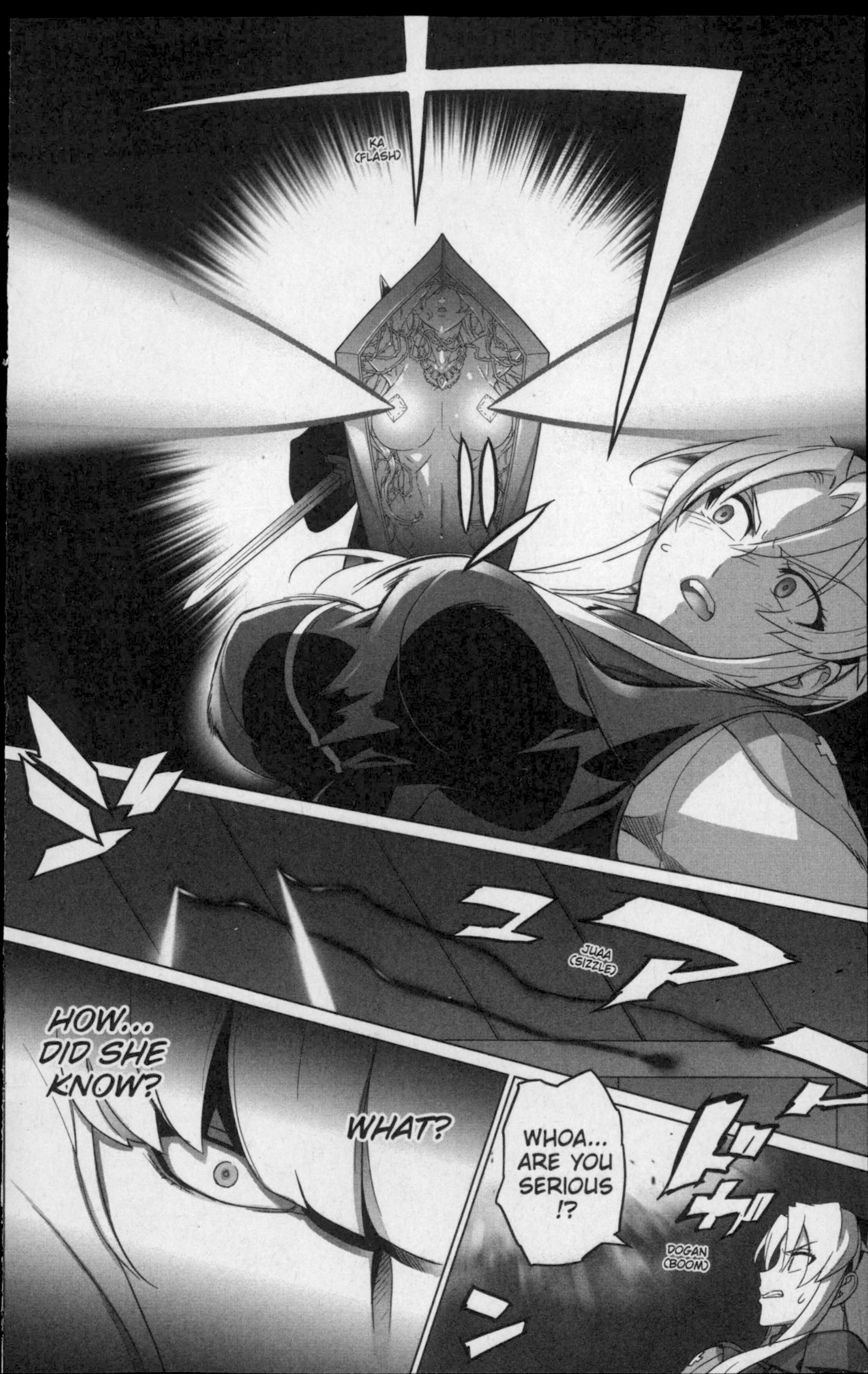
KA (FLASH)
JUAA (SIZZLE)
WHOA... ARE YOU SERIOUS!?
DOGAN (BOOM)
WHAT?
HOW... DID SHE KNOW?

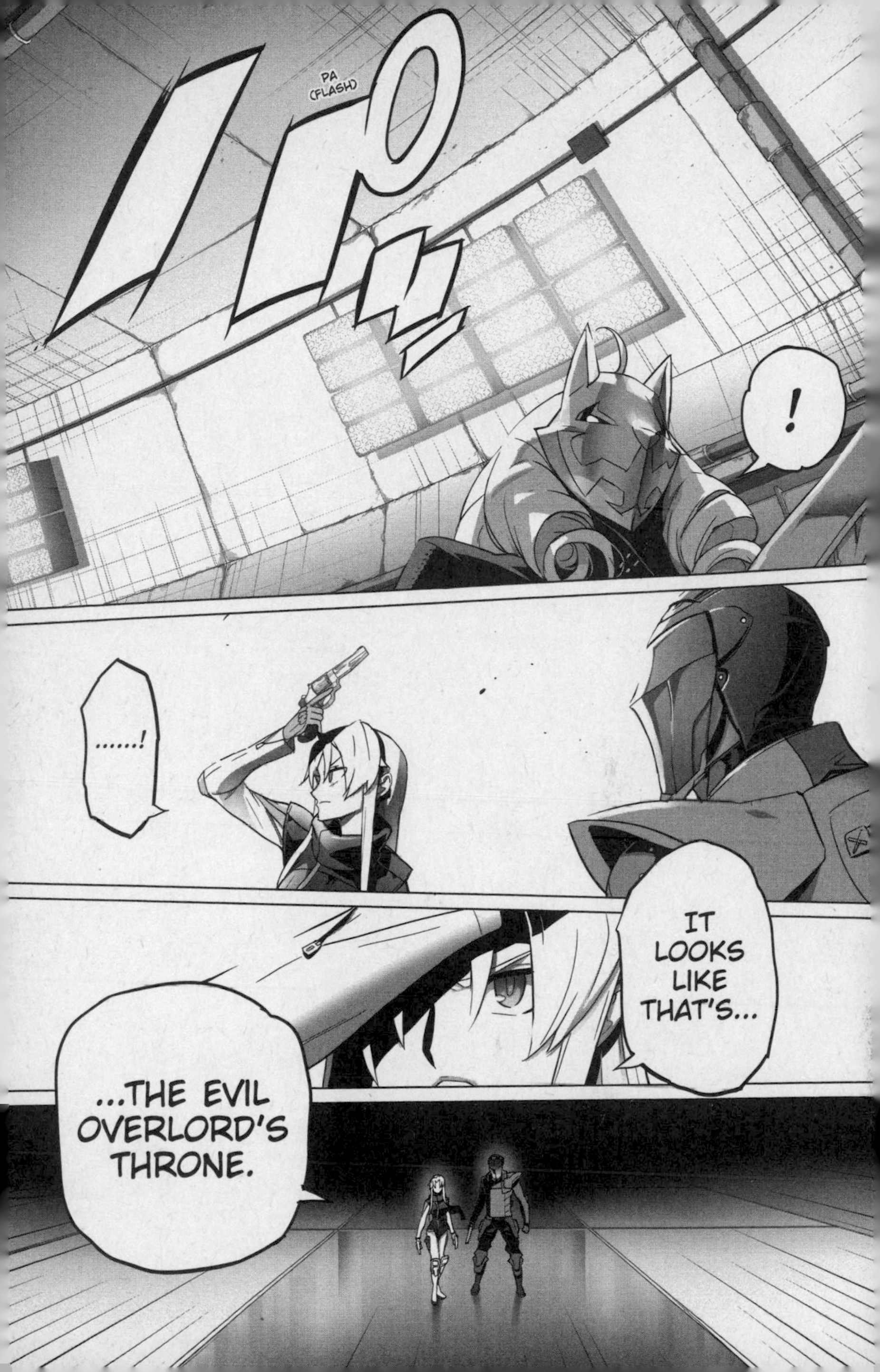
PA (FLASH)
!
......!
IT LOOKS LIKE THAT'S...
...THE EVIL OVERLORD'S THRONE.

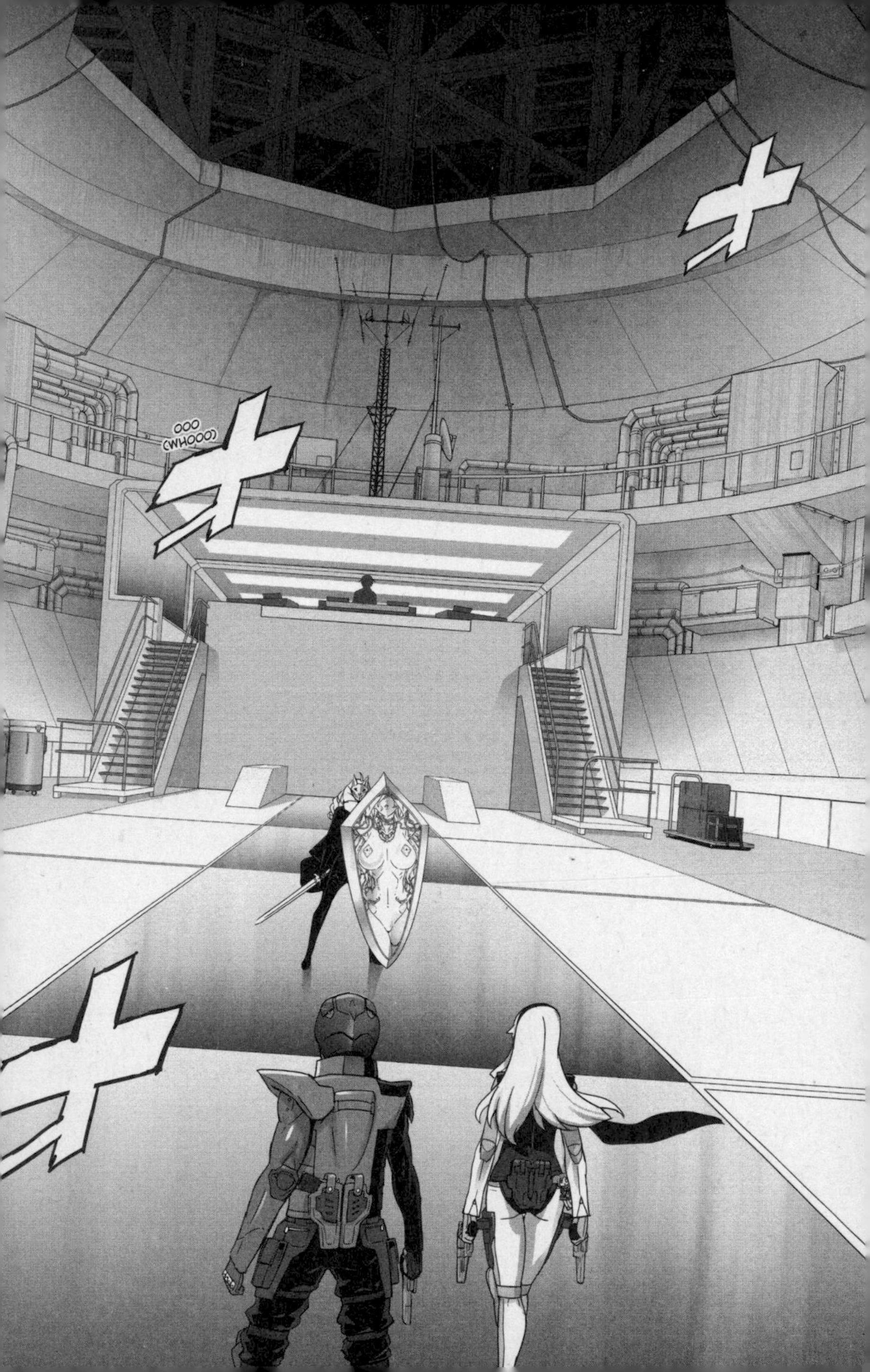
OOO
(WHOOO)

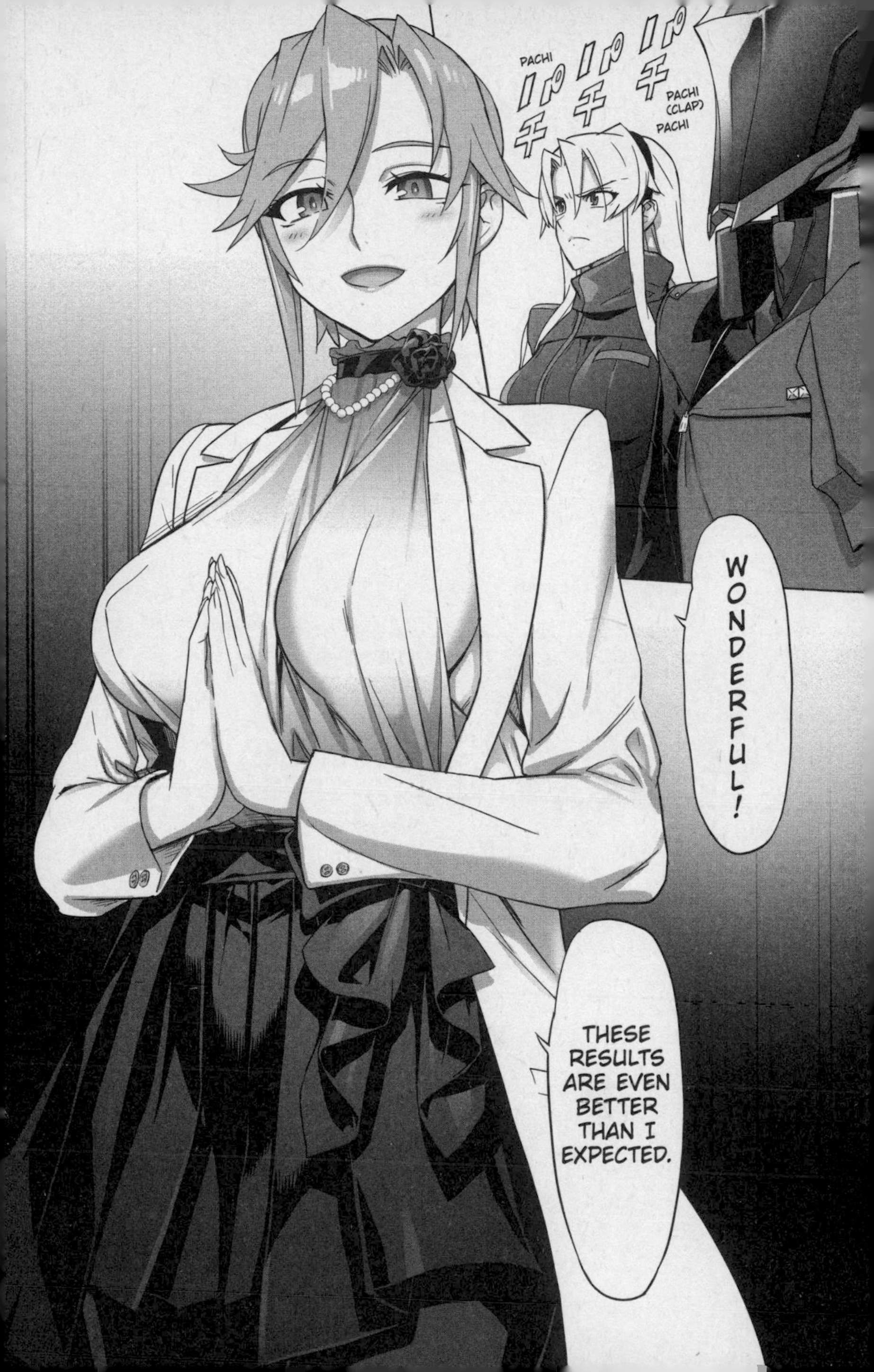
PACHI
パチパチパチ
PACHI (CLAP)
PACHI
WONDERFUL!
THESE RESULTS ARE EVEN BETTER THAN I EXPECTED.

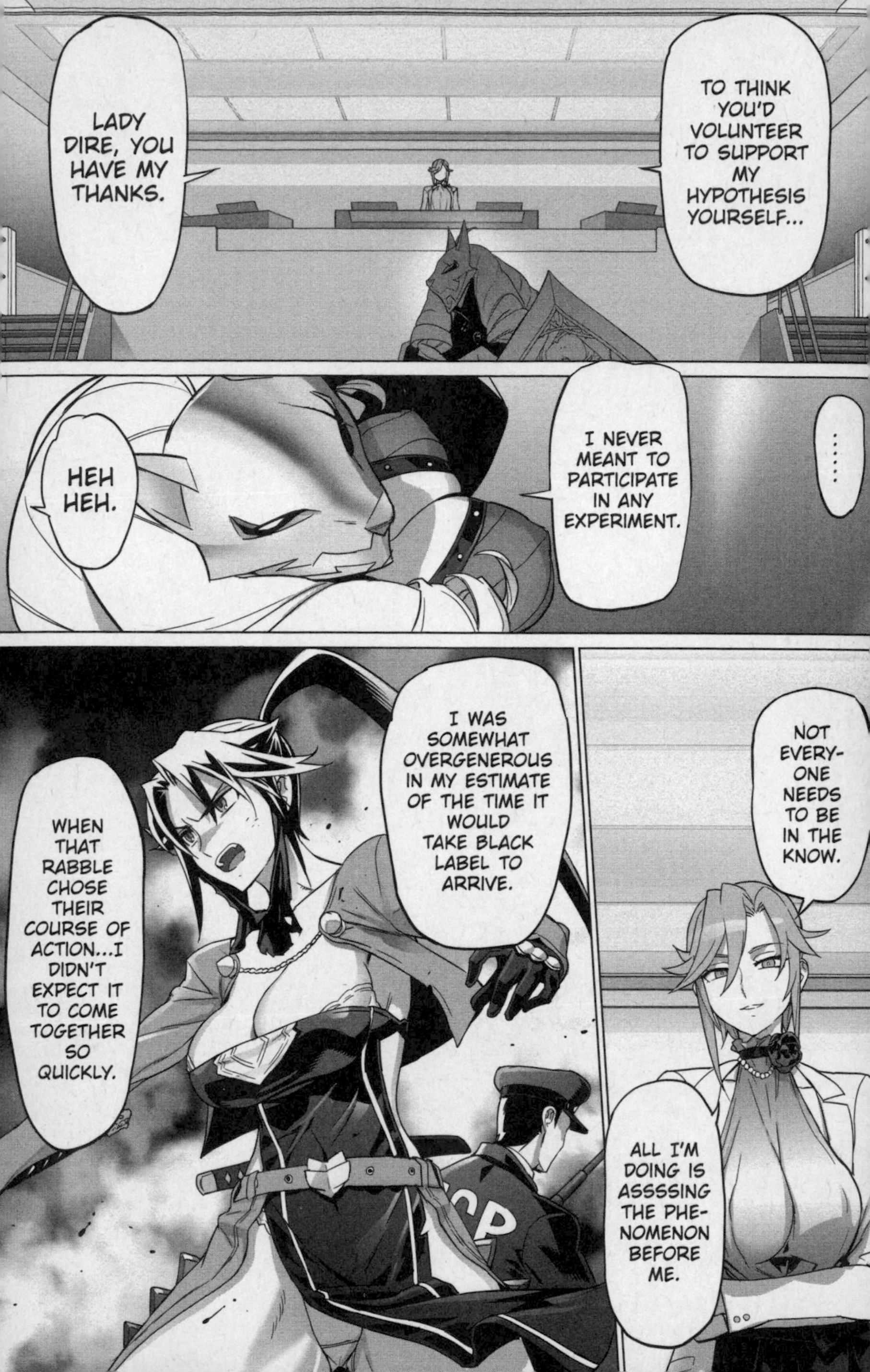
TO THINK YOU'D VOLUNTEER TO SUPPORT MY HYPOTHESIS YOURSELF...
LADY DIRE, YOU HAVE MY THANKS.
......
I NEVER MEANT TO PARTICIPATE IN ANY EXPERIMENT.
HEH HEH.
NOT EVERY-ONE NEEDS TO BE IN THE KNOW.
ALL I'M DOING IS ASSSSING THE PHE-NOMENON BEFORE ME.
I WAS SOMEWHAT OVERGENEROUS IN MY ESTIMATE OF THE TIME IT WOULD TAKE BLACK LABEL TO ARRIVE.
WHEN THAT RABBLE CHOSE THEIR COURSE OF ACTION...I DIDN'T EXPECT IT TO COME TOGETHER SO QUICKLY.
SCP

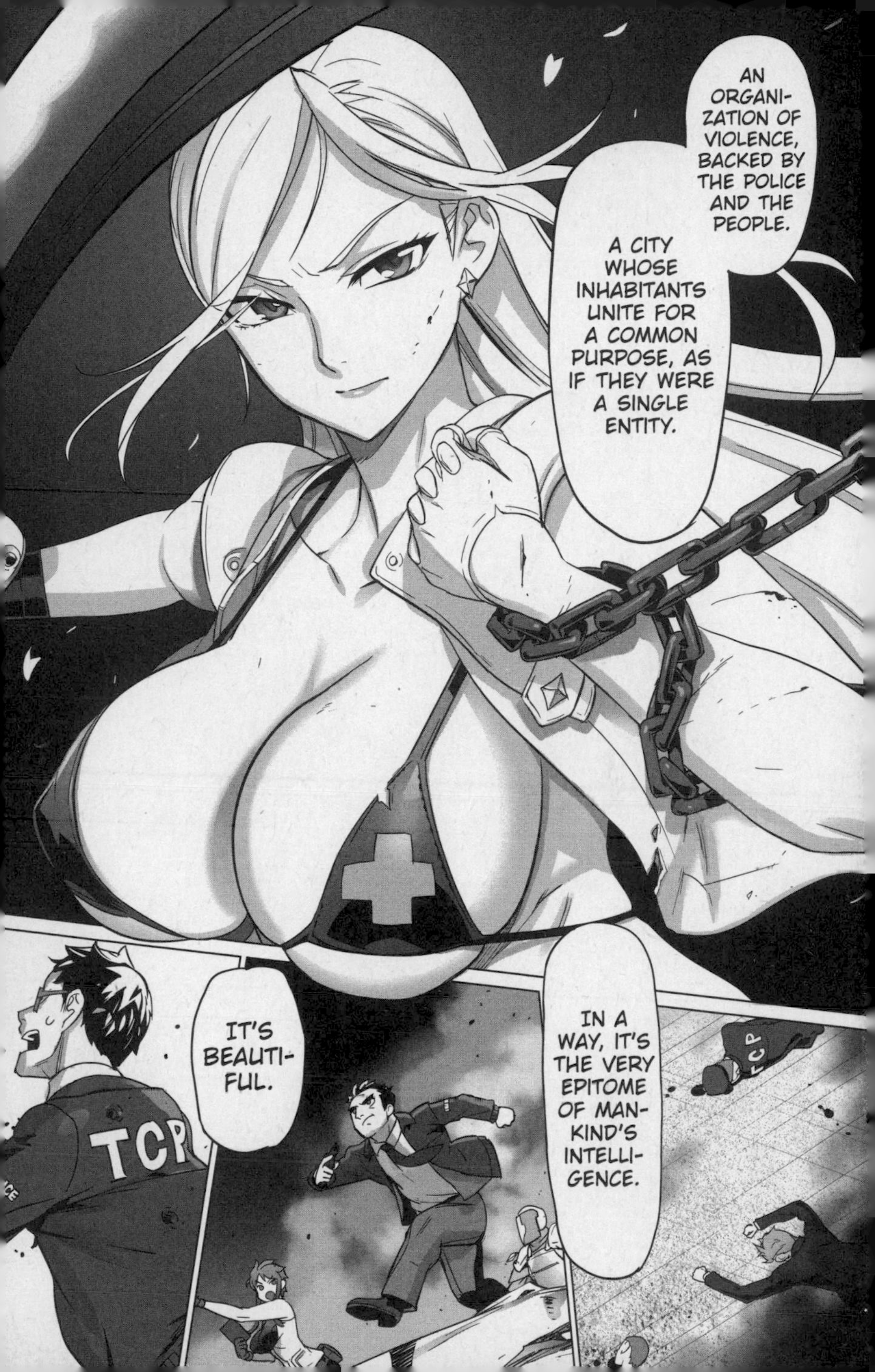
AN ORGANI-ZATION OF VIOLENCE, BACKED BY THE POLICE AND THE PEOPLE.
A CITY WHOSE INHABITANTS UNITE FOR A COMMON PURPOSE, AS IF THEY WERE A SINGLE ENTITY.
IN A WAY, IT'S THE VERY EPITOME OF MAN-KIND'S INTELLI-GENCE.
IT'S BEAUTI-FUL.
TCP
TCP

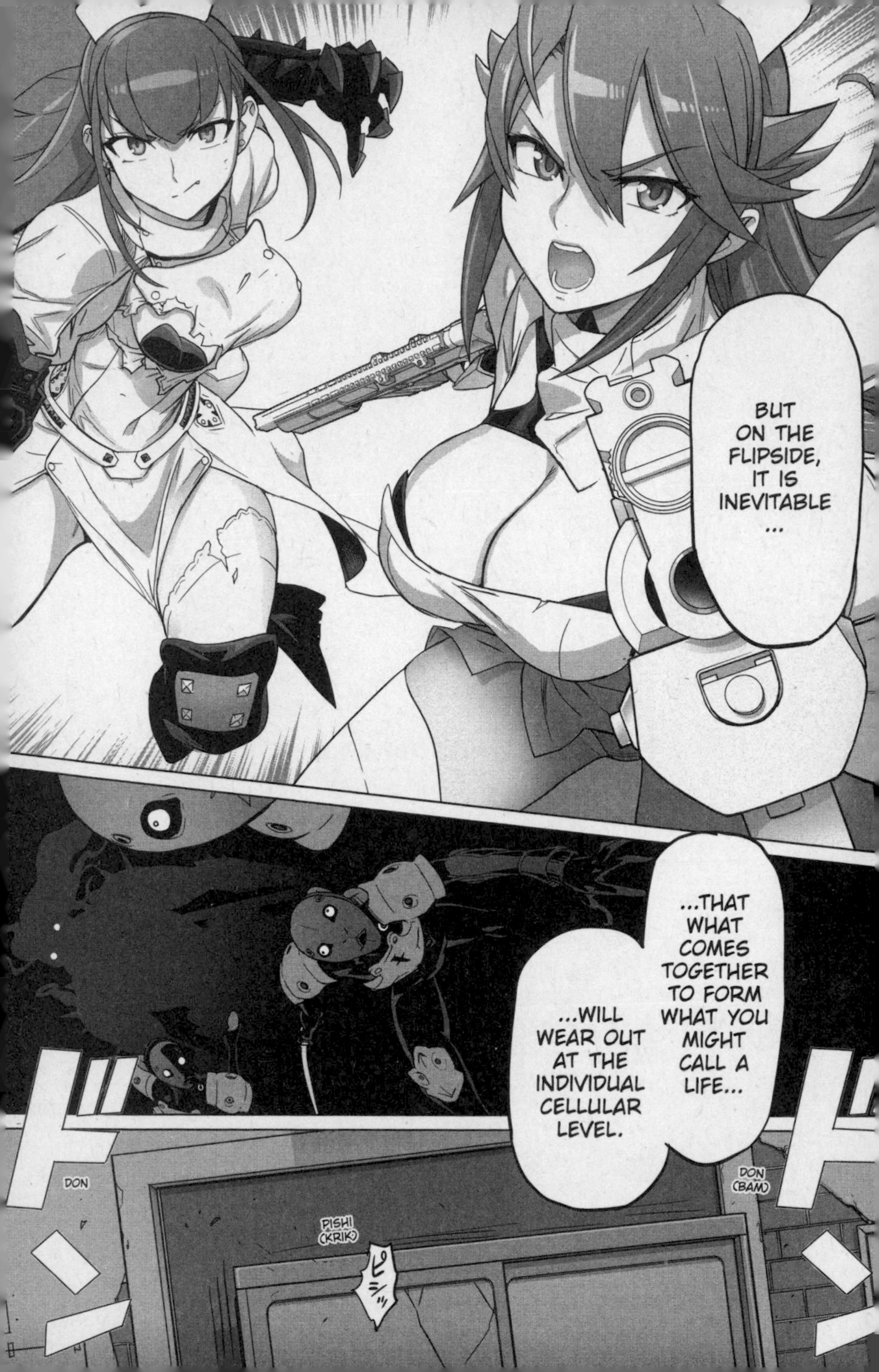
BUT ON THE FLIPSIDE, IT IS INEVITABLE ...
...THAT WHAT COMES TOGETHER TO FORM WHAT YOU MIGHT CALL A LIFE...
...WILL WEAR OUT AT THE INDIVIDUAL CELLULAR LEVEL.
DON (BAM)
PISHI (KRIK)
DON

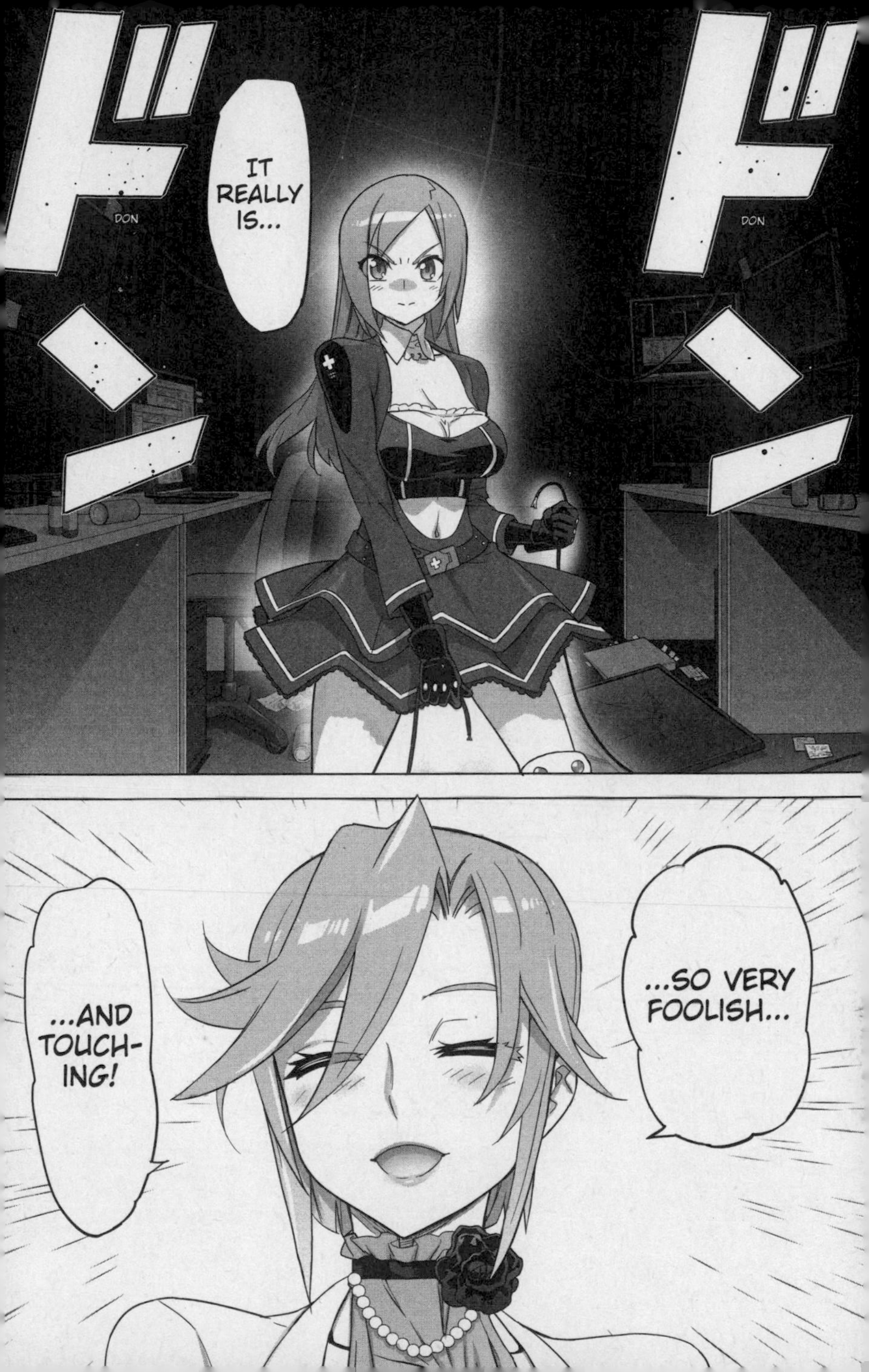
ドーン
DON
IT REALLY IS...
ドーン
DON
...SO VERY FOOLISH...
...AND TOUCH-ING!

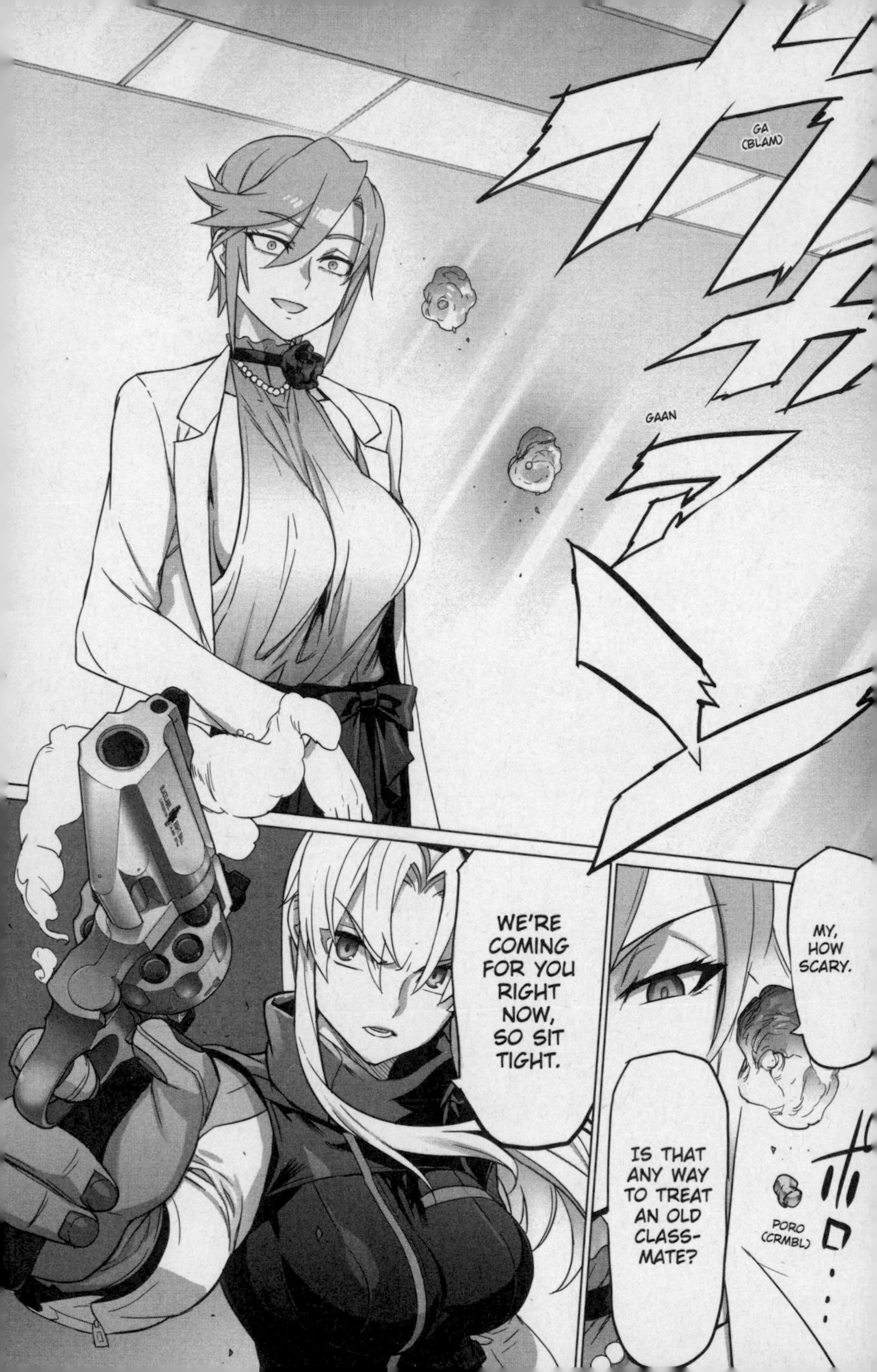
GA (BLAM)
GAAN
MY, HOW SCARY.
IS THAT ANY WAY TO TREAT AN OLD CLASS-MATE?
PORO (CRMBL)
WE'RE COMING FOR YOU RIGHT NOW, SO SIT TIGHT.

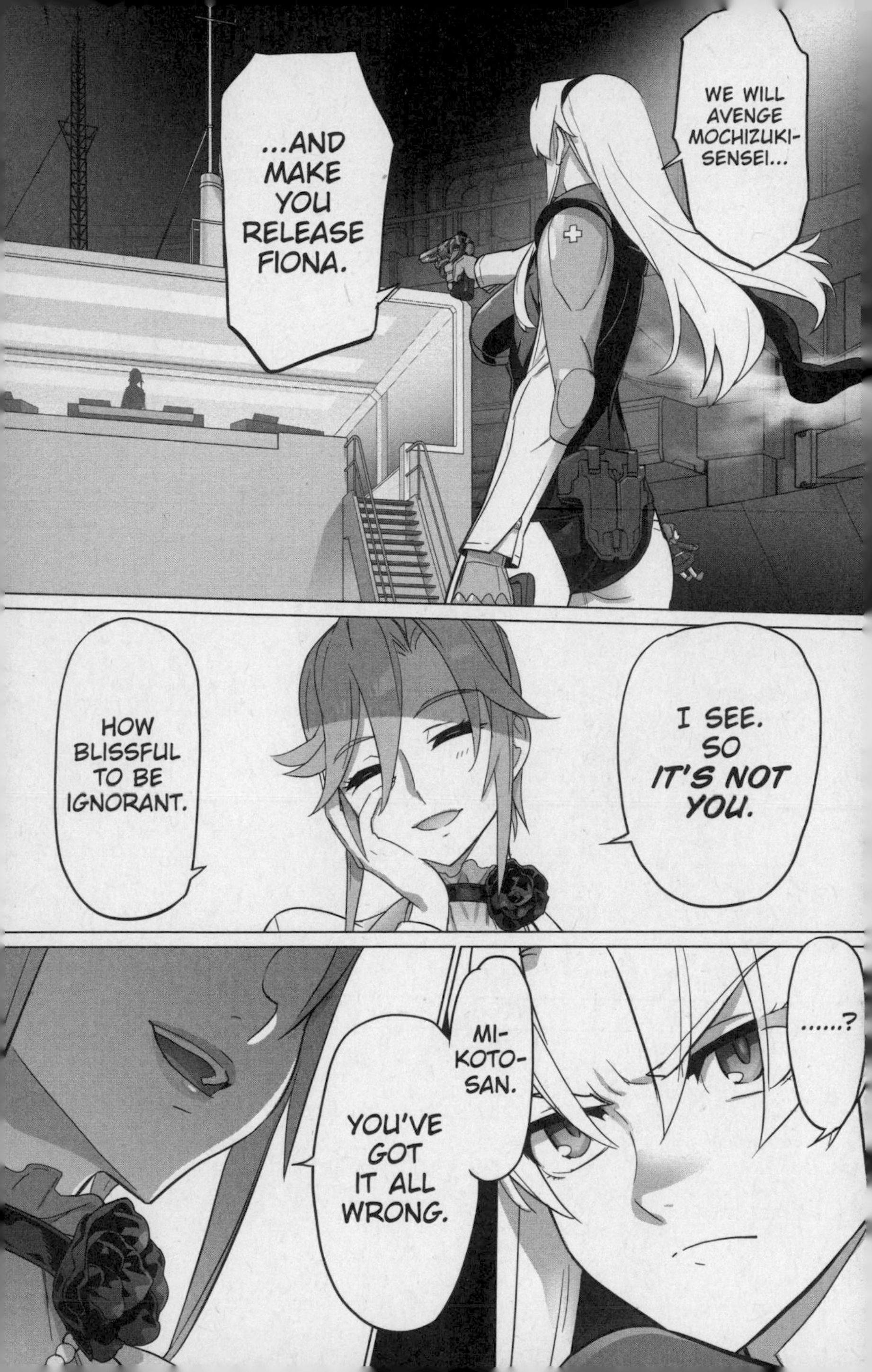

WE WILL AVENGE MOCHIZUKI-SENSEI...
...AND MAKE YOU RELEASE FIONA.
I SEE. SO IT'S NOT YOU.
HOW BLISSFUL TO BE IGNORANT.
......?
MI-KOTO-SAN.
YOU'VE GOT IT ALL WRONG.

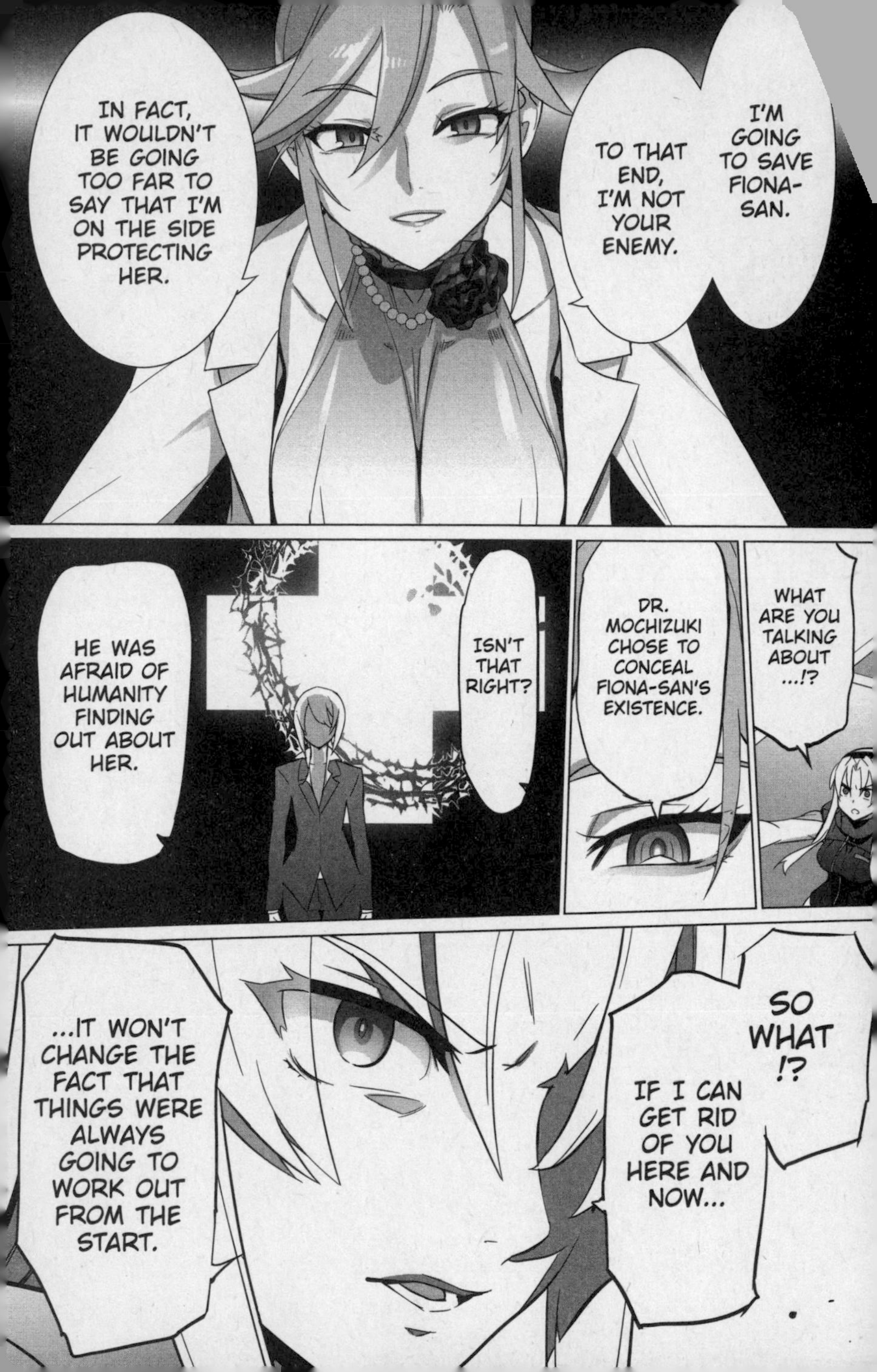
I'M GOING TO SAVE FIONA-SAN.
TO THAT END, I'M NOT YOUR ENEMY.
IN FACT, IT WOULDN'T BE GOING TOO FAR TO SAY THAT I'M ON THE SIDE PROTECTING HER.
WHAT ARE YOU TALKING ABOUT ...!?
DR. MOCHIZUKI CHOSE TO CONCEAL FIONA-SAN'S EXISTENCE.
ISN'T THAT RIGHT?
HE WAS AFRAID OF HUMANITY FINDING OUT ABOUT HER.
SO WHAT !?
IF I CAN GET RID OF YOU HERE AND NOW...
...IT WON'T CHANGE THE FACT THAT THINGS WERE ALWAYS GOING TO WORK OUT FROM THE START.

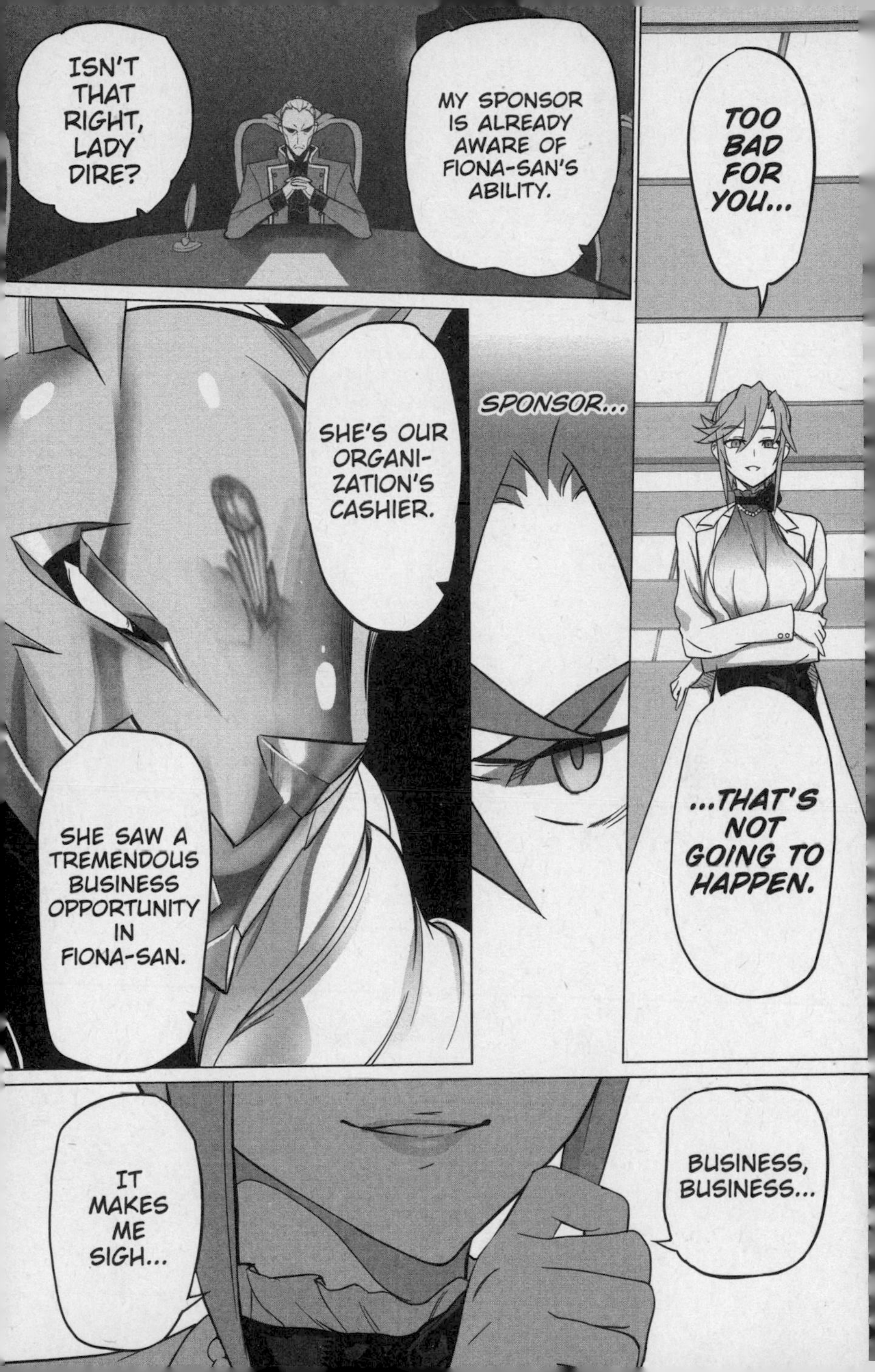
MY SPONSOR IS ALREADY AWARE OF FIONA-SAN'S ABILITY.
ISN'T THAT RIGHT, LADY DIRE?
SPONSOR...
SHE'S OUR ORGANIZATION'S CASHIER.
SHE SAW A TREMENDOUS BUSINESS OPPORTUNITY IN FIONA-SAN.
TOO BAD FOR YOU...
...THAT'S NOT GOING TO HAPPEN.
BUSINESS, BUSINESS...
IT MAKES ME SIGH...

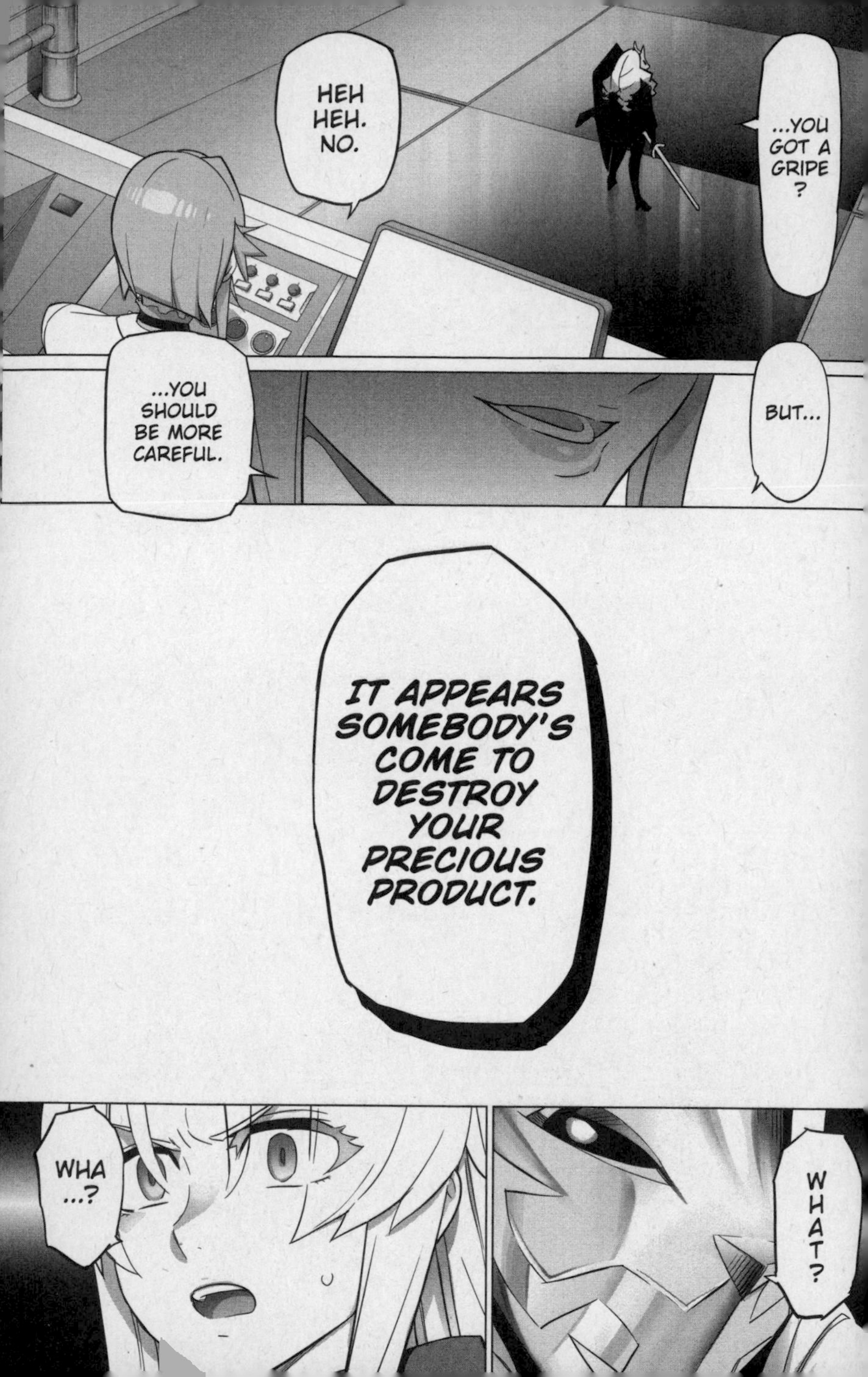
...YOU GOT A GRIPE?
HEH HEH. NO.
BUT...
...YOU SHOULD BE MORE CAREFUL.
IT APPEARS SOMEBODY'S COME TO DESTROY YOUR PRECIOUS PRODUCT.
WHAT?
WHA...?

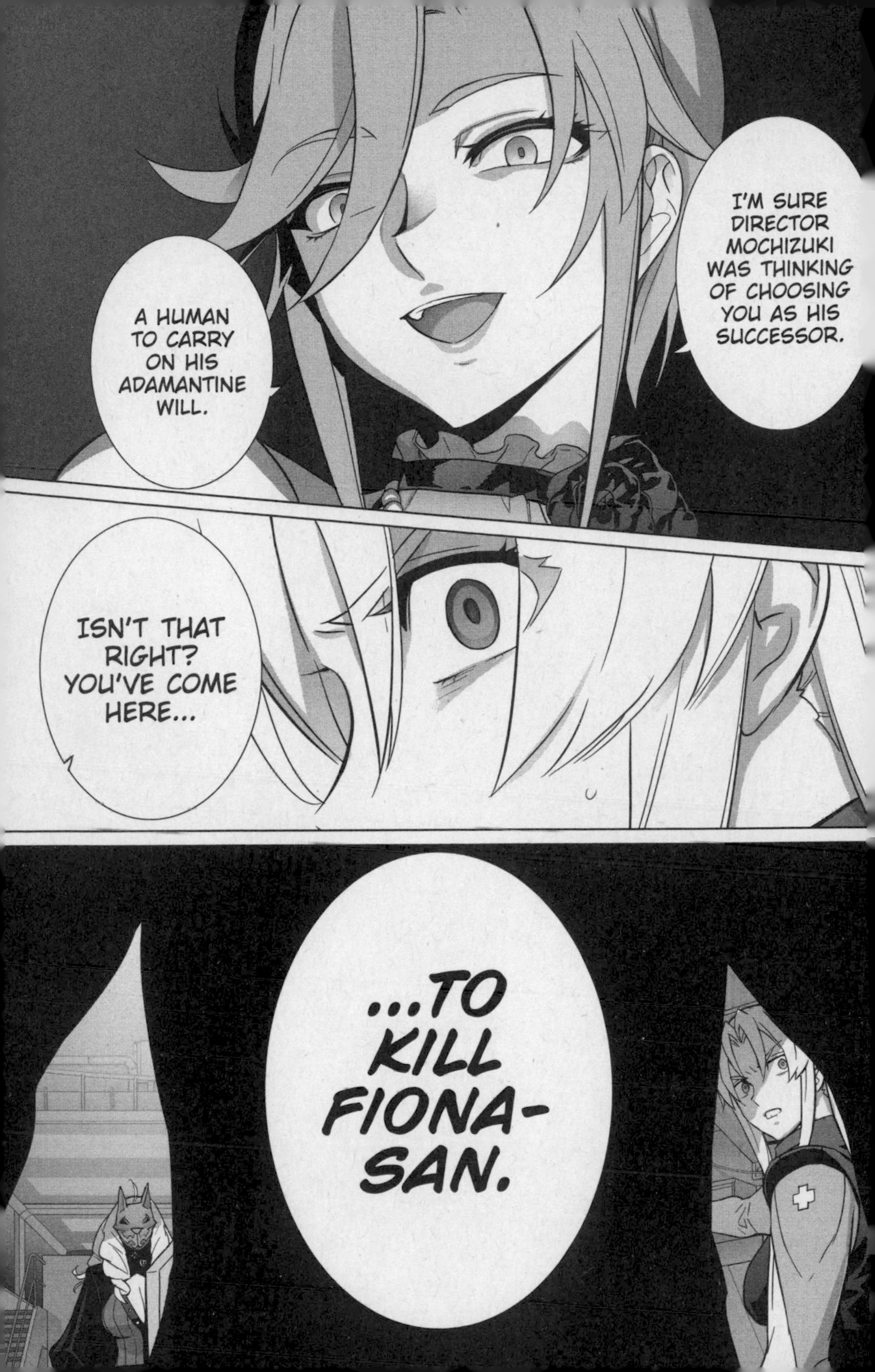
I'M SURE DIRECTOR MOCHIZUKI WAS THINKING OF CHOOSING YOU AS HIS SUCCESSOR.
A HUMAN TO CARRY ON HIS ADAMANTINE WILL.
ISN'T THAT RIGHT? YOU'VE COME HERE...
...TO KILL FIONA-SAN.

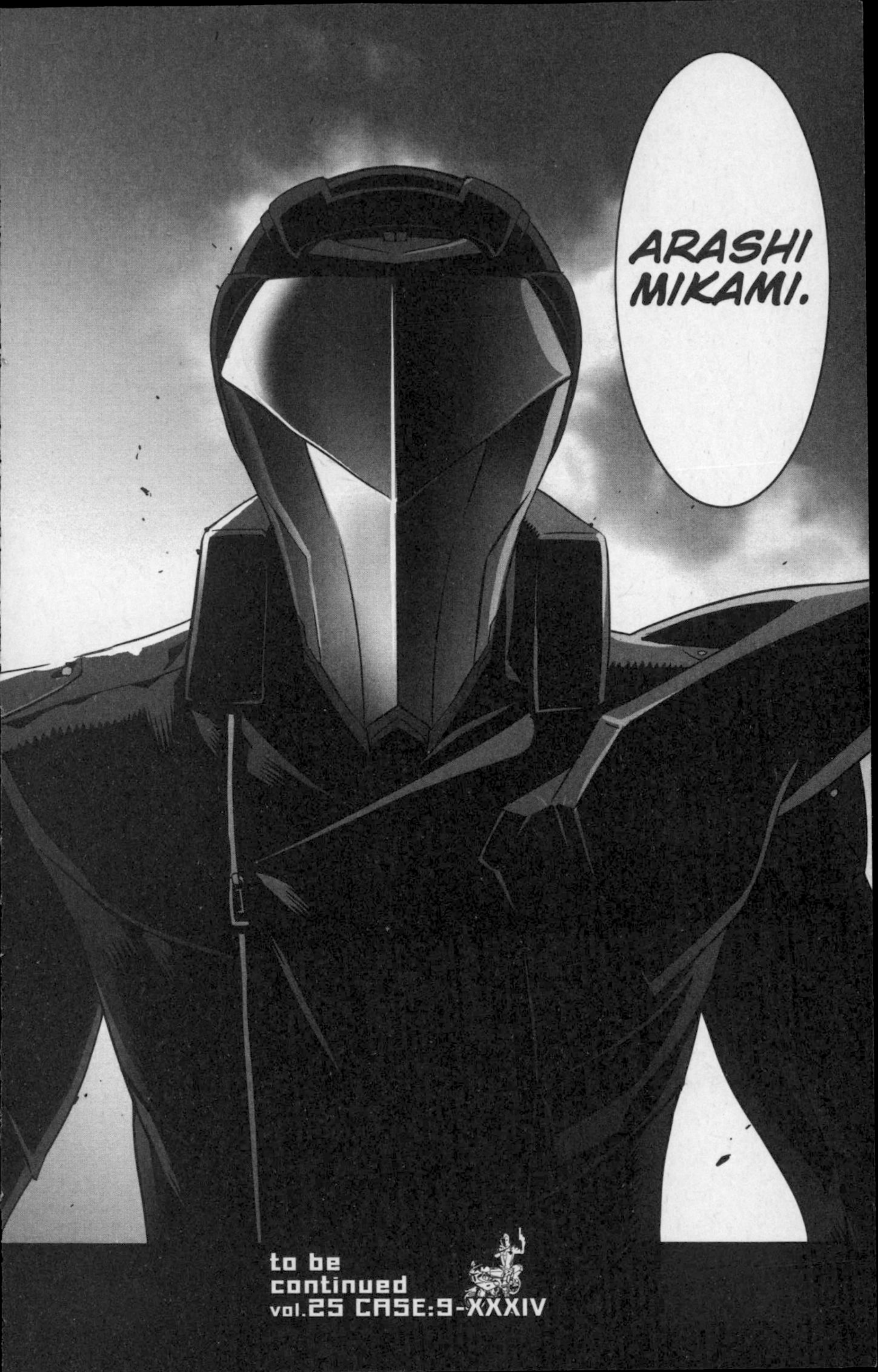
ARASHI MIKAMI.
to be continued
vol.25 CASE:9-XXXIV

TRIAGE X

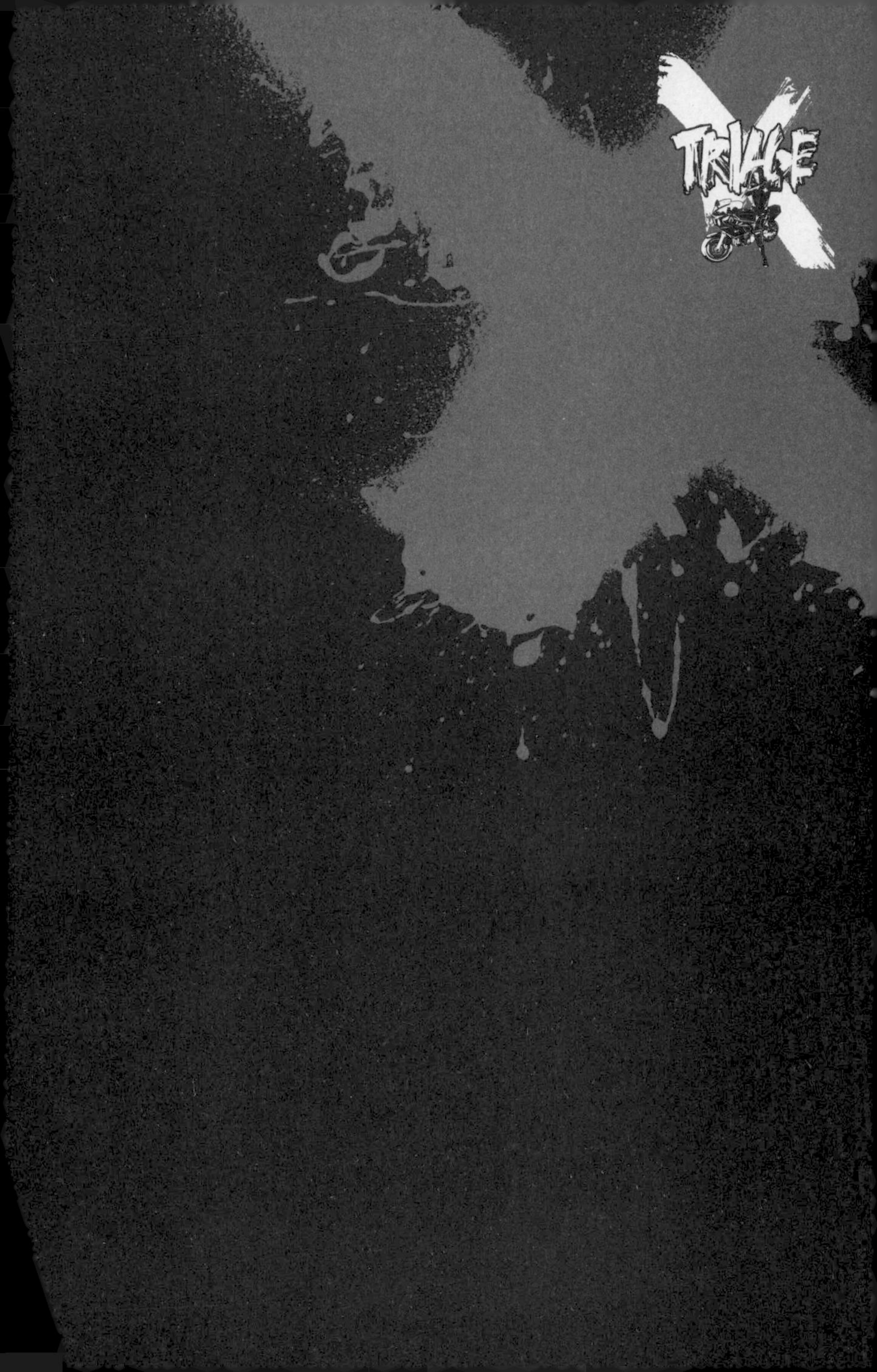
TRIAGE X

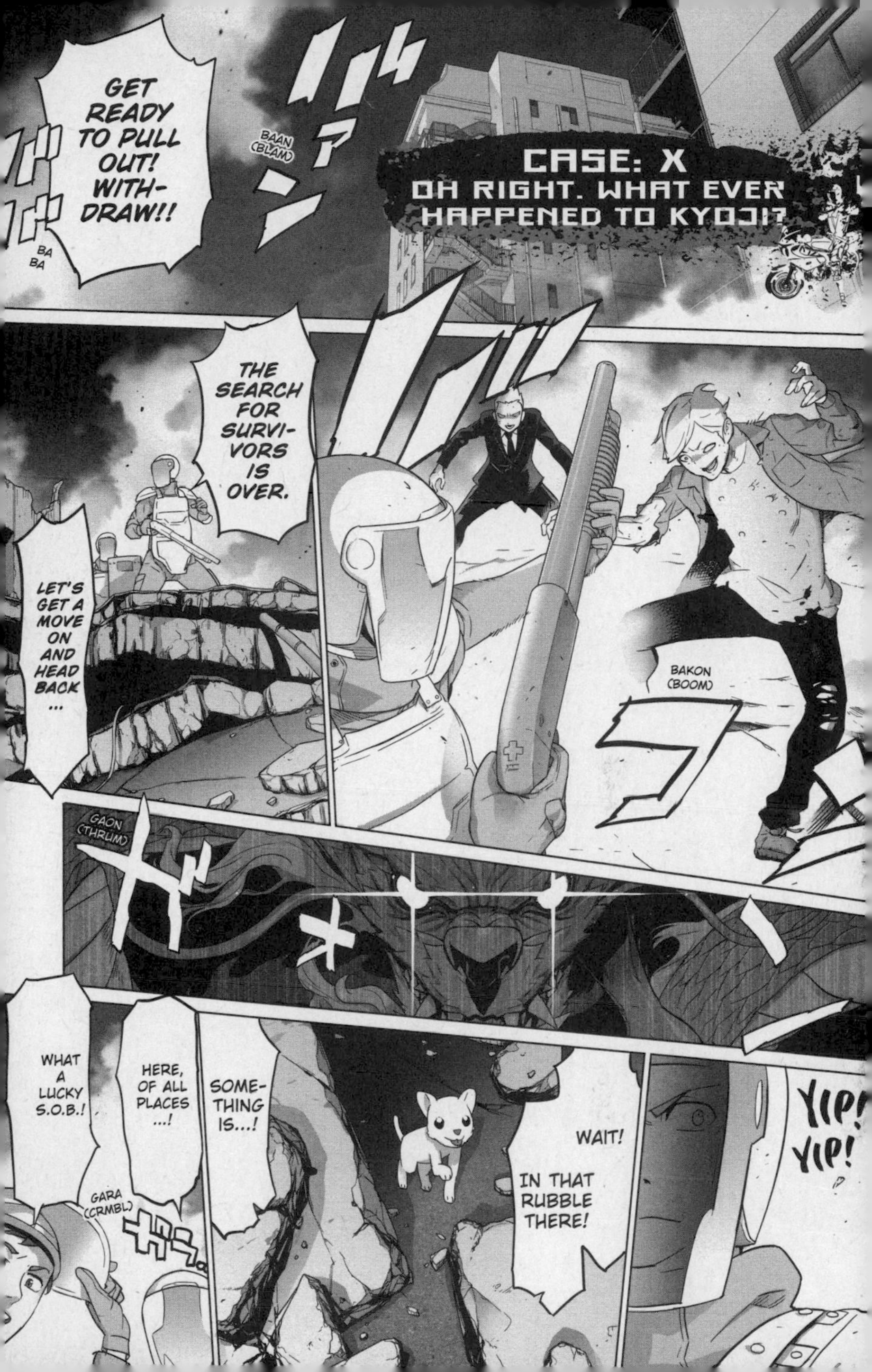
CASE: X
OH RIGHT. WHAT EVER HAPPENED TO KYOJI?
BAAN (BLAM)
GET READY TO PULL OUT! WITH-DRAW!!
BA BA
BAKON (BOOM)
THE SEARCH FOR SURVI-VORS IS OVER.
LET'S GET A MOVE ON AND HEAD BACK...
GAON (THRUM)
YIP! YIP!
WAIT!
IN THAT RUBBLE THERE!
SOME-THING IS...!
HERE, OF ALL PLACES...!
WHAT A LUCKY S.O.B.!
GARA (CRMBL)

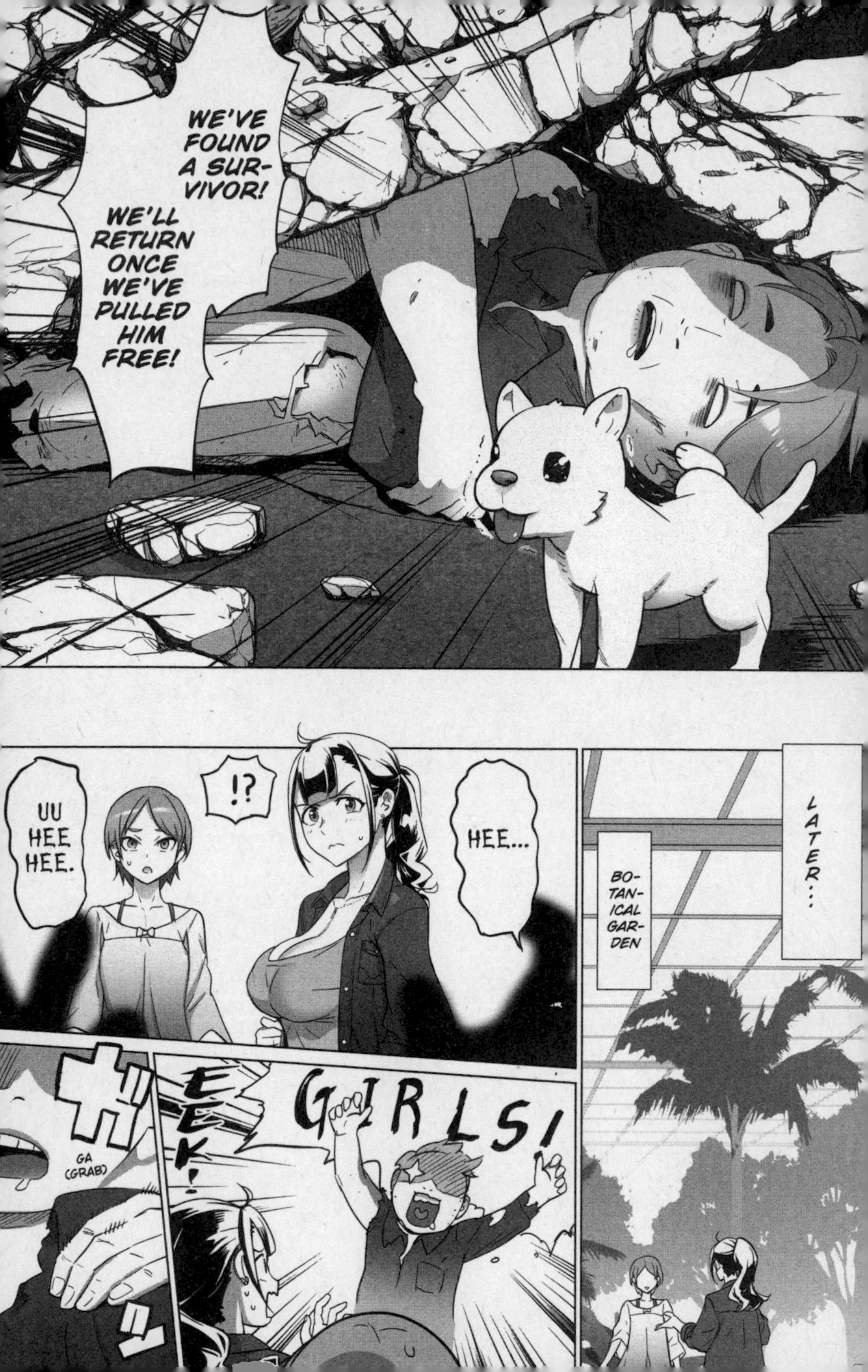
WE'VE FOUND A SUR-VIVOR!
WE'LL RETURN ONCE WE'VE PULLED HIM FREE!
LATER...
BO-TAN-ICAL GAR-DEN
HEE...
!?
UU HEE HEE.
GIRLS!
EEK!
GA (GRAB)

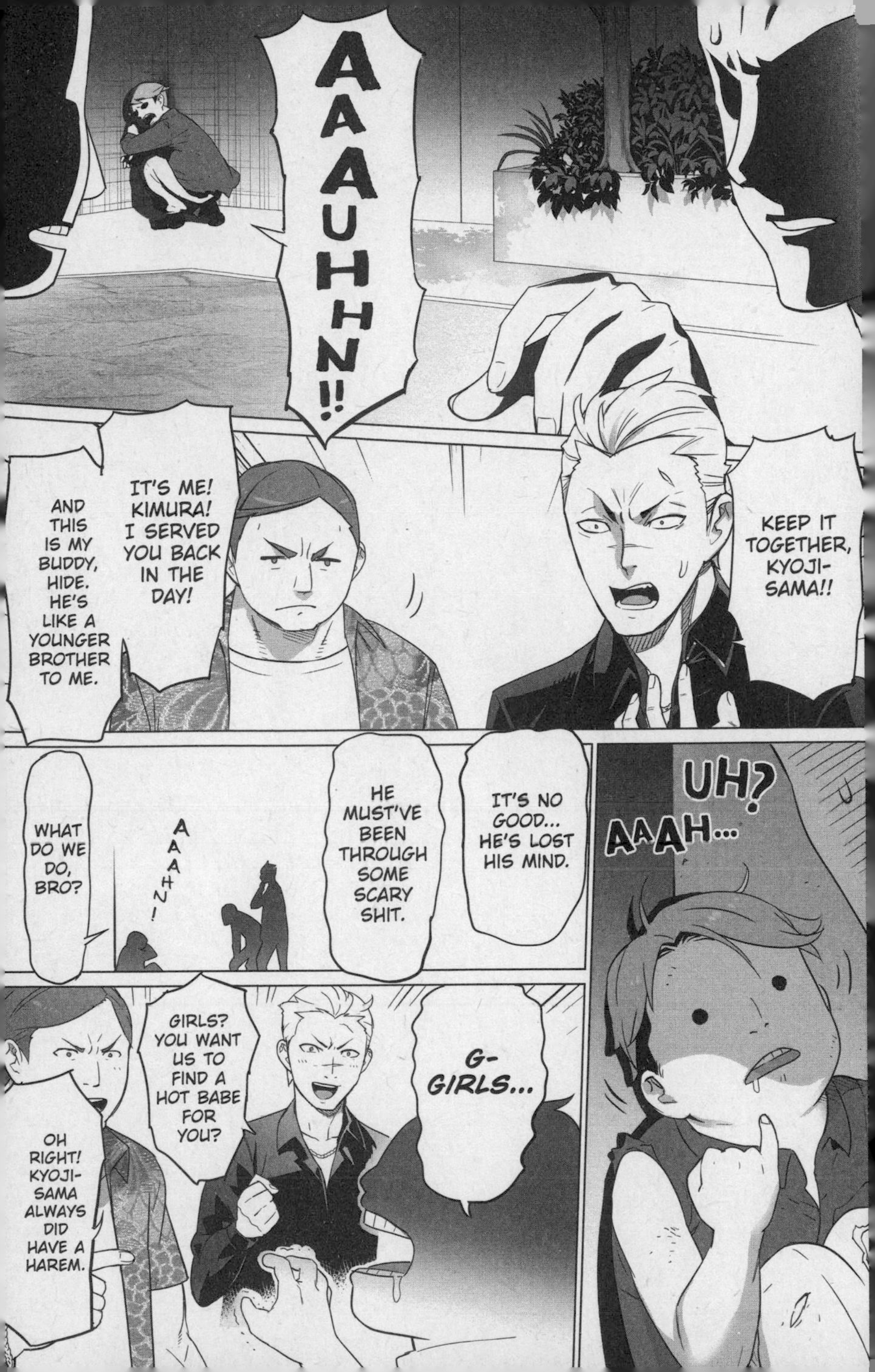
AAAUHHN!!
KEEP IT TOGETHER, KYOJI-SAMA!!
IT'S ME! KIMURA! I SERVED YOU BACK IN THE DAY!
AND THIS IS MY BUDDY, HIDE. HE'S LIKE A YOUNGER BROTHER TO ME.
UH? AAAH...
IT'S NO GOOD... HE'S LOST HIS MIND.
HE MUST'VE BEEN THROUGH SOME SCARY SHIT.
AAAHN!
WHAT DO WE DO, BRO?
G-GIRLS...
GIRLS? YOU WANT US TO FIND A HOT BABE FOR YOU?
OH RIGHT! KYOJI-SAMA ALWAYS DID HAVE A HAREM.

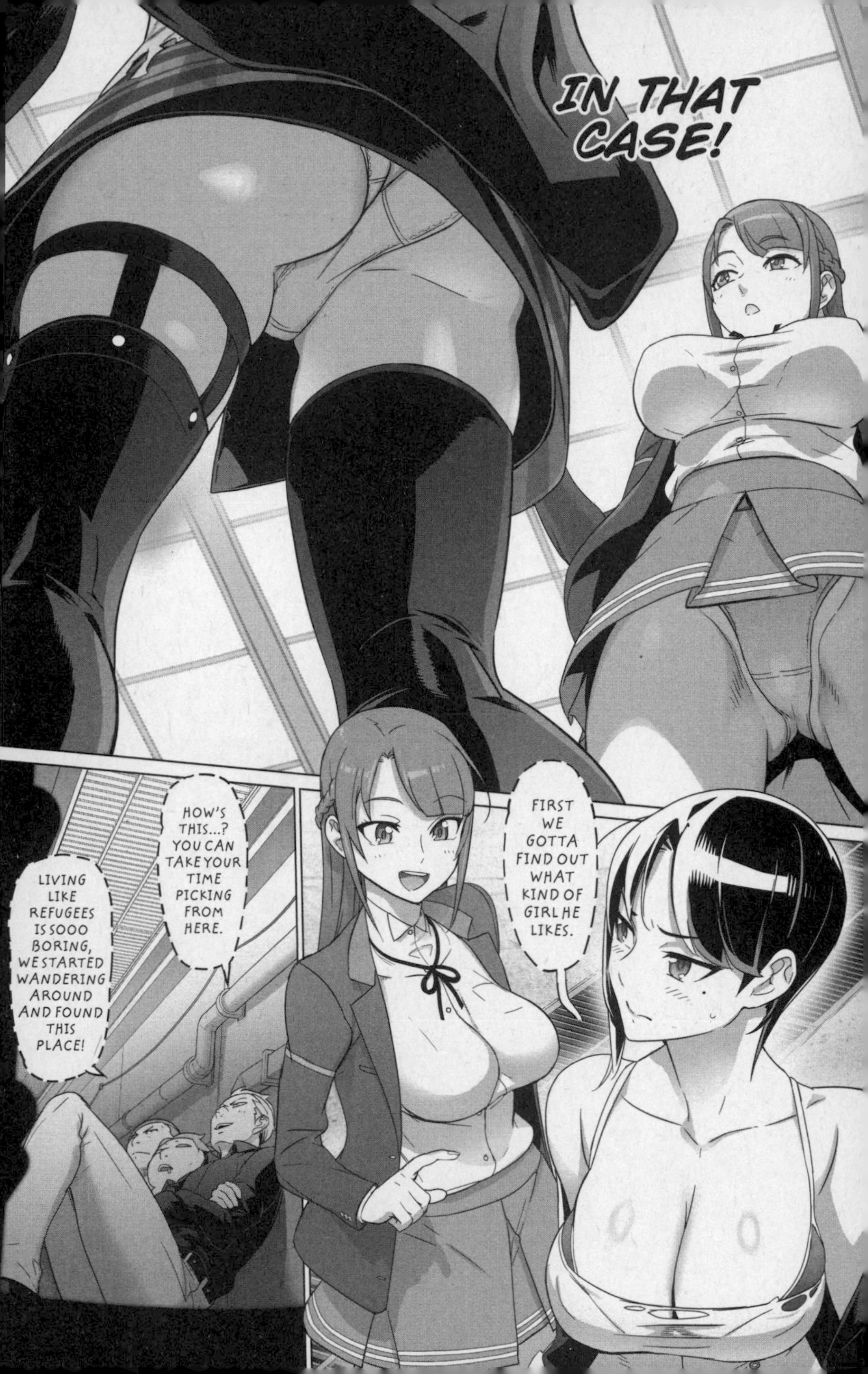
IN THAT CASE!
FIRST WE GOTTA FIND OUT WHAT KIND OF GIRL HE LIKES.
HOW'S THIS...? YOU CAN TAKE YOUR TIME PICKING FROM HERE.
LIVING LIKE REFUGEES IS SOOO BORING, WE STARTED WANDERING AROUND AND FOUND THIS PLACE!

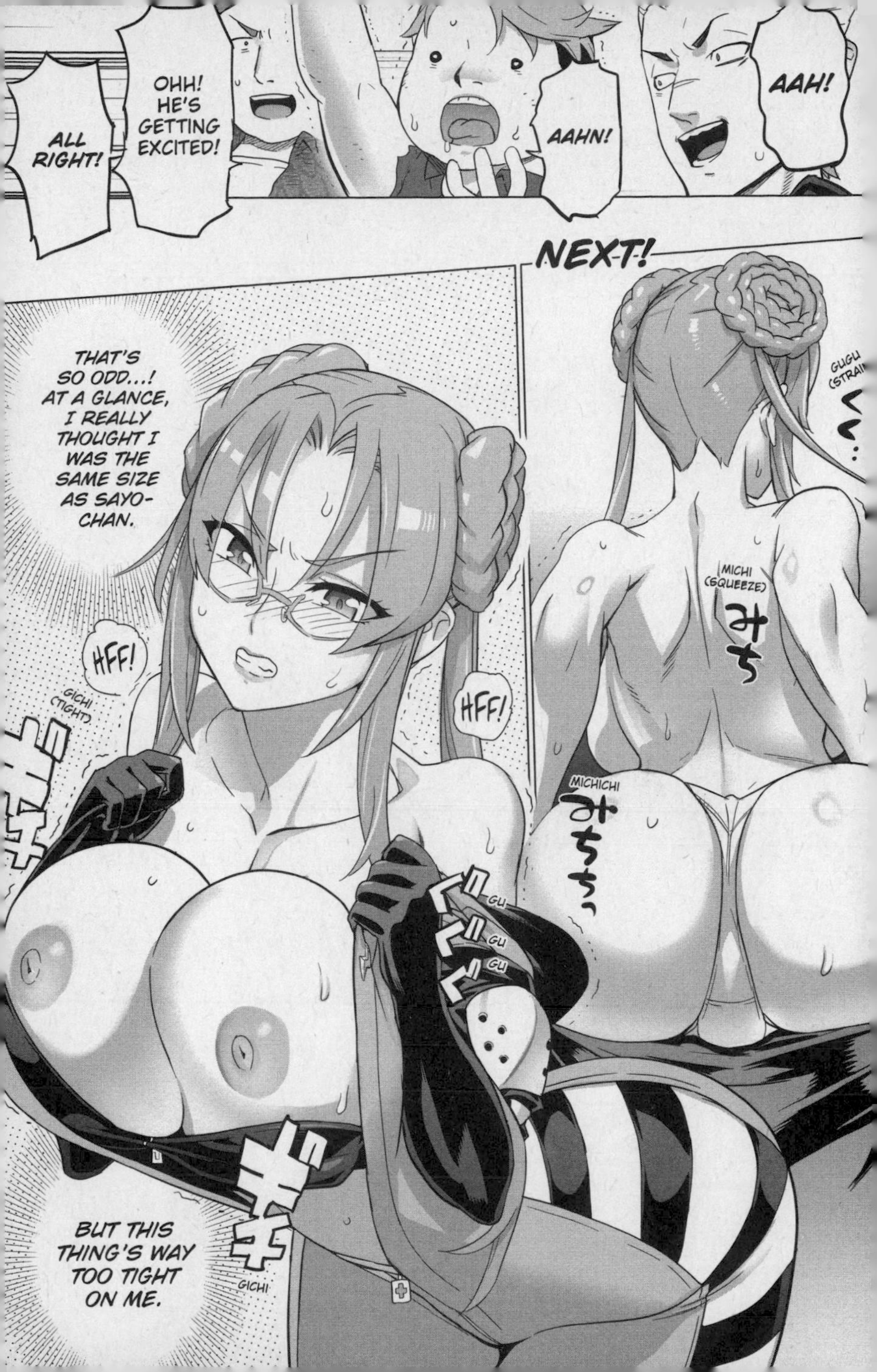
AAH!
AAHN!
OHH! HE'S GETTING EXCITED!
ALL RIGHT!
NEXT!
GUGU (STRAI
MICHI (SQUEEZE) みち
MICHICHI みちち
THAT'S SO ODD...! AT A GLANCE, I REALLY THOUGHT I WAS THE SAME SIZE AS SAYO-CHAN.
HFF!
HFF!
GICHI (TIGHT)
GU GU GU
BUT THIS THING'S WAY TOO TIGHT ON ME.
GICHI

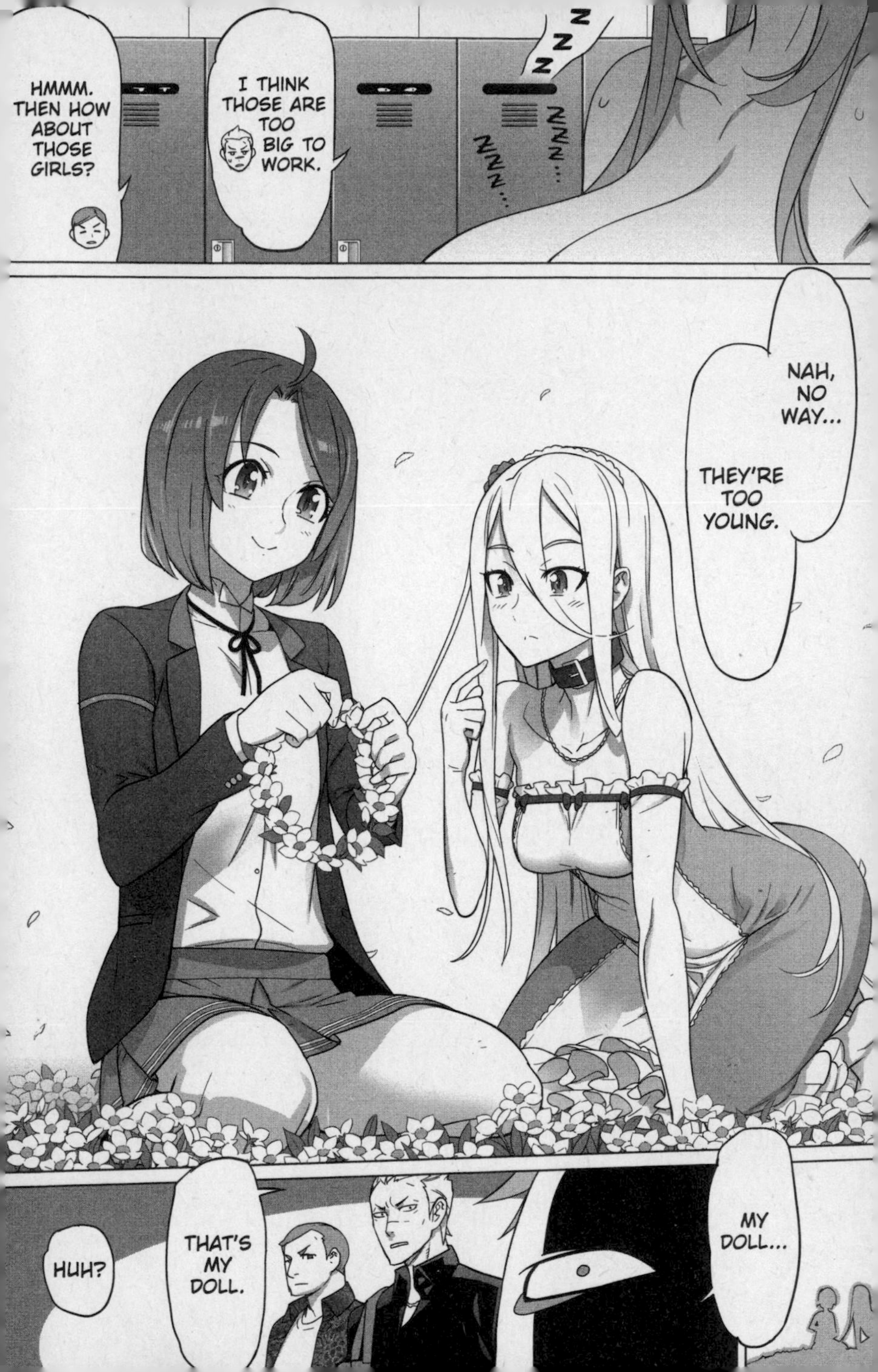

ZZZ
ZZZ...
ZZZ...
I THINK THOSE ARE TOO BIG TO WORK.
HMMM. THEN HOW ABOUT THOSE GIRLS?
NAH, NO WAY...
THEY'RE TOO YOUNG.
MY DOLL...
THAT'S MY DOLL.
HUH?

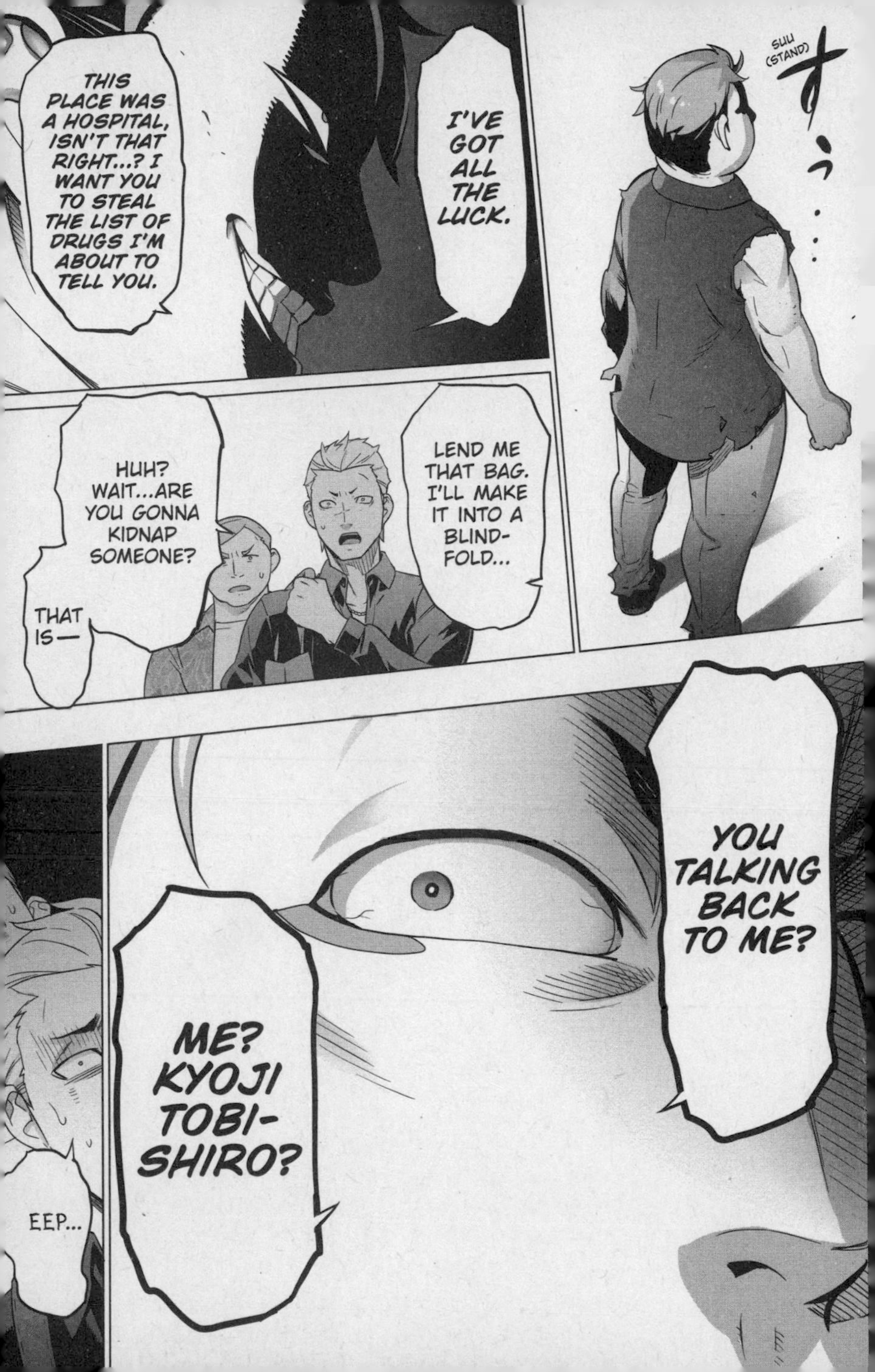
SUU (STAND)
I'VE GOT ALL THE LUCK.
THIS PLACE WAS A HOSPITAL, ISN'T THAT RIGHT...? I WANT YOU TO STEAL THE LIST OF DRUGS I'M ABOUT TO TELL YOU.
LEND ME THAT BAG. I'LL MAKE IT INTO A BLIND-FOLD...
HUH? WAIT...ARE YOU GONNA KIDNAP SOMEONE?
THAT IS—
YOU TALKING BACK TO ME?
ME? KYOJI TOBI-SHIRO?
EEP...

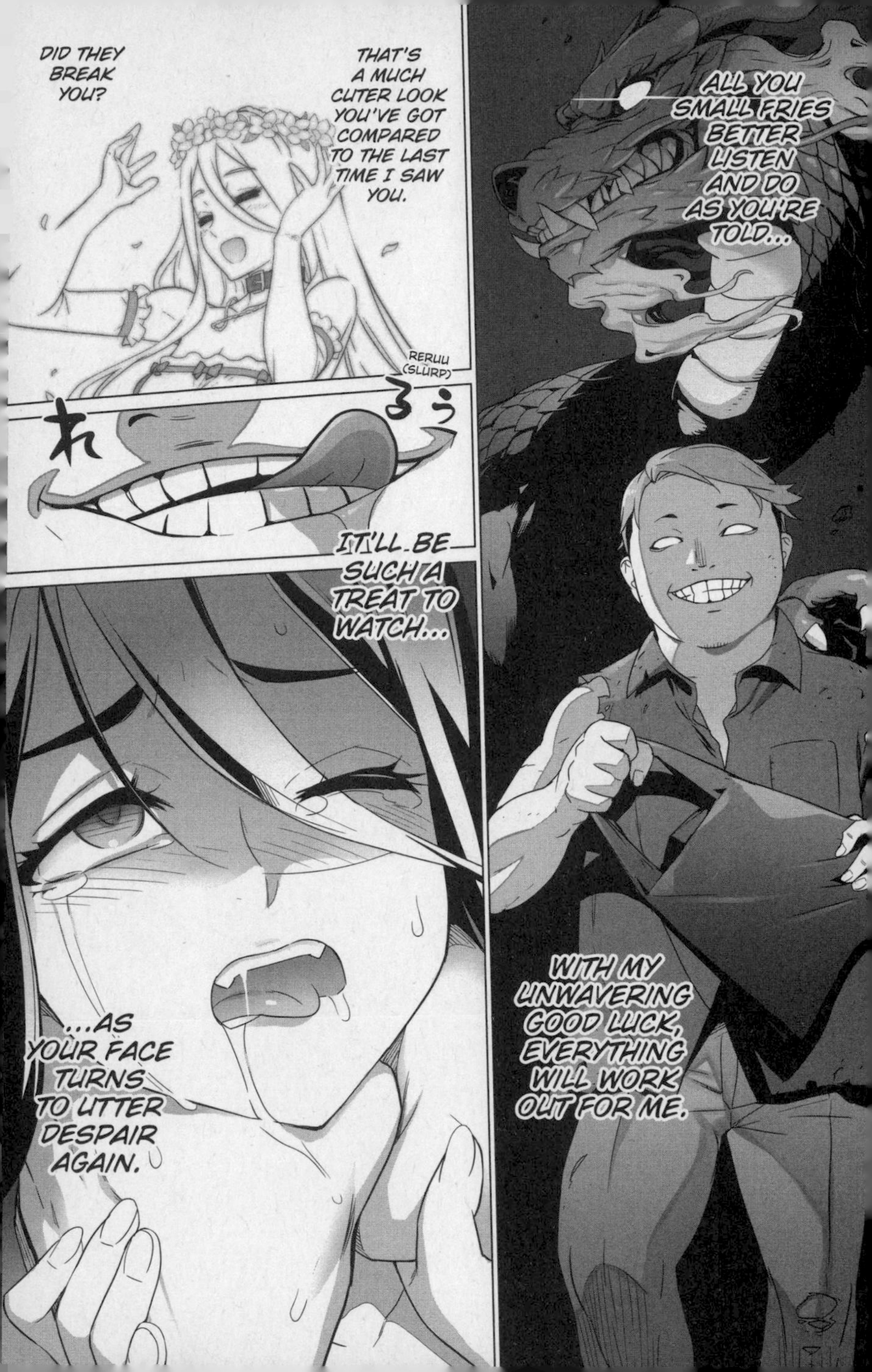
ALL YOU SMALL FRIES BETTER LISTEN AND DO AS YOU'RE TOLD...
WITH MY UNWAVERING GOOD LUCK, EVERYTHING WILL WORK OUT FOR ME.
THAT'S A MUCH CUTER LOOK YOU'VE GOT COMPARED TO THE LAST TIME I SAW YOU.
DID THEY BREAK YOU?
RERUU (SLURP)
れろぅ
IT'LL BE SUCH A TREAT TO WATCH...
...AS YOUR FACE TURNS TO UTTER DESPAIR AGAIN.

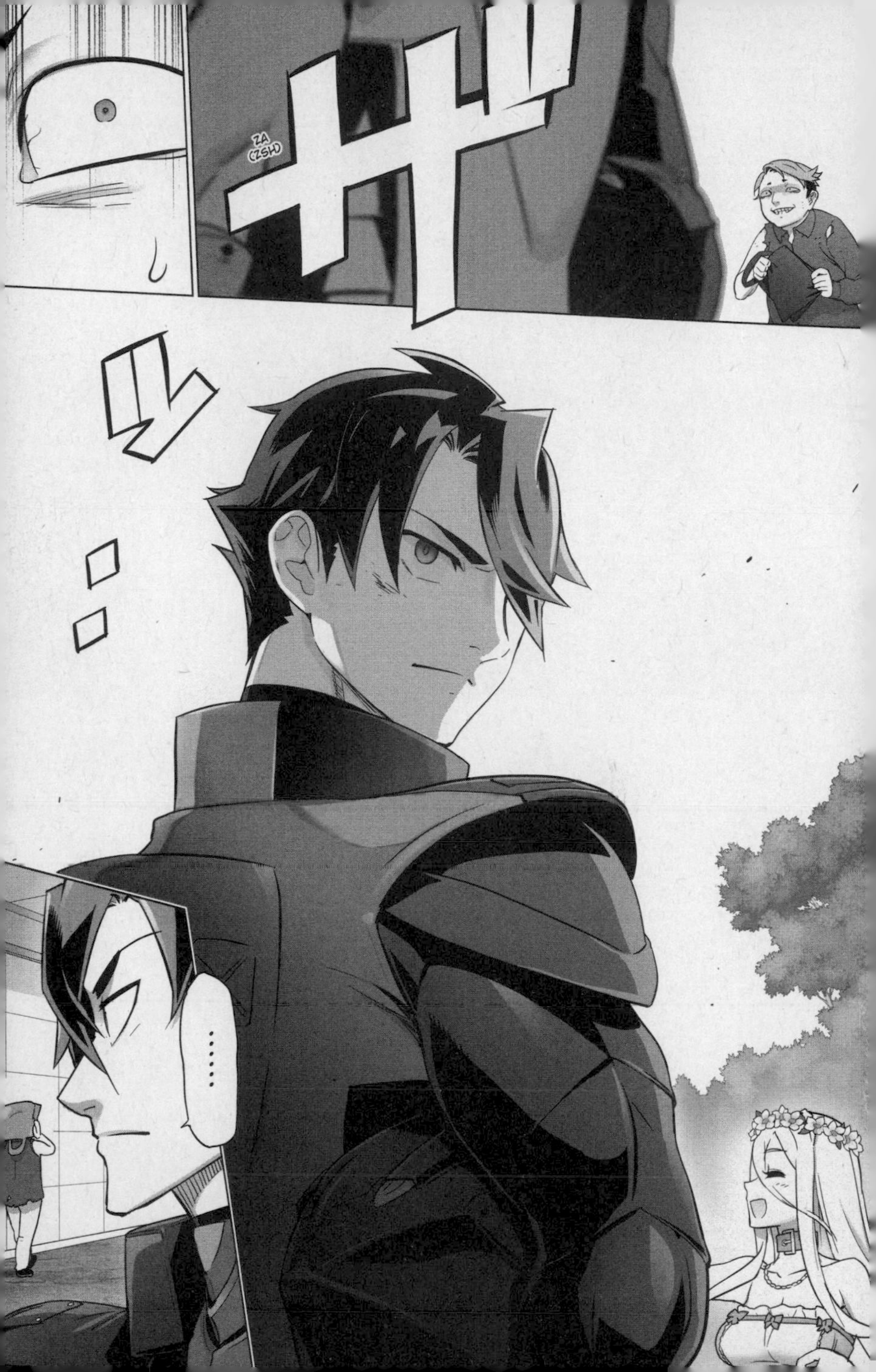

ザッ
ZA
(ZSH)
……

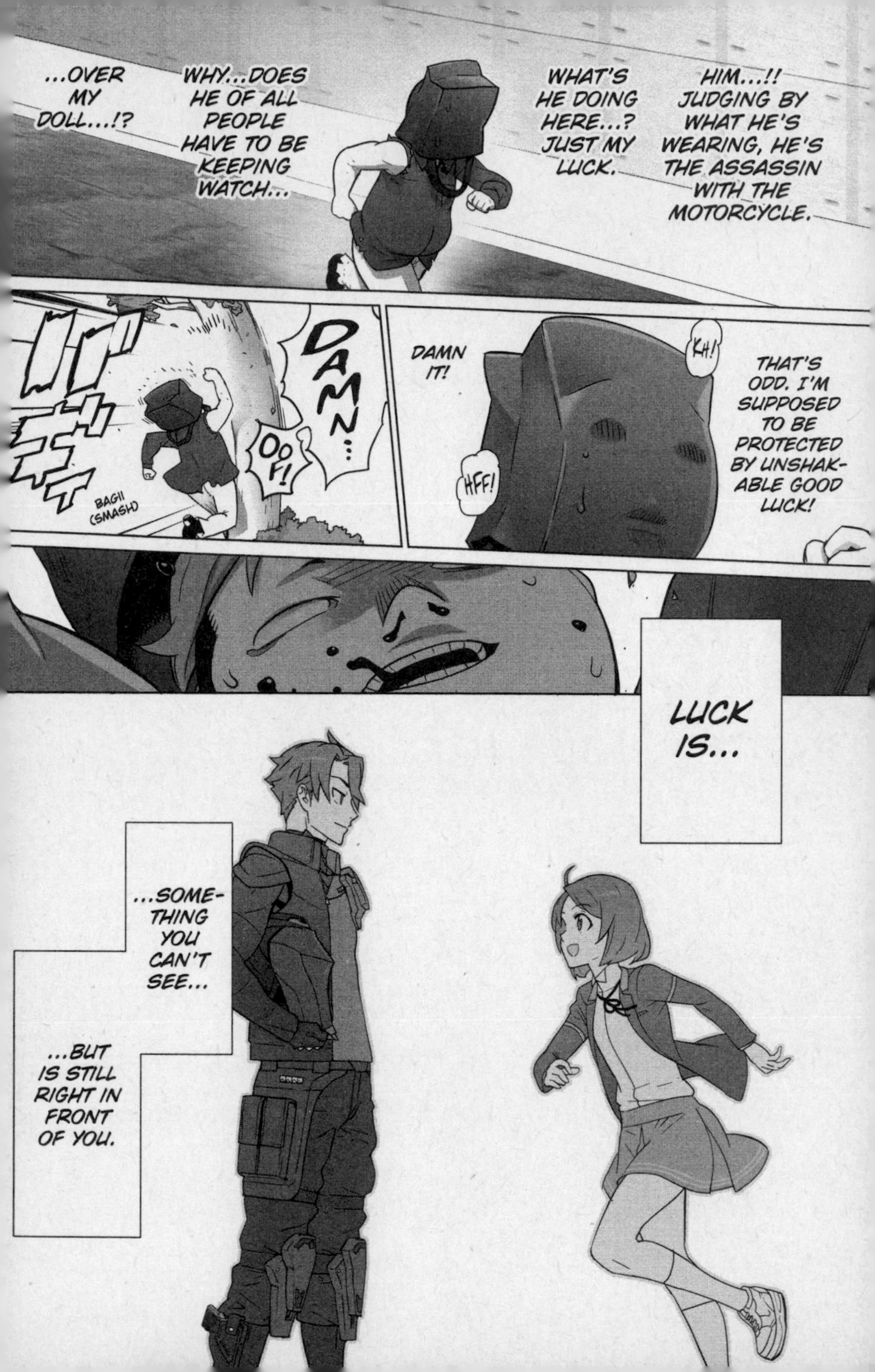
HIM...!! JUDGING BY WHAT HE'S WEARING, HE'S THE ASSASSIN WITH THE MOTORCYCLE.
WHAT'S HE DOING HERE...? JUST MY LUCK.
WHY...DOES HE OF ALL PEOPLE HAVE TO BE KEEPING WATCH...
...OVER MY DOLL...!?
KH!
THAT'S ODD. I'M SUPPOSED TO BE PROTECTED BY UNSHAK-ABLE GOOD LUCK!
DAMN IT!
HFF!
DAMN...
OOF!
BAGII (SMASH)
LUCK IS...
...SOME-THING YOU CAN'T SEE...
...BUT IS STILL RIGHT IN FRONT OF YOU.

TRIAGE X

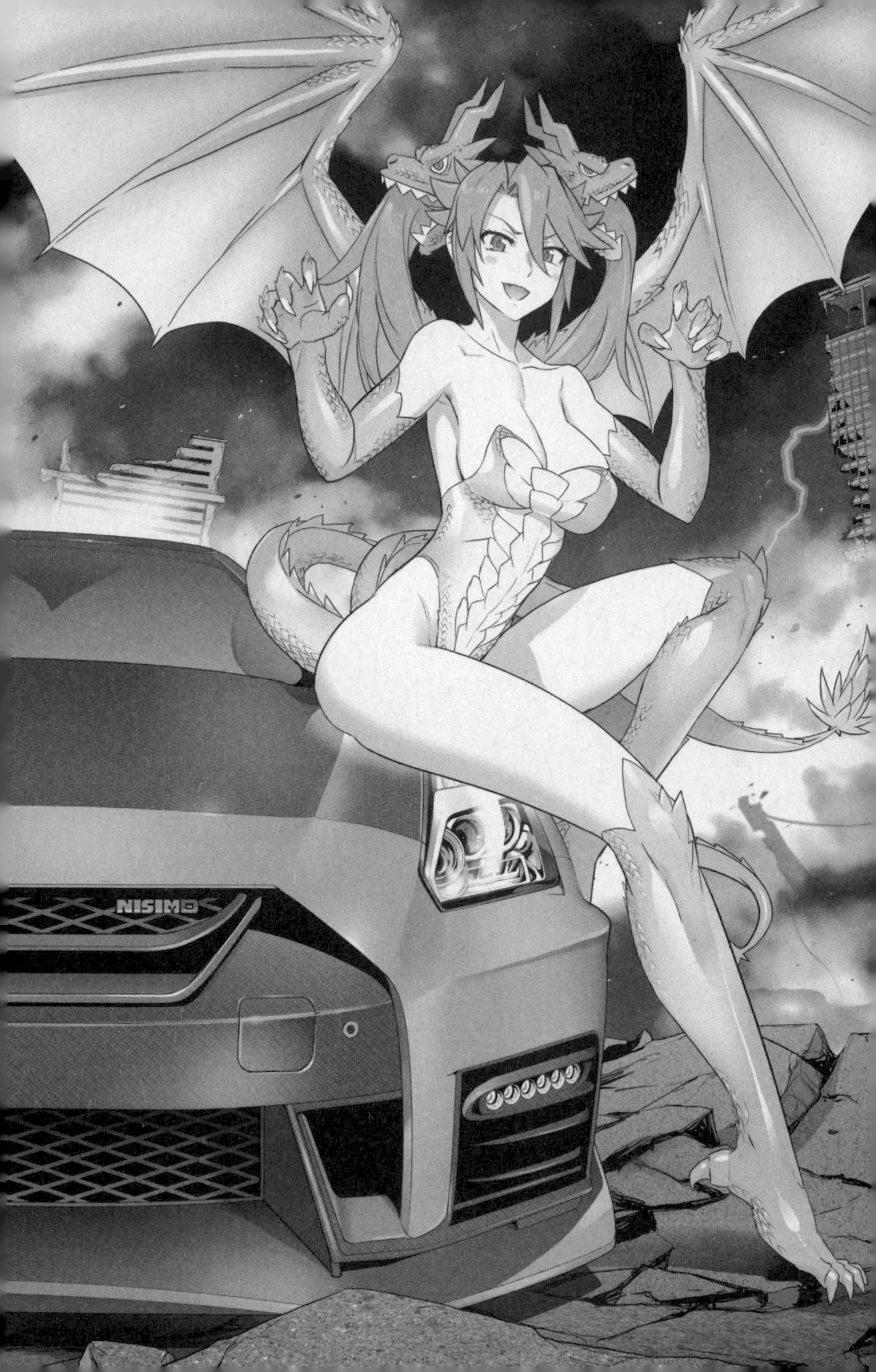
NISMO

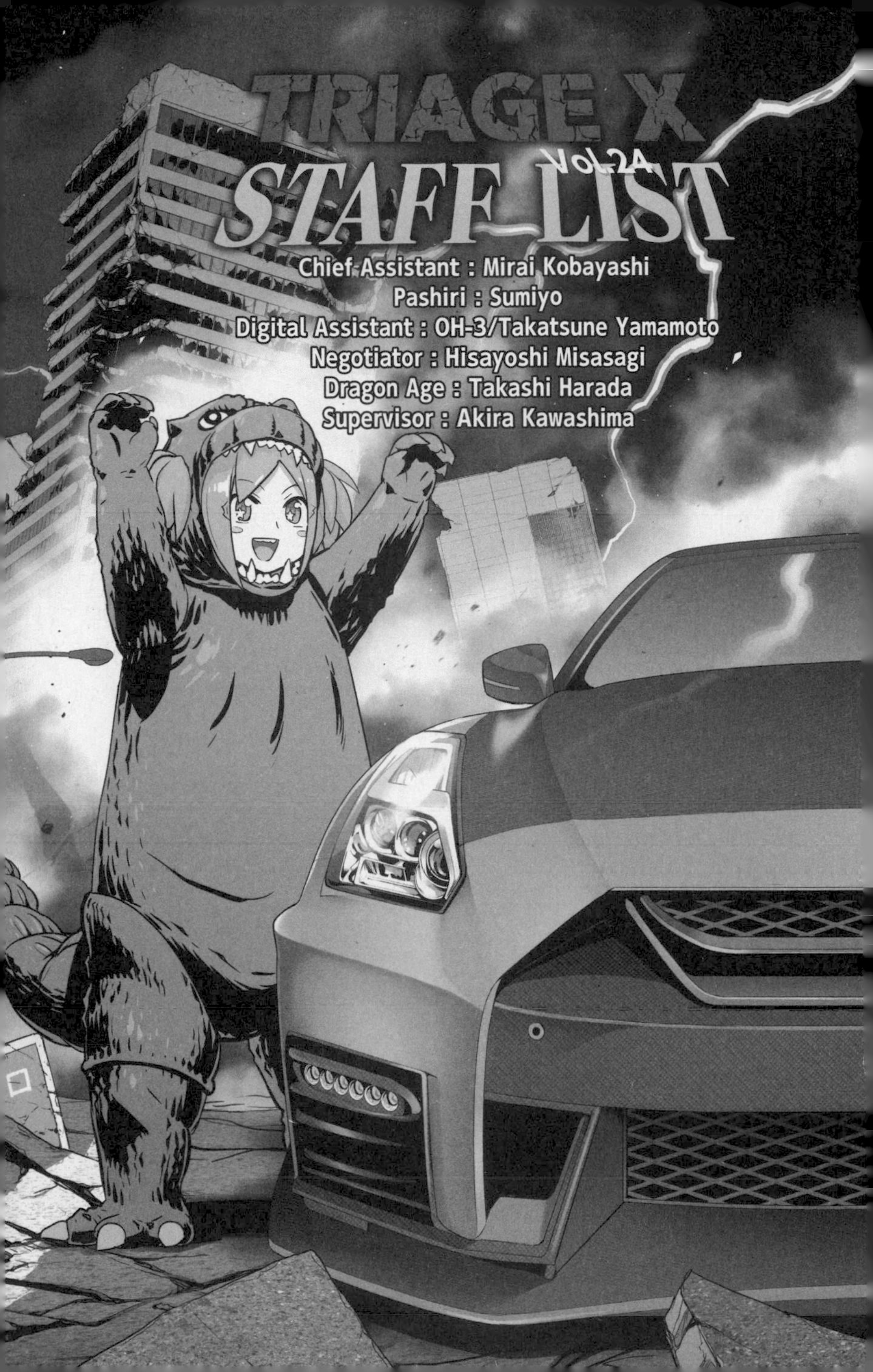
TRIAGE X
Vol.24
STAFF LIST
Chief Assistant : Mirai Kobayashi
Pashiri : Sumiyo
Digital Assistant : OH-3/Takatsune Yamamoto
Negotiator : Hisayoshi Misasagi
Dragon Age : Takashi Harada
Supervisor : Akira Kawashima

TRIAGE X ㉔

SHOUJI SATO

Translation: Christine Dashiell

Lettering: Abigail Blackman

TRIAGE X Volume 24 © Shouji Sato 2022. First published in Japan in 2022 by KADOKAWA CORPORATION, Tokyo. English translation rights arranged with KADOKAWA CORPORATION, Tokyo, through TUTTLE-MORI AGENCY, INC., Tokyo.

English translation © 2023 by Yen Press, LLC

Yen Press
150 West 30th Street, 19th Floor
New York, NY 10001

Visit us at yenpress.com
facebook.com/yenpress
twitter.com/yenpress
yenpress.tumblr.com
instagram.com/yenpress

First Yen Press Edition: January 2023
Edited by Abigail Blackman & Yen Press Editorial: Kurt Hassler
Designed by Yen Press Design: Eddy Mingki, Wendy Chan

Library of Congress Control Number: 2015952593

ISBNs: 978-1-9753-6000-9 (paperback)
       978-1-9753-6001-6 (ebook)

10 9 8 7 6 5 4 3 2 1

WOR

Printed in the United States of America